CAPTAIN AMERICA

PRISONER OF WAR

CAPTAIN AMERICA: PRISONER OF WAR. Contains material originally published in magazine form as CAPTAIN AMERICA #616-619. First printing 2011. Hardcover ISBN# 978-0-7851-5121-0. Softcover ISBN# 978-0-7851-5122-7. Published by MARVEL WORLDWIDE, INC., a subsidiary of MARVEL ENTERTAINMENT, LLC. OFFICE OF PUBLICATION: 135 West 50th Street, New York, NY 10020. Copyright © 2011 and 2012 Marvel Characters, Inc. All rights reserved. Hardcover: $24.99 per copy in the U.S. and $27.99 in Canada (GST #R127032852). Softcover: $19.99 per copy in the U.S. and $21.99 in Canada (GST #R127032852). Canadian Agreement #40668537. All characters featured in this issue and the distinctive names and likenesses thereof, and all related indicia are trademarks of Marvel Characters, Inc. No similarity between any of the names, characters, persons, and/or institutions in this magazine with those of any living or dead person or institution is intended, and any such similarity which may exist is purely coincidental. **Printed in the U.S.A.** ALAN FINE, EVP - Office of the President, Marvel Worldwide, Inc. and EVP & CMO Marvel Characters B.V.; DAN BUCKLEY, Publisher & President - Print, Animation & Digital Divisions; JOE QUESADA, Chief Creative Officer; JIM SOKOLOWSKI, Chief Operating Officer; DAVID BOGART, SVP of Business Affairs & Talent Management; TOM BREVOORT, SVP of Publishing; C.B. CEBULSKI, SVP of Creator & Content Development; DAVID GABRIEL, SVP of Publishing Sales & Circulation; MICHAEL PASCIULLO, SVP of Brand Planning & Communications; JIM O'KEEFE, VP of Operations & Logistics; DAN CARR, Executive Director of Publishing Technology; JUSTIN F. GABRIE, Director of Publishing & Editorial Operations; SUSAN CRESPI, Editorial Operations Manager; ALEX MORALES, Publishing Operations Manager; STAN LEE, Chairman Emeritus. For information regarding advertising in Marvel Comics or on Marvel.com, please contact John Dokes, SVP Integrated Sales and Marketing, at jdokes@marvel.com. For Marvel subscription inquiries, please call 800-217-9158. **Manufactured between 7/11/2011 and 8/8/2011 (hardcover), and 7/11/2011 and 2/6/2012 (softcover), by R.R. DONNELLEY, INC., SALEM, VA, USA.**

10 9 8 7 6 5 4 3 2 1

CAPTAIN AMERICA

PRISONER OF WAR

"ORIGIN"
WRITER: Ed Brubaker
ARTIST: Travis Charest
COLOR ARTIST: Justin Ponsor

"MUST THERE BE A CAPTAIN AMERICA?"
WRITER: Ed Brubaker
PENCILER: Ed McGuinness
INKERS: Dexter Vines
with **Ed McGuinness**
COLOR ARTIST: Val Staples

"GULAG"
WRITER: Ed Brubaker
ARTISTS: Mike Deodato;
Butch Guice & Stefano Gaudiano;
and Chris Samnee
COLOR ARTIST: Bettie Breitweiser
with **Rain Beredo (Part 1)**

"OPAQUE SHADOWS"
WRITER/ARTIST: Howard Chaykin
COLOR ARTIST: Edgar Delgado

"SPIN"
WRITER: Cullen Bunn
ARTIST: Jason Latour
COLOR ARTIST: Rico Renzi

"OPERATION: TOOTH FAIRY"
WRITER: Mike Benson
ARTIST: Paul Grist
COLOR ARTIST: Lee Loughridge

"THE EXHIBIT"
WRITER: Frank Tieri
ARTIST: Paul Azaceta
COLOR ARTIST: Matthew Wilson

"CROSSFIRE"
WRITERS: Kyle Higgins
& Alec Siegel
ARTIST: Pepe Larraz
COLOR ARTIST: Chris Sotomayor

COVER ARTISTS: Travis Charest (#616) &
Marko Djurdjevic (#617-619)
LETTERER: VC's Joe Caramagna
ASSOCIATE EDITOR: Lauren Sankovitch
EDITOR: Tom Brevoort

CAPTAIN AMERICA CREATED BY JOE SIMON AND JACK KIRBY

Collection Editor: Jennifer Grünwald • Editorial Assistants: James Emmett & Joe Hochstein
Assistant Editors: Alex Starbuck & Nelson Ribeiro • Editor, Special Projects: Mark D. Beazley
Senior Editor, Special Projects: Jeff Youngquist • Senior Vice President of Sales: David Gabriel
SVP of Brand Planning & Communications: Michael Pasciullo

Editor in Chief: Axel Alonso • Chief Creative Officer: Joe Quesada
Publisher: Dan Buckley • Executive Producer: Alan Fine

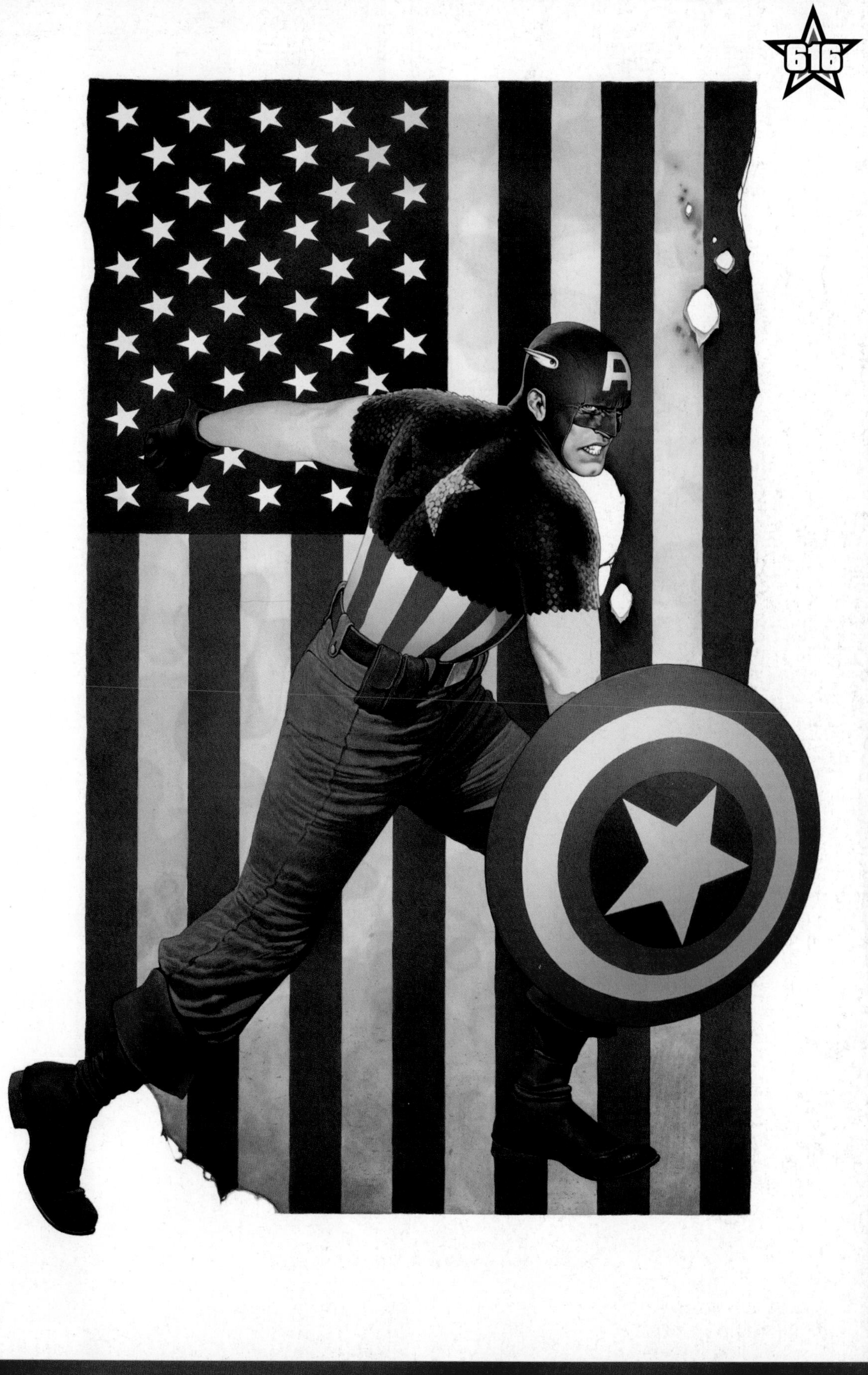
616

ORIGIN, MUST THERE BE A CAPTAIN AMERICA? & GULAG PART 1

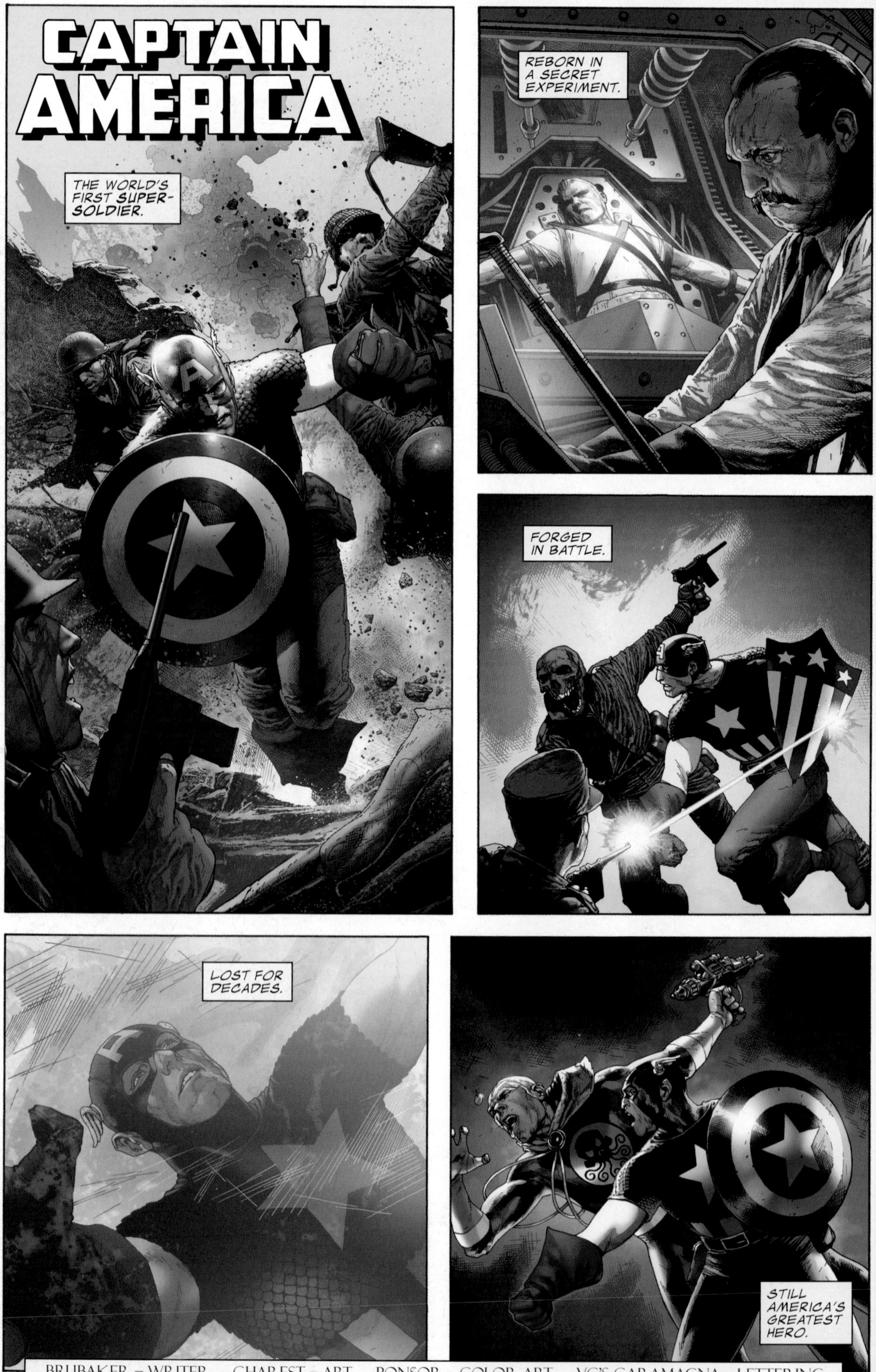
CAPTAIN AMERICA
THE WORLD'S FIRST SUPER-SOLDIER.
REBORN IN A SECRET EXPERIMENT.
FORGED IN BATTLE.
LOST FOR DECADES.
STILL AMERICA'S GREATEST HERO.

BRUBAKER – WRITER CHAREST – ART PONSOR – COLOR ART VC'S CARAMAGNA – LETTERING

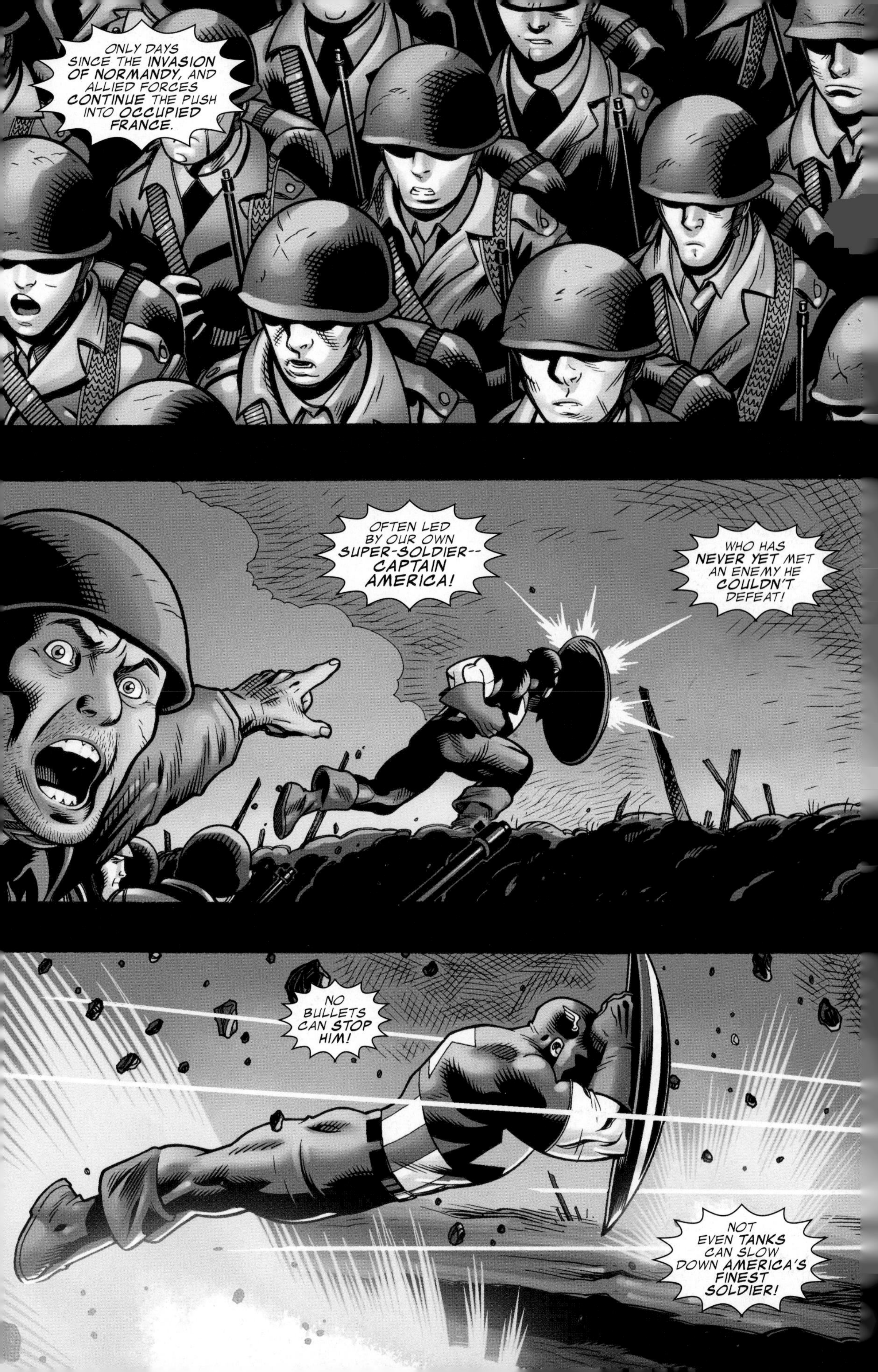
ONLY DAYS SINCE THE INVASION OF NORMANDY, AND ALLIED FORCES CONTINUE THE PUSH INTO OCCUPIED FRANCE.
OFTEN LED BY OUR OWN SUPER-SOLDIER--CAPTAIN AMERICA!
WHO HAS NEVER YET MET AN ENEMY HE COULDN'T DEFEAT!
NO BULLETS CAN STOP HIM!
NOT EVEN TANKS CAN SLOW DOWN AMERICA'S FINEST SOLDIER!

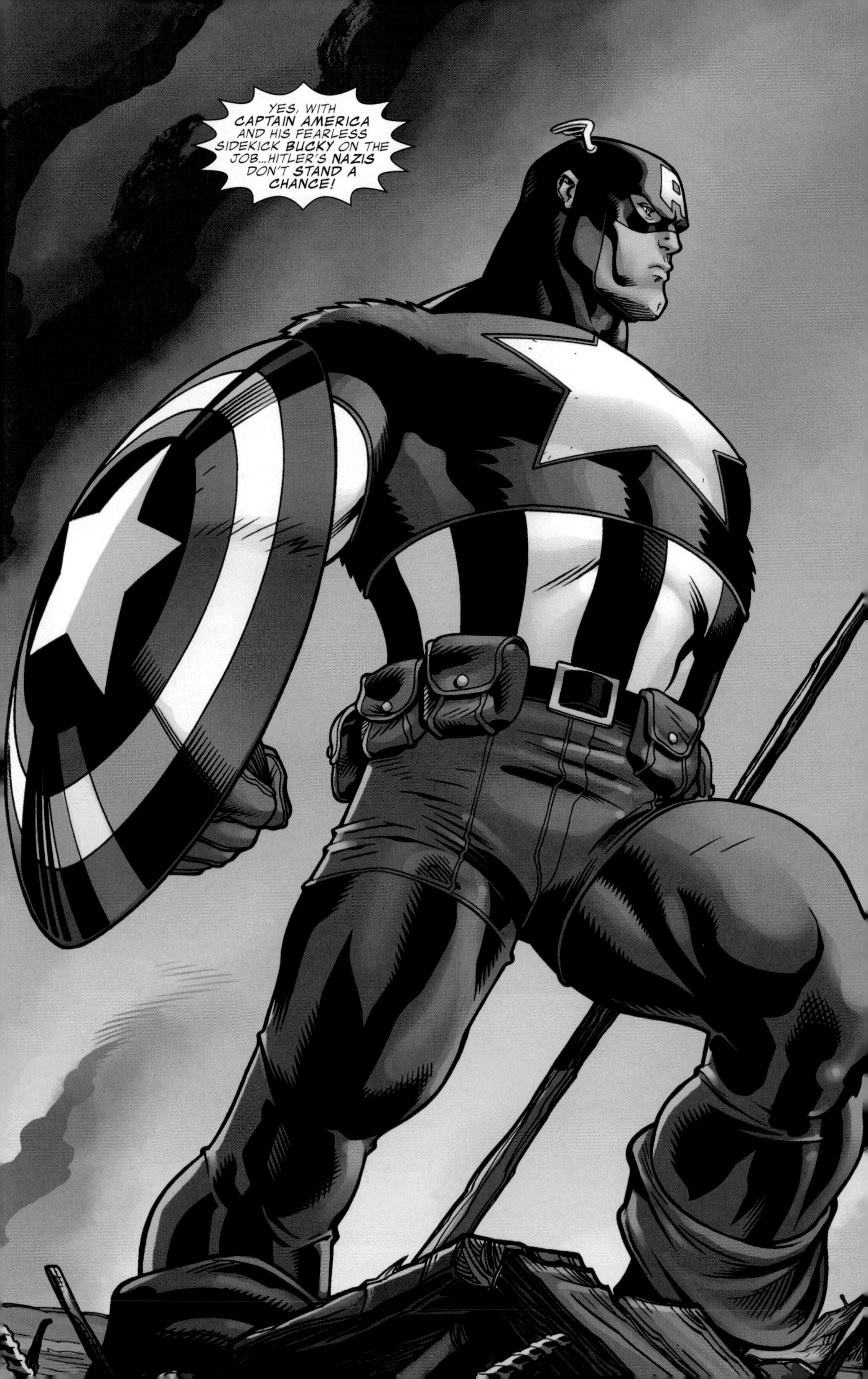
YES, WITH CAPTAIN AMERICA AND HIS FEARLESS SIDEKICK BUCKY ON THE JOB...HITLER'S NAZIS DON'T STAND A CHANCE!

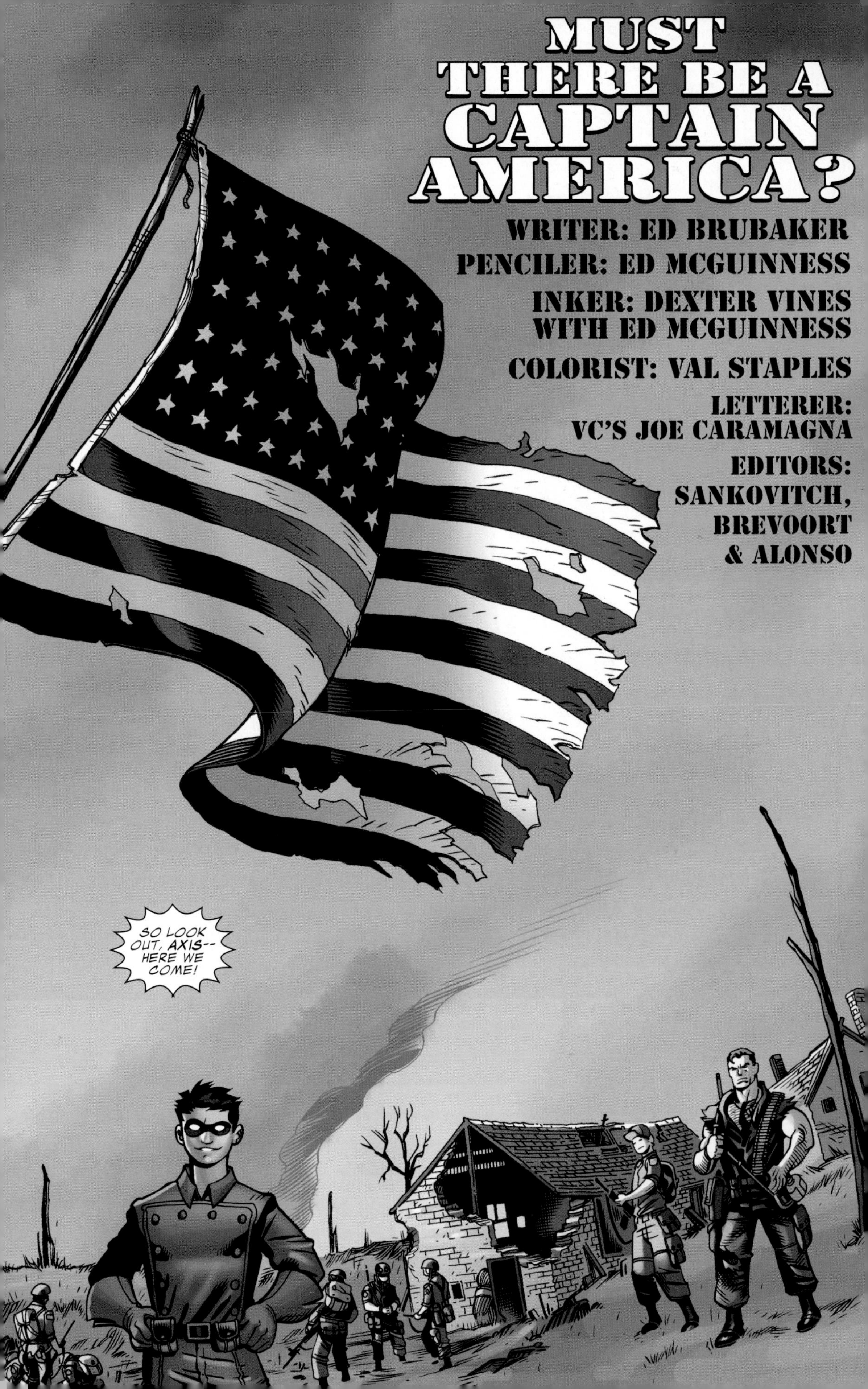
MUST THERE BE A CAPTAIN AMERICA?
WRITER: ED BRUBAKER
PENCILER: ED MCGUINNESS
INKER: DEXTER VINES WITH ED MCGUINNESS
COLORIST: VAL STAPLES
LETTERER: VC'S JOE CARAMAGNA
EDITORS: SANKOVITCH, BREVOORT & ALONSO
SO LOOK OUT, AXIS-- HERE WE COME!

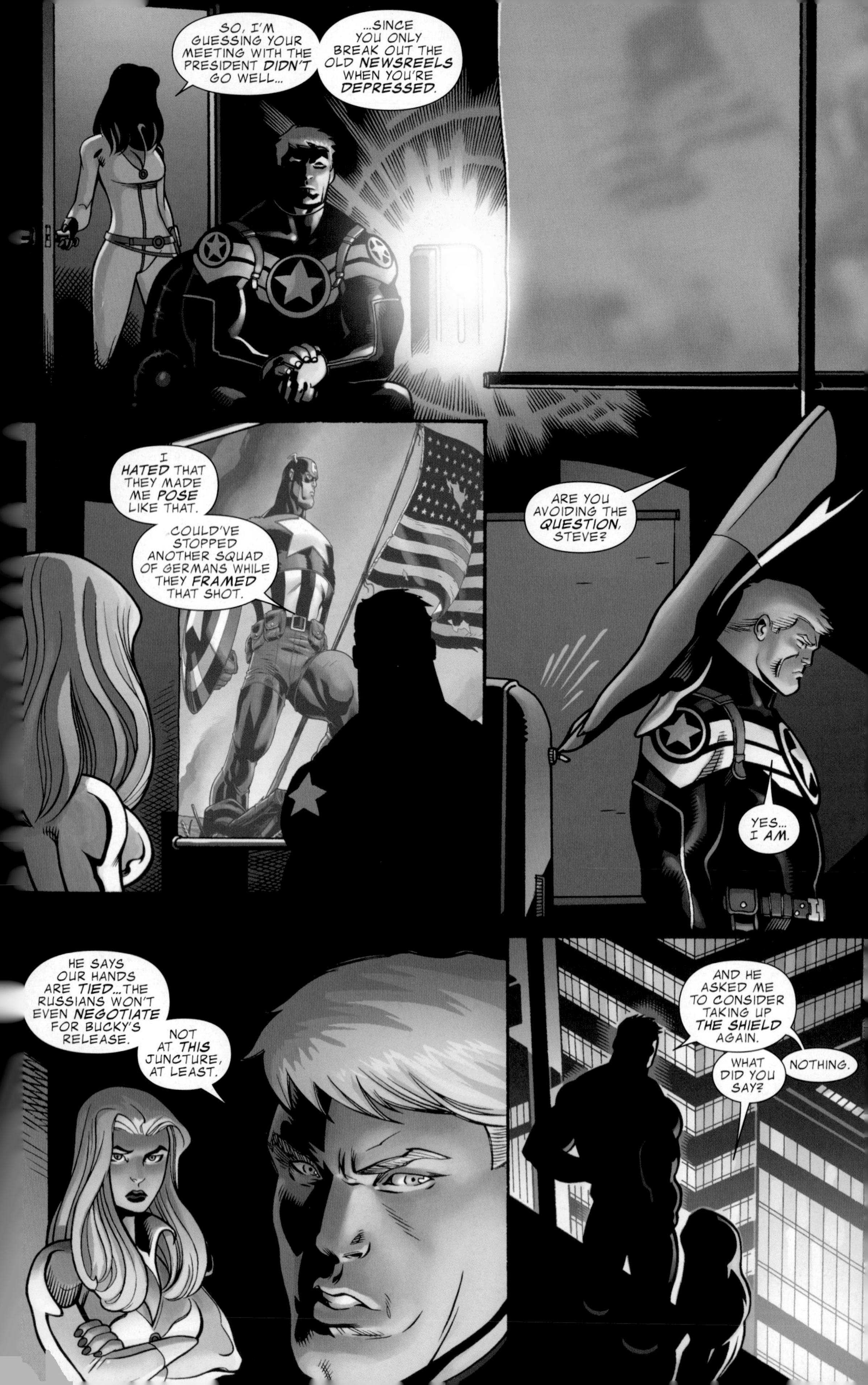
SO, I'M GUESSING YOUR MEETING WITH THE PRESIDENT DIDN'T GO WELL...
...SINCE YOU ONLY BREAK OUT THE OLD NEWSREELS WHEN YOU'RE DEPRESSED.
I HATED THAT THEY MADE ME POSE LIKE THAT.
COULD'VE STOPPED ANOTHER SQUAD OF GERMANS WHILE THEY FRAMED THAT SHOT.
ARE YOU AVOIDING THE QUESTION, STEVE?
YES... I AM.
HE SAYS OUR HANDS ARE TIED...THE RUSSIANS WON'T EVEN NEGOTIATE FOR BUCKY'S RELEASE.
NOT AT THIS JUNCTURE, AT LEAST.
AND HE ASKED ME TO CONSIDER TAKING UP THE SHIELD AGAIN.
WHAT DID YOU SAY?
NOTHING.

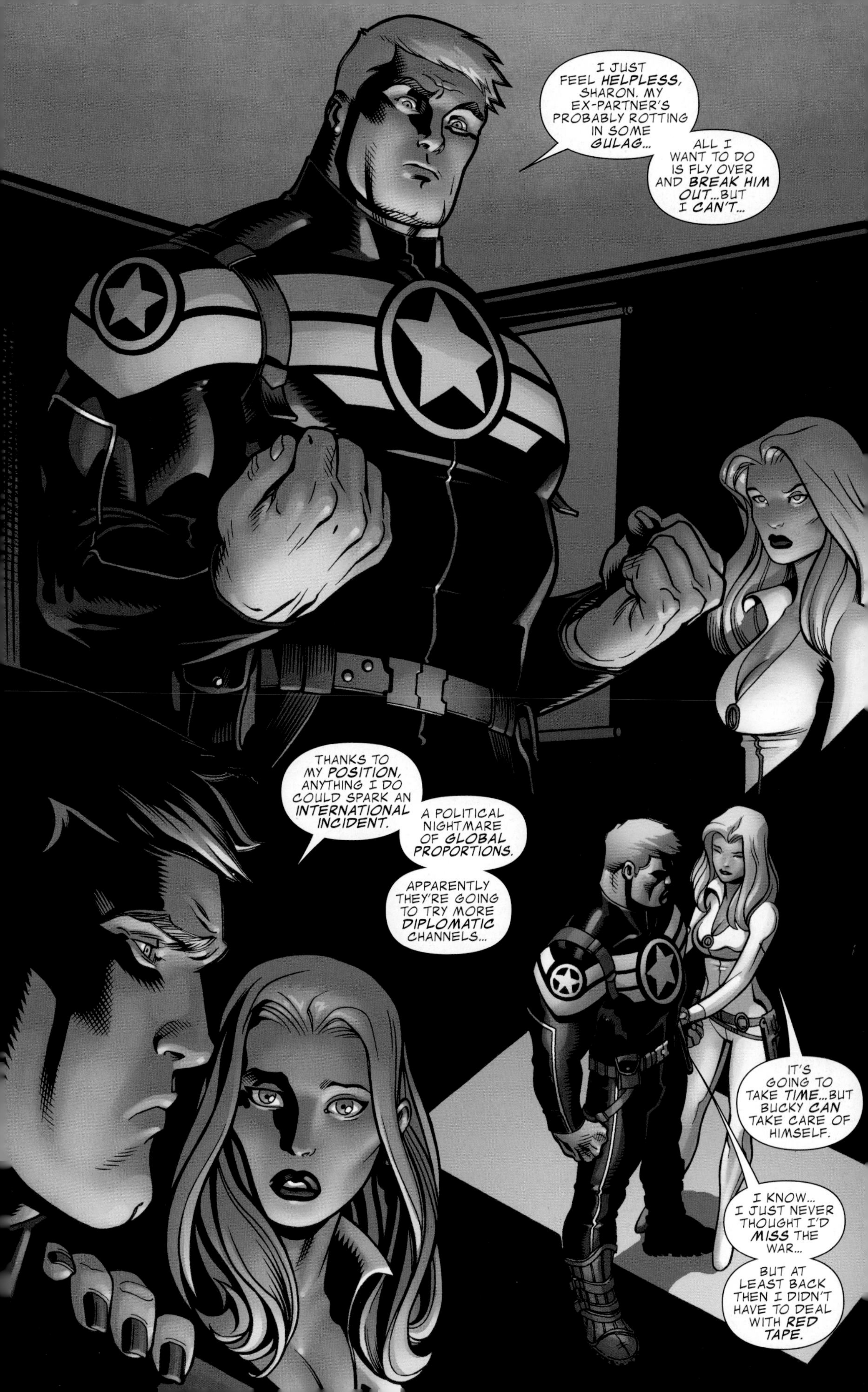
I JUST FEEL HELPLESS, SHARON. MY EX-PARTNER'S PROBABLY ROTTING IN SOME GULAG...
ALL I WANT TO DO IS FLY OVER AND BREAK HIM OUT...BUT I CAN'T...
THANKS TO MY POSITION, ANYTHING I DO COULD SPARK AN INTERNATIONAL INCIDENT.
A POLITICAL NIGHTMARE OF GLOBAL PROPORTIONS.
APPARENTLY THEY'RE GOING TO TRY MORE DIPLOMATIC CHANNELS...
IT'S GOING TO TAKE TIME...BUT BUCKY CAN TAKE CARE OF HIMSELF.
I KNOW... I JUST NEVER THOUGHT I'D MISS THE WAR...
BUT AT LEAST BACK THEN I DIDN'T HAVE TO DEAL WITH RED TAPE.

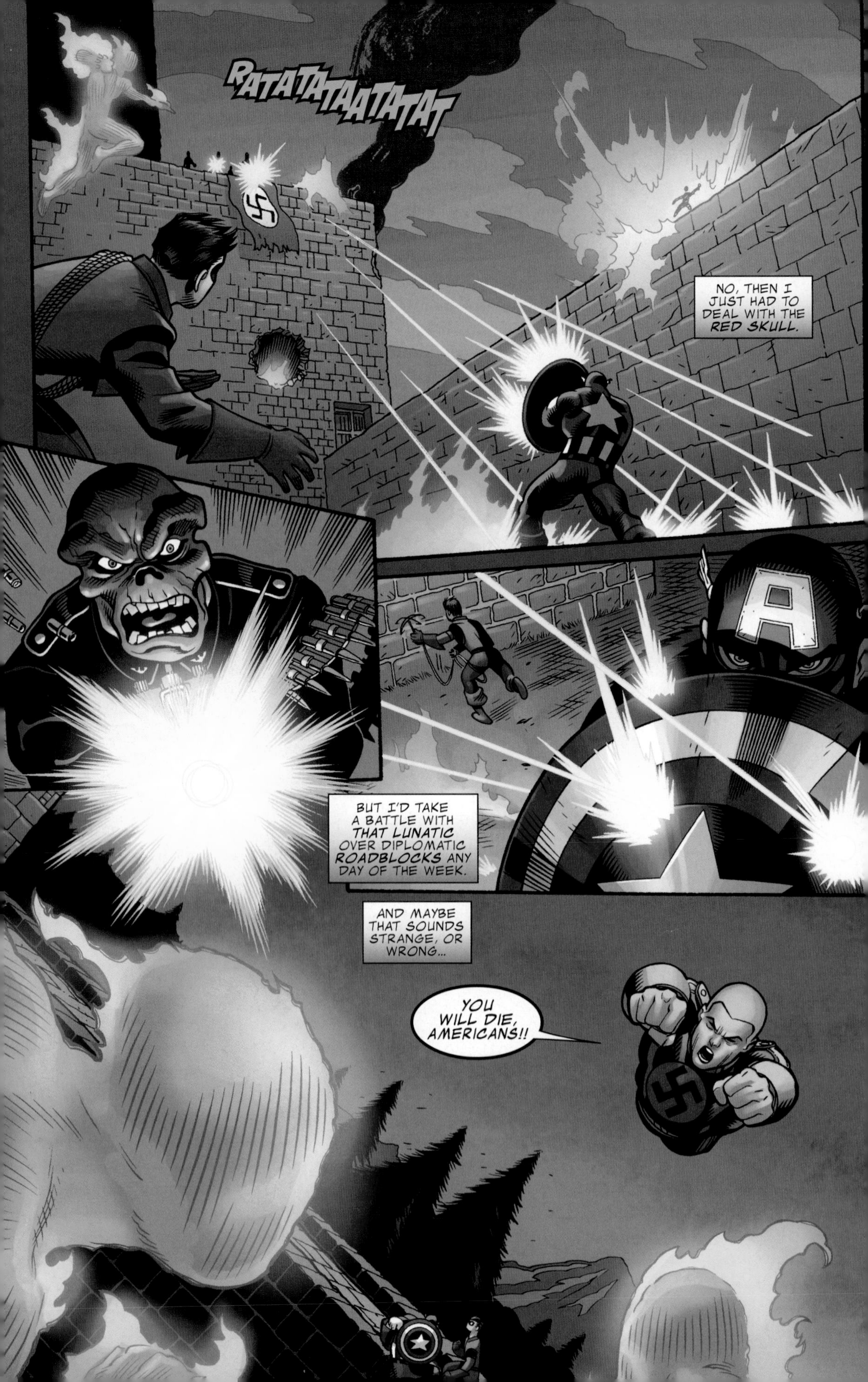
RATATATAATATAT
NO, THEN I JUST HAD TO DEAL WITH THE RED SKULL.
BUT I'D TAKE A BATTLE WITH THAT LUNATIC OVER DIPLOMATIC ROADBLOCKS ANY DAY OF THE WEEK.
AND MAYBE THAT SOUNDS STRANGE, OR WRONG...
YOU WILL DIE, AMERICANS!!

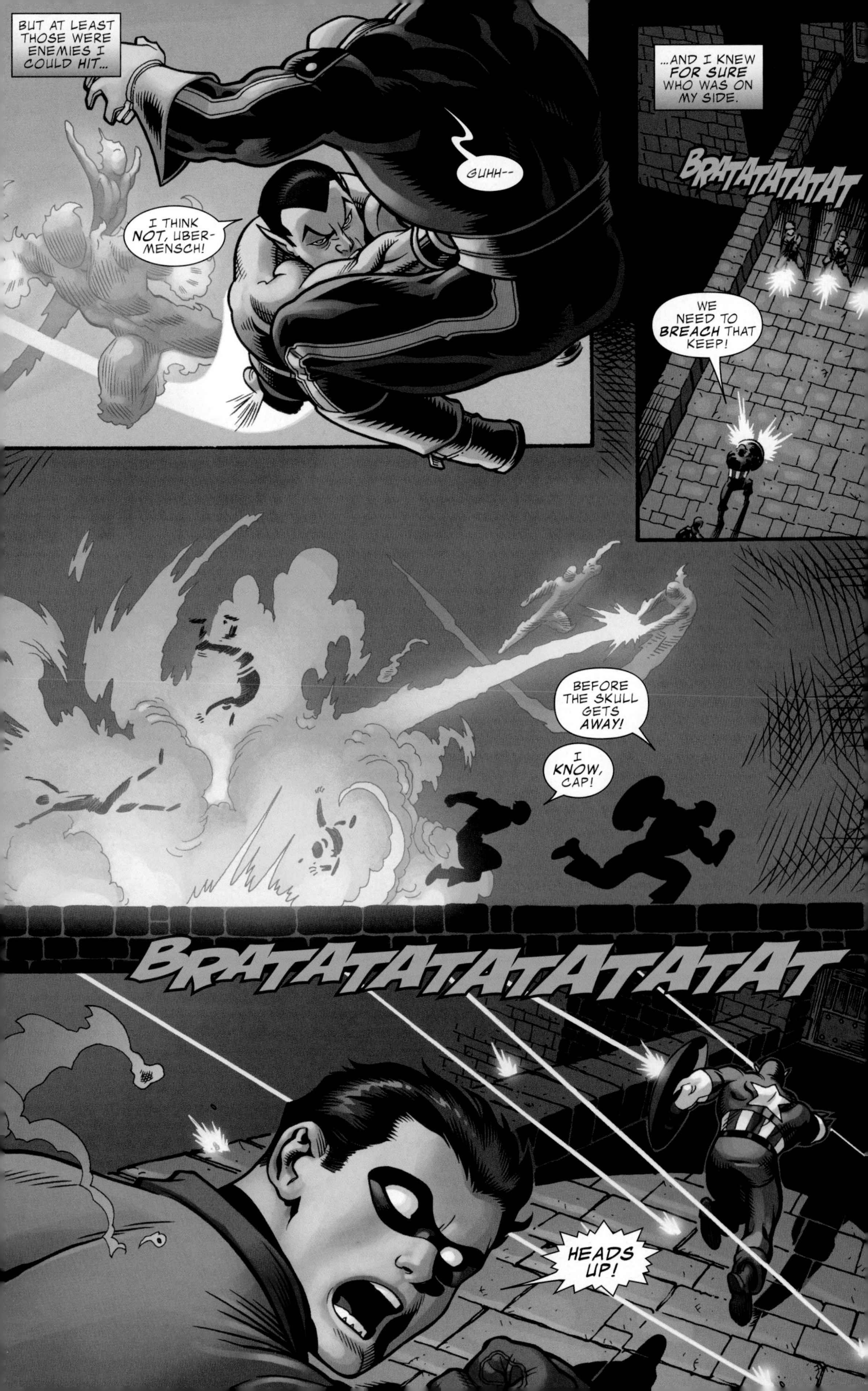
BUT AT LEAST THOSE WERE ENEMIES I COULD HIT...
GUHH--
I THINK NOT, UBER-MENSCH!
...AND I KNEW FOR SURE WHO WAS ON MY SIDE.
BRATATATATAT
WE NEED TO BREACH THAT KEEP!
BEFORE THE SKULL GETS AWAY!
I KNOW, CAP!
BRATATATATATATATAT
HEADS UP!

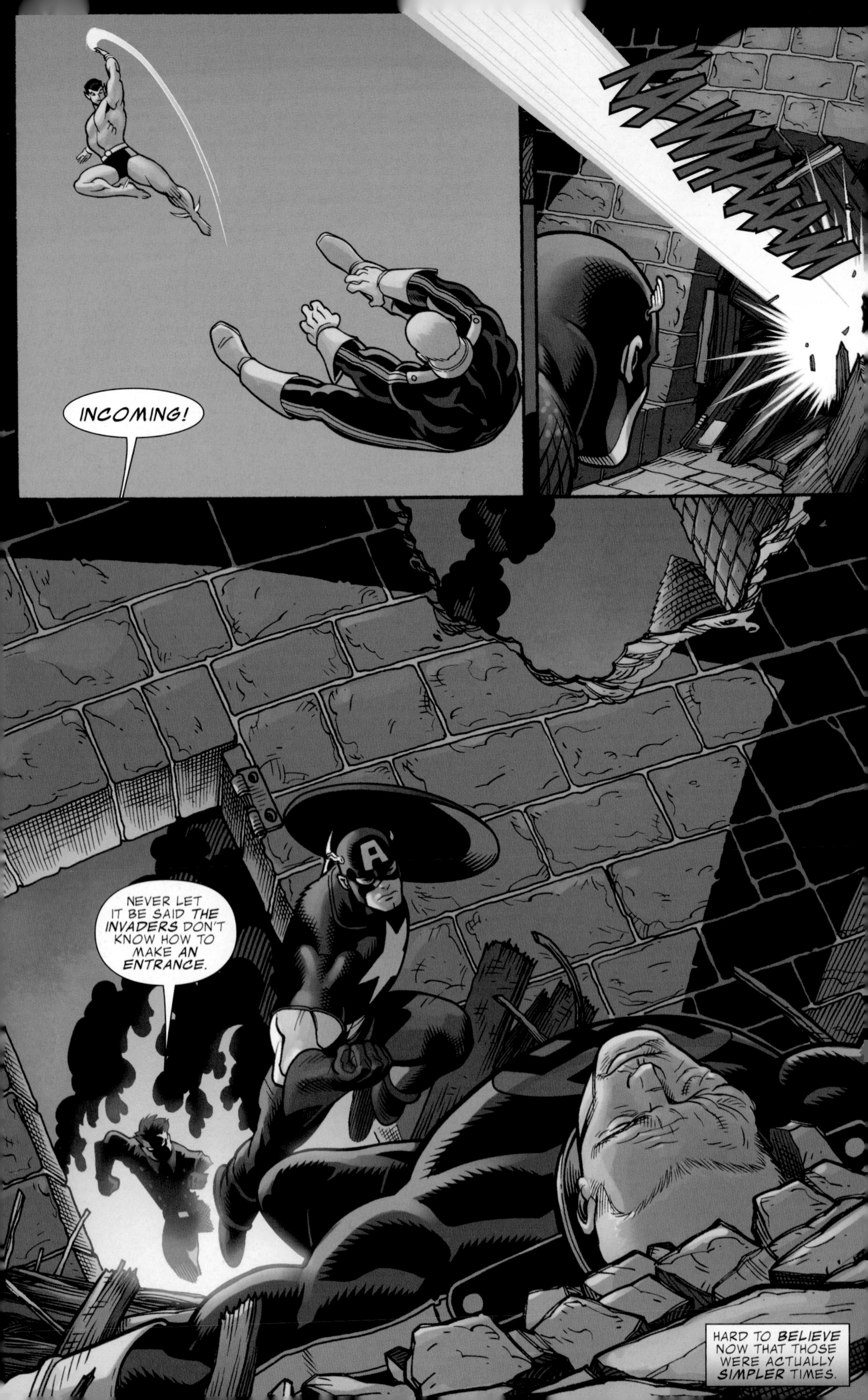
INCOMING!
KA-WHAAAM
NEVER LET IT BE SAID THE INVADERS DON'T KNOW HOW TO MAKE AN ENTRANCE.
HARD TO BELIEVE NOW THAT THOSE WERE ACTUALLY SIMPLER TIMES.

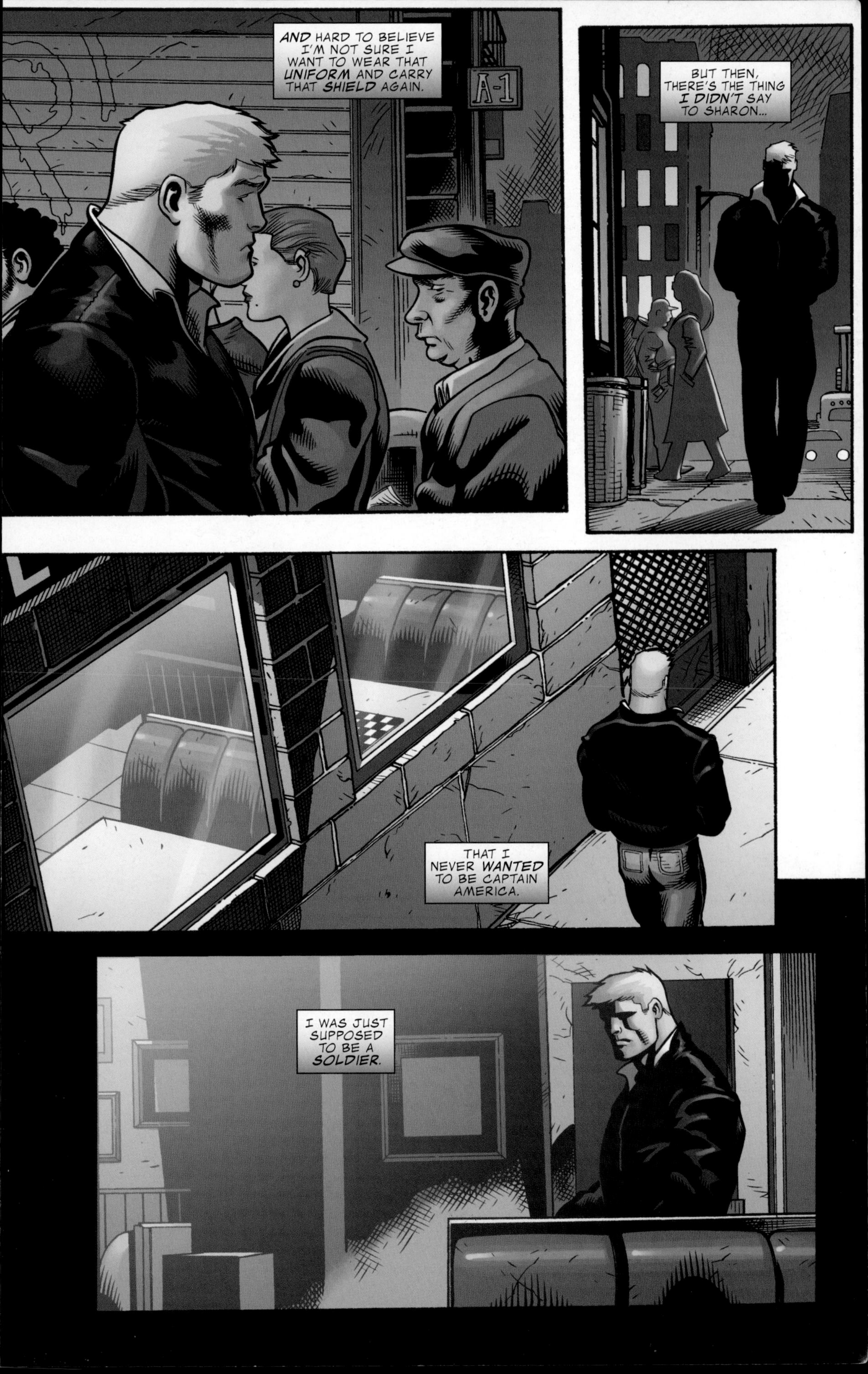
AND HARD TO BELIEVE I'M NOT SURE I WANT TO WEAR THAT UNIFORM AND CARRY THAT SHIELD AGAIN.
A-1
BUT THEN, THERE'S THE THING I DIDN'T SAY TO SHARON...
THAT I NEVER WANTED TO BE CAPTAIN AMERICA.
I WAS JUST SUPPOSED TO BE A SOLDIER.

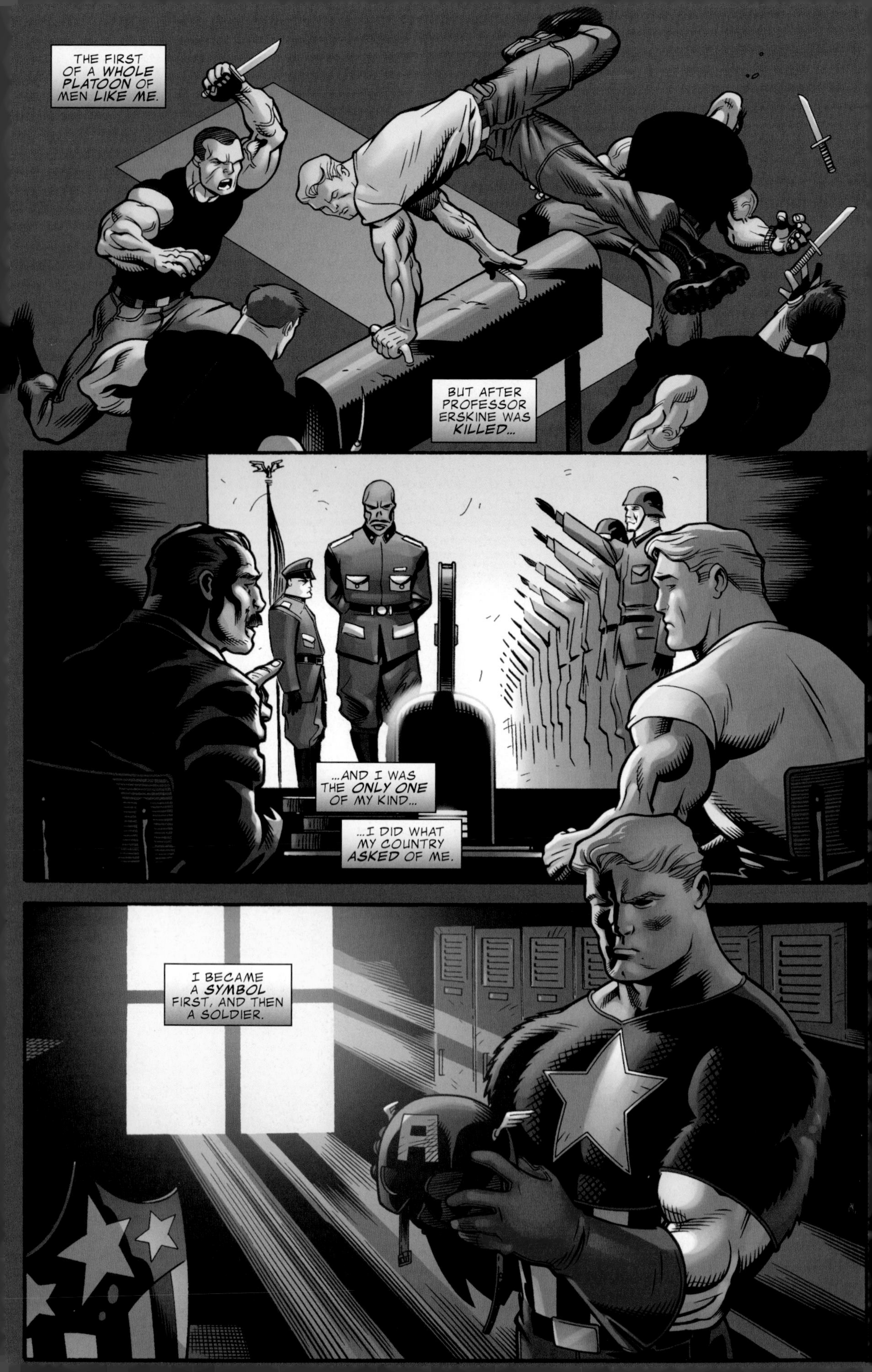
THE FIRST OF A WHOLE PLATOON OF MEN LIKE ME.
BUT AFTER PROFESSOR ERSKINE WAS KILLED...
...AND I WAS THE ONLY ONE OF MY KIND...
...I DID WHAT MY COUNTRY ASKED OF ME.
I BECAME A SYMBOL FIRST, AND THEN A SOLDIER.

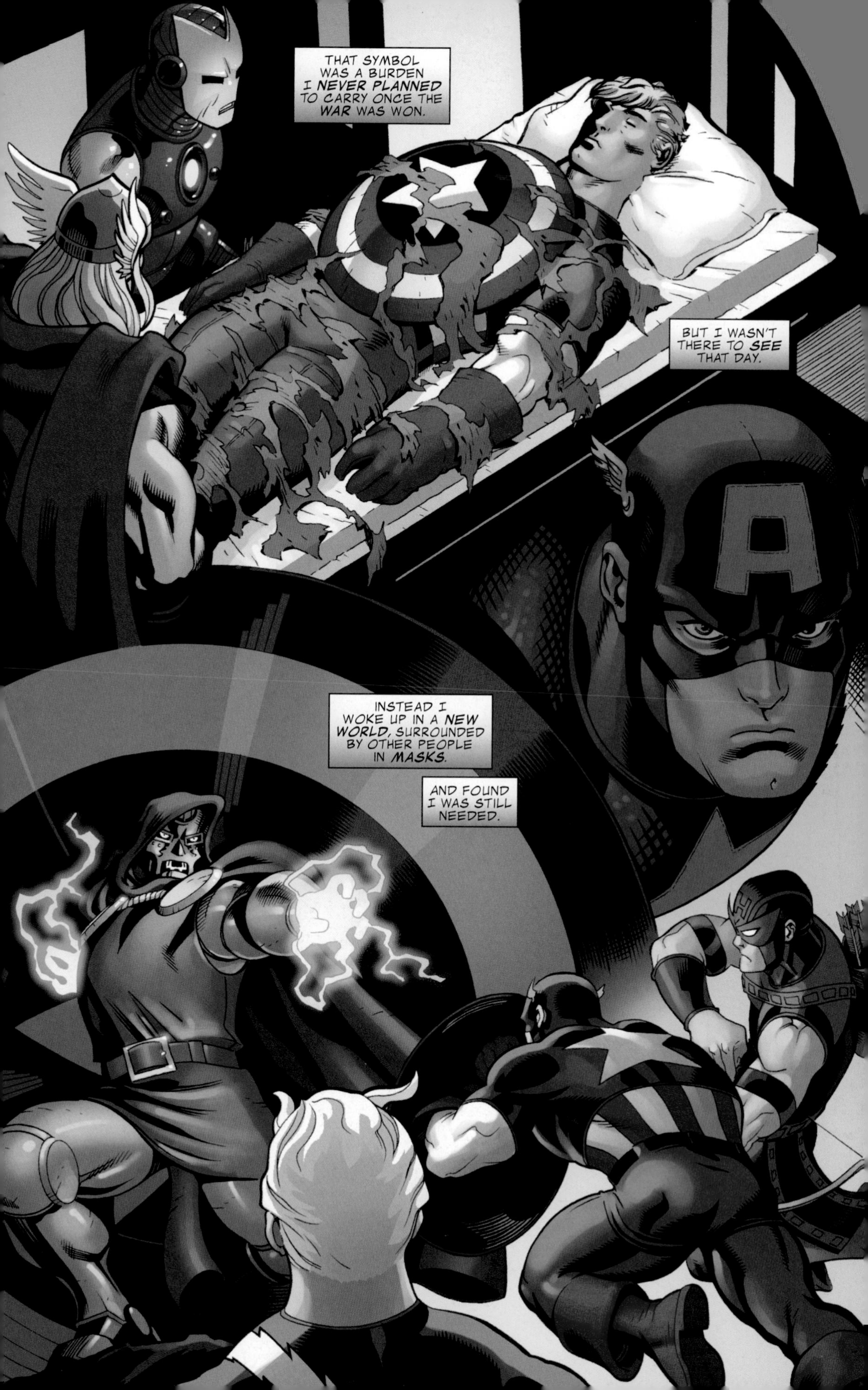
THAT SYMBOL WAS A BURDEN I NEVER PLANNED TO CARRY ONCE THE WAR WAS WON.
BUT I WASN'T THERE TO SEE THAT DAY.
INSTEAD I WOKE UP IN A NEW WORLD, SURROUNDED BY OTHER PEOPLE IN MASKS.
AND FOUND I WAS STILL NEEDED.

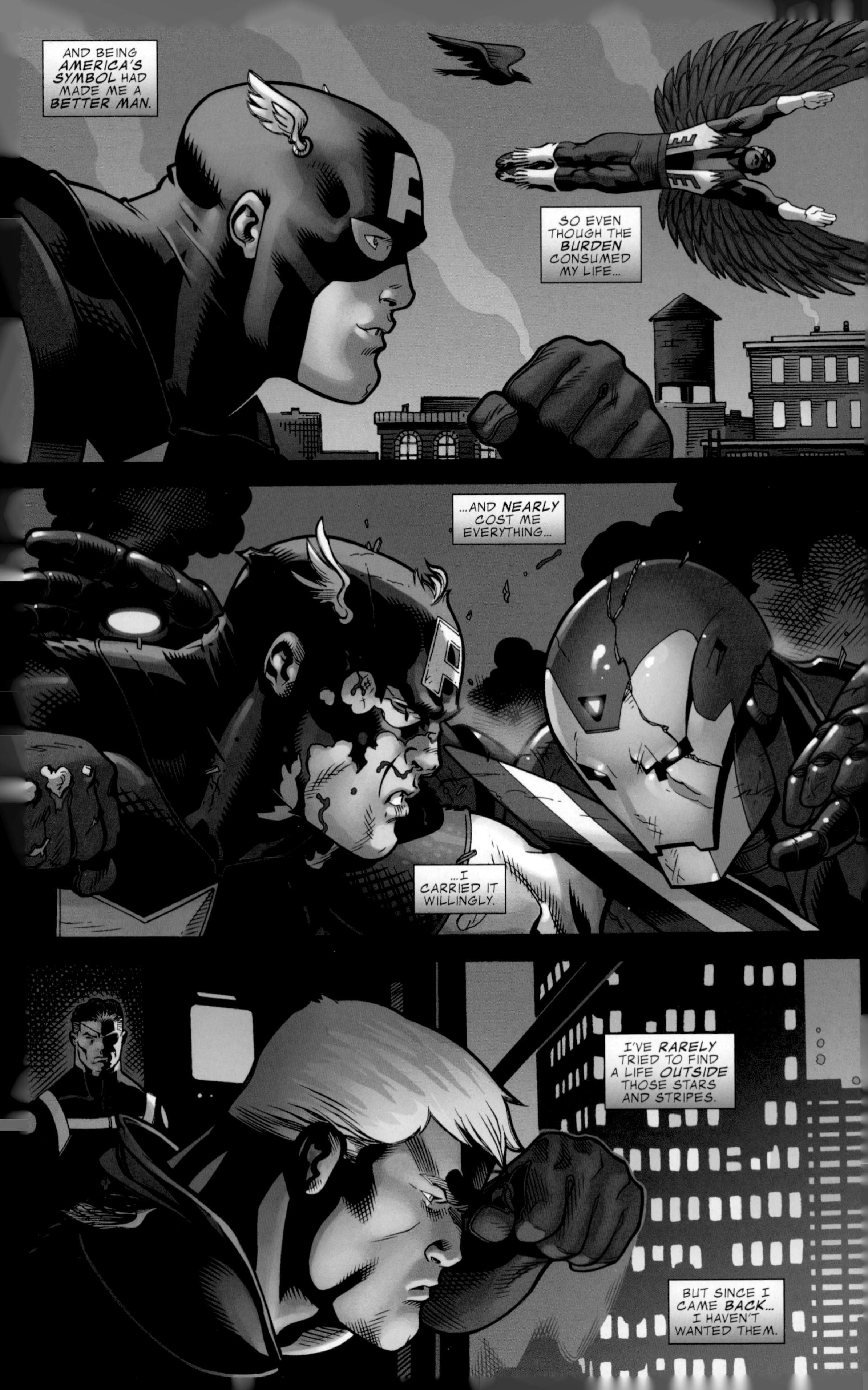
AND BEING AMERICA'S SYMBOL HAD MADE ME A BETTER MAN.
SO EVEN THOUGH THE BURDEN CONSUMED MY LIFE...
...AND NEARLY COST ME EVERYTHING...
...I CARRIED IT WILLINGLY.
I'VE RARELY TRIED TO FIND A LIFE OUTSIDE THOSE STARS AND STRIPES.
BUT SINCE I CAME BACK... I HAVEN'T WANTED THEM.

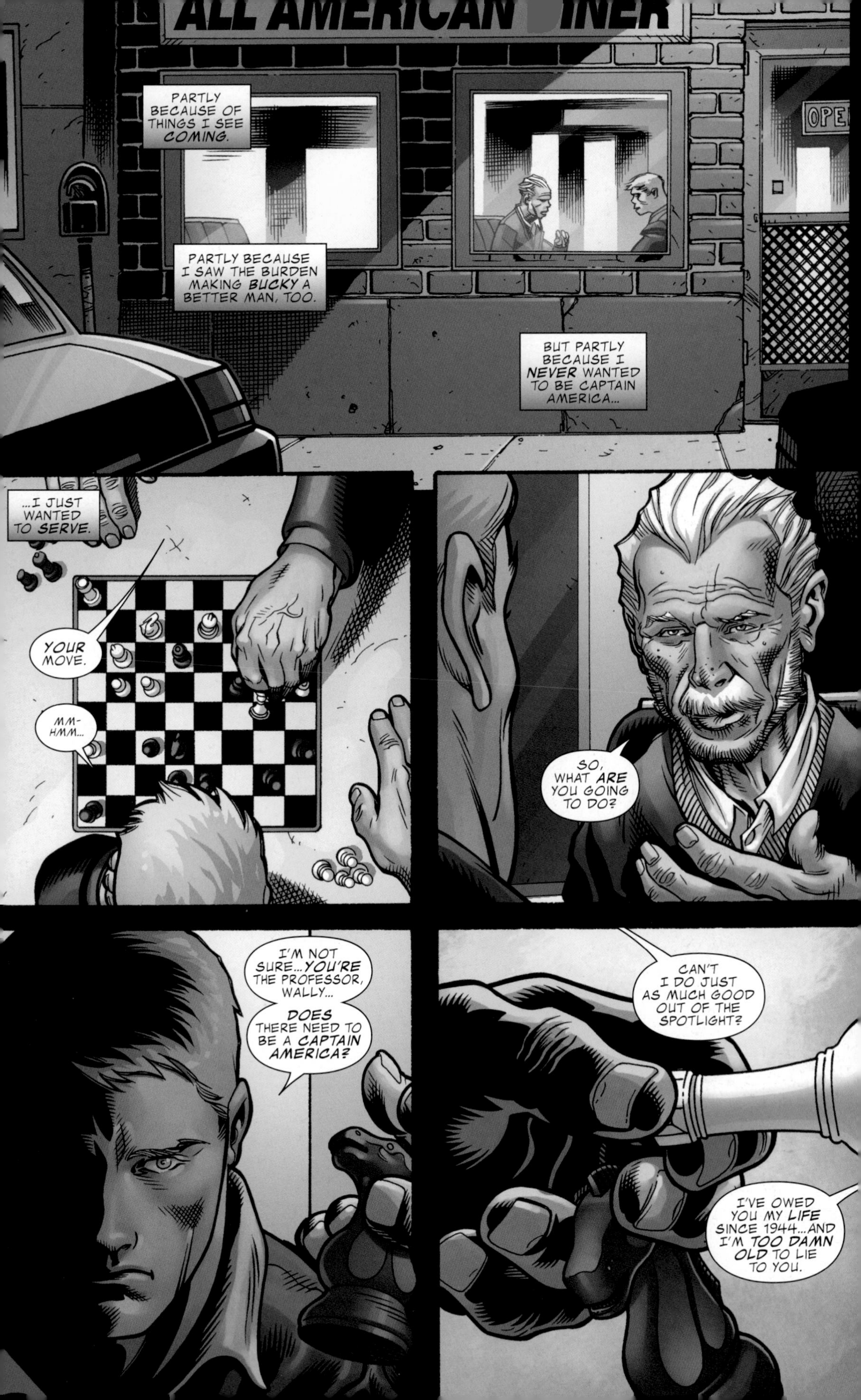
ALL AMERICAN DINER
PARTLY BECAUSE OF THINGS I SEE COMING.
PARTLY BECAUSE I SAW THE BURDEN MAKING BUCKY A BETTER MAN, TOO.
OPEN
BUT PARTLY BECAUSE I NEVER WANTED TO BE CAPTAIN AMERICA...
...I JUST WANTED TO SERVE.
YOUR MOVE.
MM-HMM...
SO, WHAT ARE YOU GOING TO DO?
I'M NOT SURE...YOU'RE THE PROFESSOR, WALLY...
DOES THERE NEED TO BE A CAPTAIN AMERICA?
CAN'T I DO JUST AS MUCH GOOD OUT OF THE SPOTLIGHT?
I'VE OWED YOU MY LIFE SINCE 1944...AND I'M TOO DAMN OLD TO LIE TO YOU.

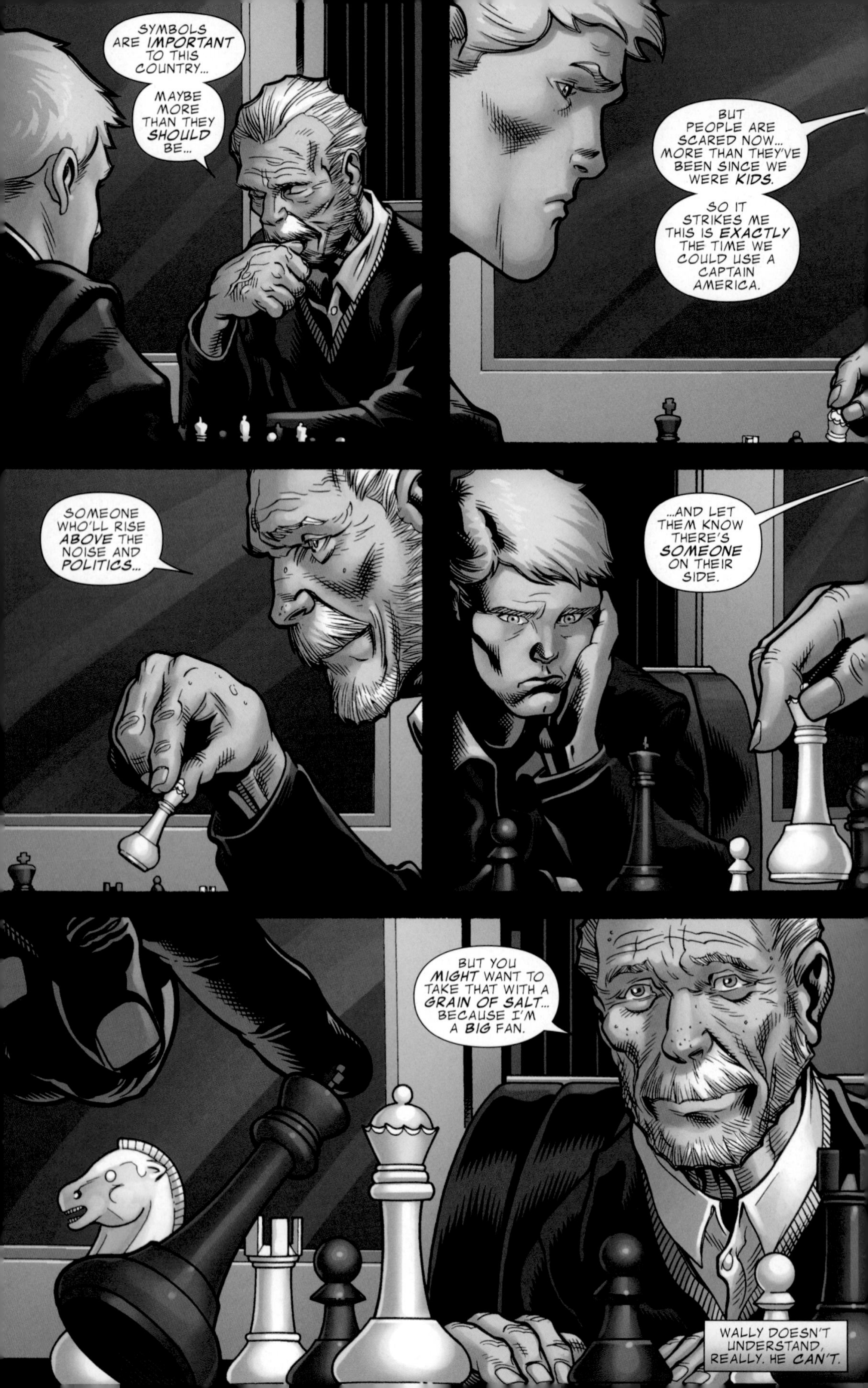
SYMBOLS ARE IMPORTANT TO THIS COUNTRY...
MAYBE MORE THAN THEY SHOULD BE...
BUT PEOPLE ARE SCARED NOW... MORE THAN THEY'VE BEEN SINCE WE WERE KIDS.
SO IT STRIKES ME THIS IS EXACTLY THE TIME WE COULD USE A CAPTAIN AMERICA.
SOMEONE WHO'LL RISE ABOVE THE NOISE AND POLITICS...
...AND LET THEM KNOW THERE'S SOMEONE ON THEIR SIDE.
BUT YOU MIGHT WANT TO TAKE THAT WITH A GRAIN OF SALT... BECAUSE I'M A BIG FAN.
WALLY DOESN'T UNDERSTAND, REALLY. HE CAN'T.

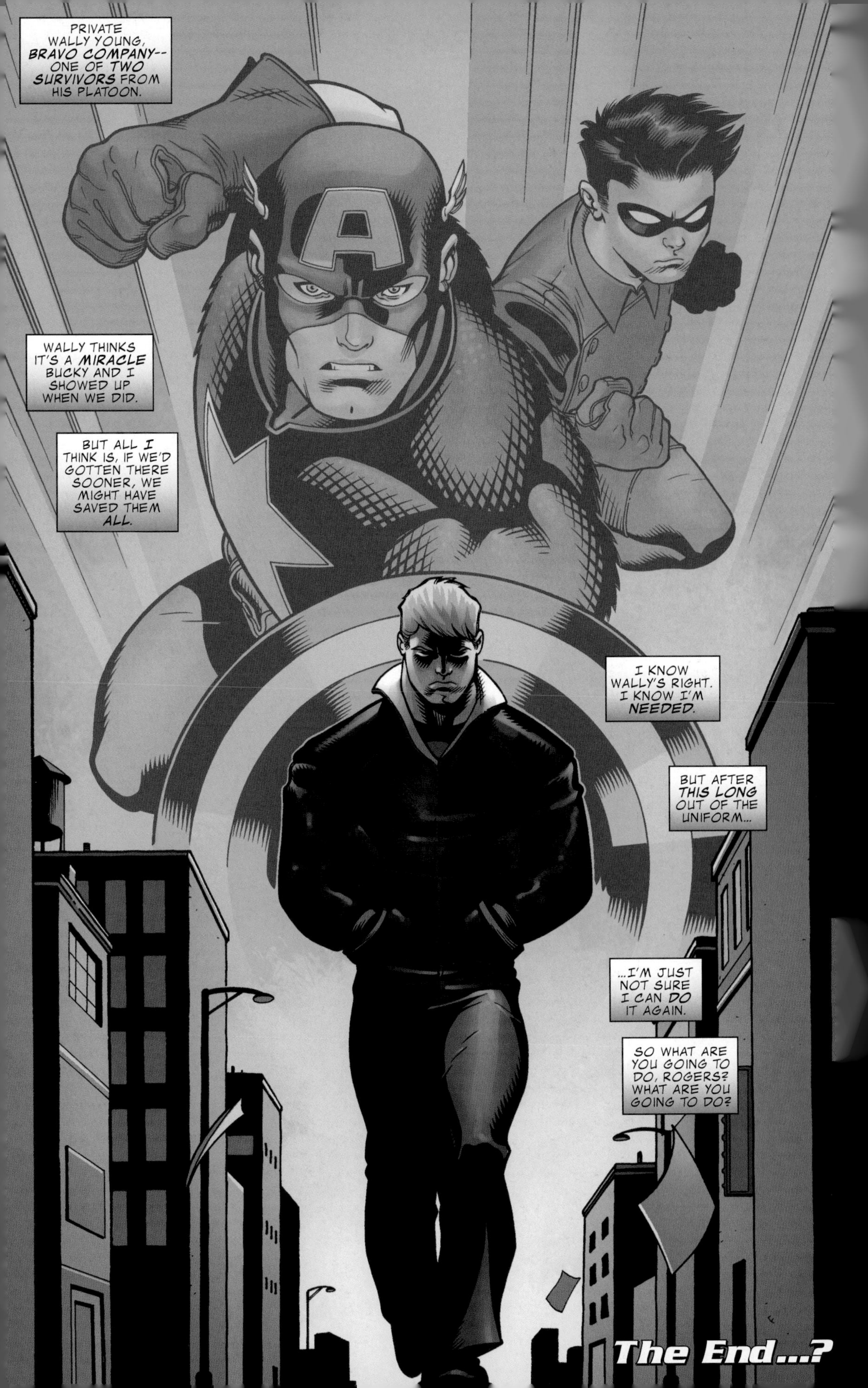
PRIVATE WALLY YOUNG, BRAVO COMPANY-- ONE OF TWO SURVIVORS FROM HIS PLATOON.
WALLY THINKS IT'S A MIRACLE BUCKY AND I SHOWED UP WHEN WE DID.
BUT ALL I THINK IS, IF WE'D GOTTEN THERE SOONER, WE MIGHT HAVE SAVED THEM ALL.
I KNOW WALLY'S RIGHT. I KNOW I'M NEEDED.
BUT AFTER THIS LONG OUT OF THE UNIFORM...
...I'M JUST NOT SURE I CAN DO IT AGAIN.
SO WHAT ARE YOU GOING TO DO, ROGERS? WHAT ARE YOU GOING TO DO?
The End...?

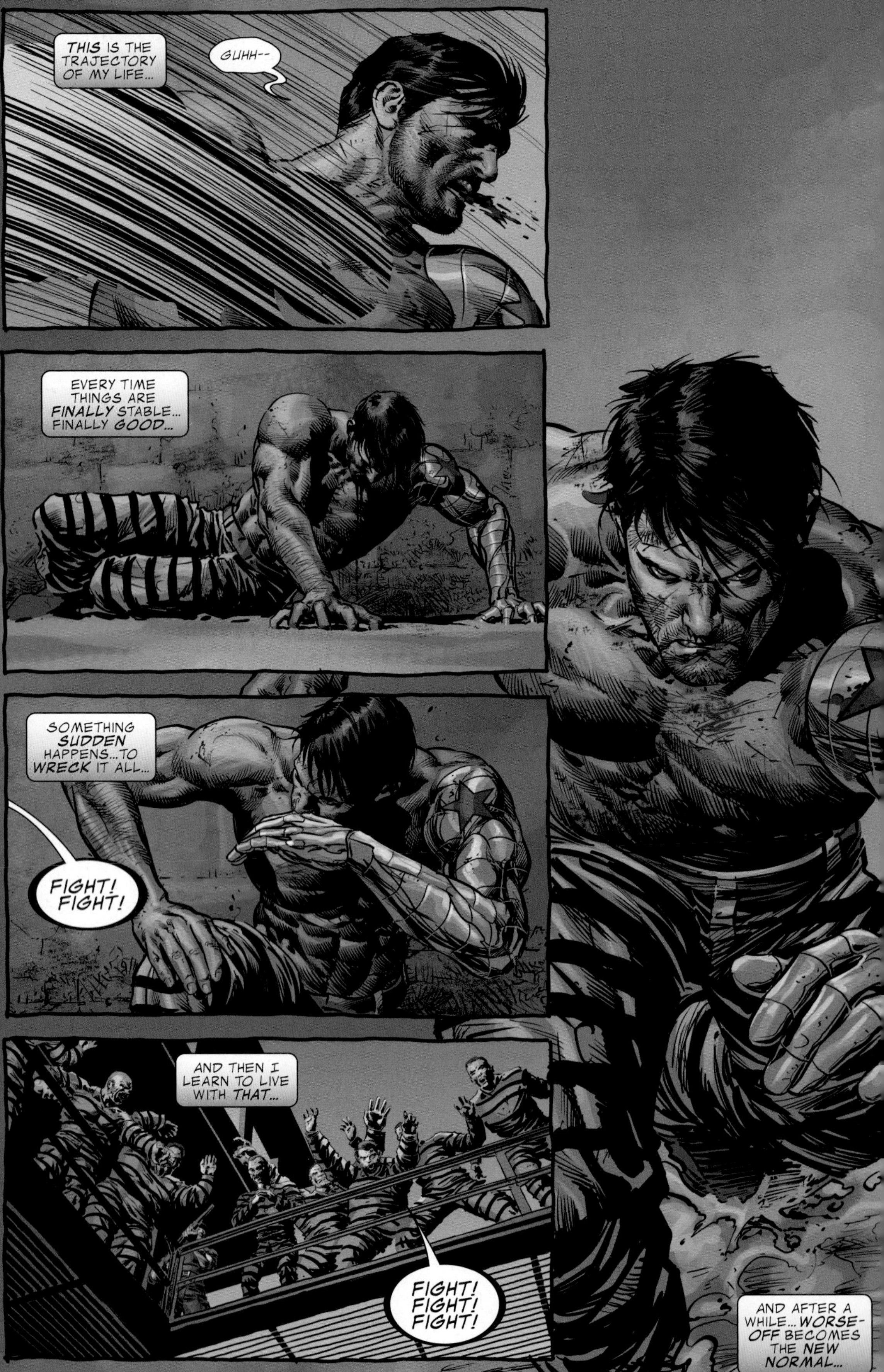
THIS IS THE TRAJECTORY OF MY LIFE...
GUHH--
EVERY TIME THINGS ARE FINALLY STABLE... FINALLY GOOD...
SOMETHING SUDDEN HAPPENS...TO WRECK IT ALL...
FIGHT! FIGHT!
AND THEN I LEARN TO LIVE WITH THAT...
FIGHT! FIGHT! FIGHT!
AND AFTER A WHILE... WORSE-OFF BECOMES THE NEW NORMAL...

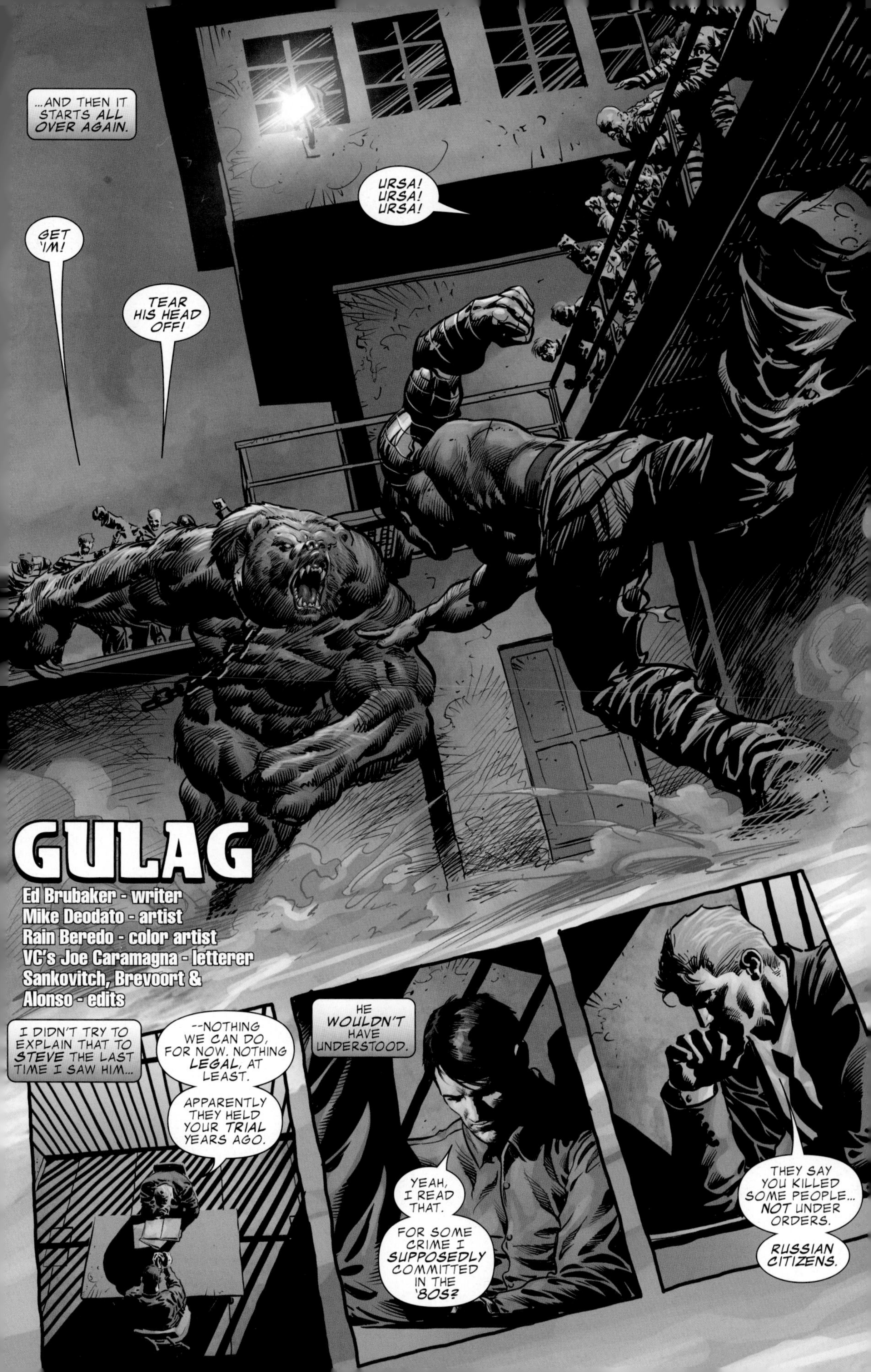
...AND THEN IT STARTS ALL OVER AGAIN.
GET 'IM!
URSA! URSA! URSA!
TEAR HIS HEAD OFF!
GULAG
Ed Brubaker - writer
Mike Deodato - artist
Rain Beredo - color artist
VC's Joe Caramagna - letterer
Sankovitch, Brevoort & Alonso - edits
I DIDN'T TRY TO EXPLAIN THAT TO STEVE THE LAST TIME I SAW HIM...
--NOTHING WE CAN DO, FOR NOW. NOTHING LEGAL, AT LEAST.
APPARENTLY THEY HELD YOUR TRIAL YEARS AGO.
HE WOULDN'T HAVE UNDERSTOOD.
YEAH, I READ THAT.
FOR SOME CRIME I SUPPOSEDLY COMMITTED IN THE '80S?
THEY SAY YOU KILLED SOME PEOPLE... NOT UNDER ORDERS.
RUSSIAN CITIZENS.

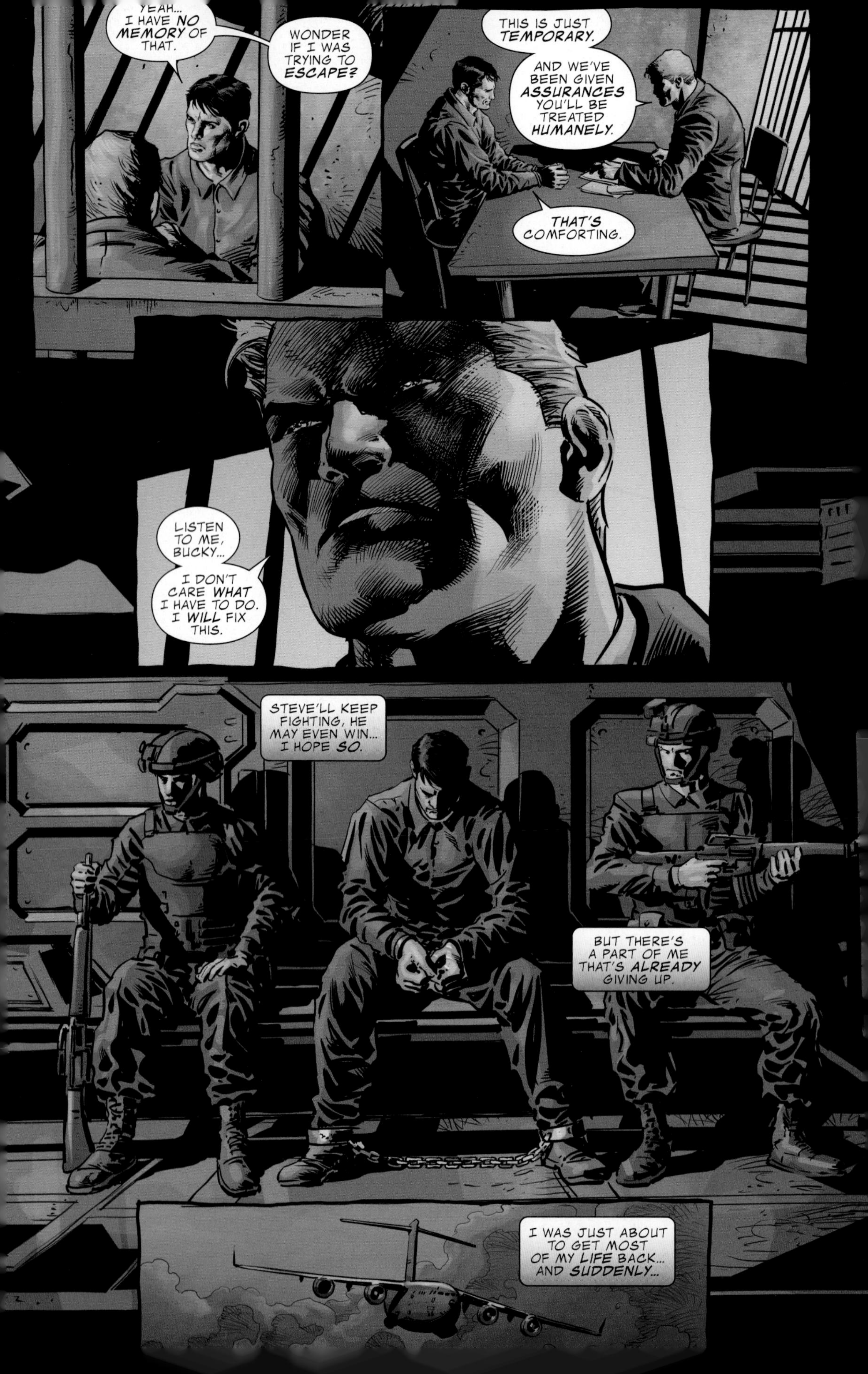
YEAH... I HAVE NO MEMORY OF THAT.
WONDER IF I WAS TRYING TO ESCAPE?
THIS IS JUST TEMPORARY.
AND WE'VE BEEN GIVEN ASSURANCES YOU'LL BE TREATED HUMANELY.
THAT'S COMFORTING.
LISTEN TO ME, BUCKY...
I DON'T CARE WHAT I HAVE TO DO. I WILL FIX THIS.
STEVE'LL KEEP FIGHTING, HE MAY EVEN WIN... I HOPE SO.
BUT THERE'S A PART OF ME THAT'S ALREADY GIVING UP.
I WAS JUST ABOUT TO GET MOST OF MY LIFE BACK... AND SUDDENLY...

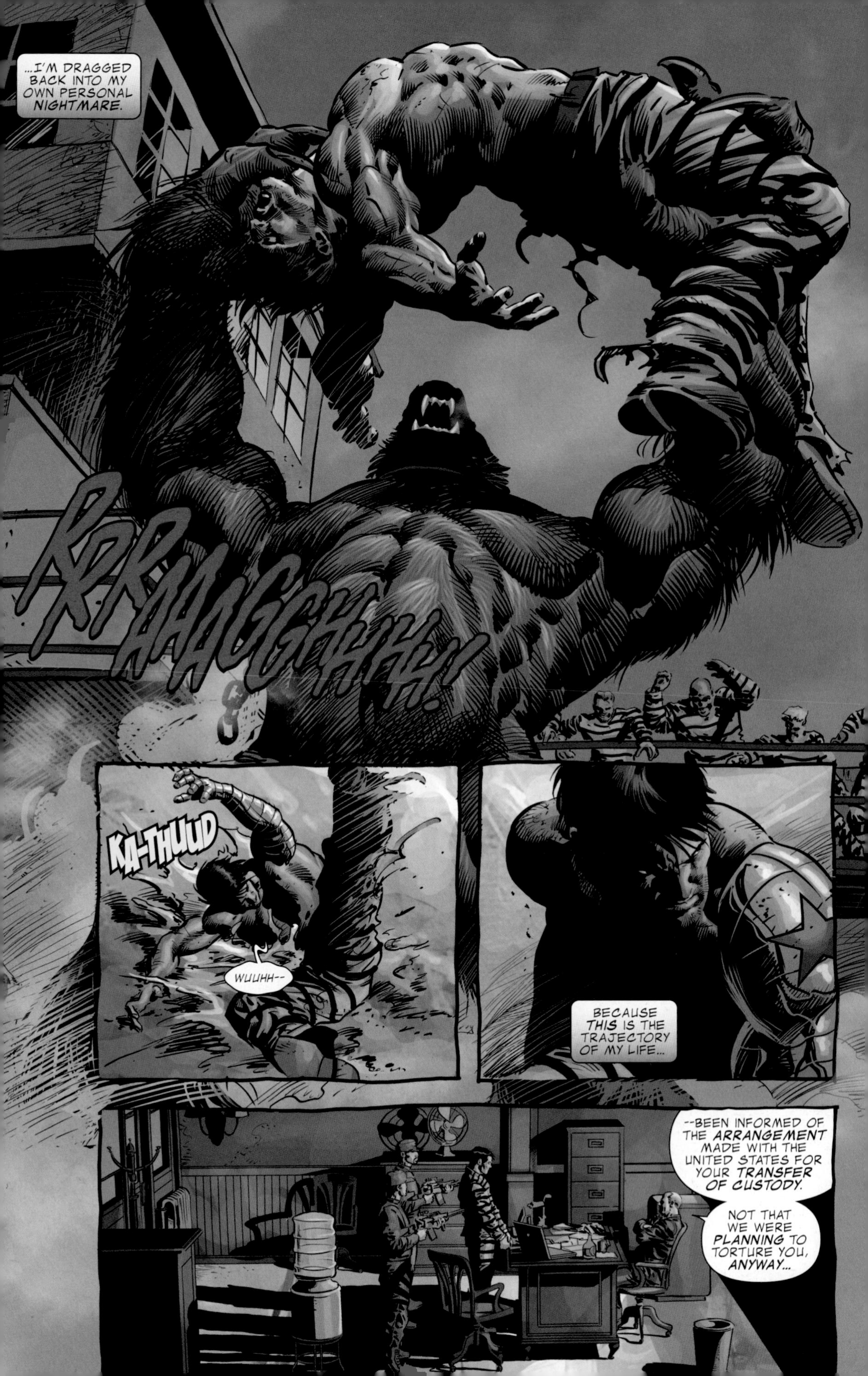
...I'M DRAGGED BACK INTO MY OWN PERSONAL NIGHTMARE.
RRRAAAGGHHHH!
KA-THUUD
WUUHH--
BECAUSE THIS IS THE TRAJECTORY OF MY LIFE...
--BEEN INFORMED OF THE ARRANGEMENT MADE WITH THE UNITED STATES FOR YOUR TRANSFER OF CUSTODY.
NOT THAT WE WERE PLANNING TO TORTURE YOU, ANYWAY...

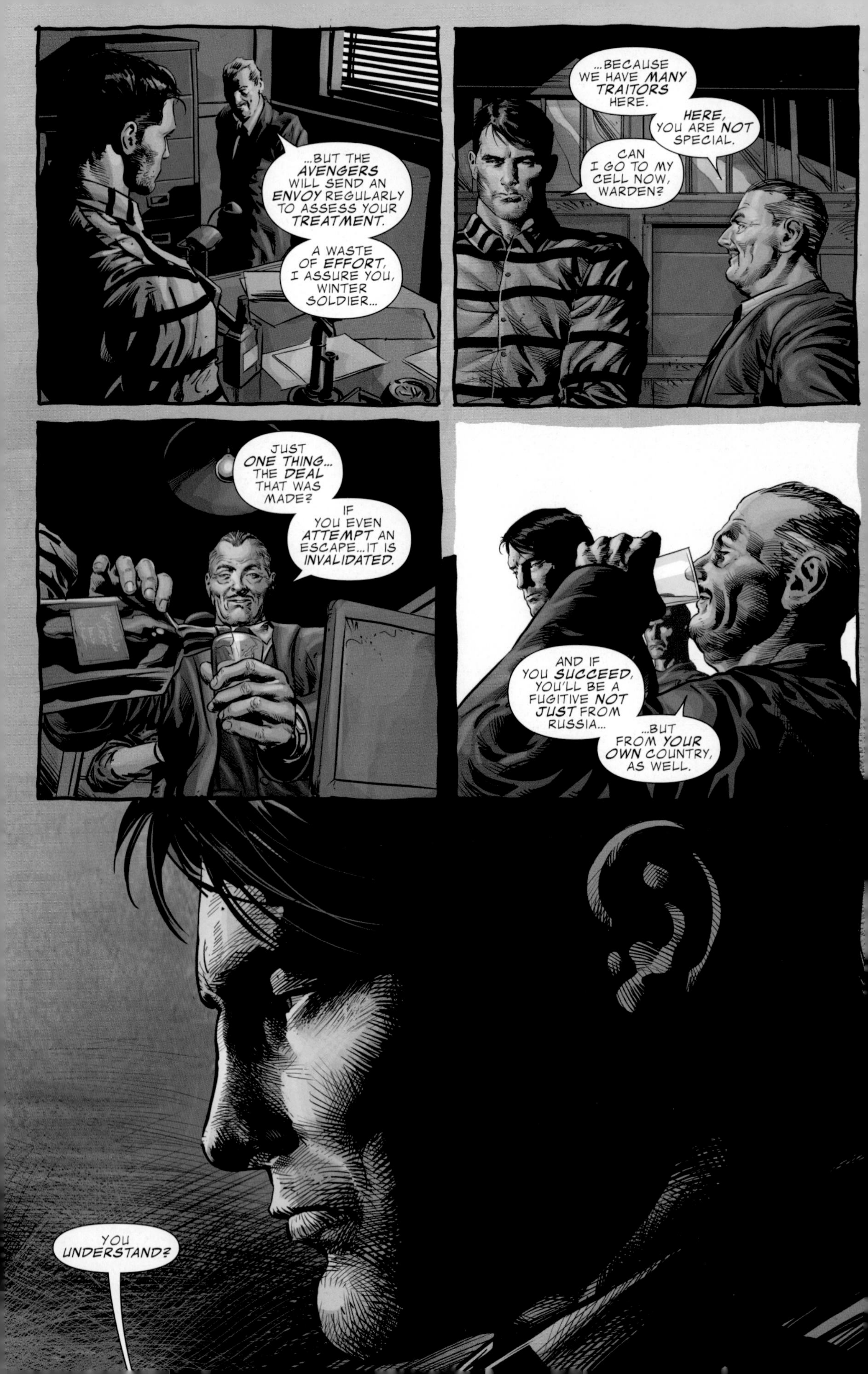
...BUT THE AVENGERS WILL SEND AN ENVOY REGULARLY TO ASSESS YOUR TREATMENT.
A WASTE OF EFFORT, I ASSURE YOU, WINTER SOLDIER...
...BECAUSE WE HAVE MANY TRAITORS HERE.
HERE, YOU ARE NOT SPECIAL.
CAN I GO TO MY CELL NOW, WARDEN?
JUST ONE THING... THE DEAL THAT WAS MADE?
IF YOU EVEN ATTEMPT AN ESCAPE...IT IS INVALIDATED.
AND IF YOU SUCCEED, YOU'LL BE A FUGITIVE NOT JUST FROM RUSSIA...
...BUT FROM YOUR OWN COUNTRY, AS WELL.
YOU UNDERSTAND?

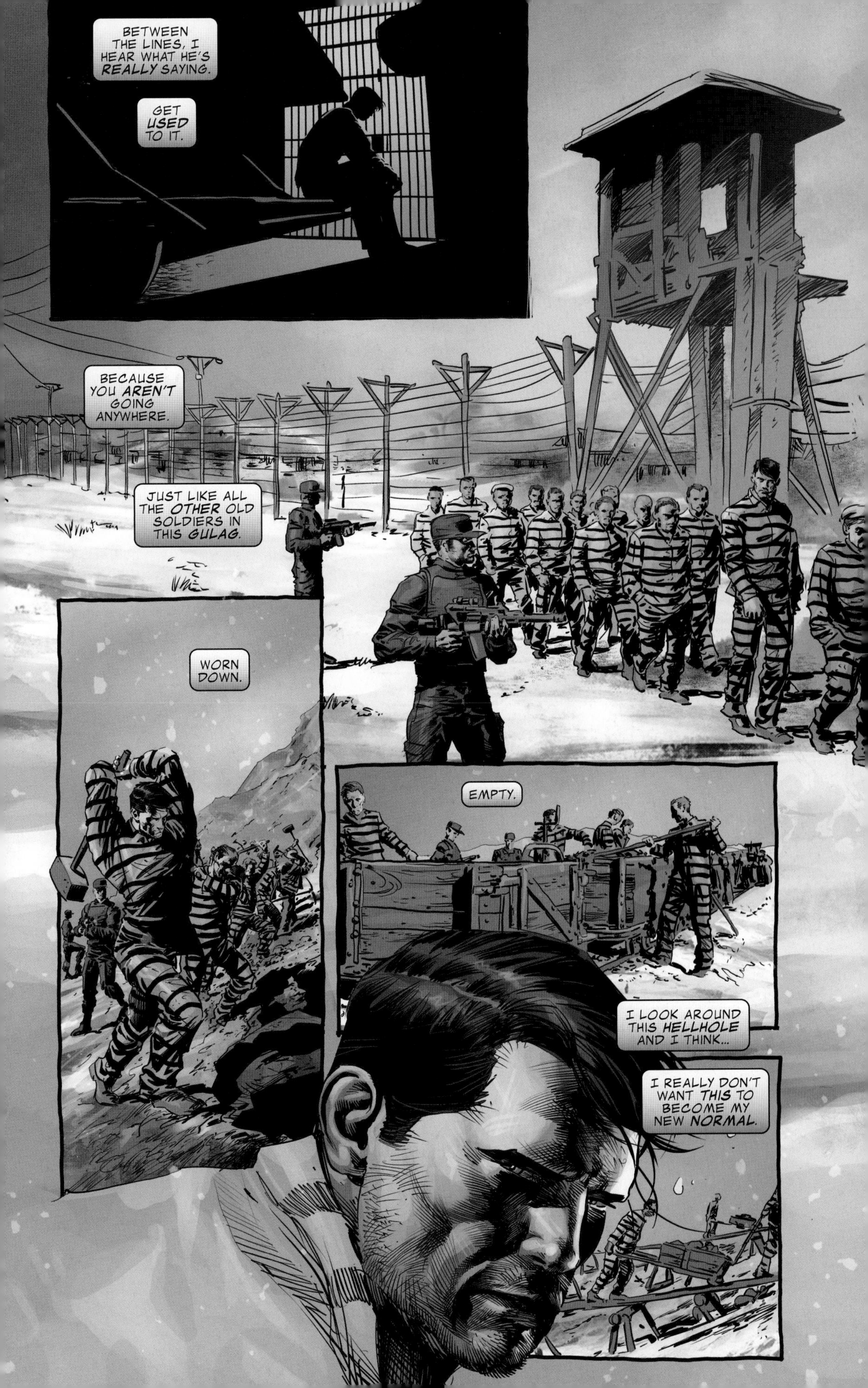
BETWEEN THE LINES, I HEAR WHAT HE'S REALLY SAYING.
GET USED TO IT.
BECAUSE YOU AREN'T GOING ANYWHERE.
JUST LIKE ALL THE OTHER OLD SOLDIERS IN THIS GULAG.
WORN DOWN.
EMPTY.
I LOOK AROUND THIS HELLHOLE AND I THINK...
I REALLY DON'T WANT THIS TO BECOME MY NEW NORMAL.

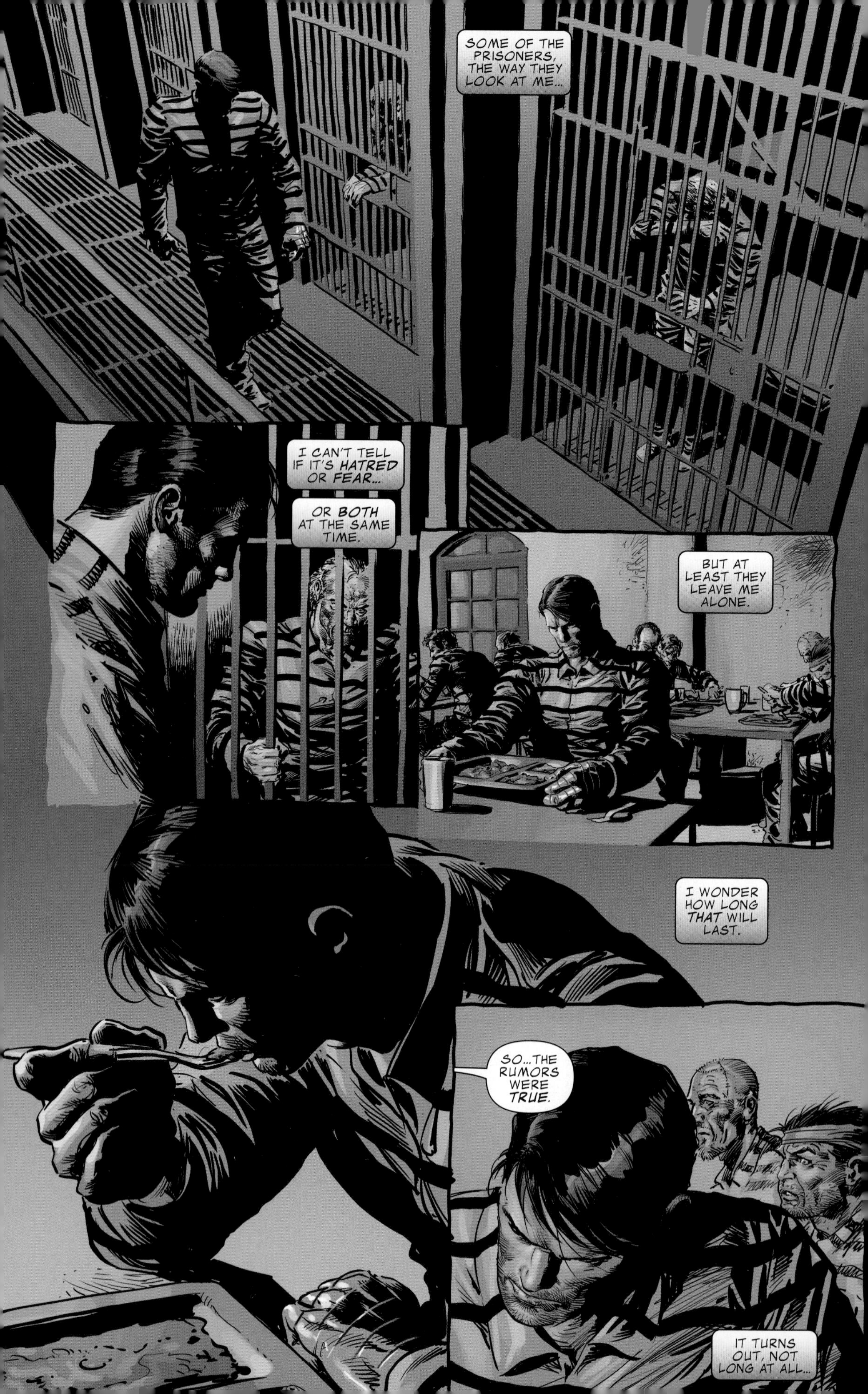
SOME OF THE PRISONERS, THE WAY THEY LOOK AT ME...
I CAN'T TELL IF IT'S *HATRED* OR *FEAR*...
OR *BOTH* AT THE SAME TIME.
BUT AT LEAST THEY LEAVE ME ALONE.
I WONDER HOW LONG *THAT* WILL LAST.
SO...THE RUMORS WERE *TRUE*.
IT TURNS OUT, NOT LONG AT ALL...

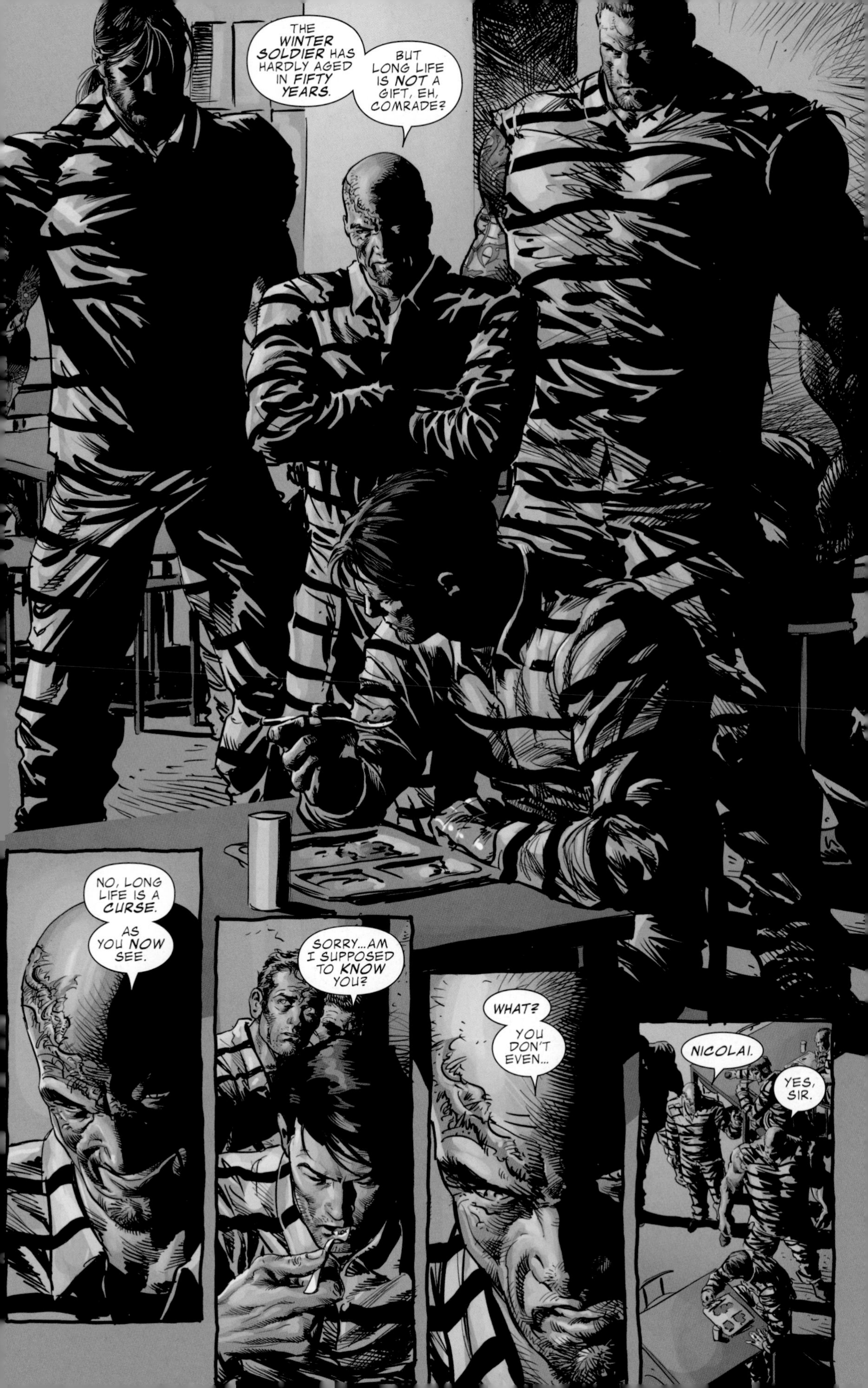
THE WINTER SOLDIER HAS HARDLY AGED IN FIFTY YEARS.
BUT LONG LIFE IS NOT A GIFT, EH, COMRADE?
NO, LONG LIFE IS A CURSE.
AS YOU NOW SEE.
SORRY...AM I SUPPOSED TO KNOW YOU?
WHAT?
YOU DON'T EVEN...
NICOLAI.
YES, SIR.

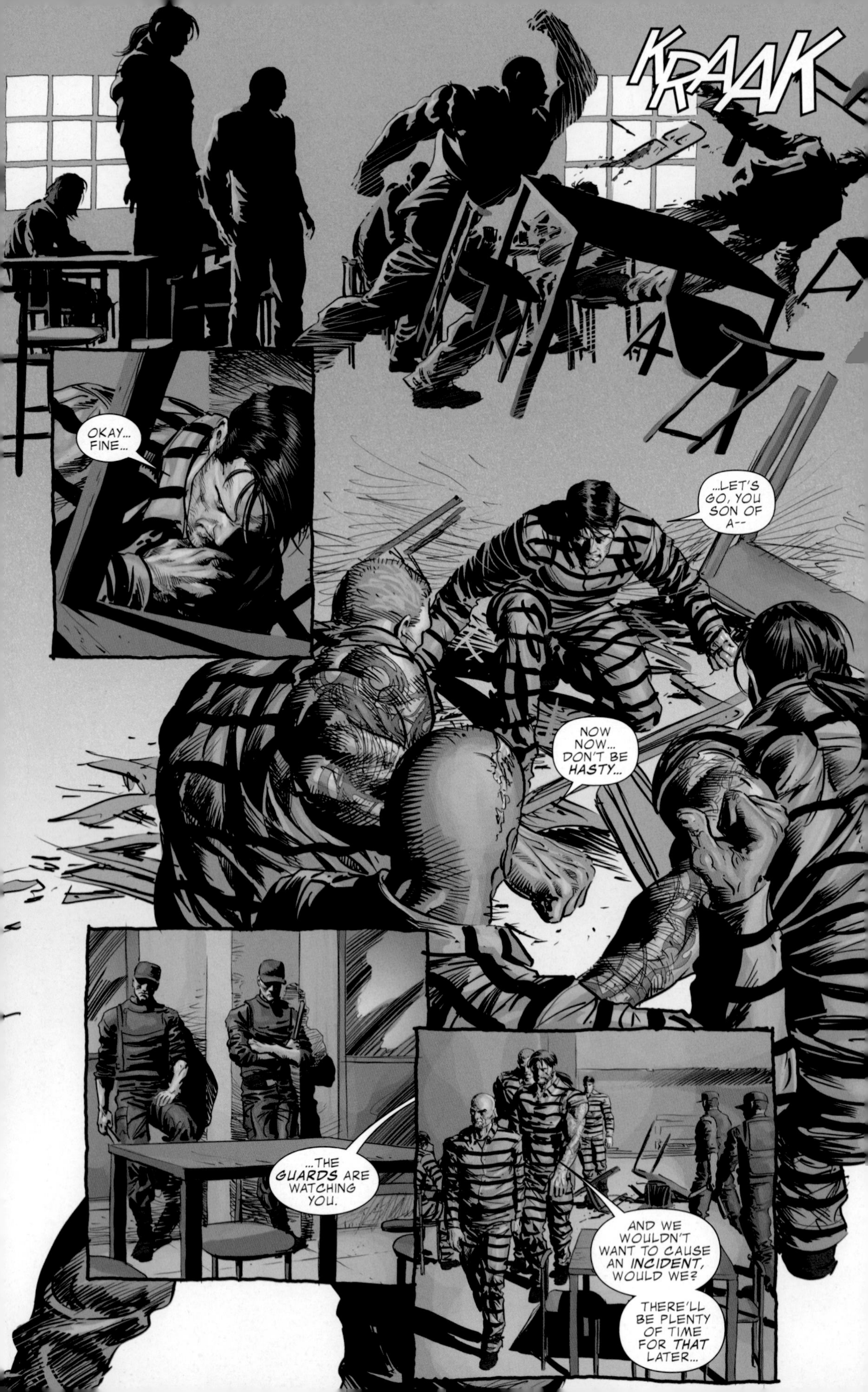
KRAAK
OKAY... FINE...
...LET'S GO, YOU SON OF A--
NOW NOW... DON'T BE HASTY...
...THE GUARDS ARE WATCHING YOU.
AND WE WOULDN'T WANT TO CAUSE AN INCIDENT, WOULD WE?
THERE'LL BE PLENTY OF TIME FOR THAT LATER...

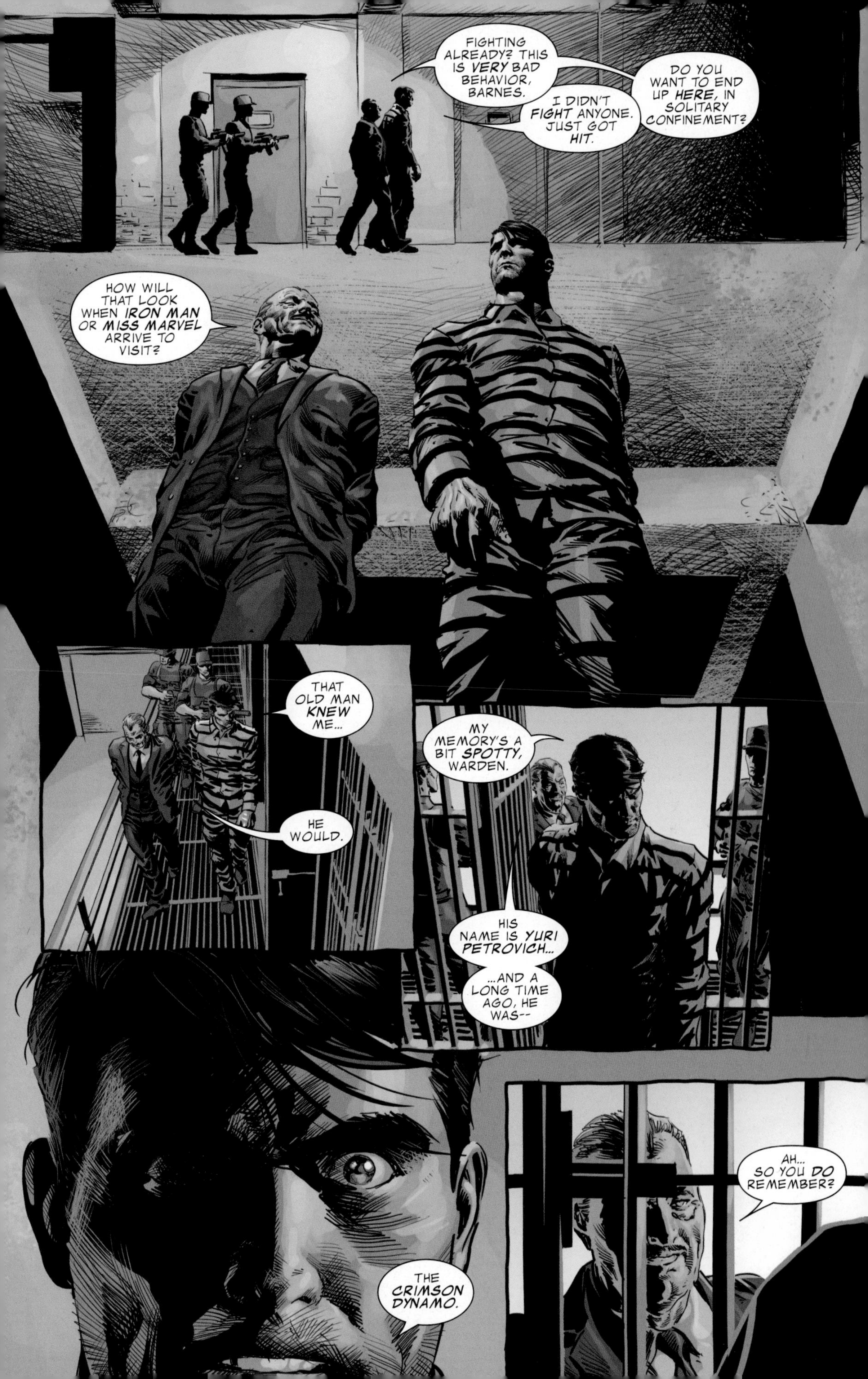
FIGHTING ALREADY? THIS IS VERY BAD BEHAVIOR, BARNES.
DO YOU WANT TO END UP HERE, IN SOLITARY CONFINEMENT?
I DIDN'T FIGHT ANYONE. JUST GOT HIT.
HOW WILL THAT LOOK WHEN IRON MAN OR MISS MARVEL ARRIVE TO VISIT?
THAT OLD MAN KNEW ME...
HE WOULD.
MY MEMORY'S A BIT SPOTTY, WARDEN.
HIS NAME IS YURI PETROVICH...
...AND A LONG TIME AGO, HE WAS--
THE CRIMSON DYNAMO.
AH... SO YOU DO REMEMBER?

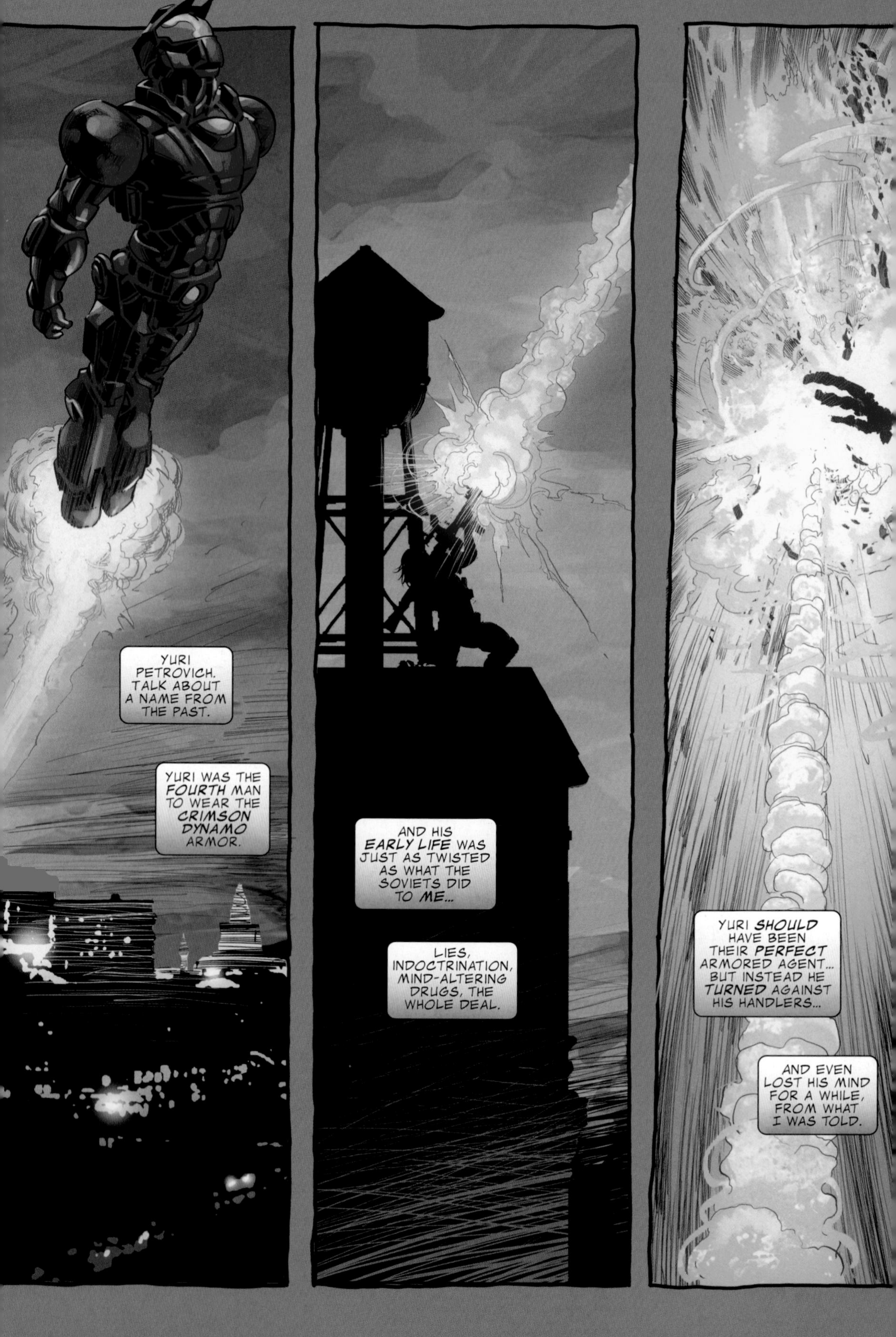
YURI PETROVICH. TALK ABOUT A NAME FROM THE PAST.
YURI WAS THE *FOURTH* MAN TO WEAR THE *CRIMSON DYNAMO* ARMOR.
AND HIS *EARLY LIFE* WAS JUST AS TWISTED AS WHAT THE SOVIETS DID TO *ME*...
LIES, INDOCTRINATION, MIND-ALTERING DRUGS, THE WHOLE DEAL.
YURI *SHOULD* HAVE BEEN THEIR *PERFECT* ARMORED AGENT... BUT INSTEAD HE *TURNED* AGAINST HIS HANDLERS...
AND EVEN LOST HIS MIND FOR A WHILE, FROM WHAT I WAS TOLD.

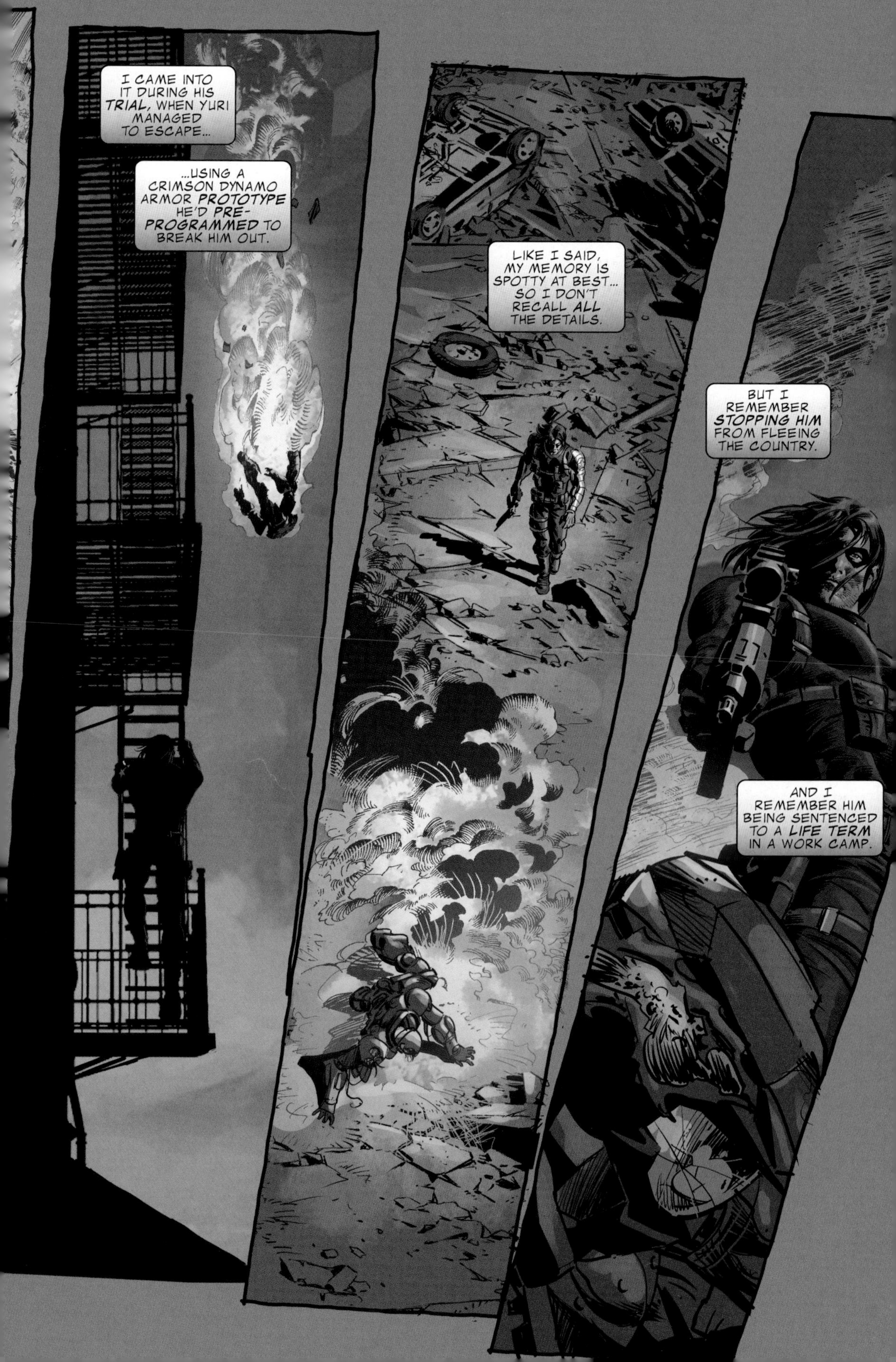
I CAME INTO IT DURING HIS TRIAL, WHEN YURI MANAGED TO ESCAPE...
...USING A CRIMSON DYNAMO ARMOR PROTOTYPE HE'D PRE-PROGRAMMED TO BREAK HIM OUT.
LIKE I SAID, MY MEMORY IS SPOTTY AT BEST... SO I DON'T RECALL ALL THE DETAILS.
BUT I REMEMBER STOPPING HIM FROM FLEEING THE COUNTRY.
AND I REMEMBER HIM BEING SENTENCED TO A LIFE TERM IN A WORK CAMP.

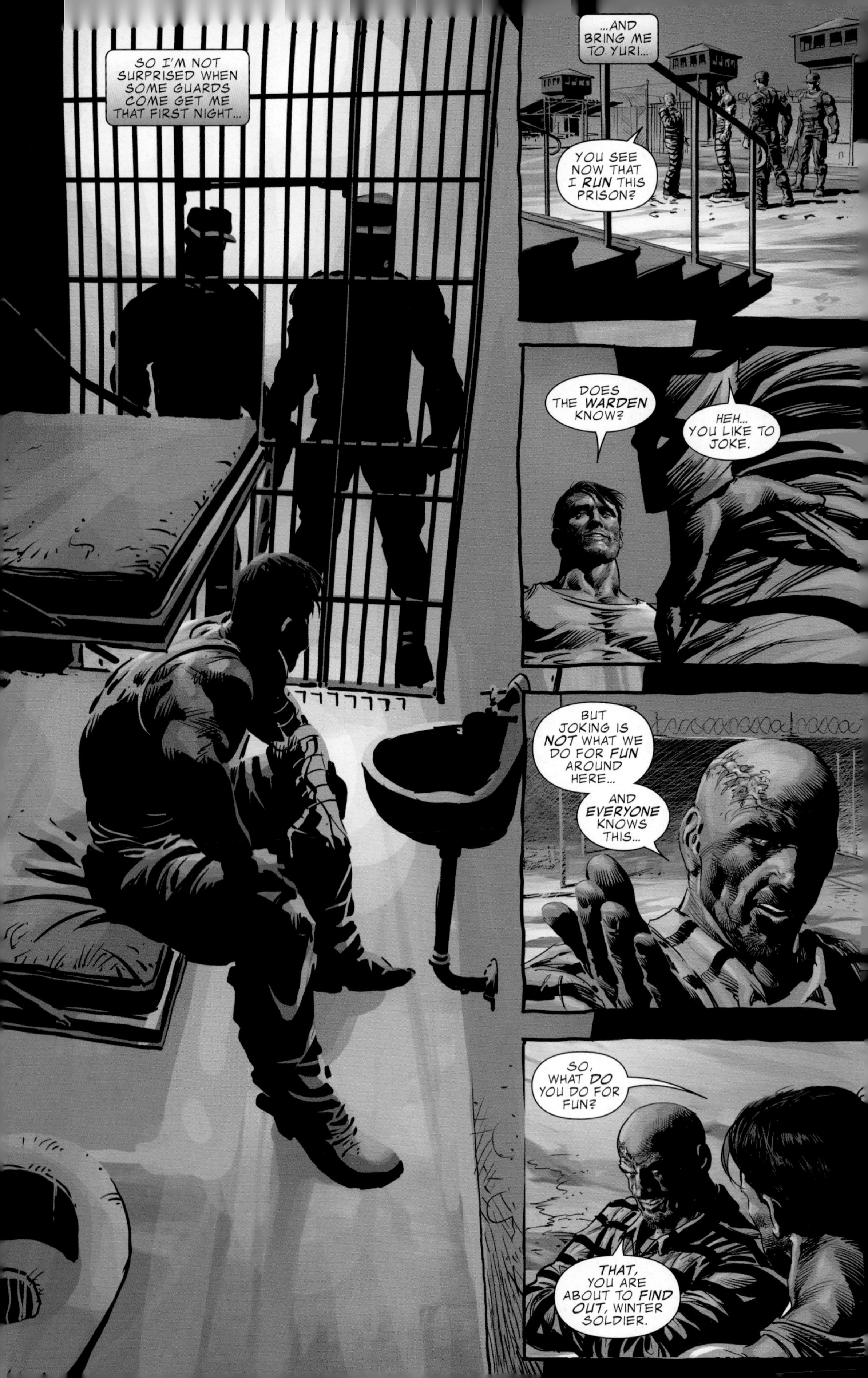
SO I'M NOT SURPRISED WHEN SOME GUARDS COME GET ME THAT FIRST NIGHT...
...AND BRING ME TO YURI...
YOU SEE NOW THAT I RUN THIS PRISON?
DOES THE WARDEN KNOW?
HEH... YOU LIKE TO JOKE.
BUT JOKING IS NOT WHAT WE DO FOR FUN AROUND HERE...
AND EVERYONE KNOWS THIS...
SO, WHAT DO YOU DO FOR FUN?
THAT, YOU ARE ABOUT TO FIND OUT, WINTER SOLDIER.

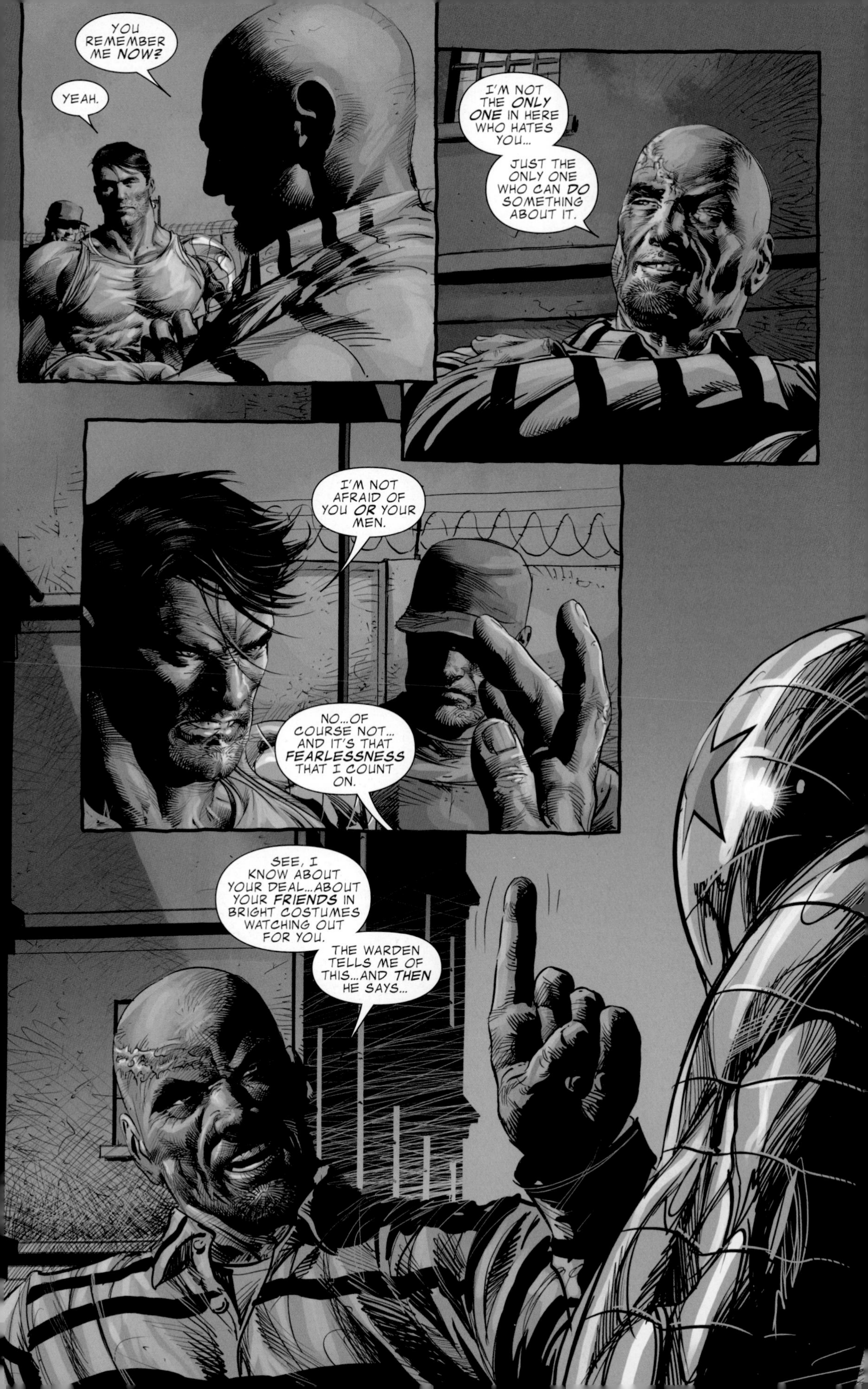
YOU REMEMBER ME NOW?
YEAH.
I'M NOT THE ONLY ONE IN HERE WHO HATES YOU...
JUST THE ONLY ONE WHO CAN DO SOMETHING ABOUT IT.
I'M NOT AFRAID OF YOU OR YOUR MEN.
NO...OF COURSE NOT... AND IT'S THAT FEARLESSNESS THAT I COUNT ON.
SEE, I KNOW ABOUT YOUR DEAL...ABOUT YOUR FRIENDS IN BRIGHT COSTUMES WATCHING OUT FOR YOU.
THE WARDEN TELLS ME OF THIS...AND THEN HE SAYS...

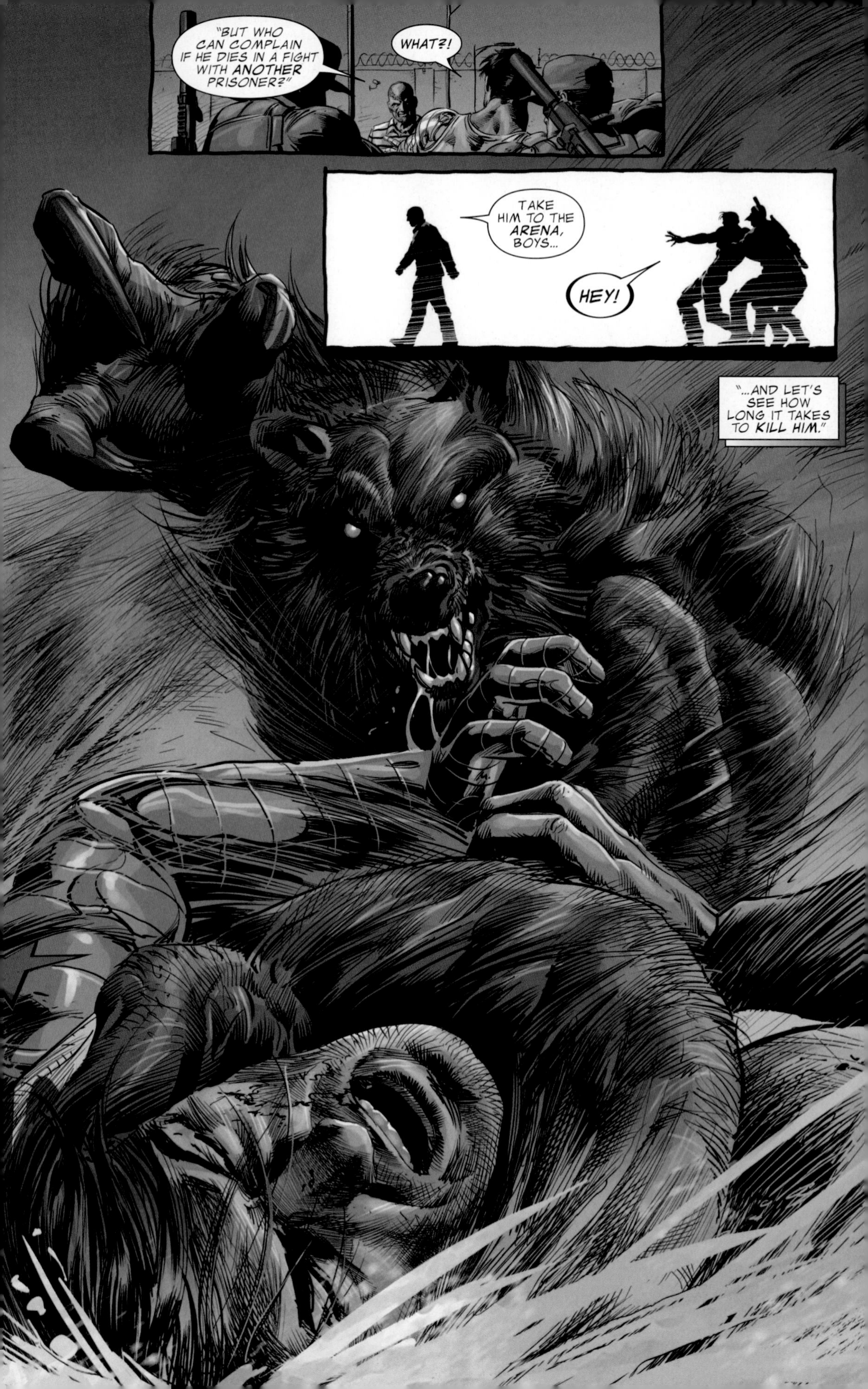
"BUT WHO CAN COMPLAIN IF HE DIES IN A FIGHT WITH ANOTHER PRISONER?"
WHAT?!
TAKE HIM TO THE ARENA, BOYS...
HEY!
"...AND LET'S SEE HOW LONG IT TAKES TO KILL HIM."

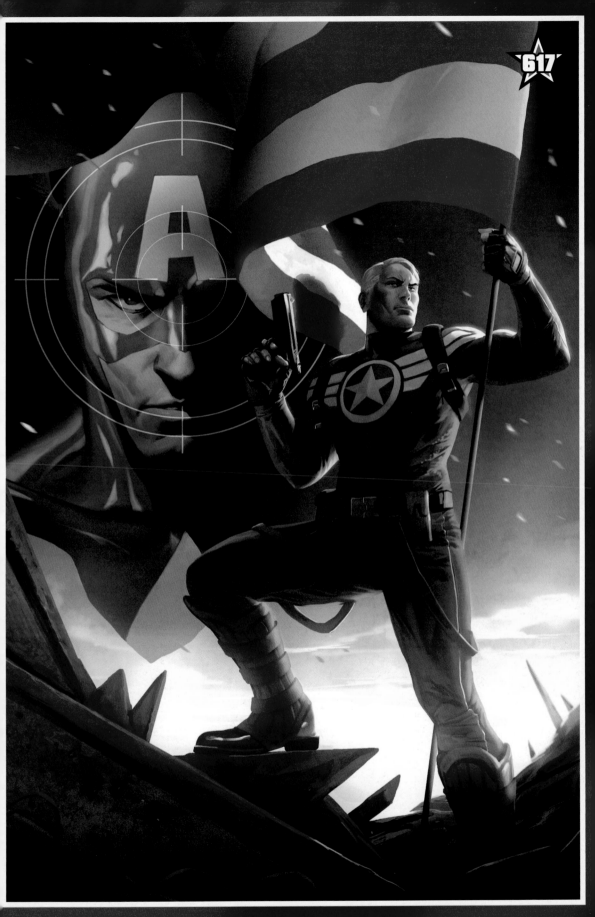

GULAG PART 2

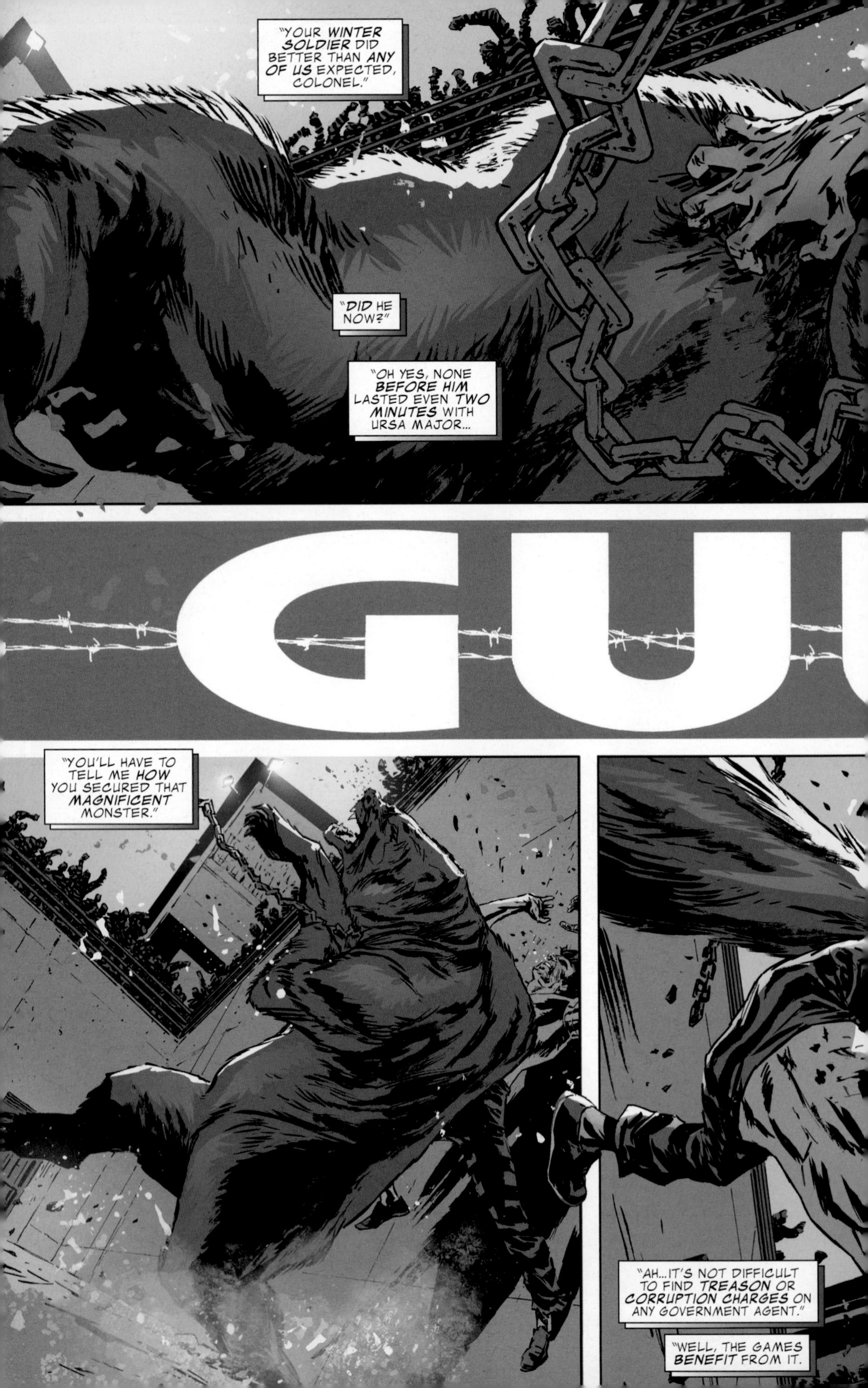
"YOUR WINTER SOLDIER DID BETTER THAN ANY OF US EXPECTED, COLONEL."
"DID HE NOW?"
"OH YES, NONE BEFORE HIM LASTED EVEN TWO MINUTES WITH URSA MAJOR...
GU
"YOU'LL HAVE TO TELL ME HOW YOU SECURED THAT MAGNIFICENT MONSTER."
"AH...IT'S NOT DIFFICULT TO FIND TREASON OR CORRUPTION CHARGES ON ANY GOVERNMENT AGENT."
"WELL, THE GAMES BENEFIT FROM IT.

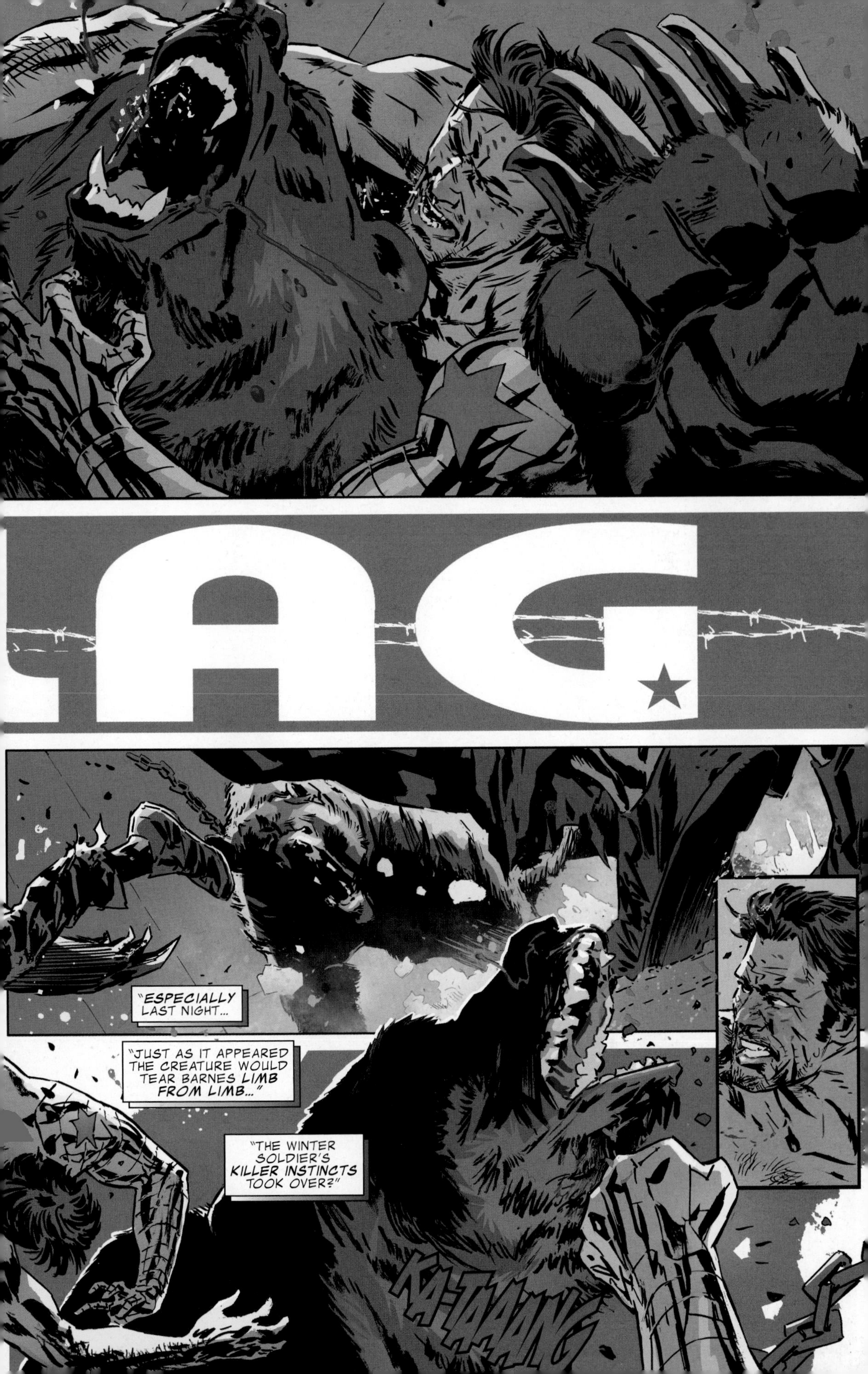
AG
"ESPECIALLY LAST NIGHT...
"JUST AS IT APPEARED THE CREATURE WOULD TEAR BARNES LIMB FROM LIMB..."
"THE WINTER SOLDIER'S KILLER INSTINCTS TOOK OVER?"
KA-TAAANG

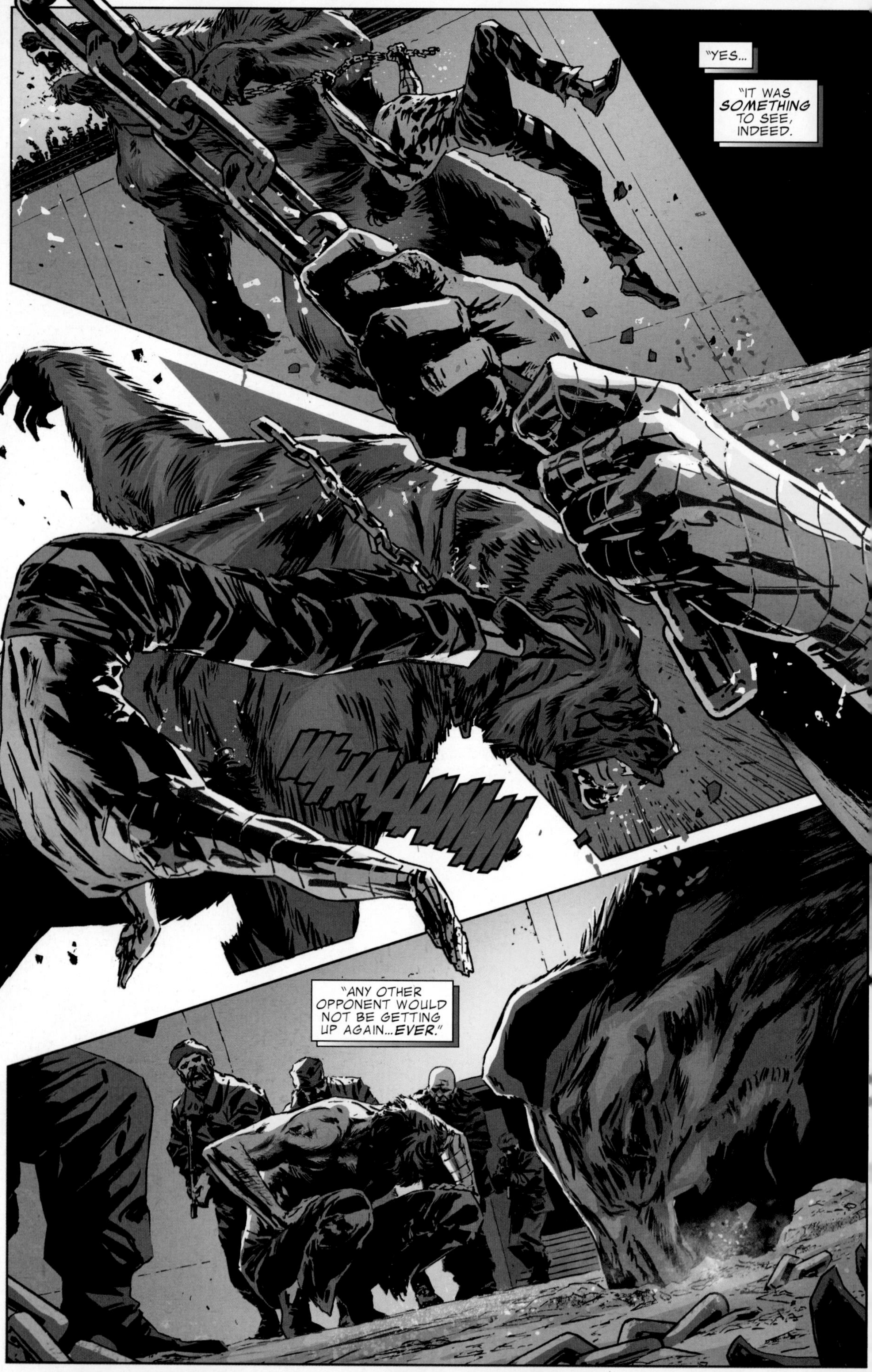
"YES...
"IT WAS SOMETHING TO SEE, INDEED.
WHAAAMM
"ANY OTHER OPPONENT WOULD NOT BE GETTING UP AGAIN...EVER."

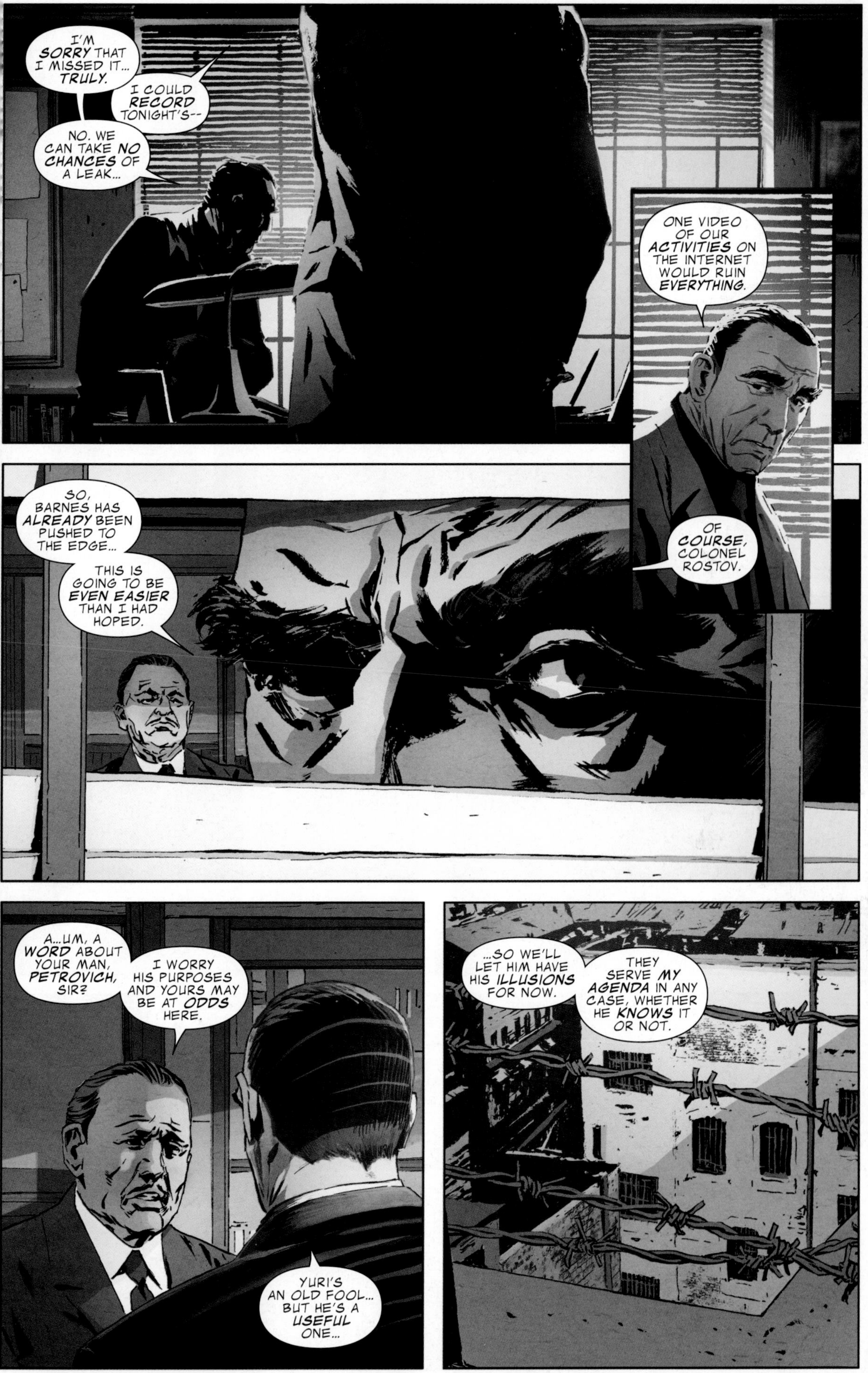
I'M SORRY THAT I MISSED IT... TRULY.
I COULD RECORD TONIGHT'S--
NO. WE CAN TAKE NO CHANCES OF A LEAK...
ONE VIDEO OF OUR ACTIVITIES ON THE INTERNET WOULD RUIN EVERYTHING.
OF COURSE, COLONEL ROSTOV.
SO, BARNES HAS ALREADY BEEN PUSHED TO THE EDGE...
THIS IS GOING TO BE EVEN EASIER THAN I HAD HOPED.
A...UM, A WORD ABOUT YOUR MAN, PETROVICH, SIR?
I WORRY HIS PURPOSES AND YOURS MAY BE AT ODDS HERE.
YURI'S AN OLD FOOL... BUT HE'S A USEFUL ONE...
...SO WE'LL LET HIM HAVE HIS ILLUSIONS FOR NOW.
THEY SERVE MY AGENDA IN ANY CASE, WHETHER HE KNOWS IT OR NOT.

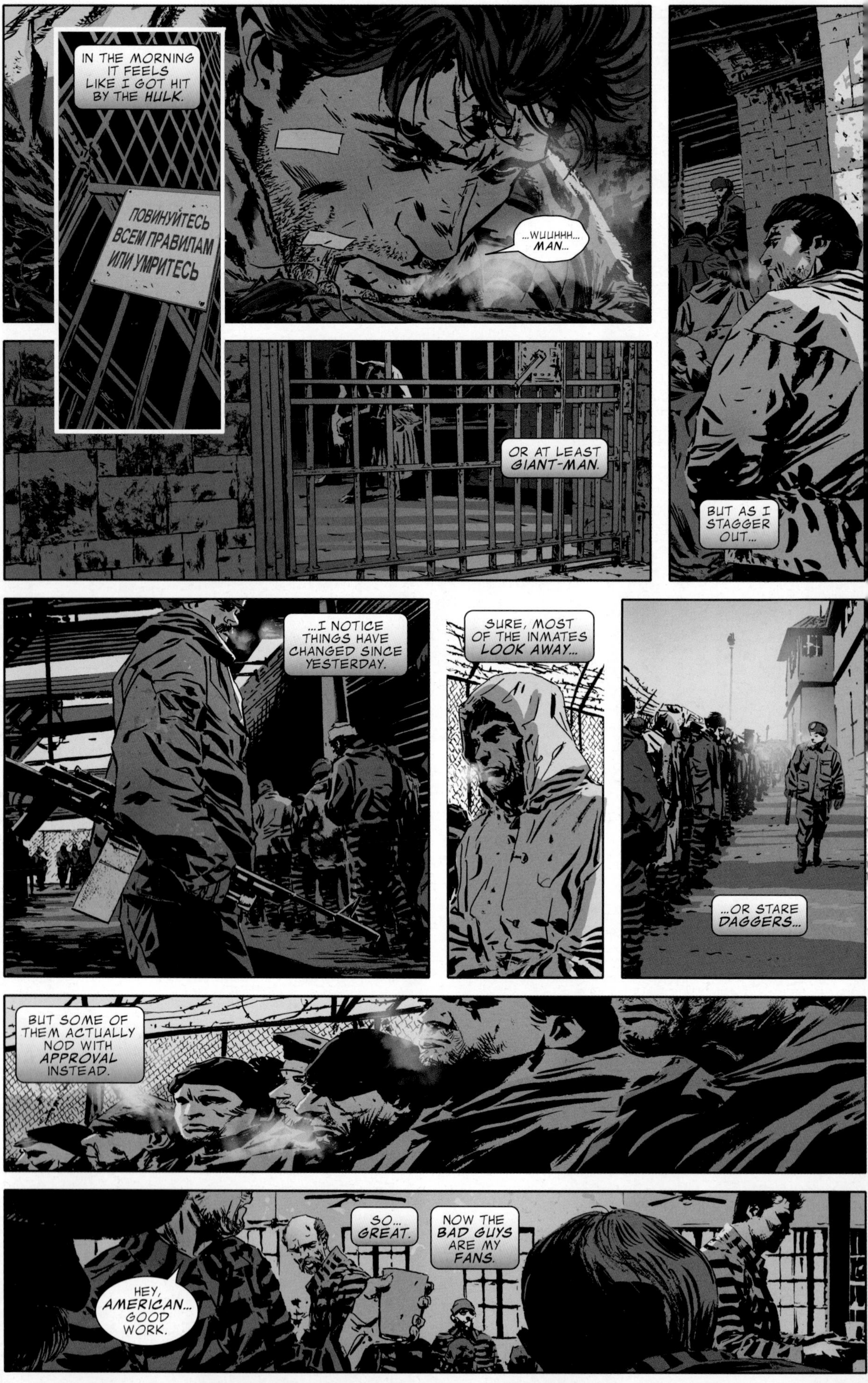
IN THE MORNING IT FEELS LIKE I GOT HIT BY THE HULK.
ПОВИНУЙТЕСЬ ВСЕМ ПРАВИЛАМ ИЛИ УМРИТЕСЬ
...WUUHHH... MAN...
OR AT LEAST GIANT-MAN.
BUT AS I STAGGER OUT...
...I NOTICE THINGS HAVE CHANGED SINCE YESTERDAY.
SURE, MOST OF THE INMATES LOOK AWAY...
...OR STARE DAGGERS...
BUT SOME OF THEM ACTUALLY NOD WITH APPROVAL INSTEAD.
HEY, AMERICAN... GOOD WORK.
SO... GREAT.
NOW THE BAD GUYS ARE MY FANS.

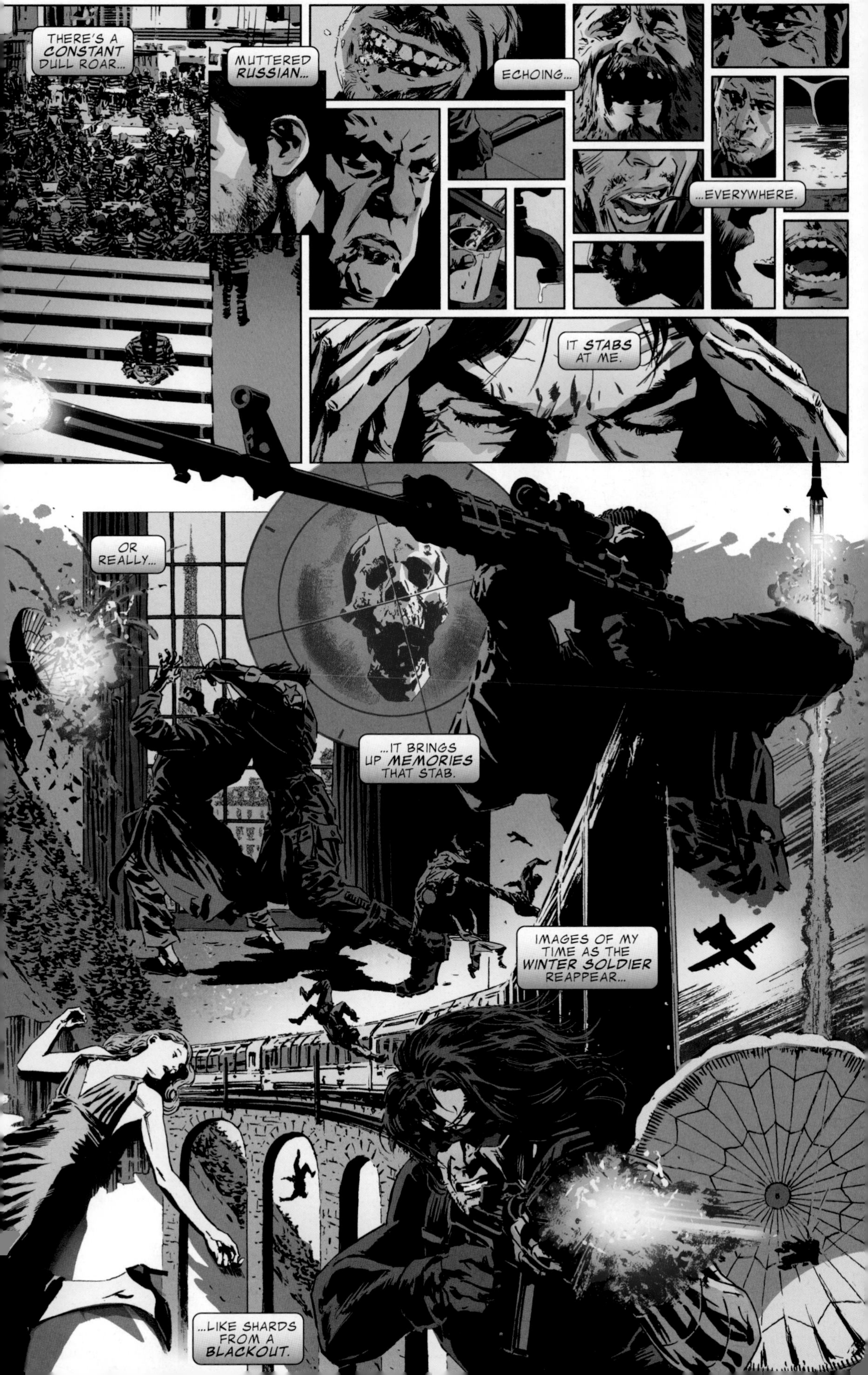
THERE'S A CONSTANT DULL ROAR...
MUTTERED RUSSIAN...
ECHOING...
...EVERYWHERE.
IT STABS AT ME.
OR REALLY...
...IT BRINGS UP MEMORIES THAT STAB.
IMAGES OF MY TIME AS THE WINTER SOLDIER REAPPEAR...
...LIKE SHARDS FROM A BLACKOUT.

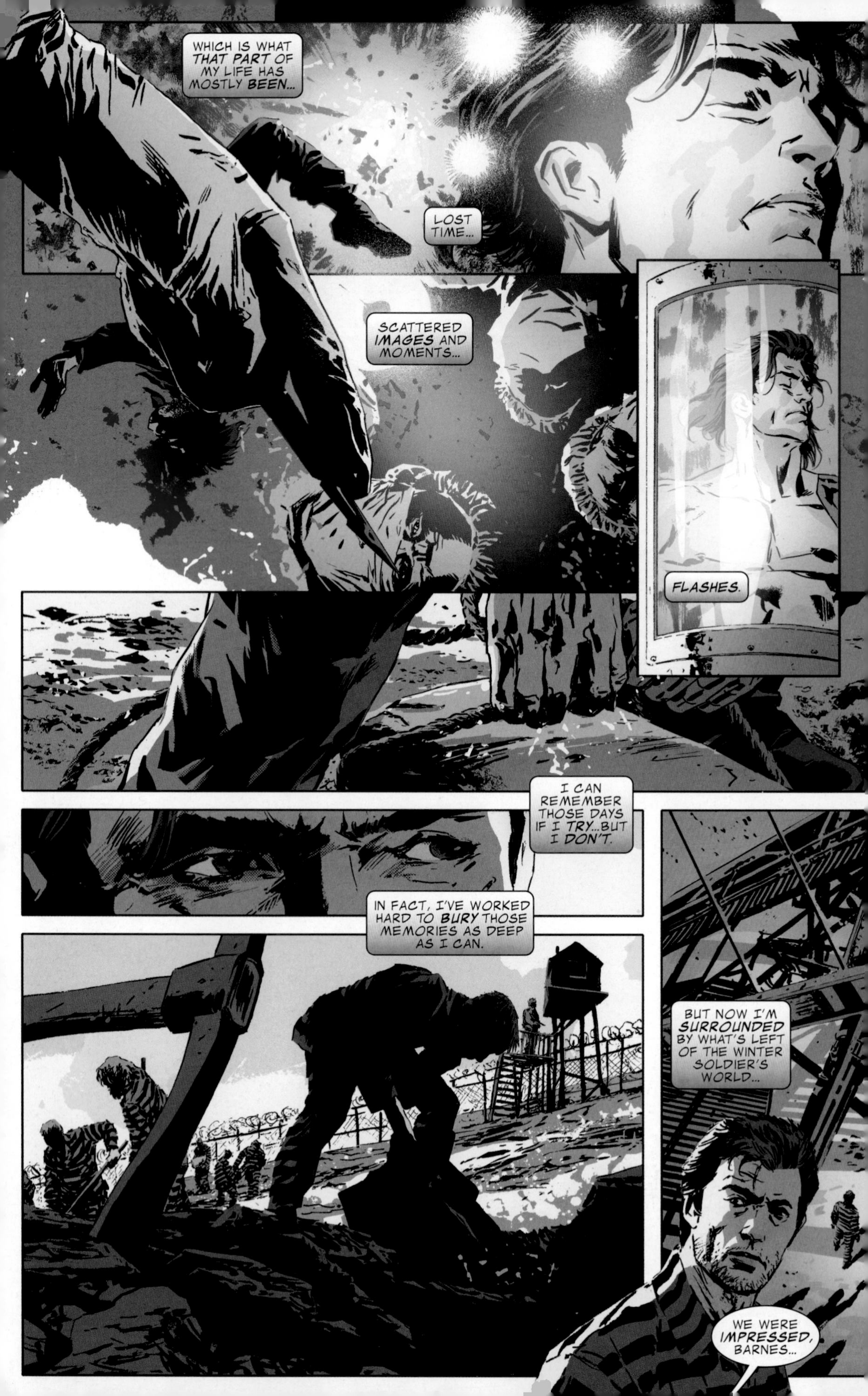
WHICH IS WHAT THAT PART OF MY LIFE HAS MOSTLY BEEN...
LOST TIME...
SCATTERED IMAGES AND MOMENTS...
FLASHES.
I CAN REMEMBER THOSE DAYS IF I TRY...BUT I DON'T.
IN FACT, I'VE WORKED HARD TO BURY THOSE MEMORIES AS DEEP AS I CAN.
BUT NOW I'M SURROUNDED BY WHAT'S LEFT OF THE WINTER SOLDIER'S WORLD...
WE WERE IMPRESSED, BARNES...

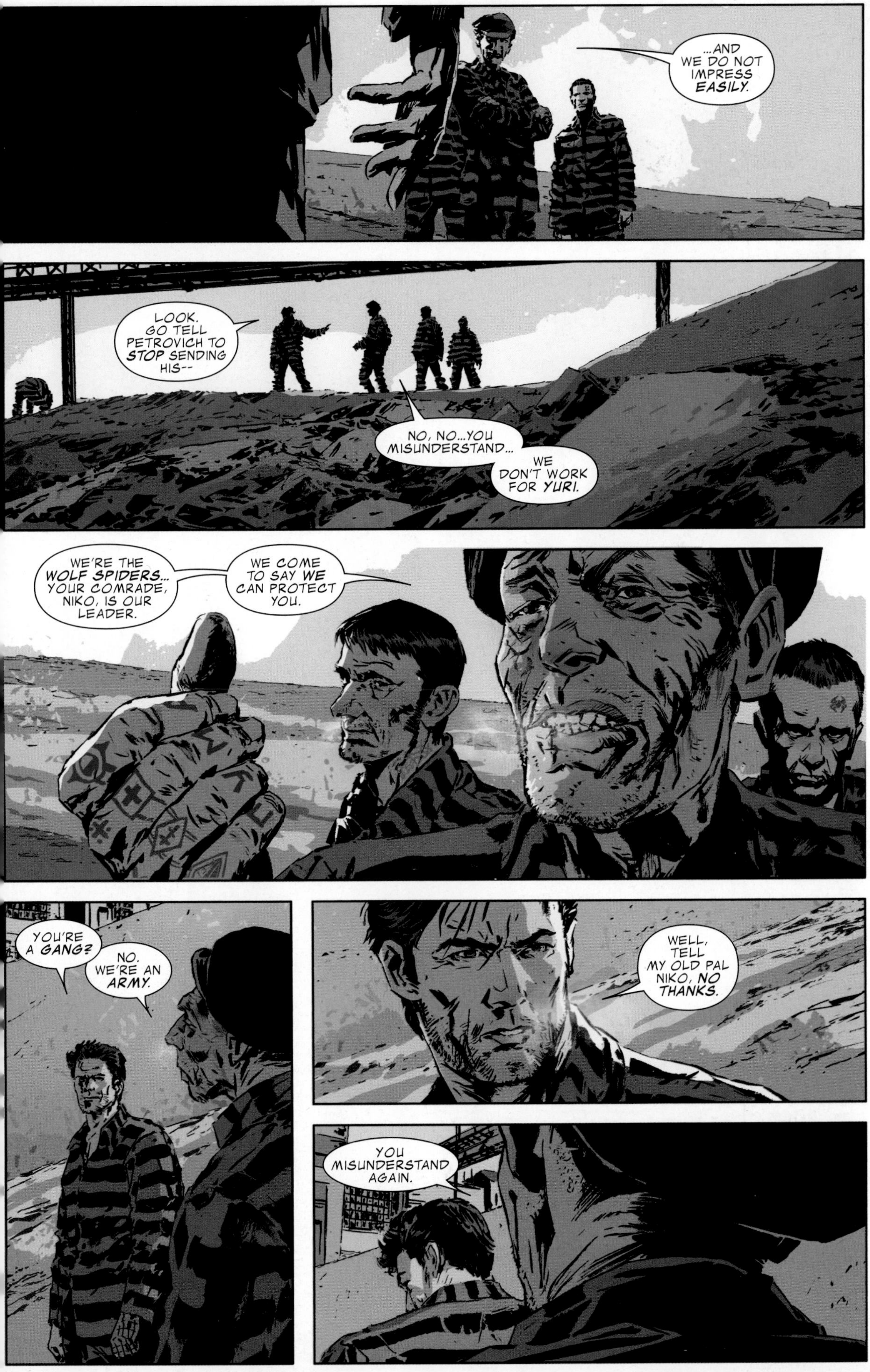
...AND WE DO NOT IMPRESS EASILY.
LOOK. GO TELL PETROVICH TO STOP SENDING HIS--
NO, NO...YOU MISUNDERSTAND...
WE DON'T WORK FOR YURI.
WE'RE THE WOLF SPIDERS... YOUR COMRADE, NIKO, IS OUR LEADER.
WE COME TO SAY WE CAN PROTECT YOU.
YOU'RE A GANG?
NO. WE'RE AN ARMY.
WELL, TELL MY OLD PAL NIKO, NO THANKS.
YOU MISUNDERSTAND AGAIN.

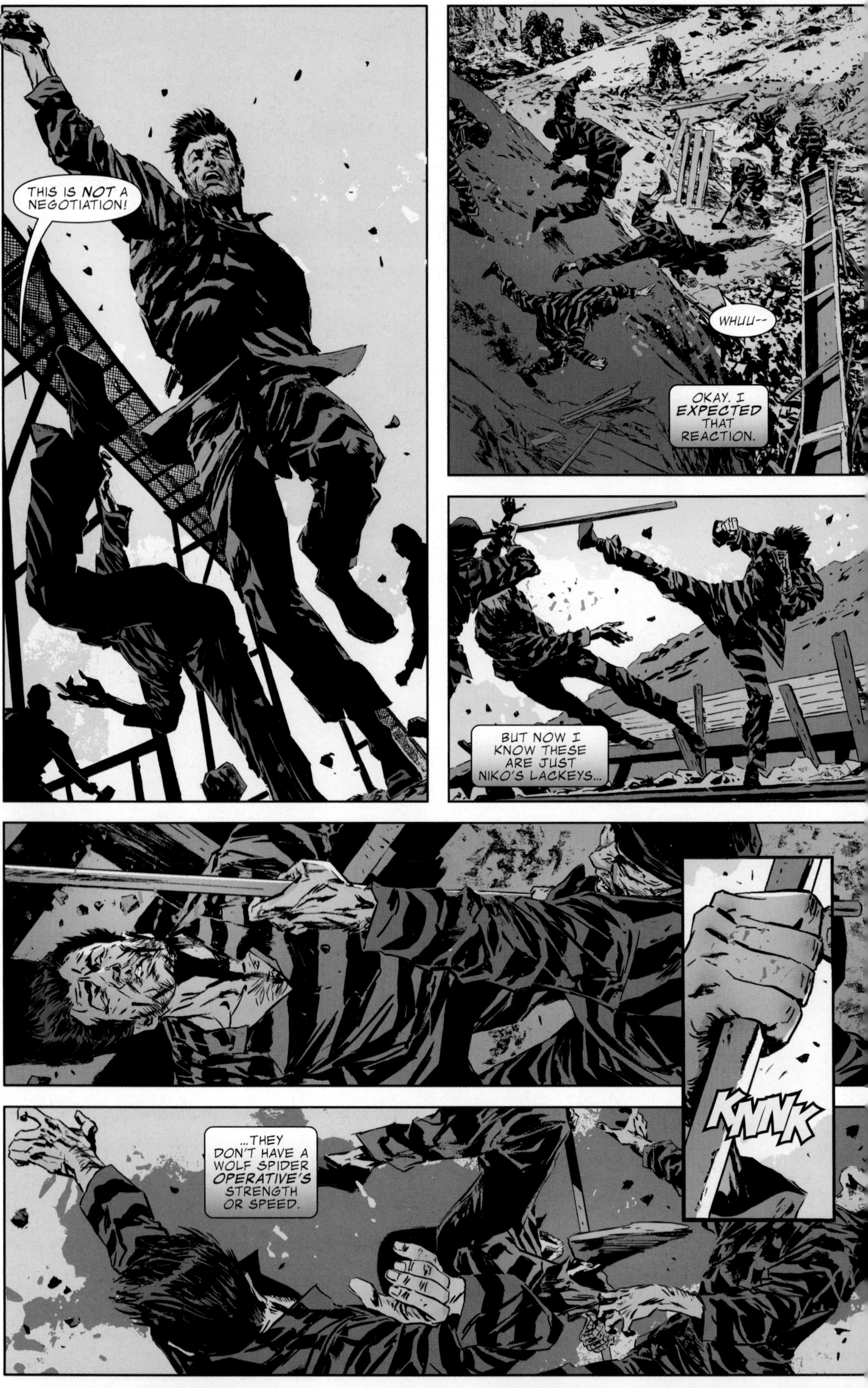
THIS IS NOT A NEGOTIATION!
WHUU--
OKAY. I EXPECTED THAT REACTION.
BUT NOW I KNOW THESE ARE JUST NIKO'S LACKEYS...
KNNK
...THEY DON'T HAVE A WOLF SPIDER OPERATIVE'S STRENGTH OR SPEED.

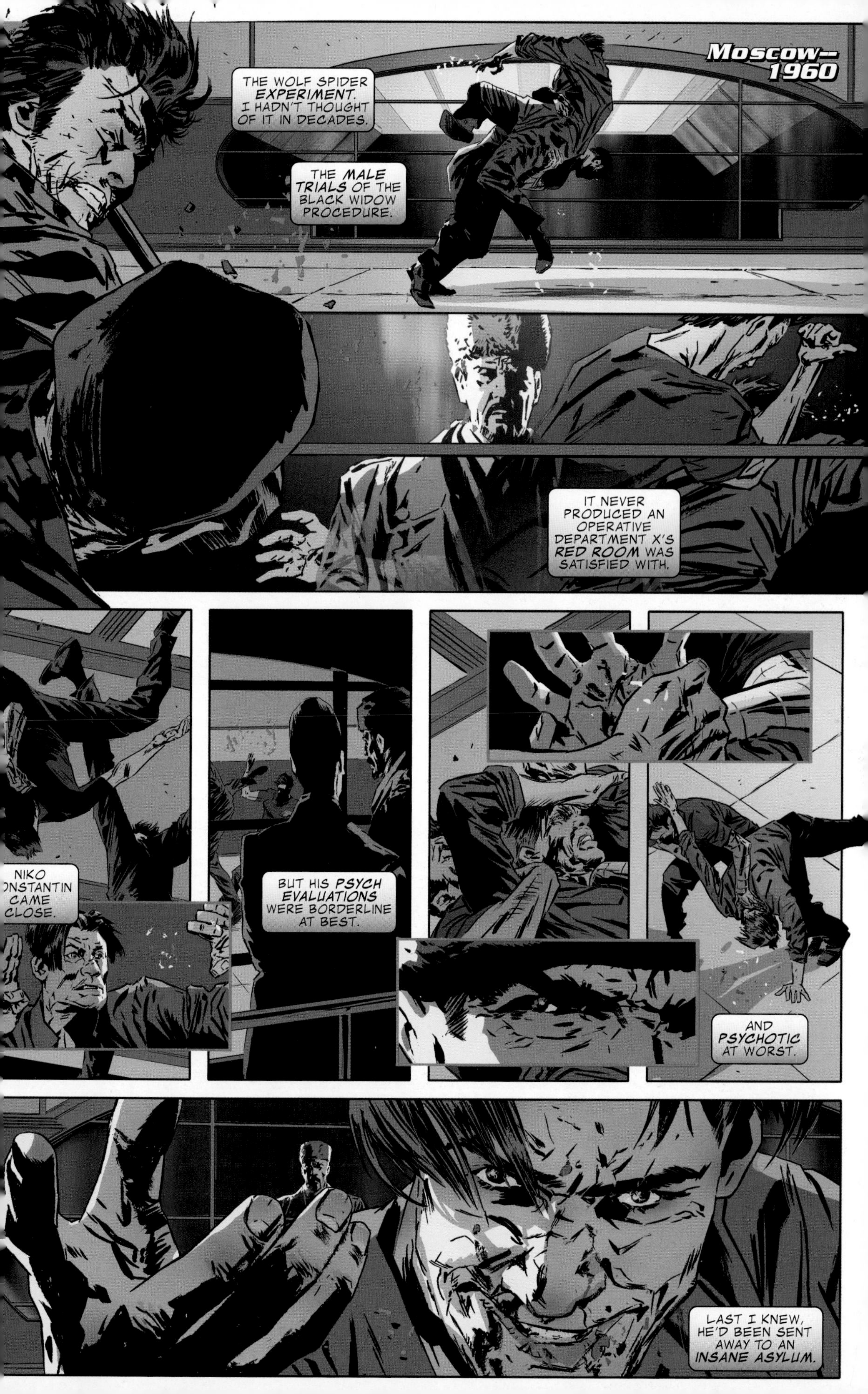
Moscow-- 1960
THE WOLF SPIDER EXPERIMENT. I HADN'T THOUGHT OF IT IN DECADES.
THE MALE TRIALS OF THE BLACK WIDOW PROCEDURE.
IT NEVER PRODUCED AN OPERATIVE DEPARTMENT X'S RED ROOM WAS SATISFIED WITH.
NIKO ONSTANTIN CAME CLOSE.
BUT HIS PSYCH EVALUATIONS WERE BORDERLINE AT BEST.
AND PSYCHOTIC AT WORST.
LAST I KNEW, HE'D BEEN SENT AWAY TO AN INSANE ASYLUM.

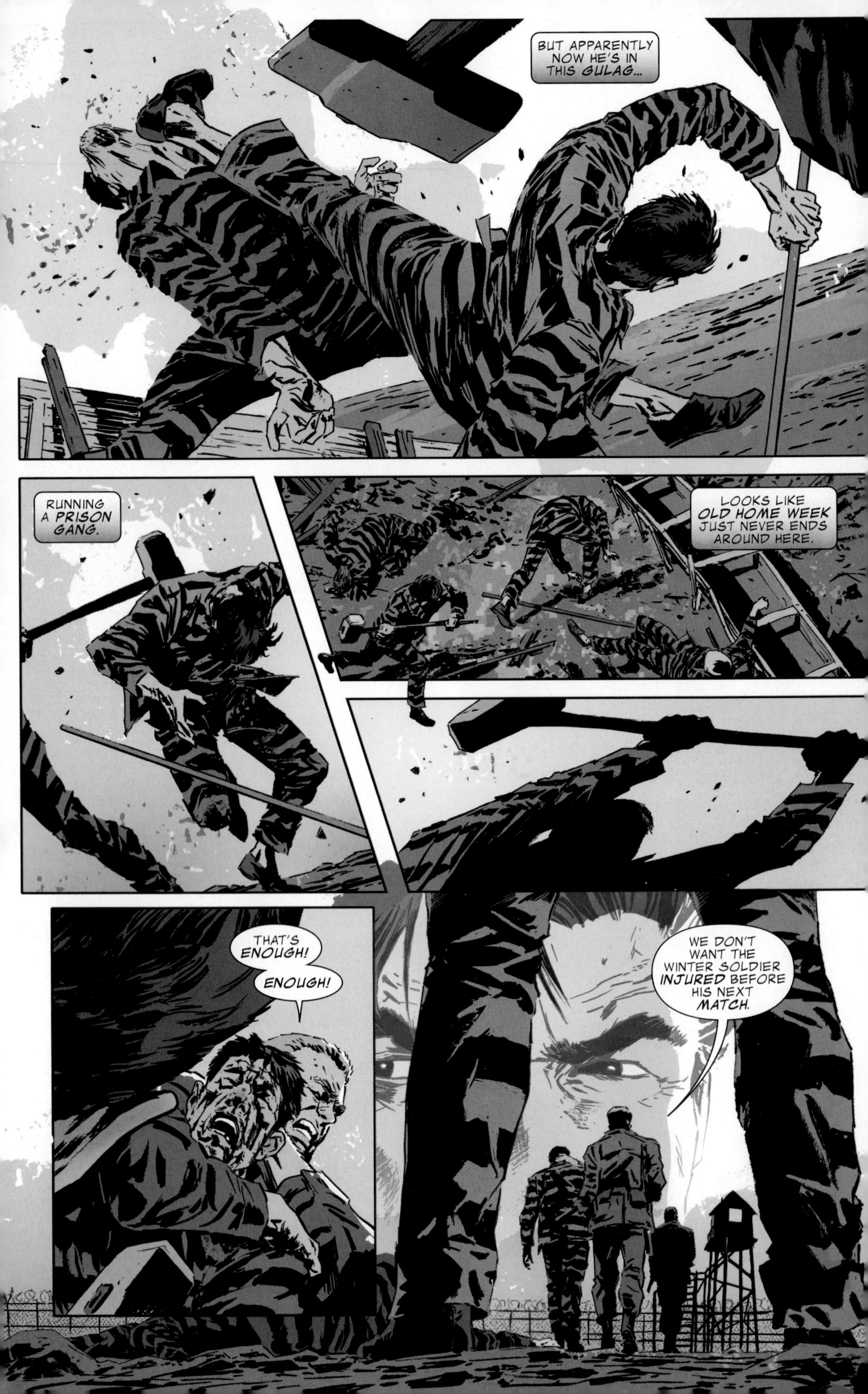
BUT APPARENTLY NOW HE'S IN THIS GULAG...
RUNNING A PRISON GANG.
LOOKS LIKE OLD HOME WEEK JUST NEVER ENDS AROUND HERE.
THAT'S ENOUGH!
ENOUGH!
WE DON'T WANT THE WINTER SOLDIER INJURED BEFORE HIS NEXT MATCH.

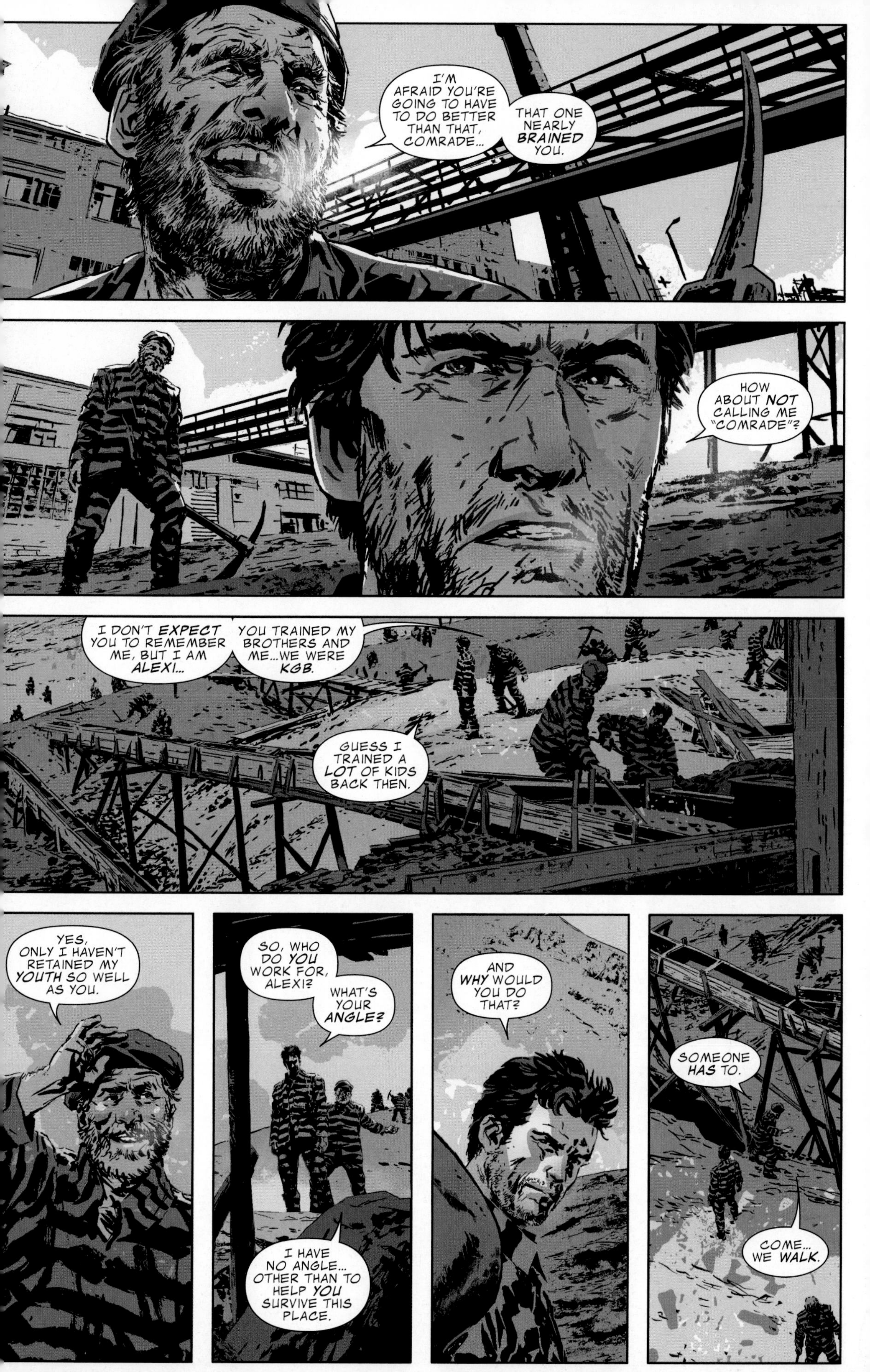
I'M AFRAID YOU'RE GOING TO HAVE TO DO BETTER THAN THAT, COMRADE...
THAT ONE NEARLY BRAINED YOU.
HOW ABOUT NOT CALLING ME "COMRADE"?
I DON'T EXPECT YOU TO REMEMBER ME, BUT I AM ALEXI...
YOU TRAINED MY BROTHERS AND ME...WE WERE KGB.
GUESS I TRAINED A LOT OF KIDS BACK THEN.
YES, ONLY I HAVEN'T RETAINED MY YOUTH SO WELL AS YOU.
SO, WHO DO YOU WORK FOR, ALEXI?
WHAT'S YOUR ANGLE?
I HAVE NO ANGLE... OTHER THAN TO HELP YOU SURVIVE THIS PLACE.
AND WHY WOULD YOU DO THAT?
SOMEONE HAS TO.
COME... WE WALK.

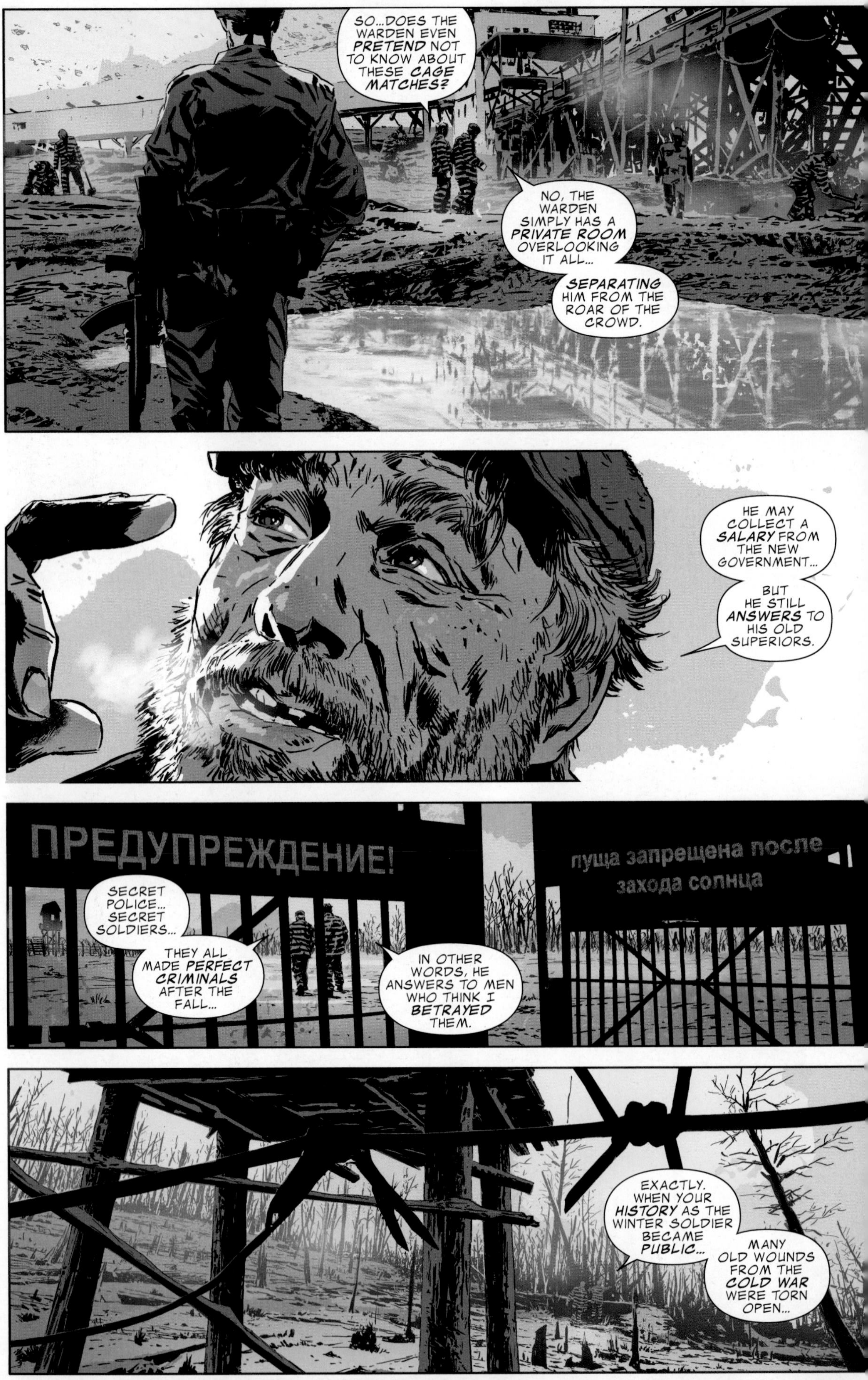
SO...DOES THE WARDEN EVEN PRETEND NOT TO KNOW ABOUT THESE CAGE MATCHES?
NO, THE WARDEN SIMPLY HAS A PRIVATE ROOM OVERLOOKING IT ALL...
SEPARATING HIM FROM THE ROAR OF THE CROWD.
HE MAY COLLECT A SALARY FROM THE NEW GOVERNMENT...
BUT HE STILL ANSWERS TO HIS OLD SUPERIORS.
ПРЕДУПРЕЖДЕНИЕ!
пуща запрещена после захода солнца
SECRET POLICE... SECRET SOLDIERS...
THEY ALL MADE PERFECT CRIMINALS AFTER THE FALL...
IN OTHER WORDS, HE ANSWERS TO MEN WHO THINK I BETRAYED THEM.
EXACTLY. WHEN YOUR HISTORY AS THE WINTER SOLDIER BECAME PUBLIC...
MANY OLD WOUNDS FROM THE COLD WAR WERE TORN OPEN...

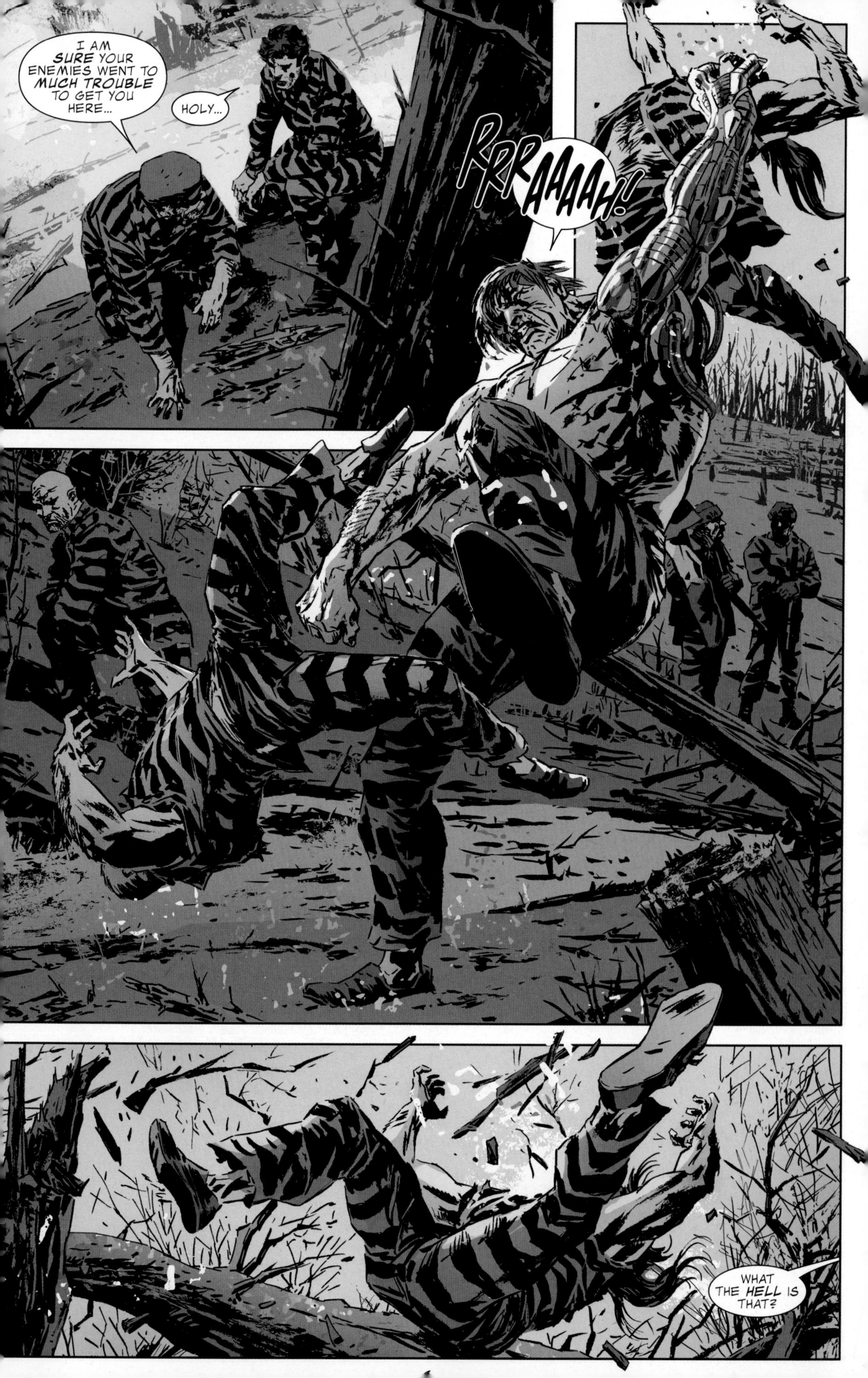
I AM SURE YOUR ENEMIES WENT TO MUCH TROUBLE TO GET YOU HERE...
HOLY...
RRRAAAAAH!
WHAT THE HELL IS THAT?

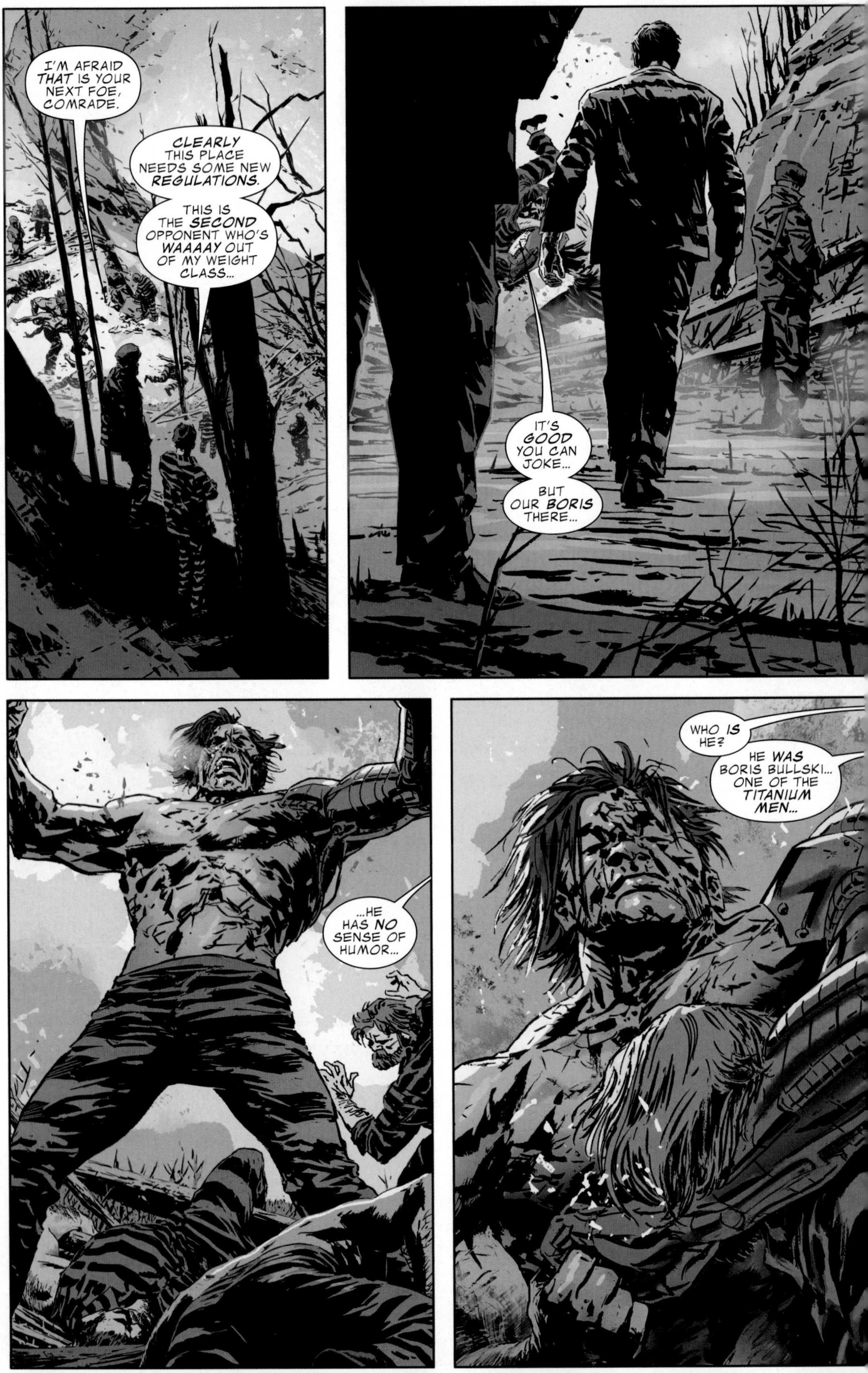
I'M AFRAID THAT IS YOUR NEXT FOE, COMRADE.
CLEARLY THIS PLACE NEEDS SOME NEW REGULATIONS.
THIS IS THE SECOND OPPONENT WHO'S WAAAAY OUT OF MY WEIGHT CLASS...
IT'S GOOD YOU CAN JOKE...
BUT OUR BORIS THERE...
...HE HAS NO SENSE OF HUMOR...
WHO IS HE?
HE WAS BORIS BULLSKI... ONE OF THE TITANIUM MEN...

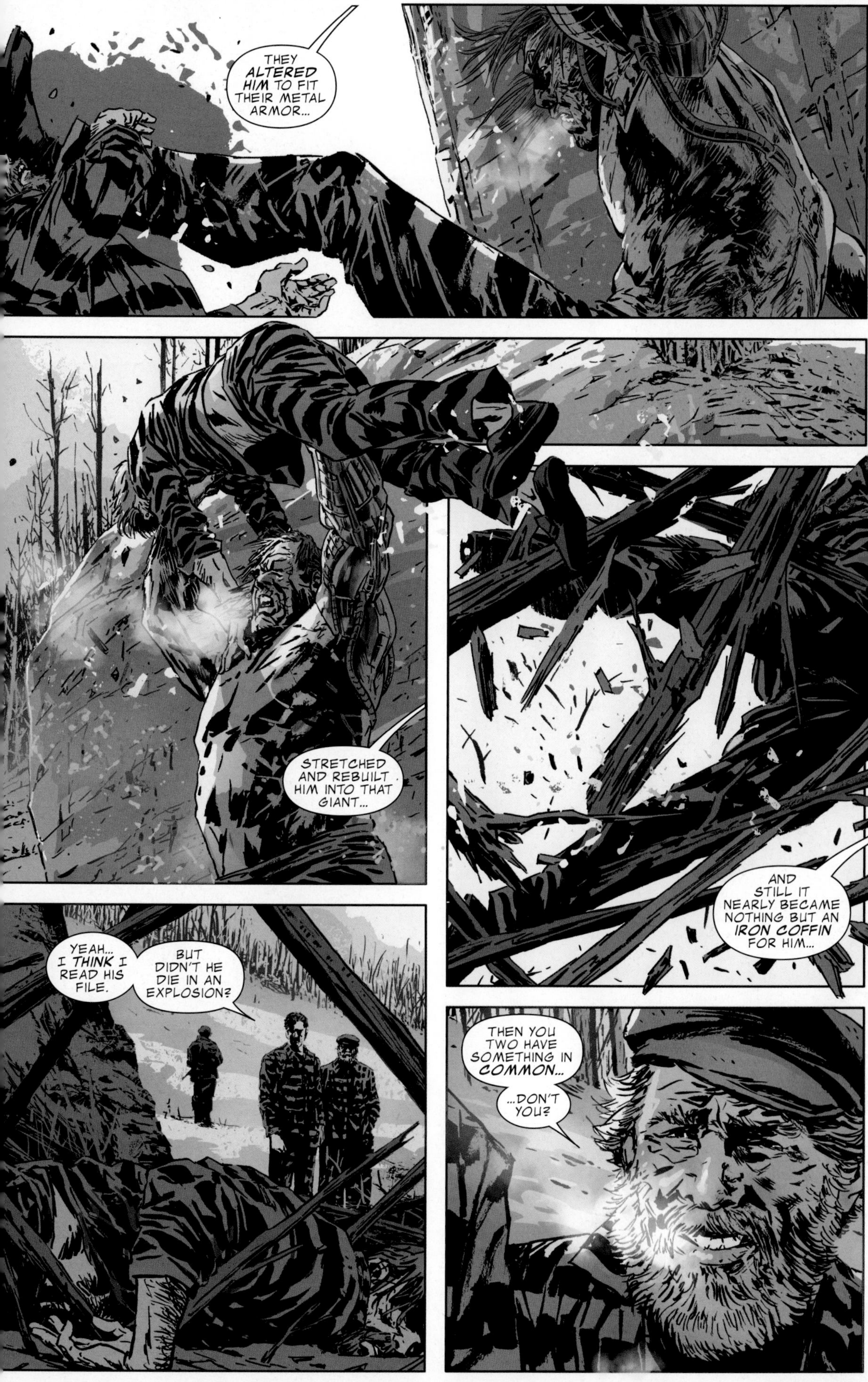
THEY ALTERED HIM TO FIT THEIR METAL ARMOR...
STRETCHED AND REBUILT HIM INTO THAT GIANT...
AND STILL IT NEARLY BECAME NOTHING BUT AN IRON COFFIN FOR HIM...
YEAH... I THINK I READ HIS FILE.
BUT DIDN'T HE DIE IN AN EXPLOSION?
THEN YOU TWO HAVE SOMETHING IN COMMON...
...DON'T YOU?

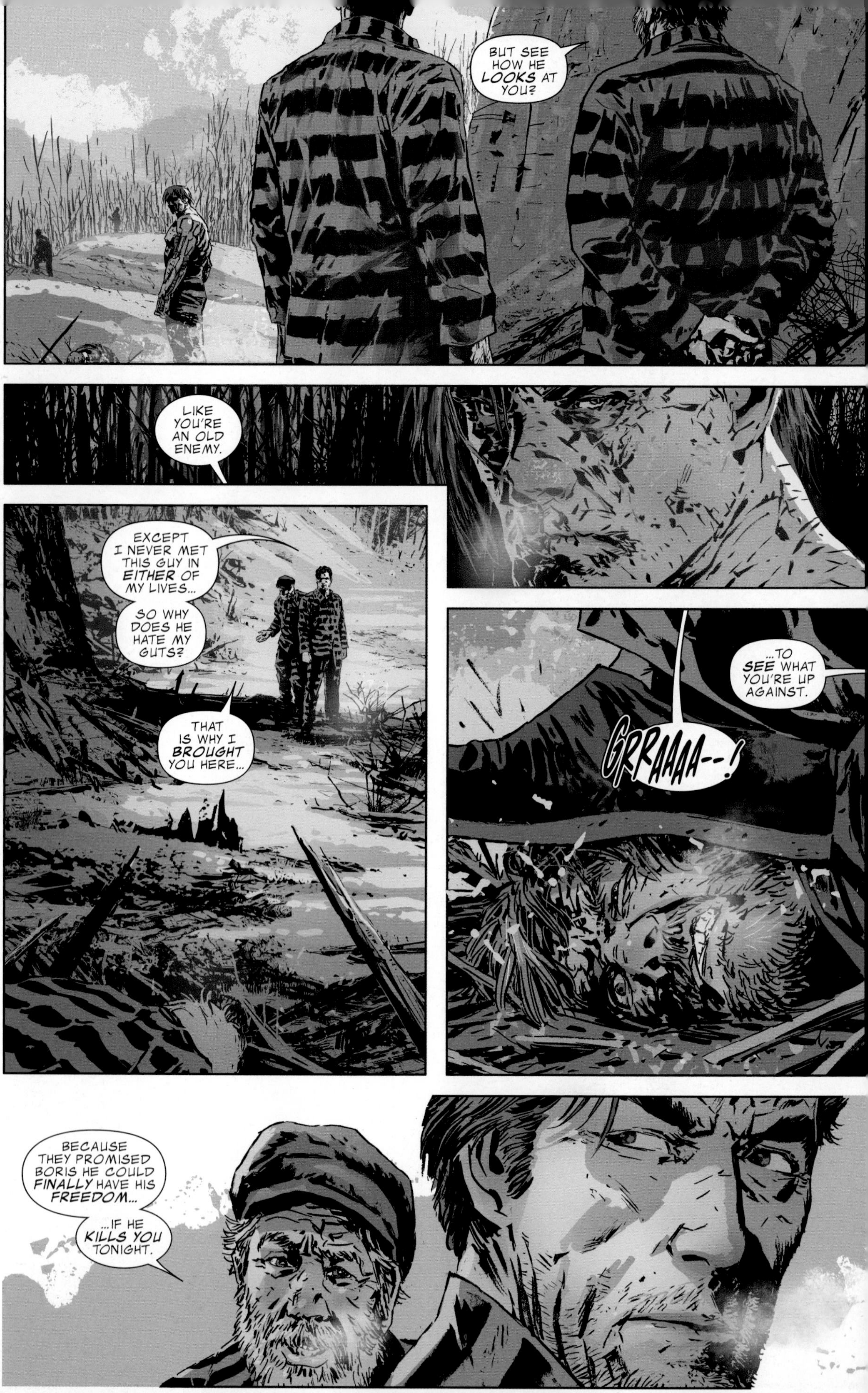
BUT SEE HOW HE LOOKS AT YOU?
LIKE YOU'RE AN OLD ENEMY.
EXCEPT I NEVER MET THIS GUY IN EITHER OF MY LIVES...
SO WHY DOES HE HATE MY GUTS?
THAT IS WHY I BROUGHT YOU HERE...
...TO SEE WHAT YOU'RE UP AGAINST.
GRRAAAA--!
BECAUSE THEY PROMISED BORIS HE COULD FINALLY HAVE HIS FREEDOM...
...IF HE KILLS YOU TONIGHT.

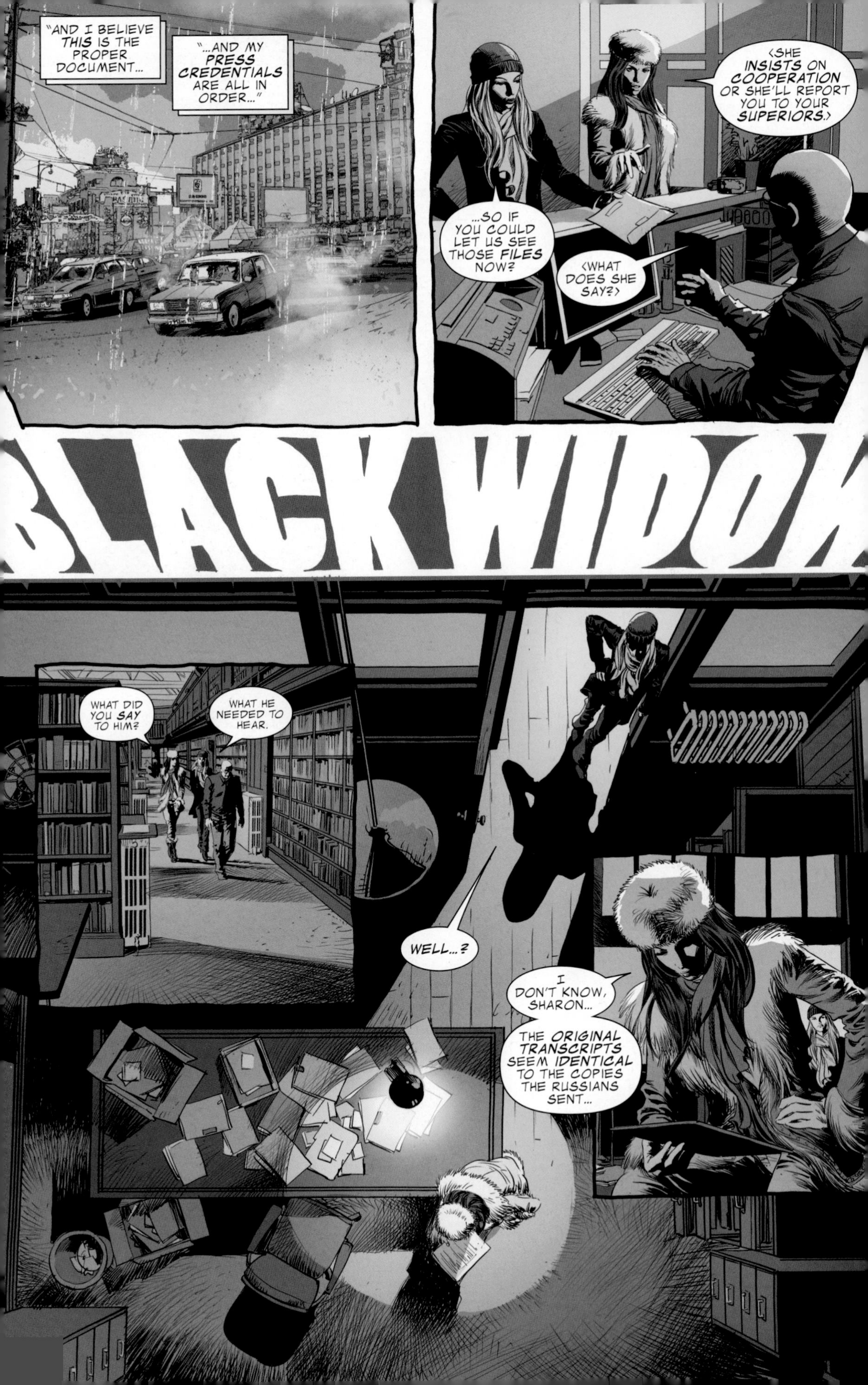
"AND I BELIEVE THIS IS THE PROPER DOCUMENT...
"...AND MY PRESS CREDENTIALS ARE ALL IN ORDER..."
‹SHE INSISTS ON COOPERATION OR SHE'LL REPORT YOU TO YOUR SUPERIORS.›
...SO IF YOU COULD LET US SEE THOSE FILES NOW?
‹WHAT DOES SHE SAY?›
BLACK WIDOW
WHAT DID YOU SAY TO HIM?
WHAT HE NEEDED TO HEAR.
WELL...?
I DON'T KNOW, SHARON...
THE ORIGINAL TRANSCRIPTS SEEM IDENTICAL TO THE COPIES THE RUSSIANS SENT...

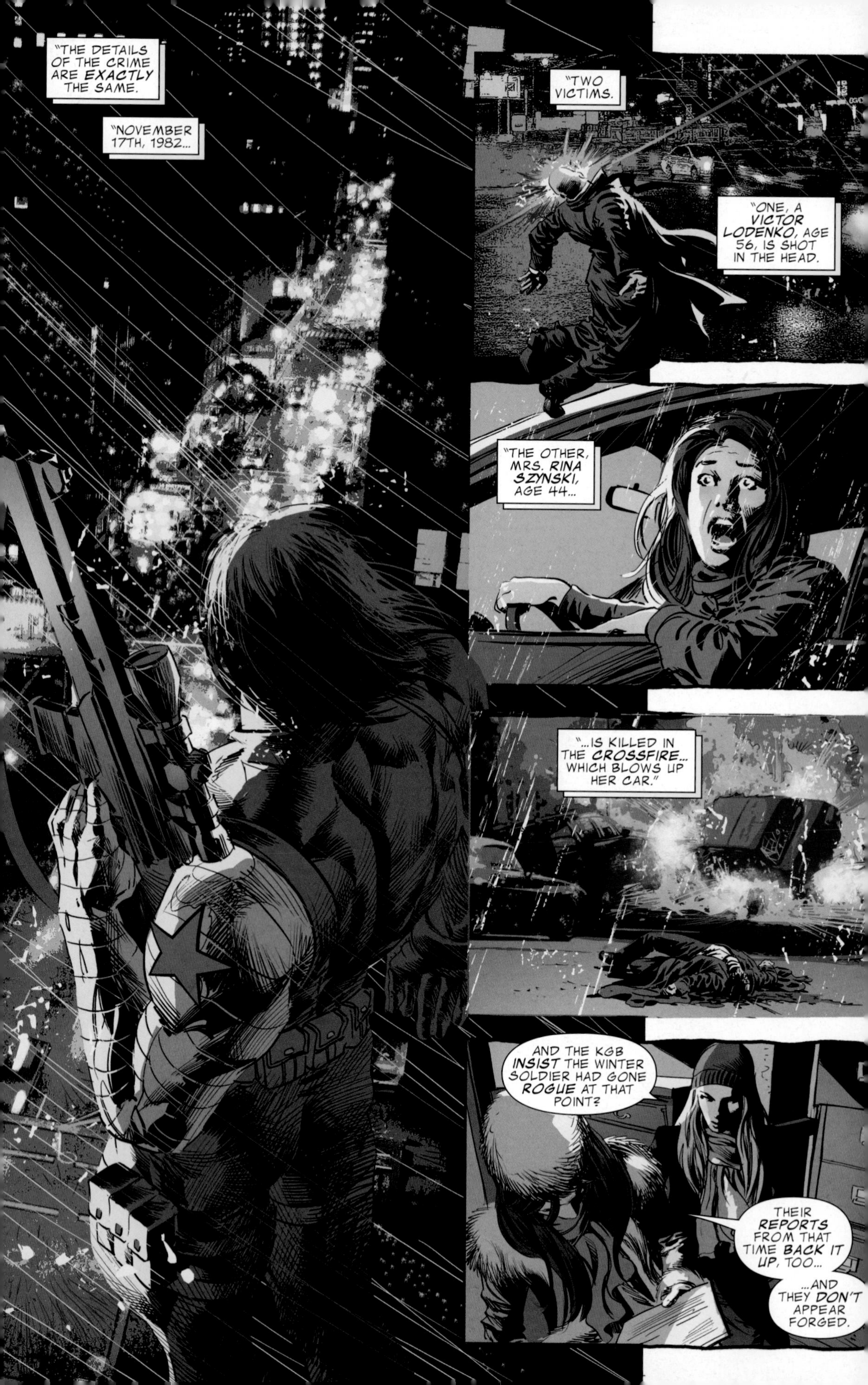
"THE DETAILS OF THE CRIME ARE EXACTLY THE SAME.
"NOVEMBER 17TH, 1982...
"TWO VICTIMS.
"ONE, A VICTOR LODENKO, AGE 56, IS SHOT IN THE HEAD.
"THE OTHER, MRS. RINA SZYNSKI, AGE 44...
"...IS KILLED IN THE CROSSFIRE... WHICH BLOWS UP HER CAR."
AND THE KGB INSIST THE WINTER SOLDIER HAD GONE ROGUE AT THAT POINT?
THEIR REPORTS FROM THAT TIME BACK IT UP, TOO...
...AND THEY DON'T APPEAR FORGED.

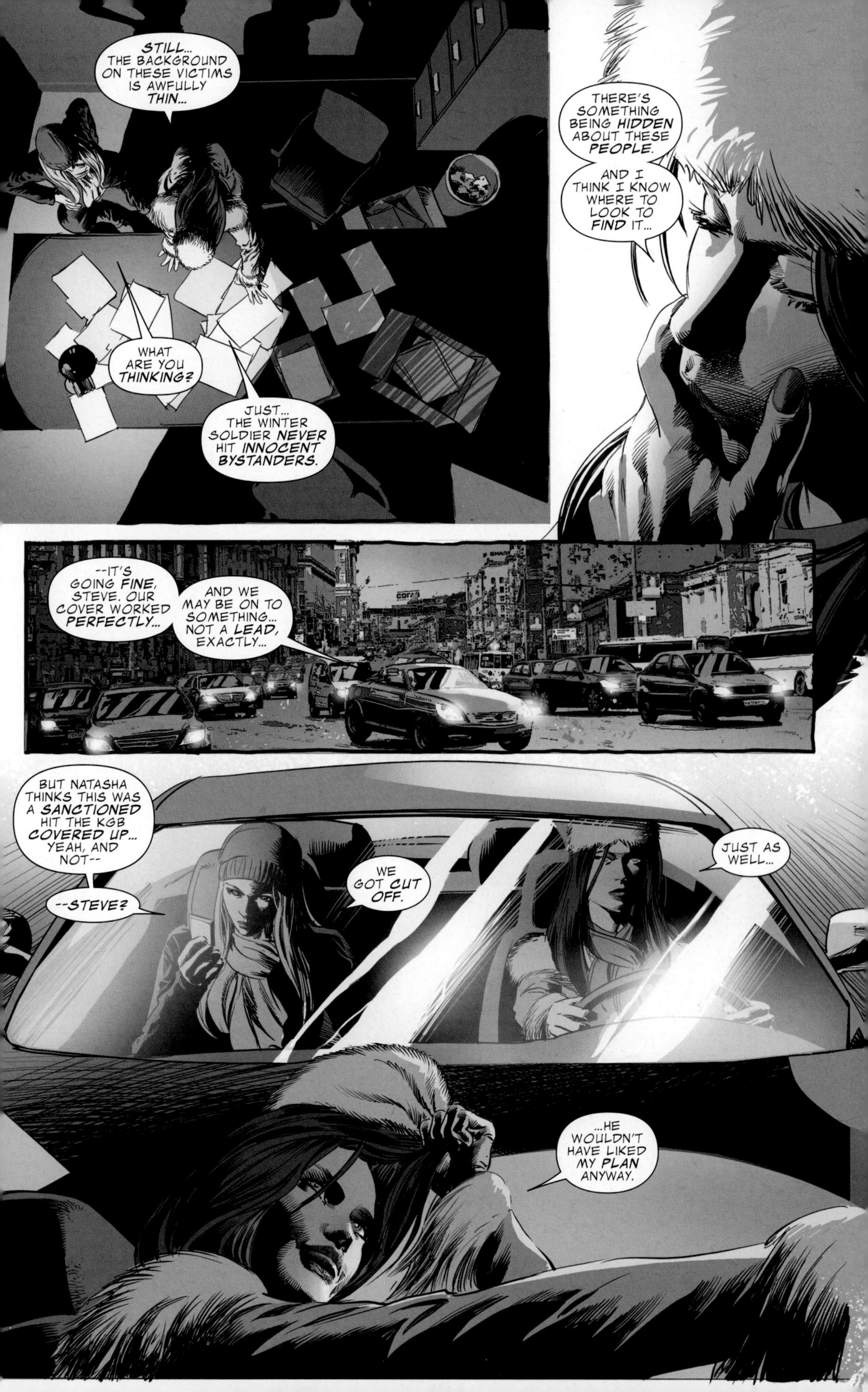
STILL... THE BACKGROUND ON THESE VICTIMS IS AWFULLY THIN...
WHAT ARE YOU THINKING?
JUST... THE WINTER SOLDIER NEVER HIT INNOCENT BYSTANDERS.
THERE'S SOMETHING BEING HIDDEN ABOUT THESE PEOPLE.
AND I THINK I KNOW WHERE TO LOOK TO FIND IT...
--IT'S GOING FINE, STEVE. OUR COVER WORKED PERFECTLY...
AND WE MAY BE ON TO SOMETHING... NOT A LEAD, EXACTLY...
BUT NATASHA THINKS THIS WAS A SANCTIONED HIT THE KGB COVERED UP... YEAH, AND NOT--
--STEVE?
WE GOT CUT OFF.
JUST AS WELL...
...HE WOULDN'T HAVE LIKED MY PLAN ANYWAY.

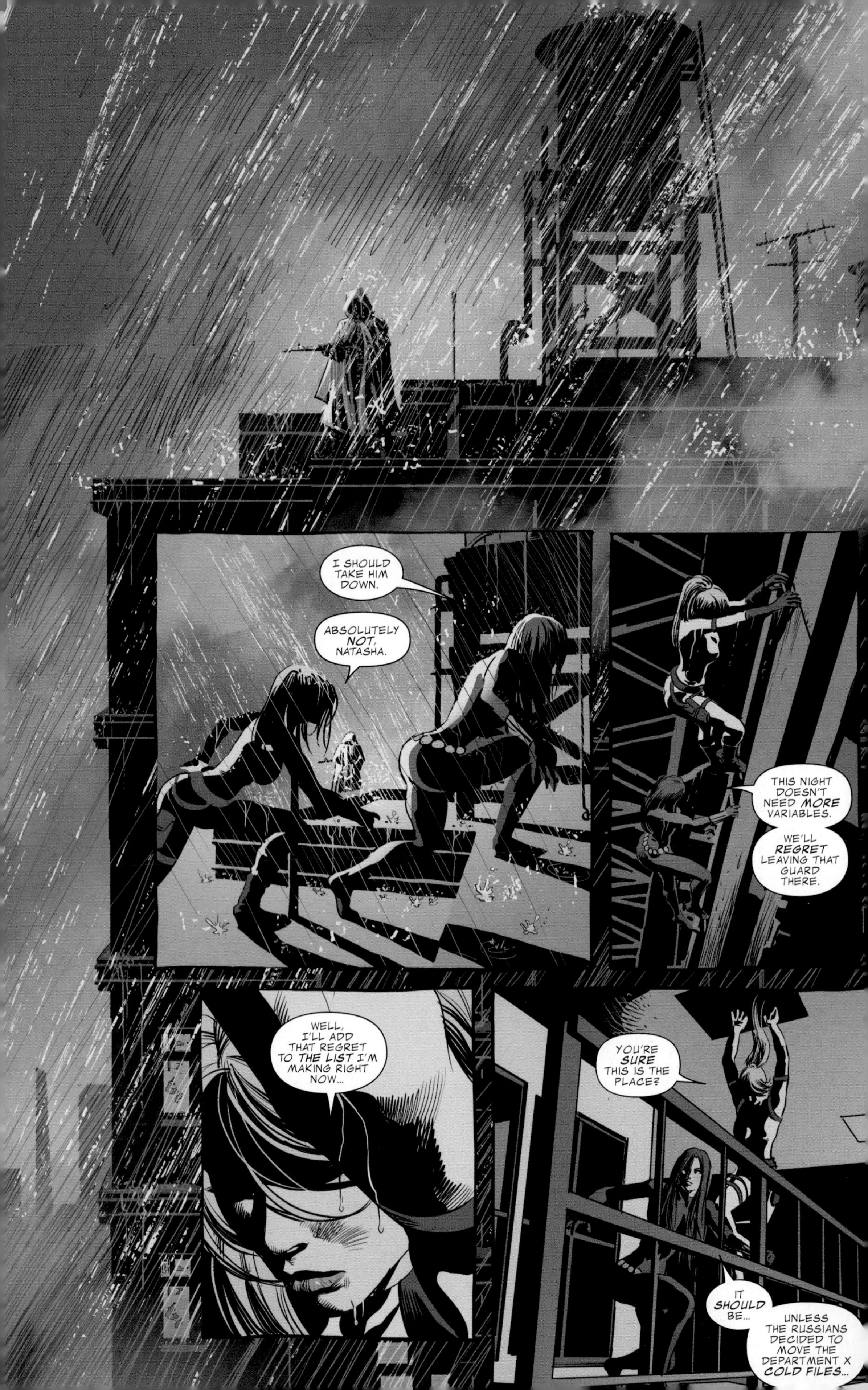
I SHOULD TAKE HIM DOWN.
ABSOLUTELY NOT, NATASHA.
THIS NIGHT DOESN'T NEED MORE VARIABLES.
WE'LL REGRET LEAVING THAT GUARD THERE.
WELL, I'LL ADD THAT REGRET TO THE LIST I'M MAKING RIGHT NOW...
YOU'RE SURE THIS IS THE PLACE?
IT SHOULD BE...
UNLESS THE RUSSIANS DECIDED TO MOVE THE DEPARTMENT X COLD FILES...

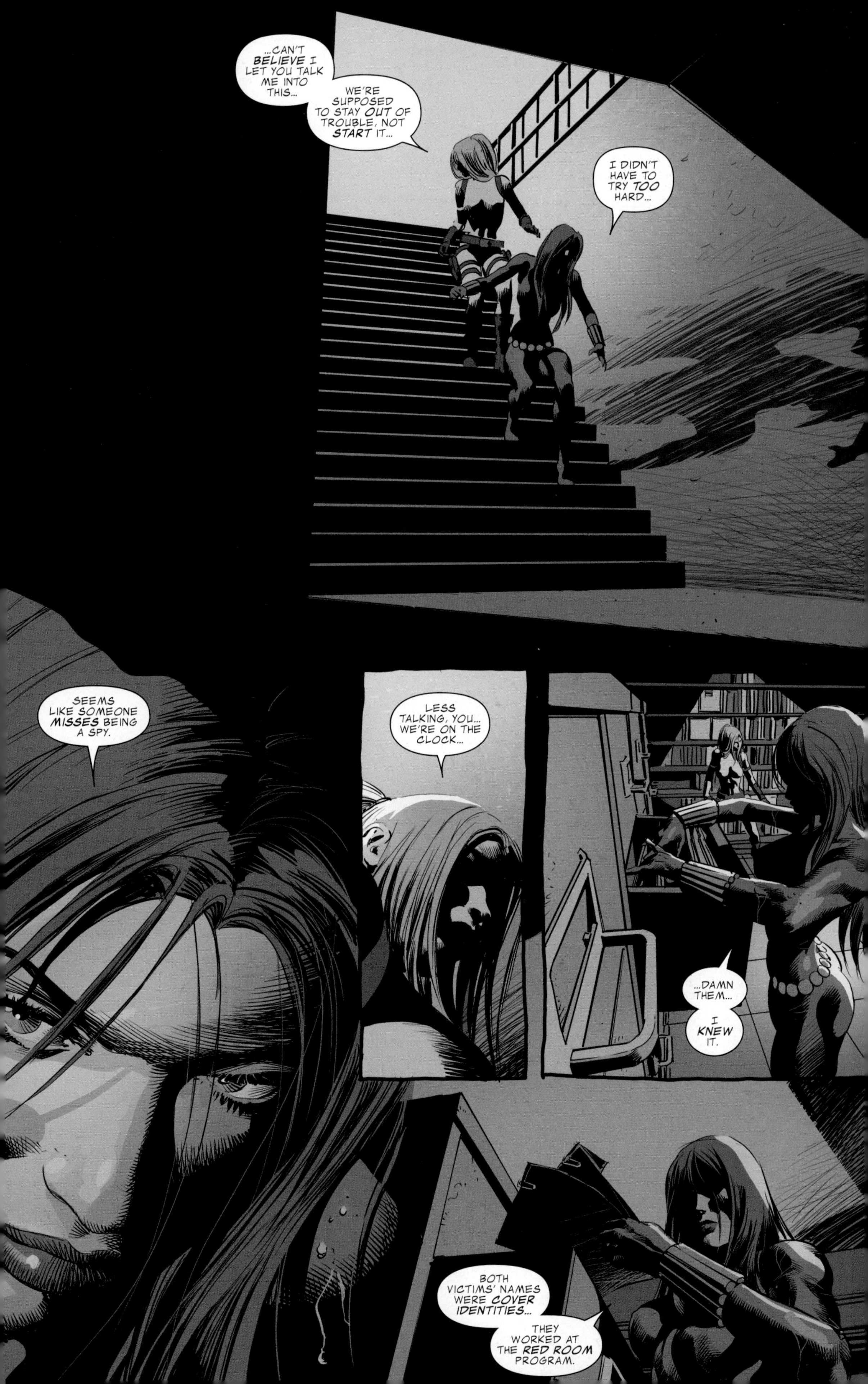
...CAN'T BELIEVE I LET YOU TALK ME INTO THIS...
WE'RE SUPPOSED TO STAY OUT OF TROUBLE, NOT START IT...
I DIDN'T HAVE TO TRY TOO HARD...
SEEMS LIKE SOMEONE MISSES BEING A SPY.
LESS TALKING, YOU... WE'RE ON THE CLOCK...
...DAMN THEM...
I KNEW IT.
BOTH VICTIMS' NAMES WERE COVER IDENTITIES...
THEY WORKED AT THE RED ROOM PROGRAM.

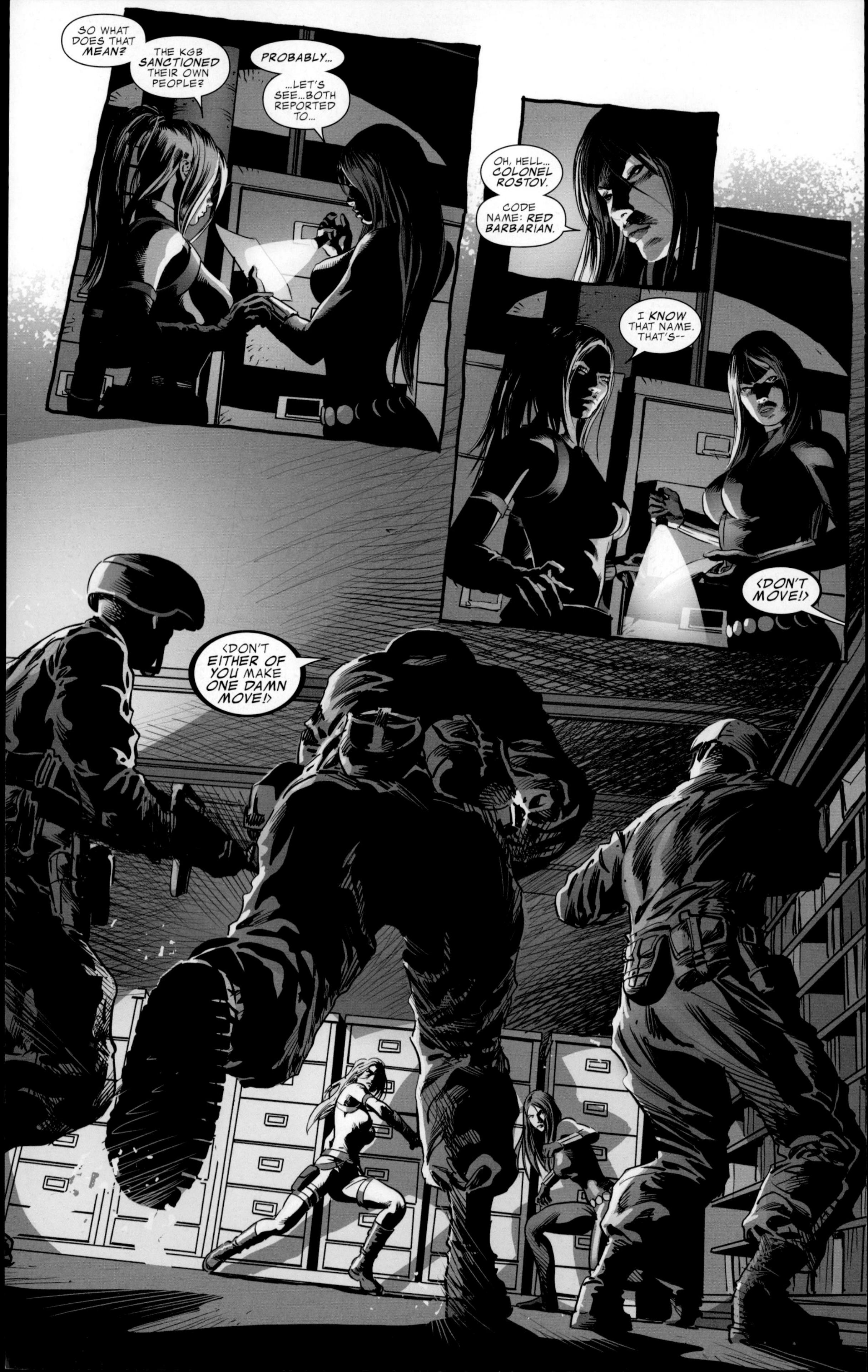
SO WHAT DOES THAT MEAN?
THE KGB SANCTIONED THEIR OWN PEOPLE?
PROBABLY...
...LET'S SEE...BOTH REPORTED TO...
OH, HELL... COLONEL ROSTOV.
CODE NAME: RED BARBARIAN.
I KNOW THAT NAME. THAT'S--
<DON'T MOVE!>
<DON'T EITHER OF YOU MAKE ONE DAMN MOVE!>

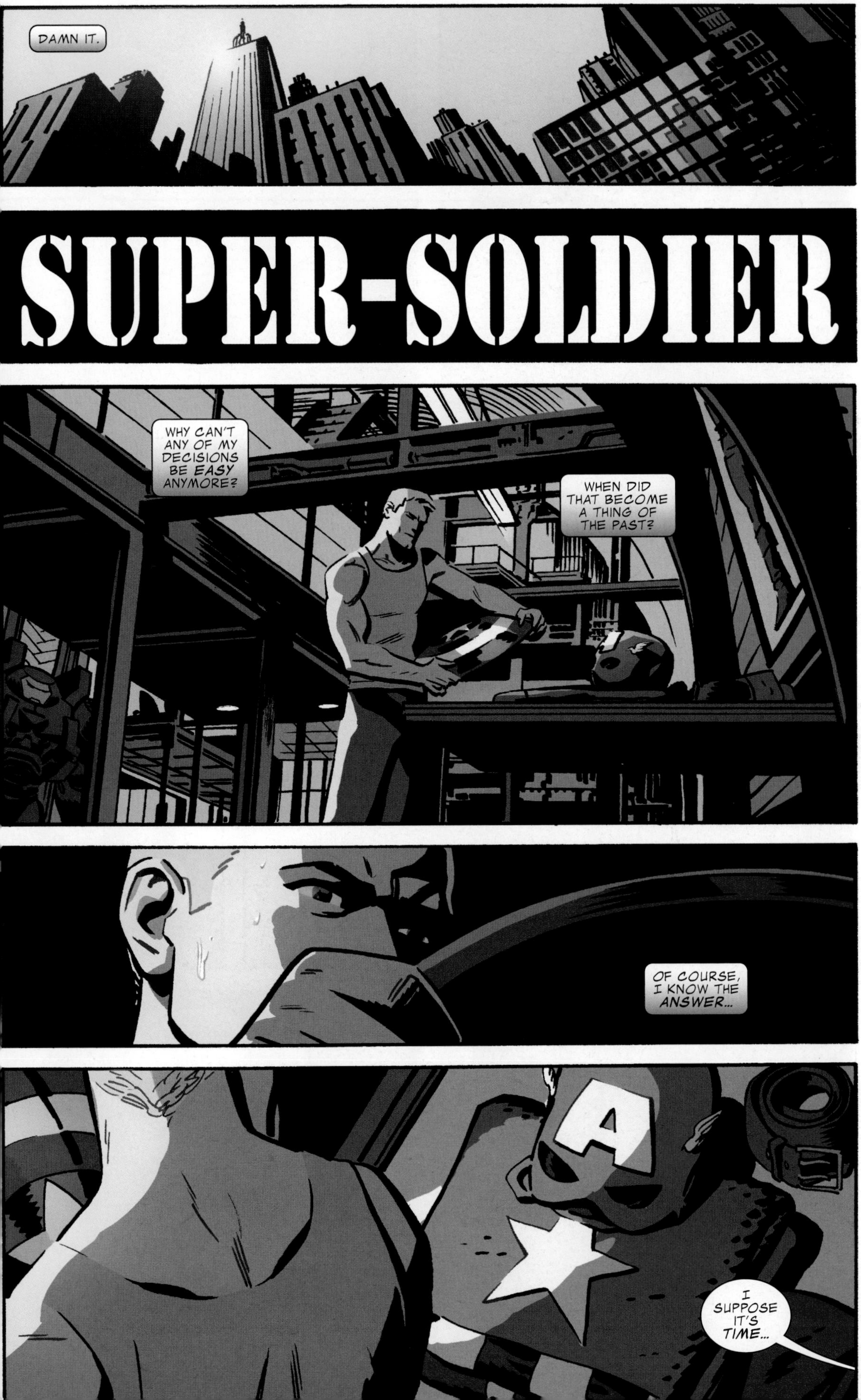
DAMN IT.
SUPER-SOLDIER
WHY CAN'T ANY OF MY DECISIONS BE EASY ANYMORE?
WHEN DID THAT BECOME A THING OF THE PAST?
OF COURSE, I KNOW THE ANSWER...
I SUPPOSE IT'S TIME...

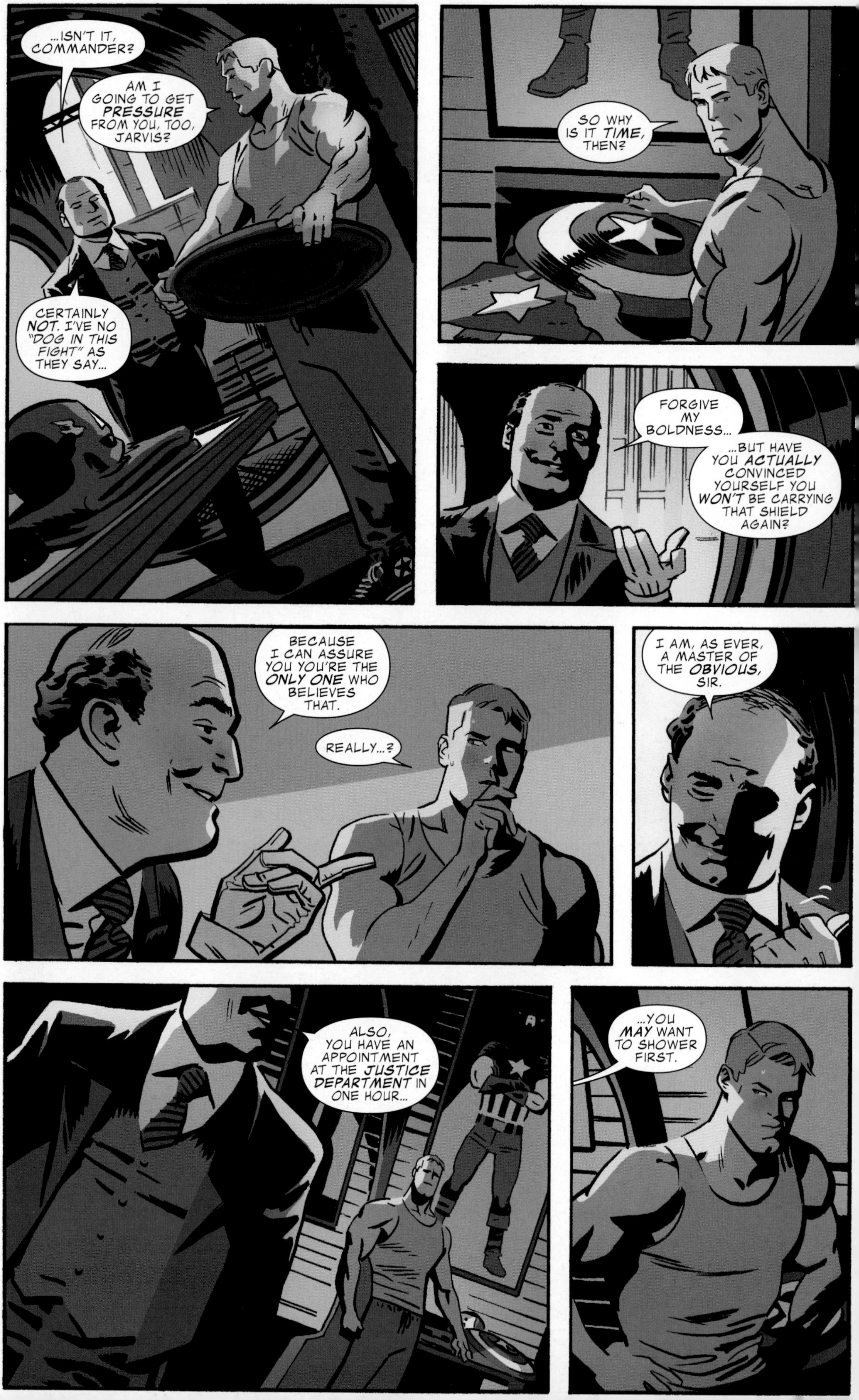
...ISN'T IT, COMMANDER?
AM I GOING TO GET PRESSURE FROM YOU, TOO, JARVIS?
CERTAINLY NOT. I'VE NO "DOG IN THIS FIGHT" AS THEY SAY...
SO WHY IS IT TIME, THEN?
FORGIVE MY BOLDNESS...
...BUT HAVE YOU ACTUALLY CONVINCED YOURSELF YOU WON'T BE CARRYING THAT SHIELD AGAIN?
BECAUSE I CAN ASSURE YOU YOU'RE THE ONLY ONE WHO BELIEVES THAT.
REALLY...?
I AM, AS EVER, A MASTER OF THE OBVIOUS, SIR.
ALSO, YOU HAVE AN APPOINTMENT AT THE JUSTICE DEPARTMENT IN ONE HOUR...
...YOU MAY WANT TO SHOWER FIRST.

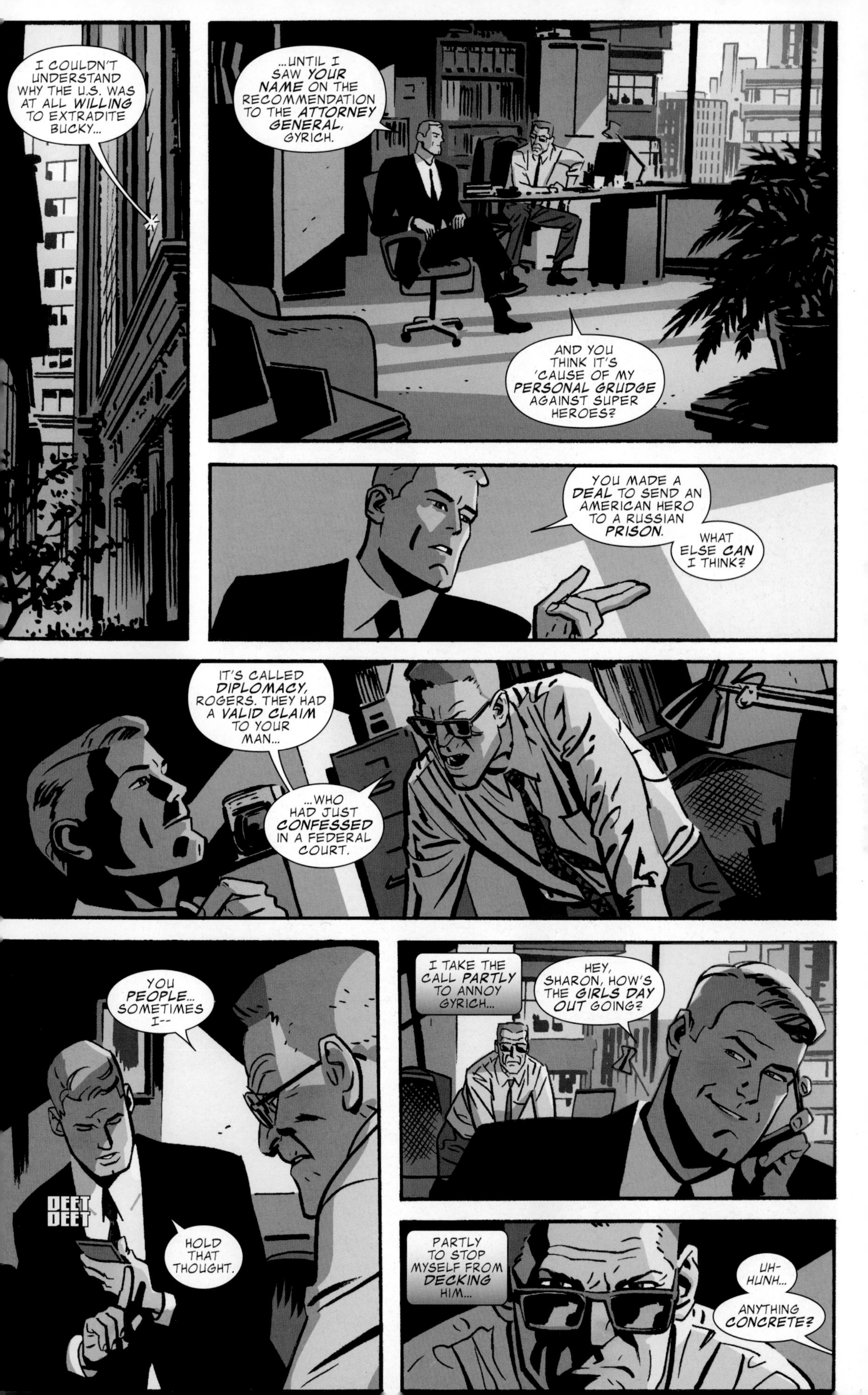
I COULDN'T UNDERSTAND WHY THE U.S. WAS AT ALL WILLING TO EXTRADITE BUCKY...
...UNTIL I SAW YOUR NAME ON THE RECOMMENDATION TO THE ATTORNEY GENERAL, GYRICH.
AND YOU THINK IT'S 'CAUSE OF MY PERSONAL GRUDGE AGAINST SUPER HEROES?
YOU MADE A DEAL TO SEND AN AMERICAN HERO TO A RUSSIAN PRISON.
WHAT ELSE CAN I THINK?
IT'S CALLED DIPLOMACY, ROGERS. THEY HAD A VALID CLAIM TO YOUR MAN...
...WHO HAD JUST CONFESSED IN A FEDERAL COURT.
YOU PEOPLE... SOMETIMES I--
DEET DEET
HOLD THAT THOUGHT.
I TAKE THE CALL PARTLY TO ANNOY GYRICH...
HEY, SHARON, HOW'S THE GIRLS DAY OUT GOING?
PARTLY TO STOP MYSELF FROM DECKING HIM...
UH-HUNH...
ANYTHING CONCRETE?

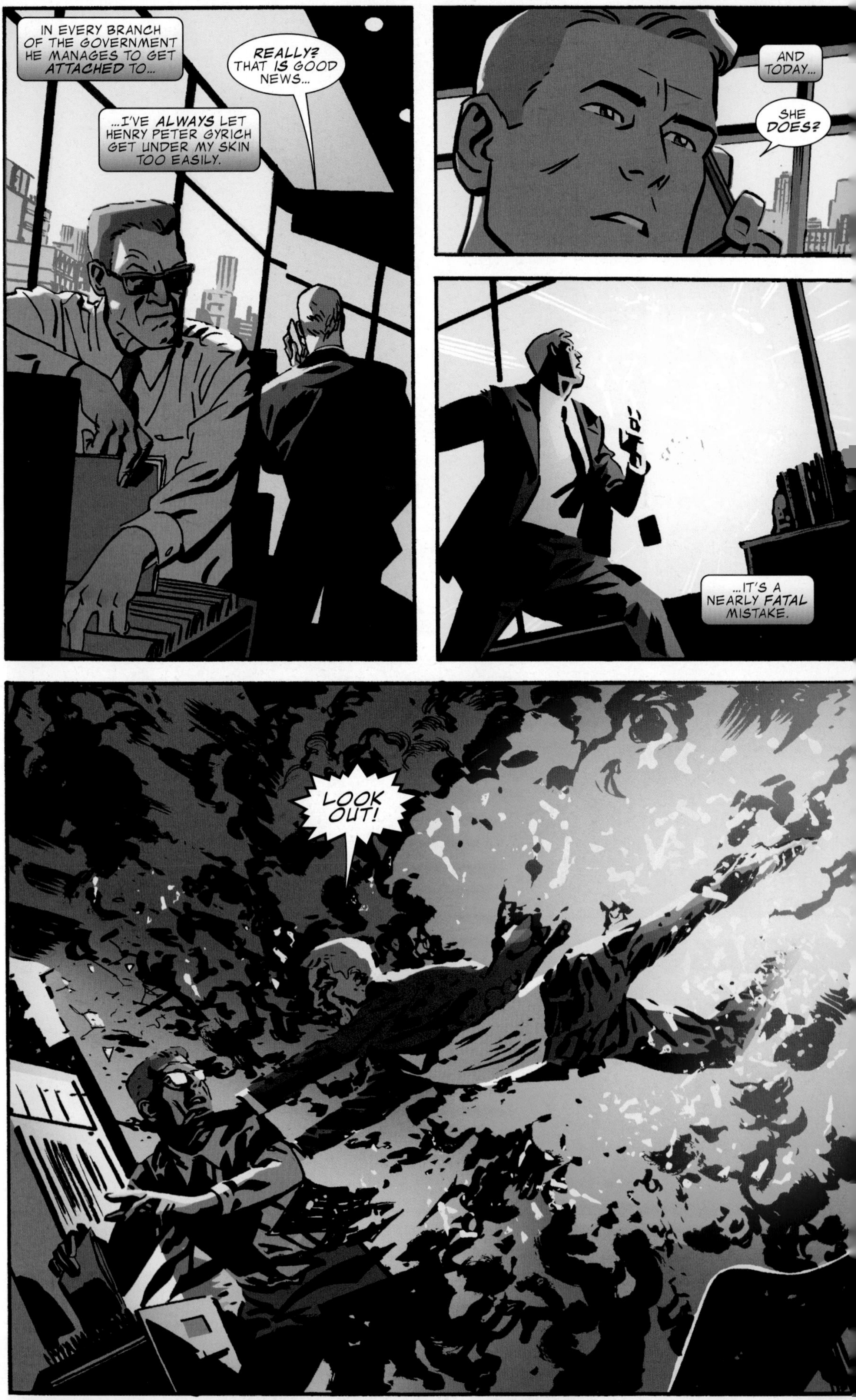
IN EVERY BRANCH OF THE GOVERNMENT HE MANAGES TO GET ATTACHED TO...
...I'VE ALWAYS LET HENRY PETER GYRICH GET UNDER MY SKIN TOO EASILY.
REALLY? THAT IS GOOD NEWS...
AND TODAY...
SHE DOES?
...IT'S A NEARLY FATAL MISTAKE.
LOOK OUT!

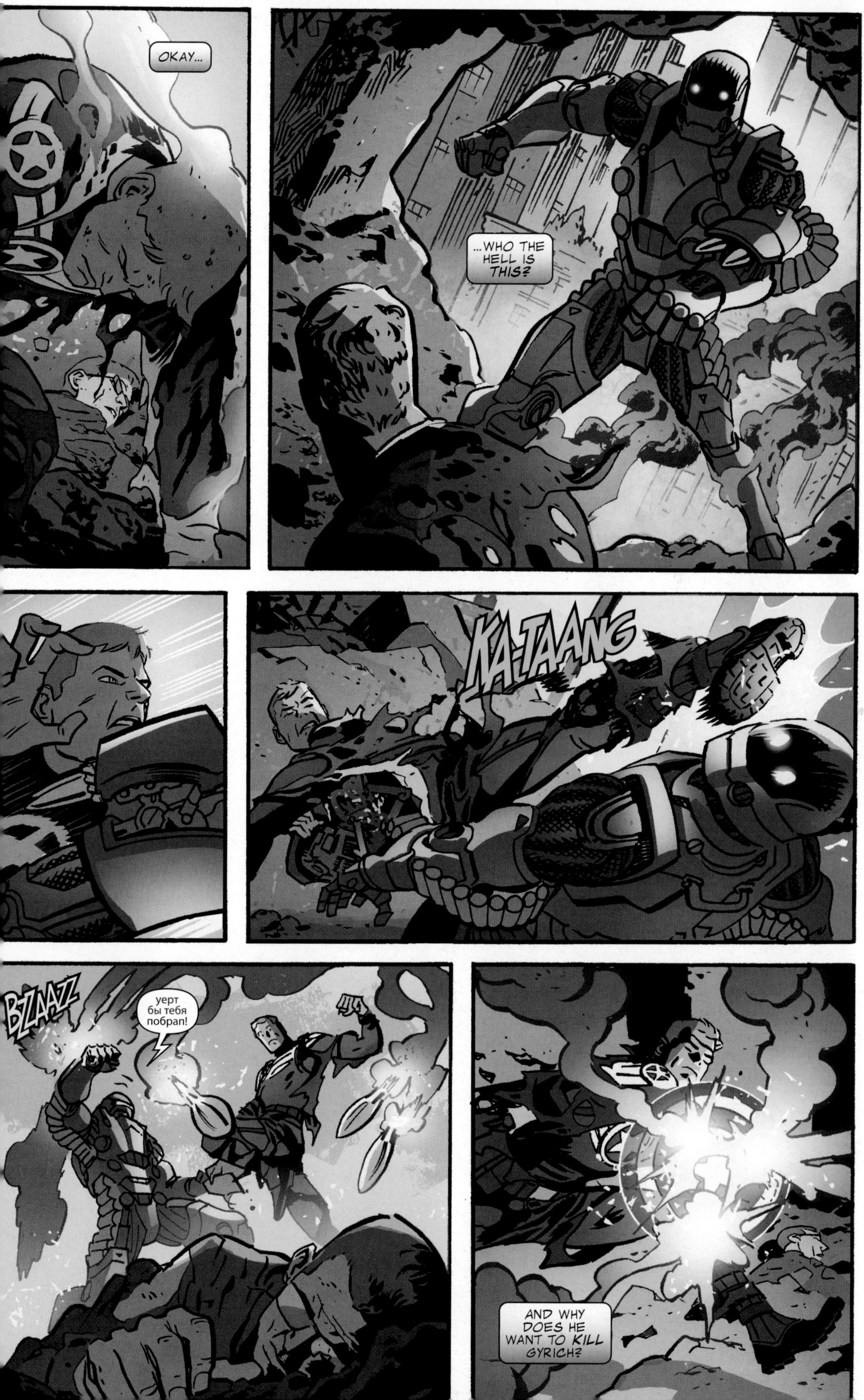
OKAY...
...WHO THE HELL IS THIS?
KA-TAANG
BZZAAZZ
уерт бы тебя побрап!
AND WHY DOES HE WANT TO KILL GYRICH?

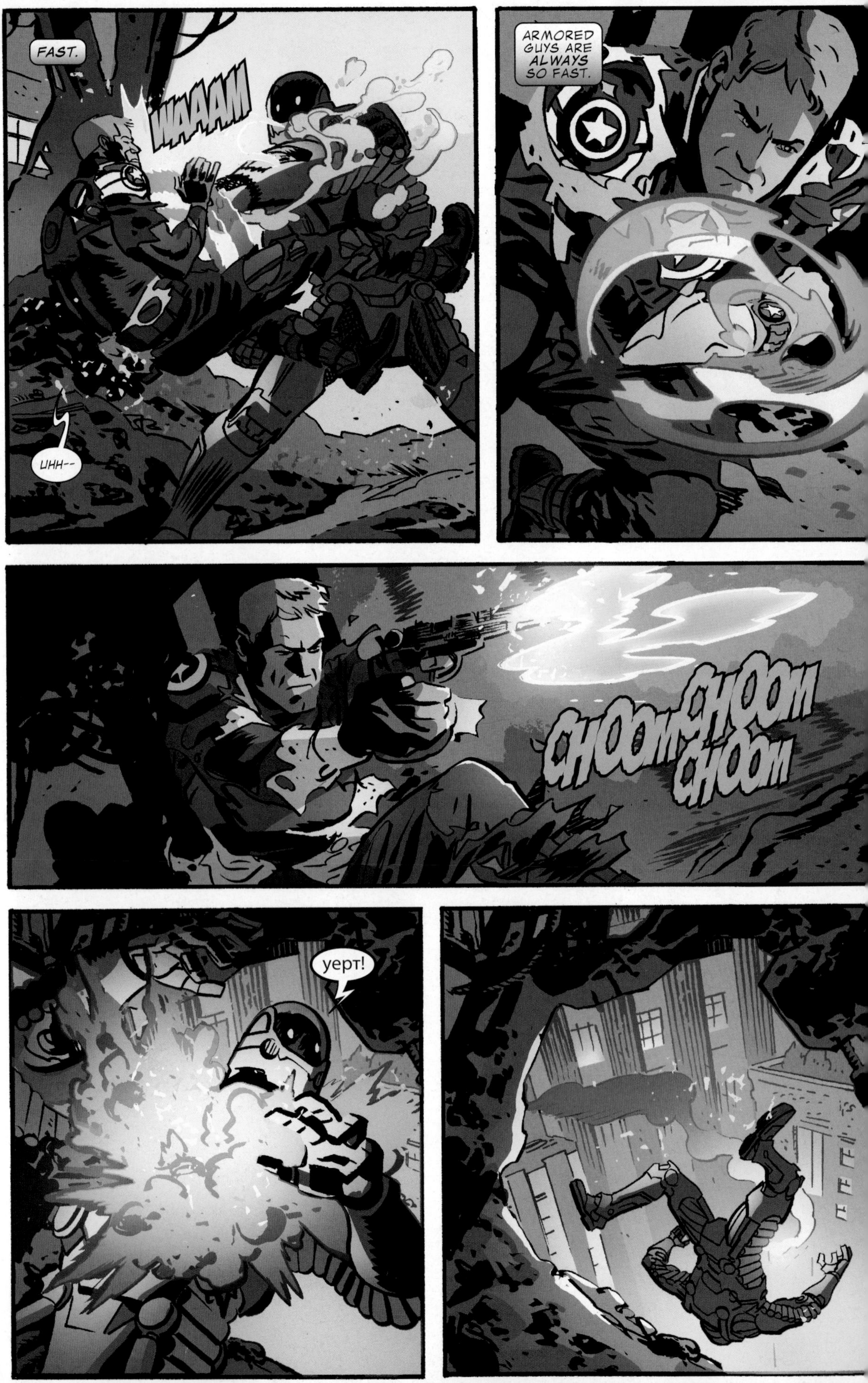
FAST.
WAAAM
UHH--
ARMORED GUYS ARE ALWAYS SO FAST.
CHOOM CHOOM CHOOM CHOOM
yeрт!

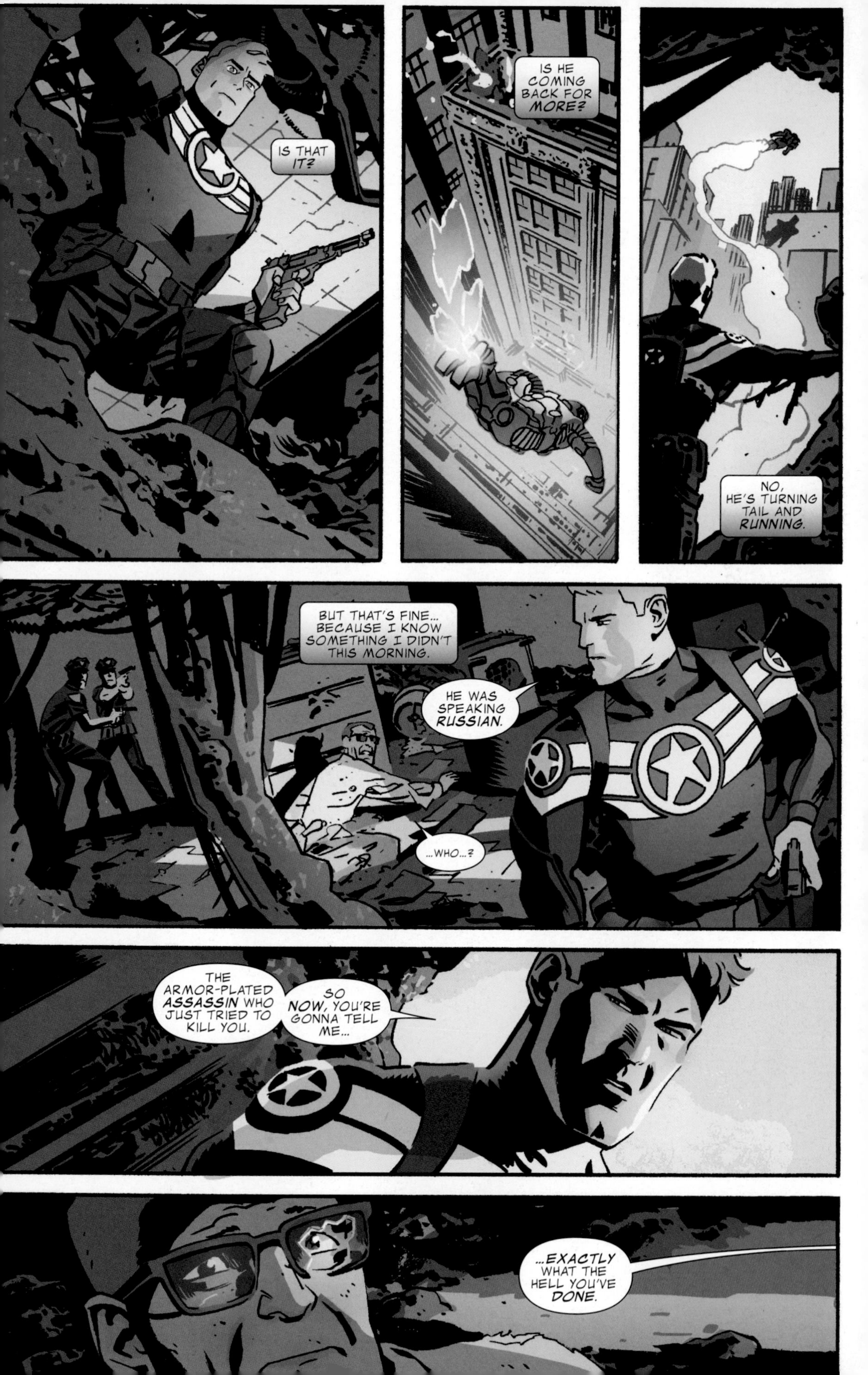
IS THAT IT?
IS HE COMING BACK FOR MORE?
NO, HE'S TURNING TAIL AND RUNNING.
BUT THAT'S FINE... BECAUSE I KNOW SOMETHING I DIDN'T THIS MORNING.
HE WAS SPEAKING RUSSIAN.
...WHO...?
THE ARMOR-PLATED ASSASSIN WHO JUST TRIED TO KILL YOU.
SO NOW, YOU'RE GONNA TELL ME...
...EXACTLY WHAT THE HELL YOU'VE DONE.

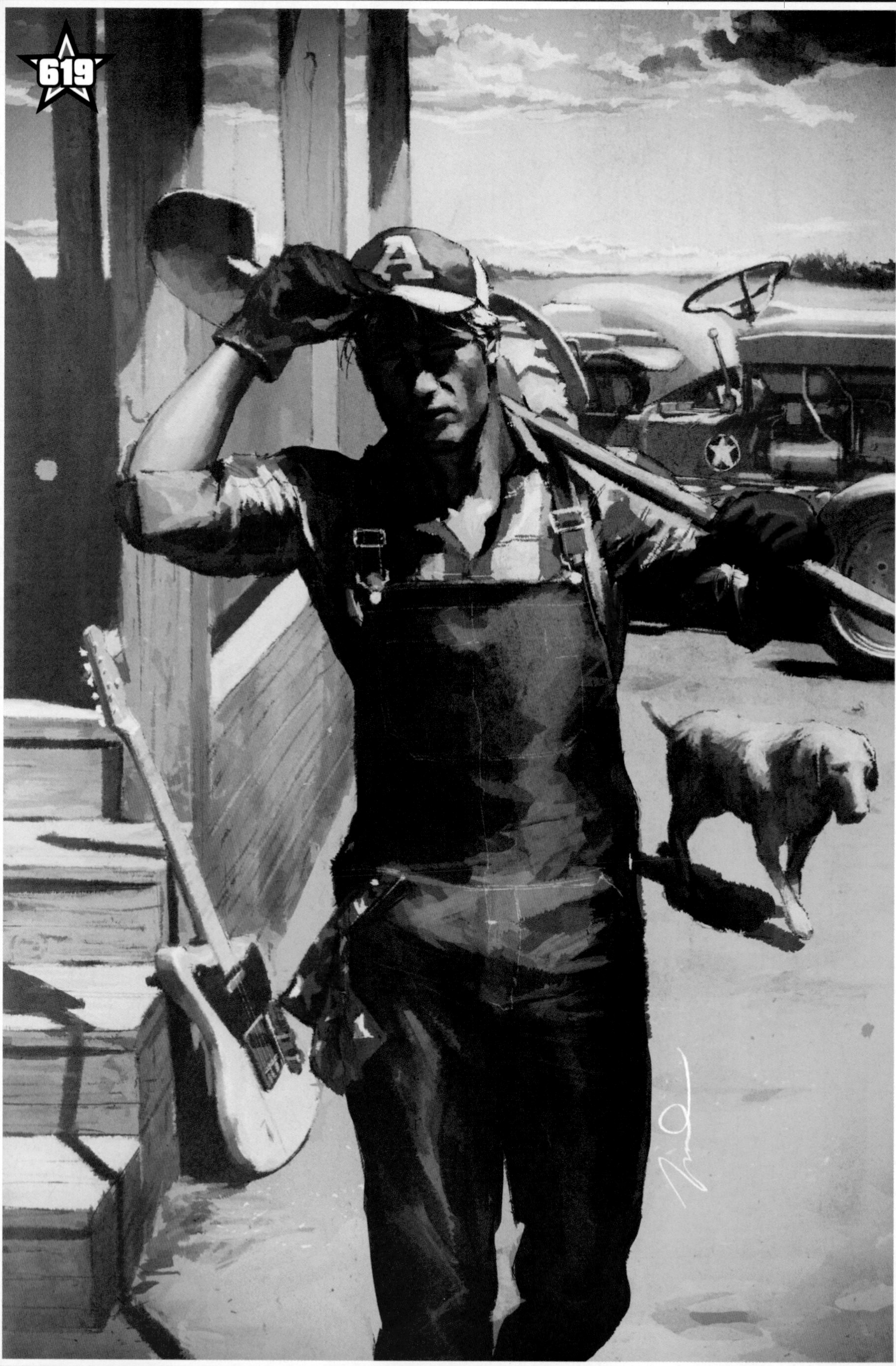
619

I AM CAPTAIN AMERICA VARIANT
BY GERALD PAREL

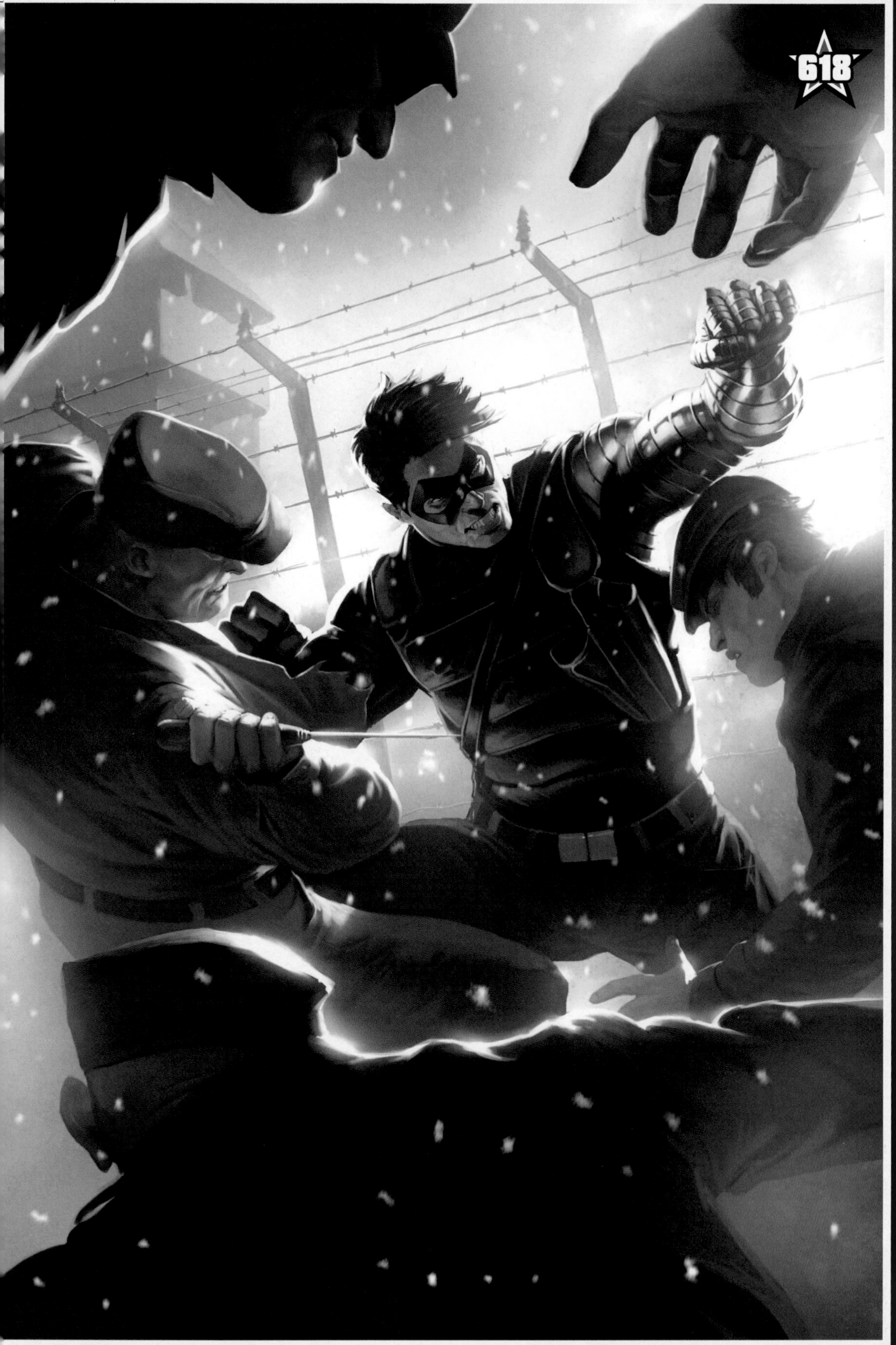
618

GULAG PART 3

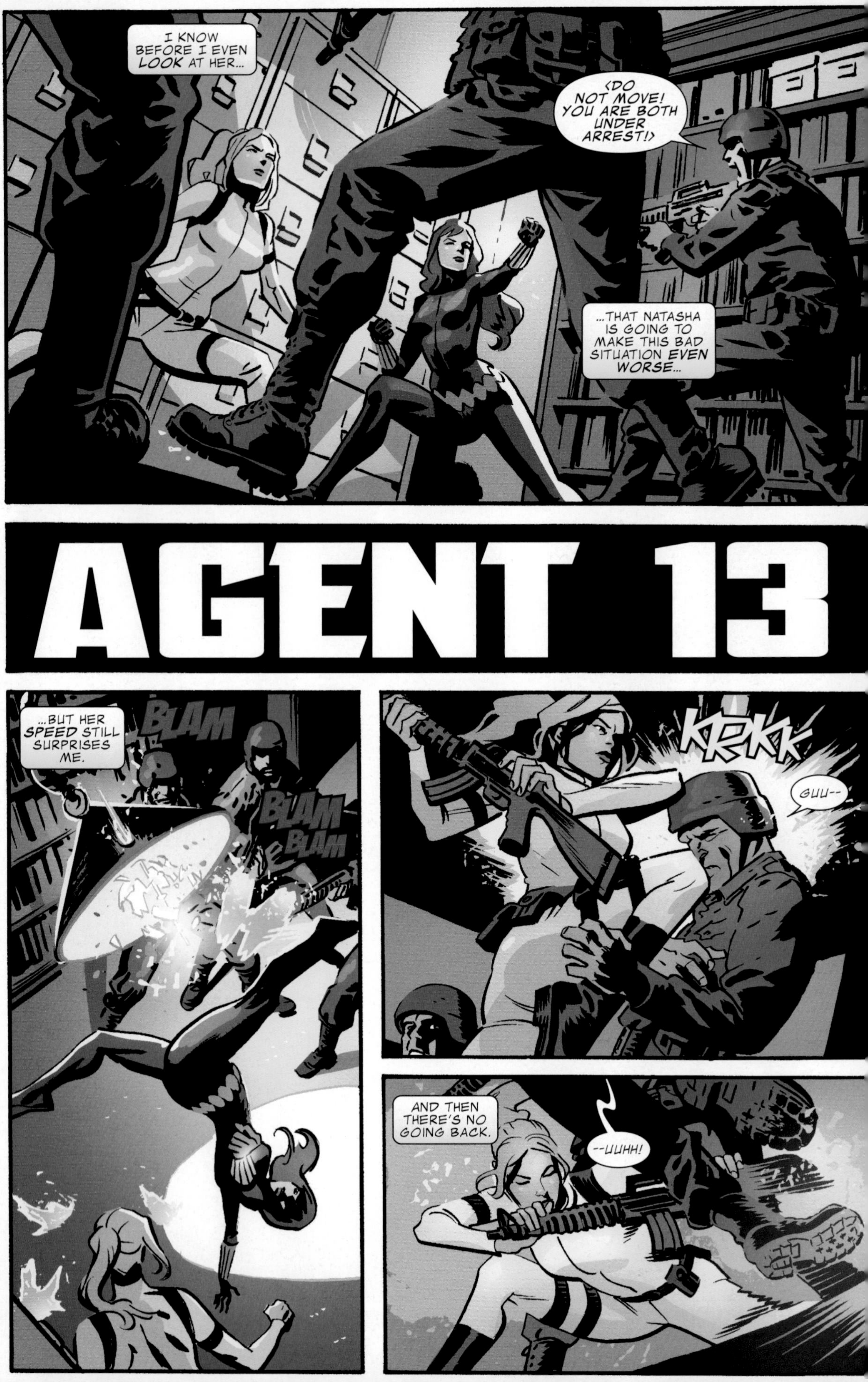
I KNOW BEFORE I EVEN LOOK AT HER...
<DO NOT MOVE! YOU ARE BOTH UNDER ARREST!>
...THAT NATASHA IS GOING TO MAKE THIS BAD SITUATION EVEN WORSE...
AGENT 13
...BUT HER SPEED STILL SURPRISES ME.
BLAM
BLAM
BLAM
KRKK
GUU--
AND THEN THERE'S NO GOING BACK.
--UUHH!

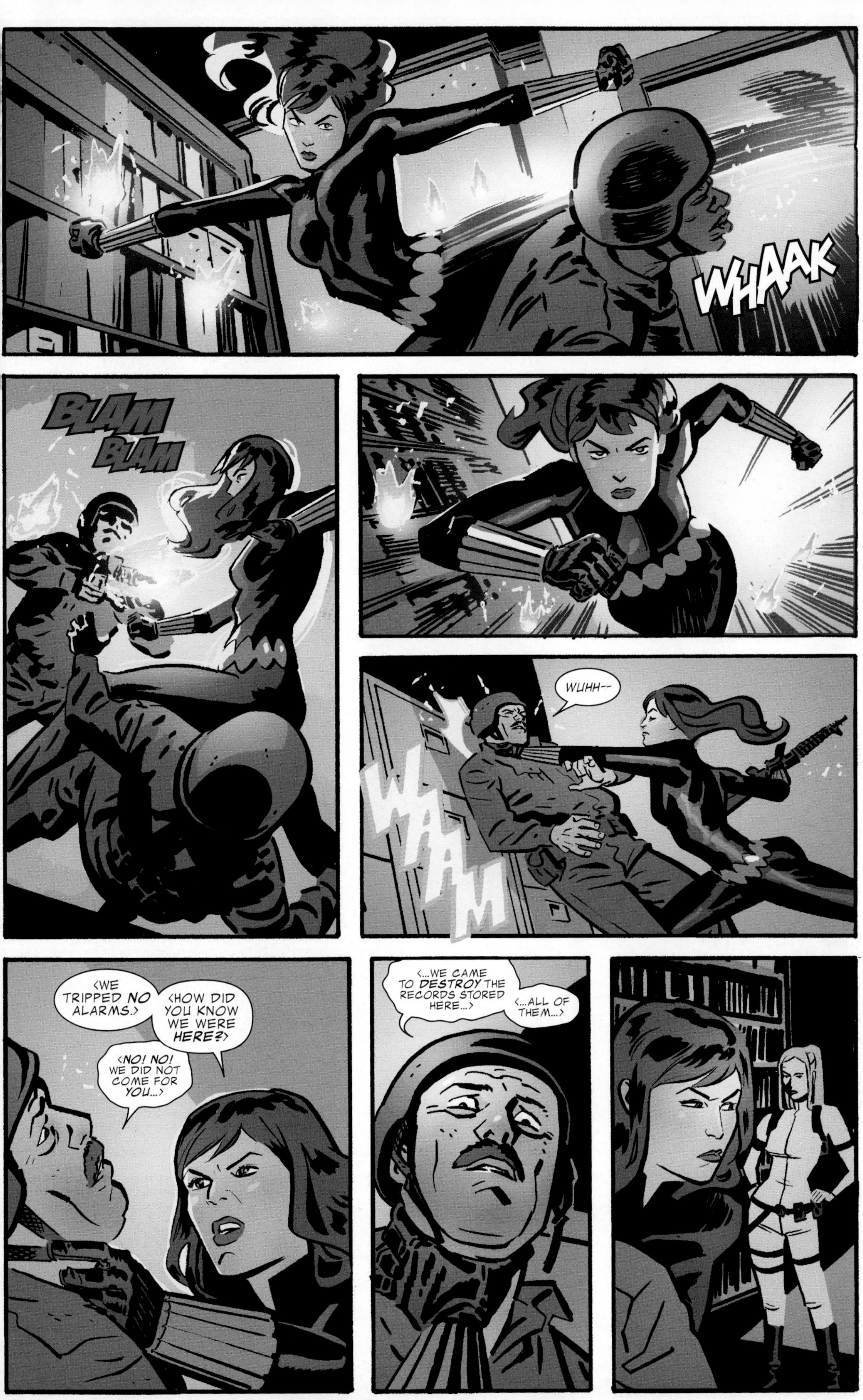
WHAAK
BLAM
BLAM
WUHH--
WHAM
<WE TRIPPED NO ALARMS.>
<HOW DID YOU KNOW WE WERE HERE?>
<NO! NO! WE DID NOT COME FOR YOU...>
<...WE CAME TO DESTROY THE RECORDS STORED HERE...>
<...ALL OF THEM...>

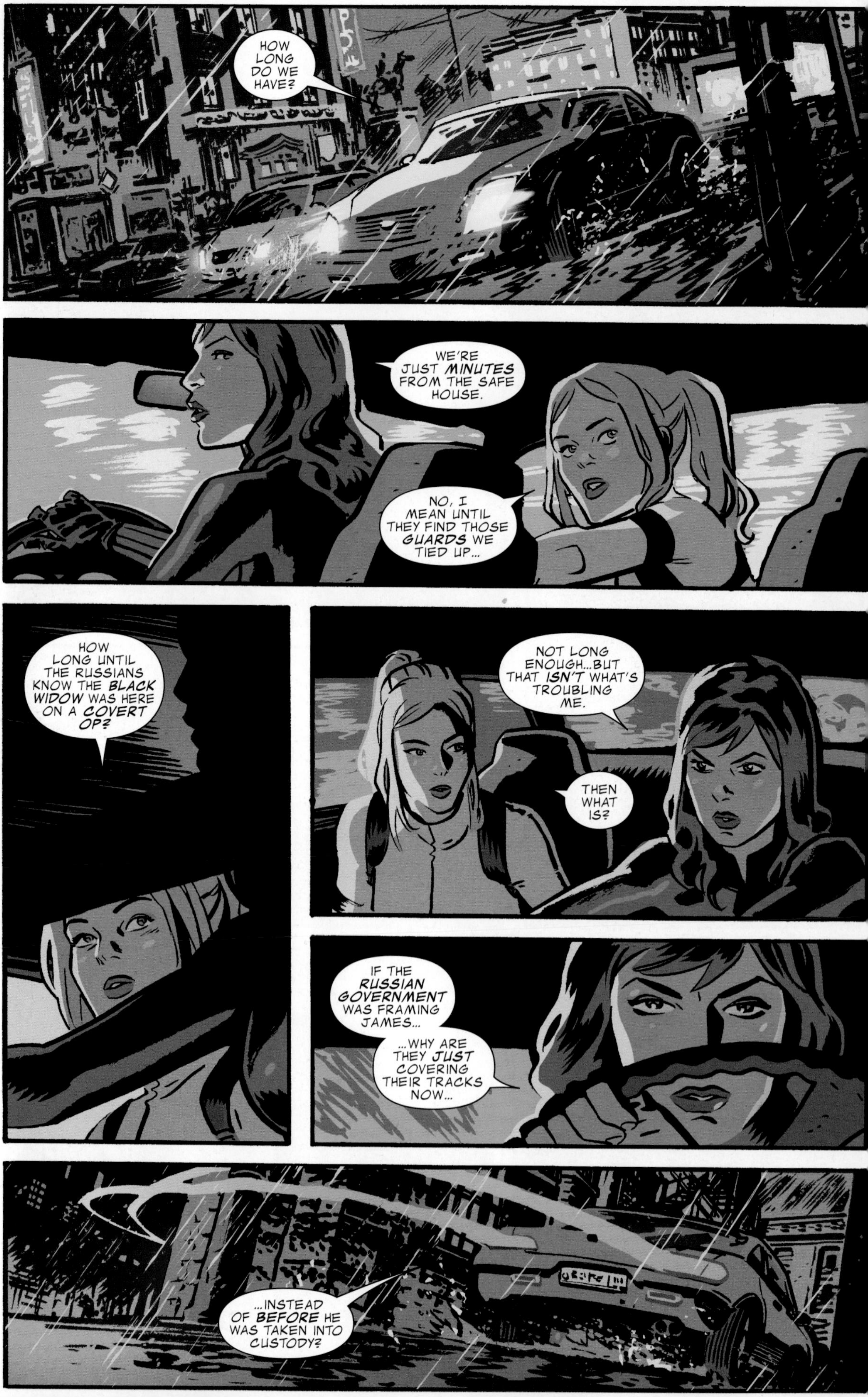
HOW LONG DO WE HAVE?
WE'RE JUST MINUTES FROM THE SAFE HOUSE.
NO, I MEAN UNTIL THEY FIND THOSE GUARDS WE TIED UP...
HOW LONG UNTIL THE RUSSIANS KNOW THE BLACK WIDOW WAS HERE ON A COVERT OP?
NOT LONG ENOUGH...BUT THAT ISN'T WHAT'S TROUBLING ME.
THEN WHAT IS?
IF THE RUSSIAN GOVERNMENT WAS FRAMING JAMES...
...WHY ARE THEY JUST COVERING THEIR TRACKS NOW...
...INSTEAD OF BEFORE HE WAS TAKEN INTO CUSTODY?

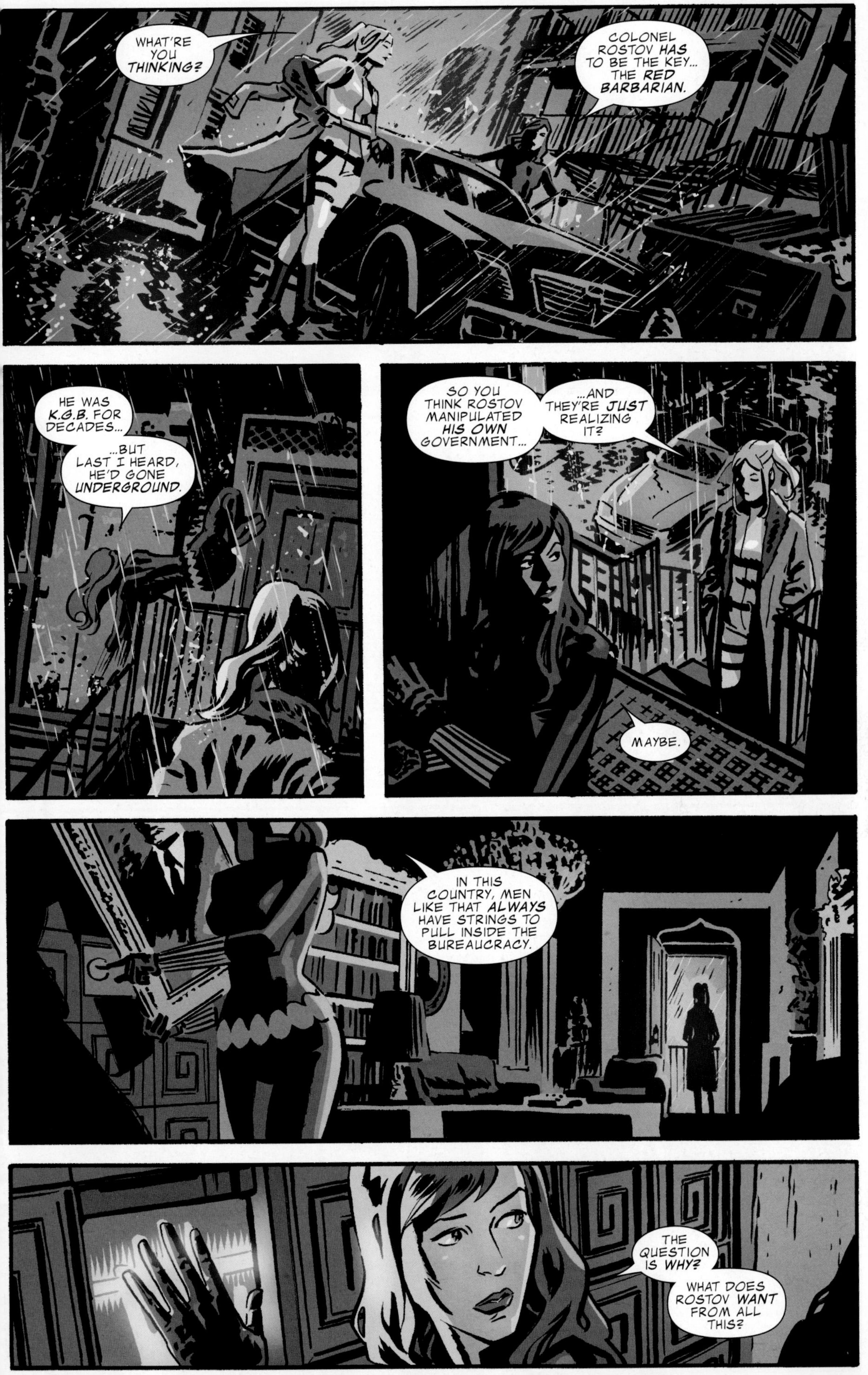
WHAT'RE YOU THINKING?
COLONEL ROSTOV HAS TO BE THE KEY... THE RED BARBARIAN.
HE WAS K.G.B. FOR DECADES...
...BUT LAST I HEARD, HE'D GONE UNDERGROUND.
SO YOU THINK ROSTOV MANIPULATED HIS OWN GOVERNMENT...
...AND THEY'RE JUST REALIZING IT?
MAYBE.
IN THIS COUNTRY, MEN LIKE THAT ALWAYS HAVE STRINGS TO PULL INSIDE THE BUREAUCRACY.
THE QUESTION IS WHY?
WHAT DOES ROSTOV WANT FROM ALL THIS?

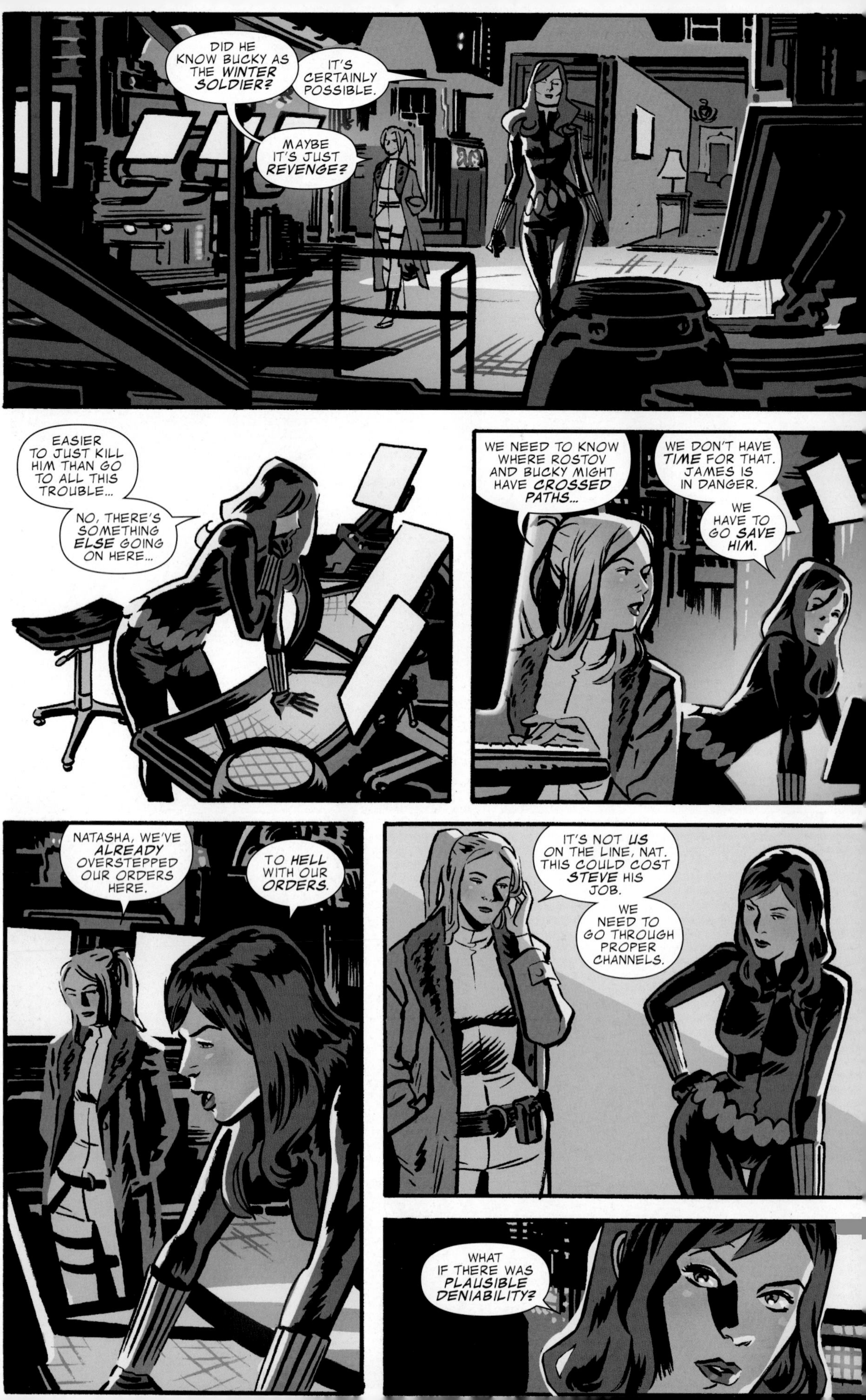
DID HE KNOW BUCKY AS THE WINTER SOLDIER?
IT'S CERTAINLY POSSIBLE.
MAYBE IT'S JUST REVENGE?
EASIER TO JUST KILL HIM THAN GO TO ALL THIS TROUBLE...
NO, THERE'S SOMETHING ELSE GOING ON HERE...
WE NEED TO KNOW WHERE ROSTOV AND BUCKY MIGHT HAVE CROSSED PATHS...
WE DON'T HAVE TIME FOR THAT. JAMES IS IN DANGER.
WE HAVE TO GO SAVE HIM.
NATASHA, WE'VE ALREADY OVERSTEPPED OUR ORDERS HERE.
TO HELL WITH OUR ORDERS.
IT'S NOT US ON THE LINE, NAT. THIS COULD COST STEVE HIS JOB.
WE NEED TO GO THROUGH PROPER CHANNELS.
WHAT IF THERE WAS PLAUSIBLE DENIABILITY?

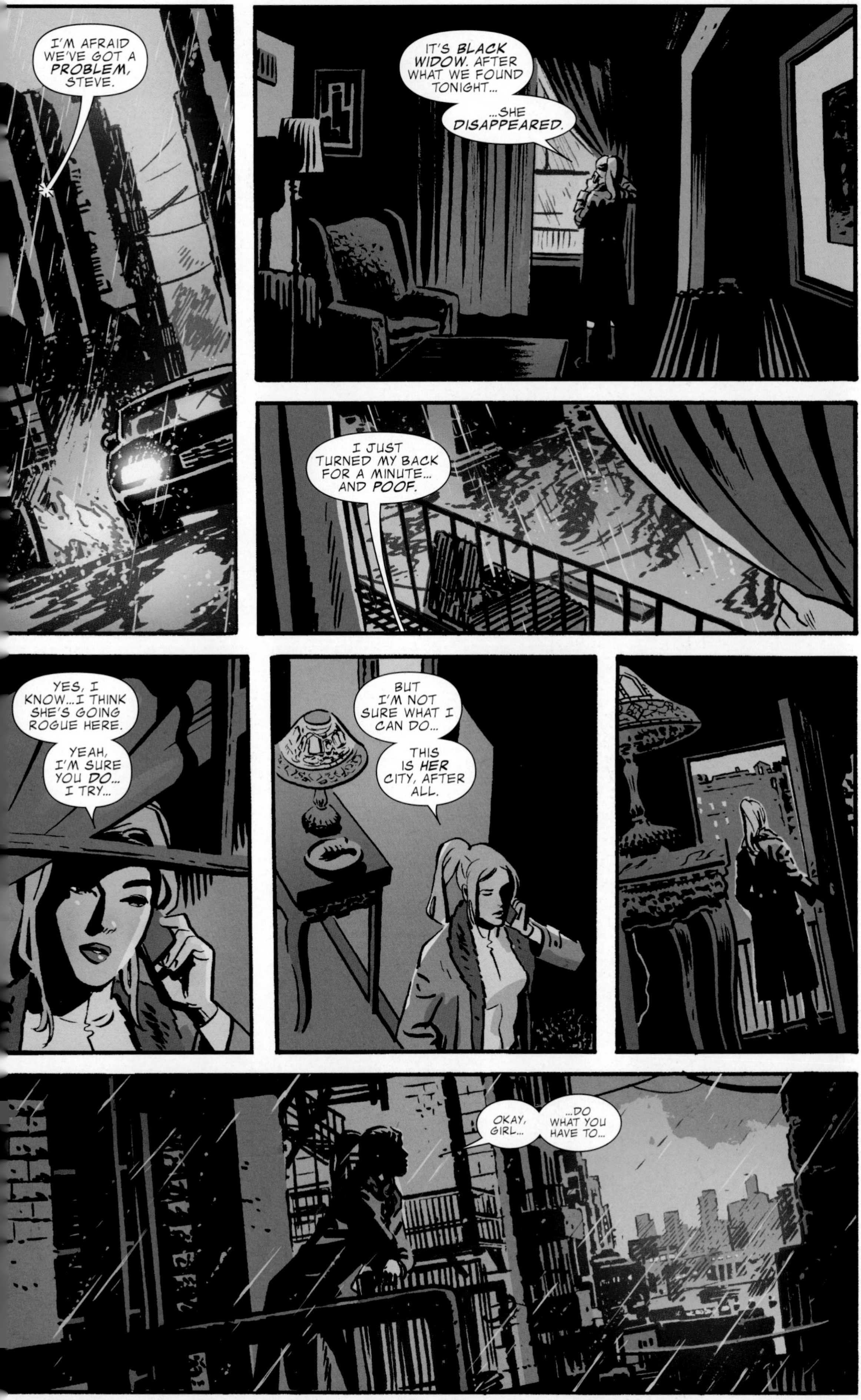
I'M AFRAID WE'VE GOT A PROBLEM, STEVE.
IT'S BLACK WIDOW. AFTER WHAT WE FOUND TONIGHT...
...SHE DISAPPEARED.
I JUST TURNED MY BACK FOR A MINUTE... AND POOF.
YES, I KNOW...I THINK SHE'S GOING ROGUE HERE.
YEAH, I'M SURE YOU DO... I TRY...
BUT I'M NOT SURE WHAT I CAN DO...
THIS IS HER CITY, AFTER ALL.
OKAY, GIRL...
...DO WHAT YOU HAVE TO...

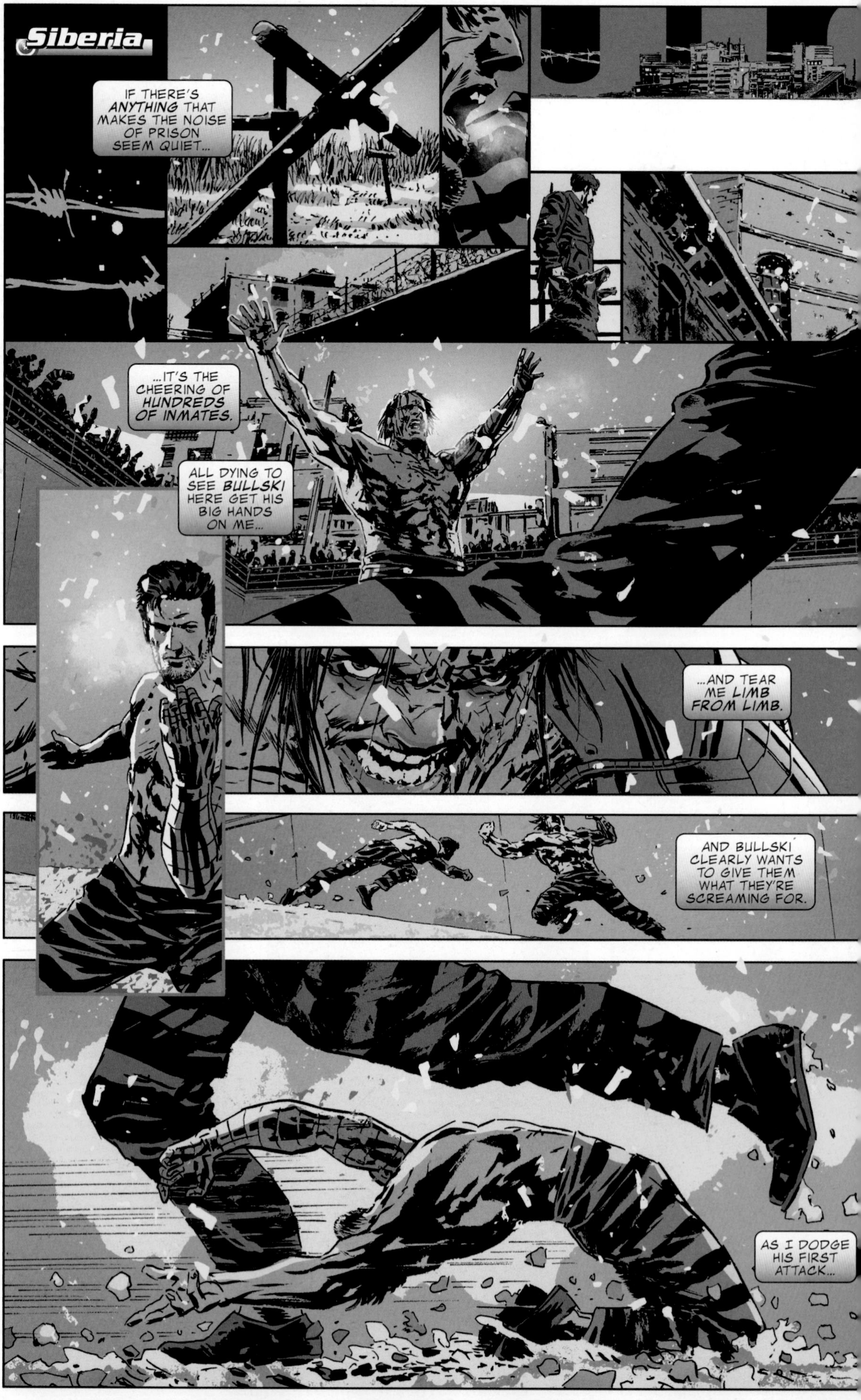
Siberia
IF THERE'S ANYTHING THAT MAKES THE NOISE OF PRISON SEEM QUIET...
...IT'S THE CHEERING OF HUNDREDS OF INMATES.
ALL DYING TO SEE BULLSKI HERE GET HIS BIG HANDS ON ME...
...AND TEAR ME LIMB FROM LIMB.
AND BULLSKI CLEARLY WANTS TO GIVE THEM WHAT THEY'RE SCREAMING FOR.
AS I DODGE HIS FIRST ATTACK...

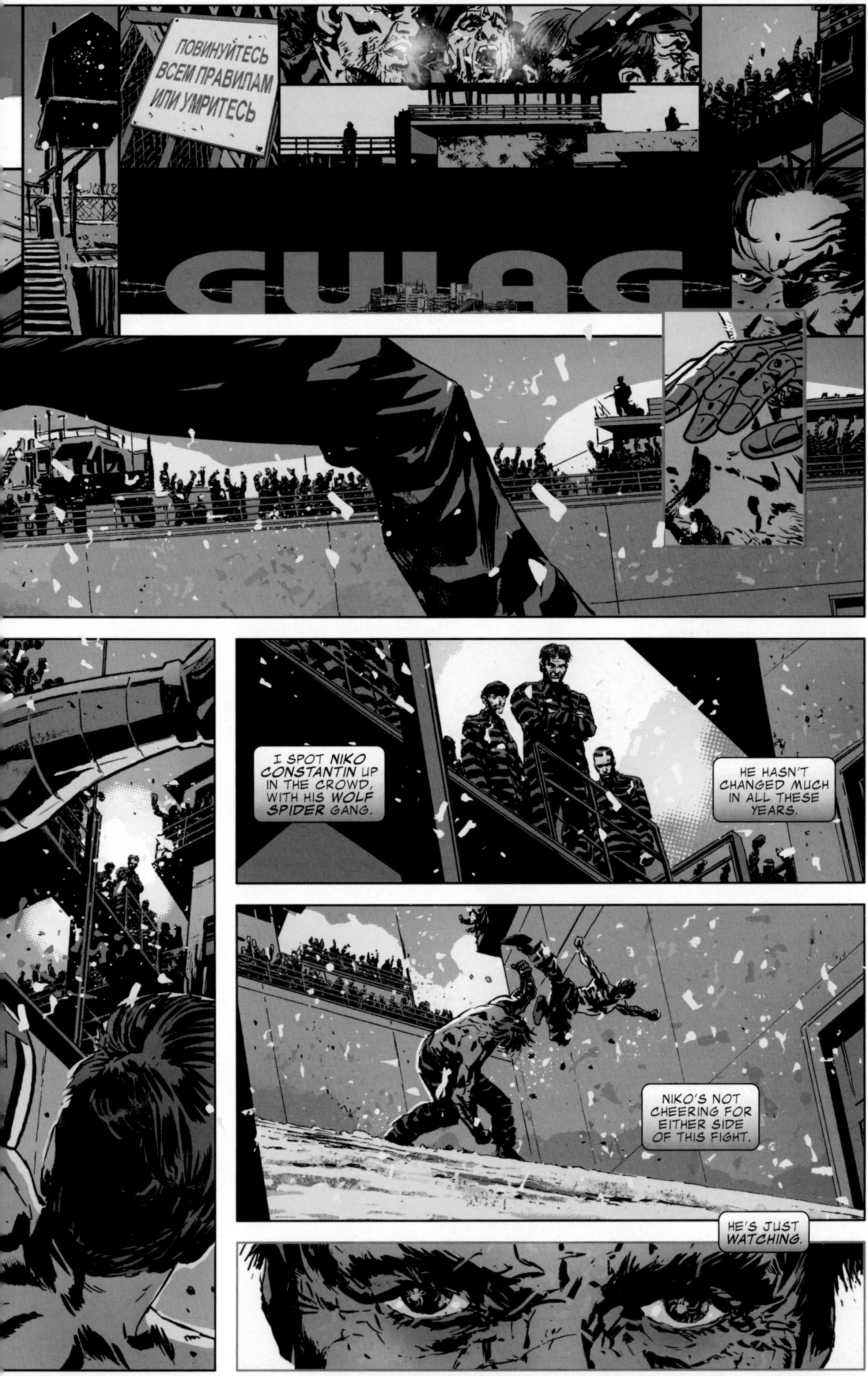

ПОВИНУЙТЕСЬ ВСЕМ ПРАВИЛАМ ИЛИ УМРИТЕСЬ
GULAG
I SPOT NIKO CONSTANTIN UP IN THE CROWD, WITH HIS WOLF SPIDER GANG.
HE HASN'T CHANGED MUCH IN ALL THESE YEARS.
NIKO'S NOT CHEERING FOR EITHER SIDE OF THIS FIGHT.
HE'S JUST WATCHING.

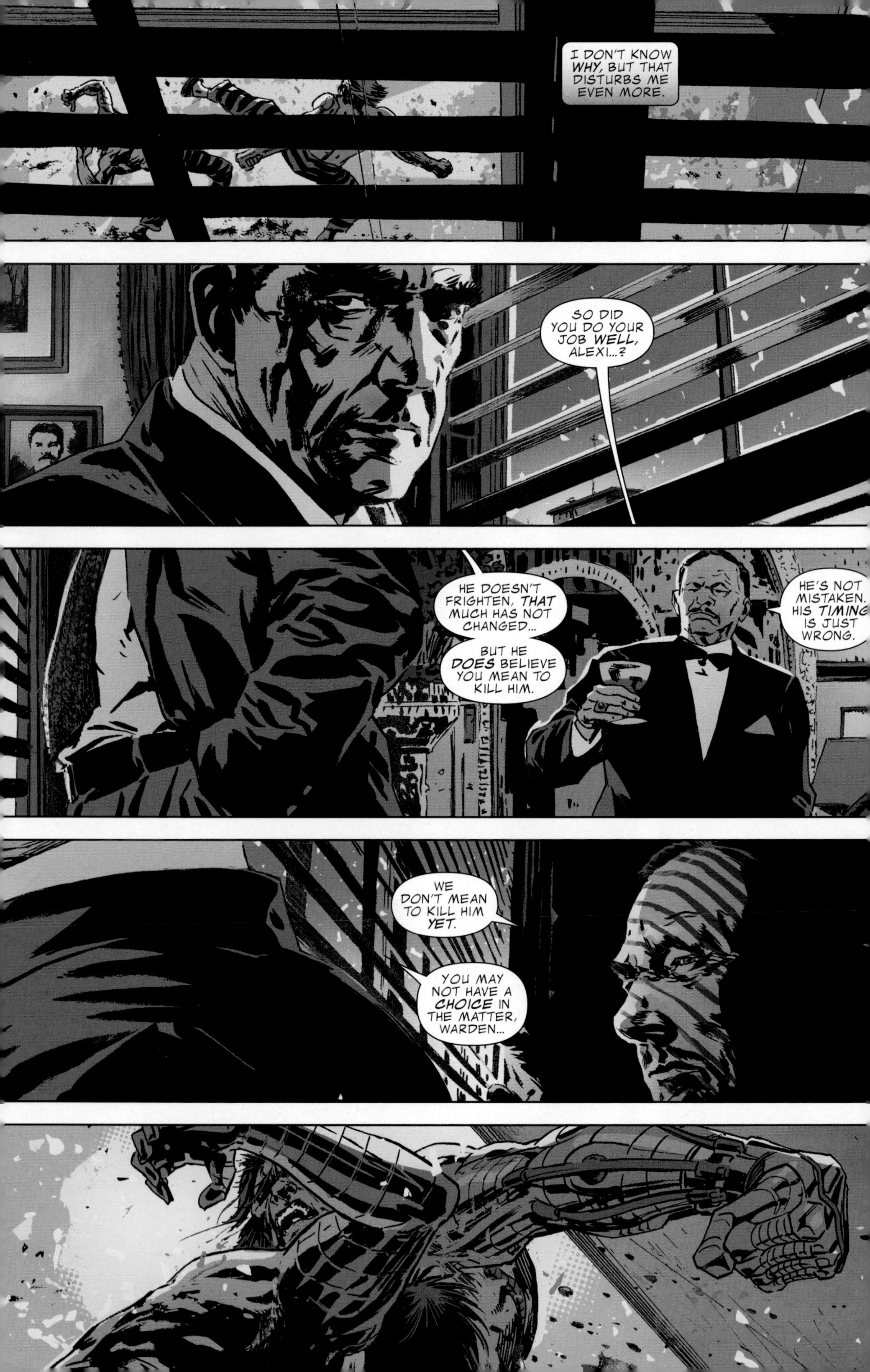
I DON'T KNOW WHY, BUT THAT DISTURBS ME EVEN MORE.
SO DID YOU DO YOUR JOB WELL, ALEXI...?
HE DOESN'T FRIGHTEN, THAT MUCH HAS NOT CHANGED...
BUT HE DOES BELIEVE YOU MEAN TO KILL HIM.
HE'S NOT MISTAKEN. HIS TIMING IS JUST WRONG.
WE DON'T MEAN TO KILL HIM YET.
YOU MAY NOT HAVE A CHOICE IN THE MATTER, WARDEN...

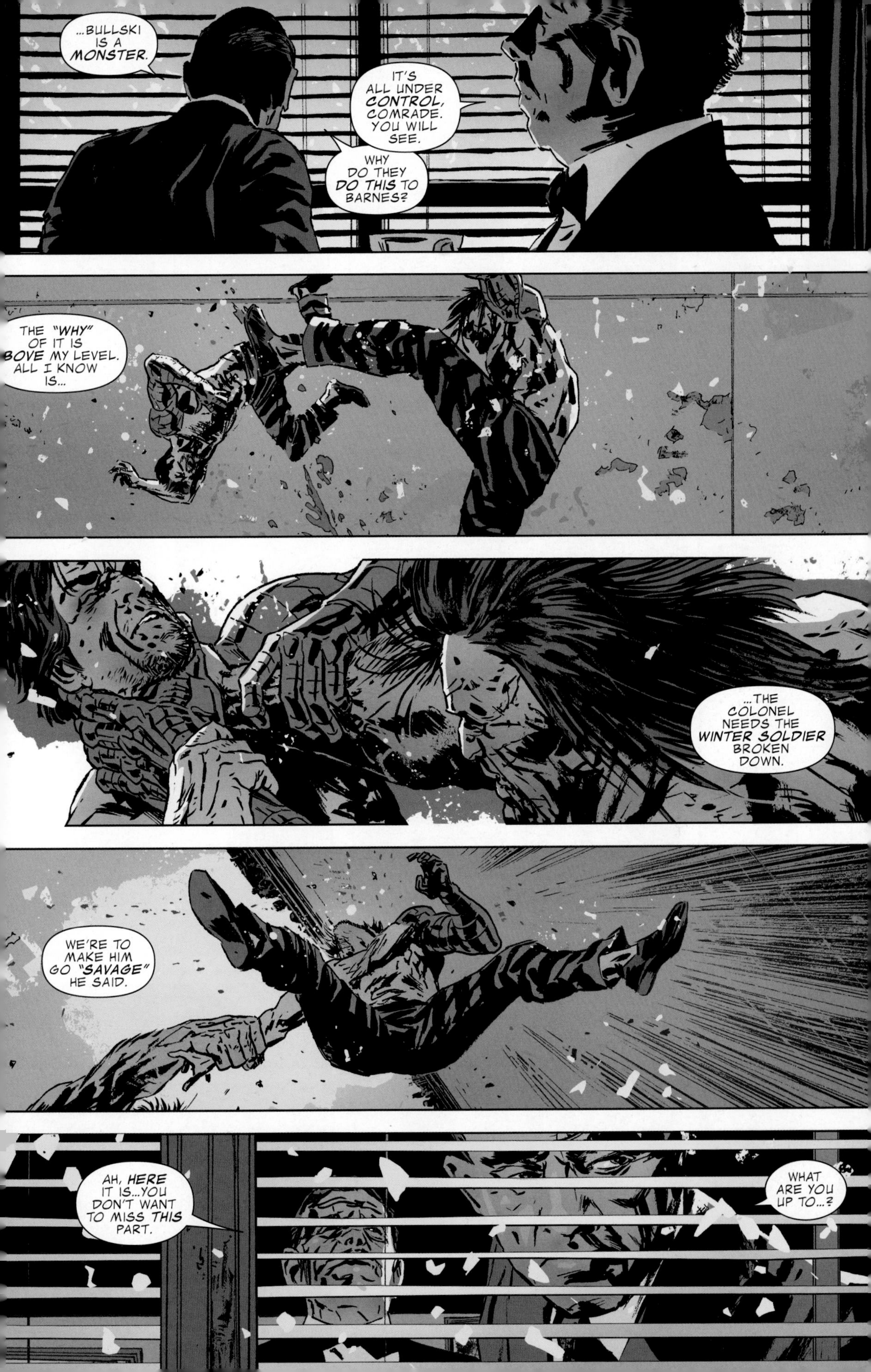
...BULLSKI IS A MONSTER.
IT'S ALL UNDER CONTROL, COMRADE. YOU WILL SEE.
WHY DO THEY DO THIS TO BARNES?
THE "WHY" OF IT IS BOVE MY LEVEL. ALL I KNOW IS...
...THE COLONEL NEEDS THE WINTER SOLDIER BROKEN DOWN.
WE'RE TO MAKE HIM GO "SAVAGE" HE SAID.
AH, HERE IT IS...YOU DON'T WANT TO MISS THIS PART.
WHAT ARE YOU UP TO...?

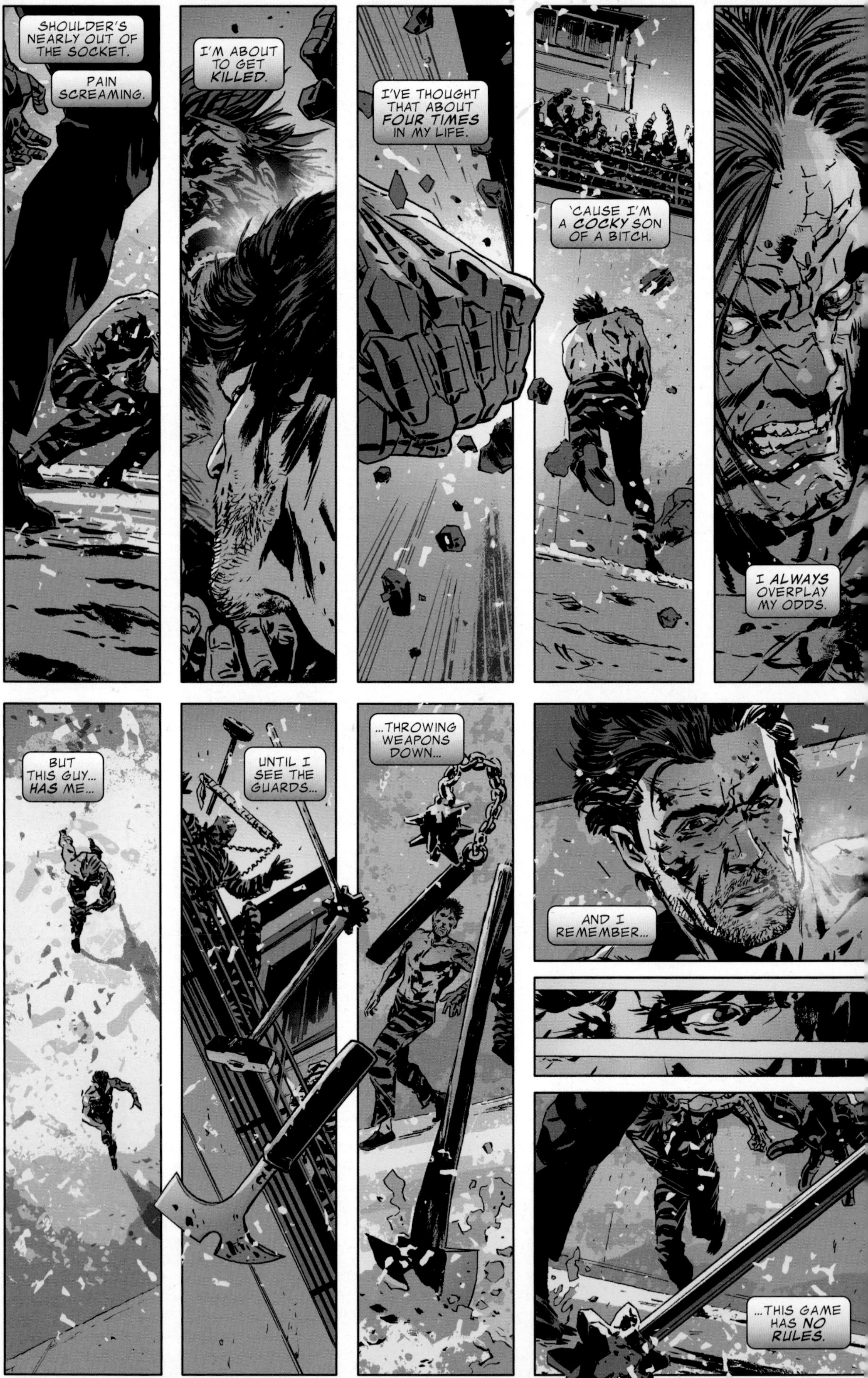
SHOULDER'S NEARLY OUT OF THE SOCKET.
PAIN SCREAMING.
I'M ABOUT TO GET KILLED.
I'VE THOUGHT THAT ABOUT FOUR TIMES IN MY LIFE.
'CAUSE I'M A COCKY SON OF A BITCH.
I ALWAYS OVERPLAY MY ODDS.
BUT THIS GUY... HAS ME...
UNTIL I SEE THE GUARDS...
...THROWING WEAPONS DOWN...
AND I REMEMBER...
...THIS GAME HAS NO RULES.

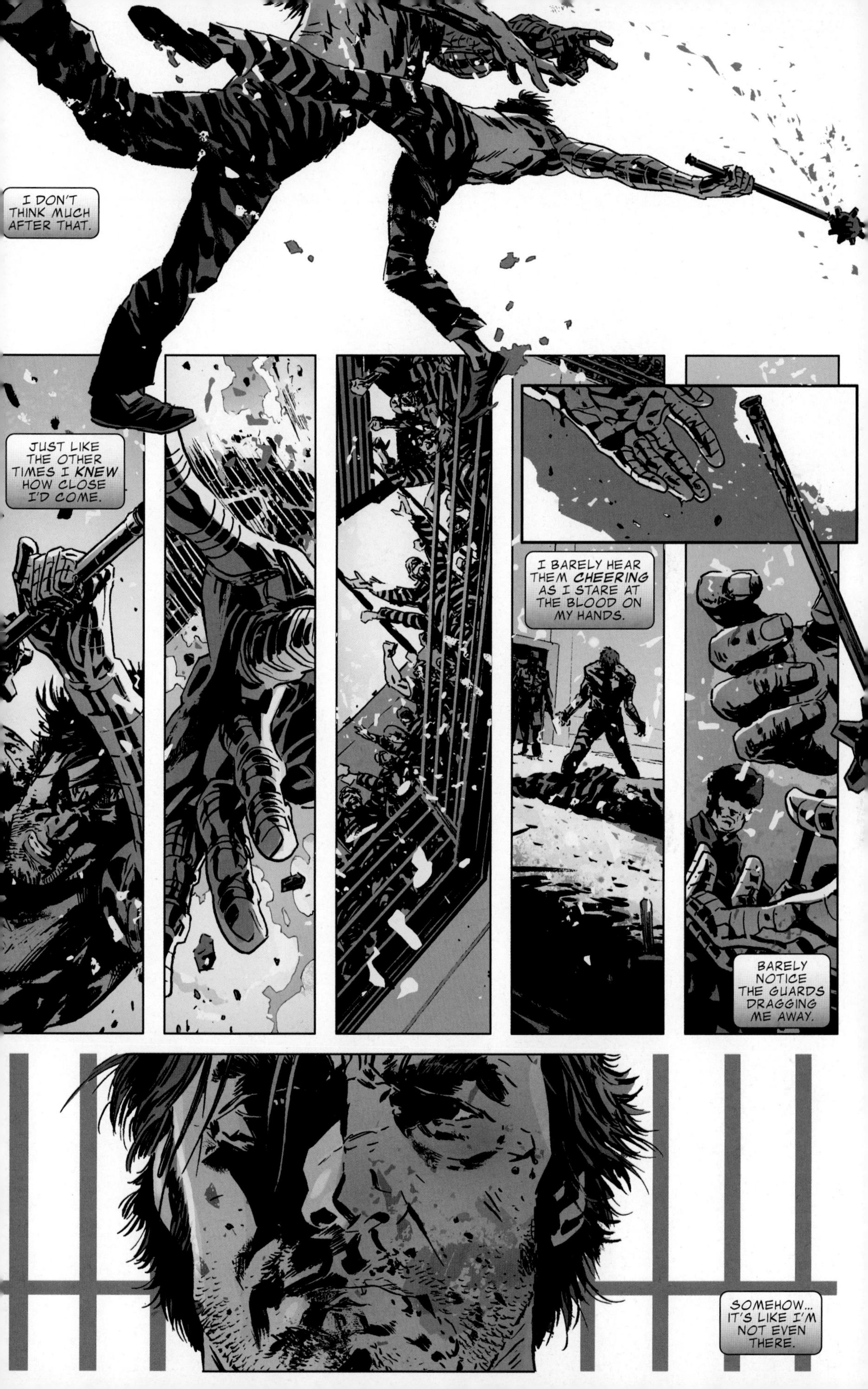
I DON'T THINK MUCH AFTER THAT.
JUST LIKE THE OTHER TIMES I KNEW HOW CLOSE I'D COME.
I BARELY HEAR THEM CHEERING AS I STARE AT THE BLOOD ON MY HANDS.
BARELY NOTICE THE GUARDS DRAGGING ME AWAY.
SOMEHOW... IT'S LIKE I'M NOT EVEN THERE.

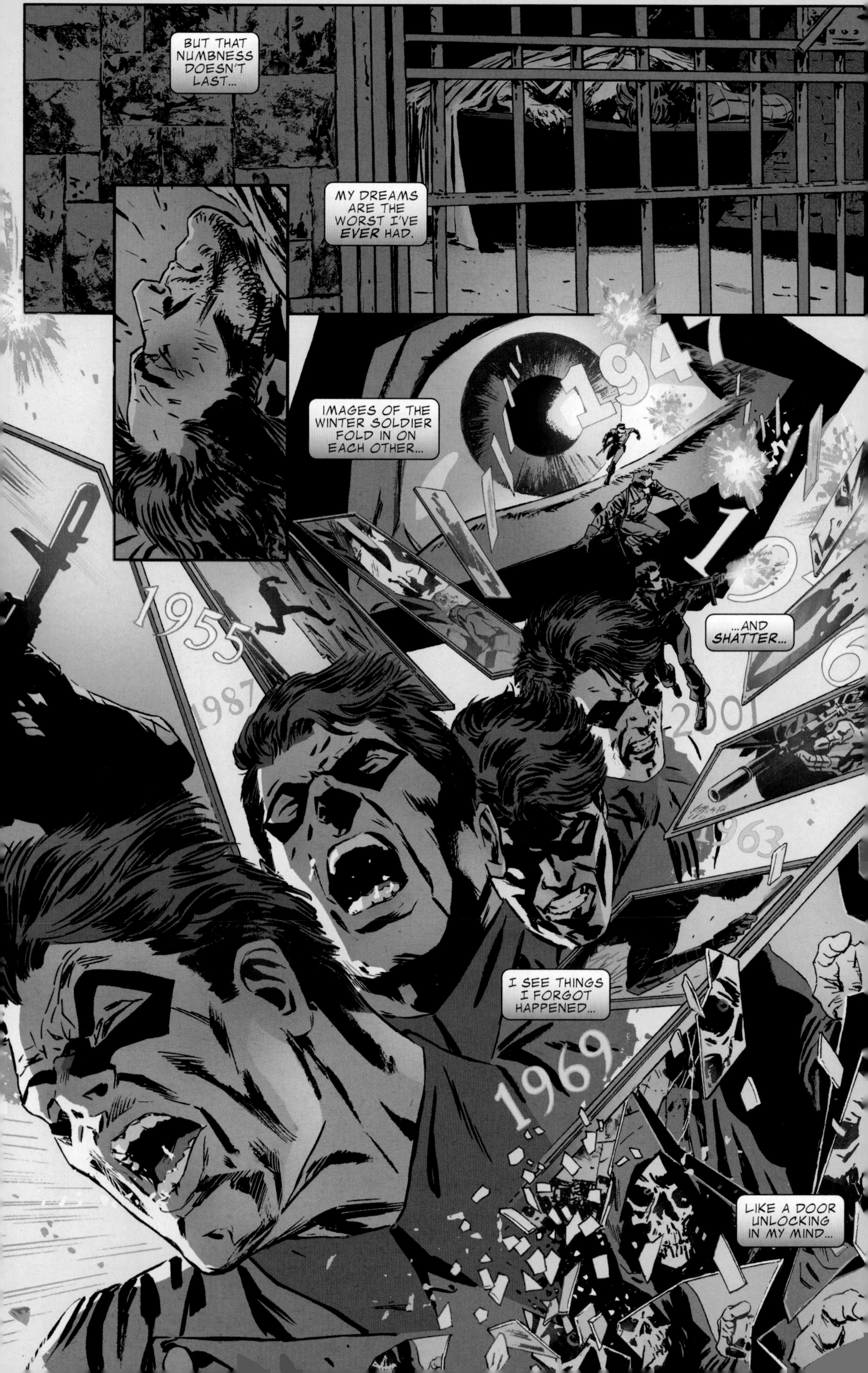
BUT THAT NUMBNESS DOESN'T LAST...
MY DREAMS ARE THE WORST I'VE EVER HAD.
IMAGES OF THE WINTER SOLDIER FOLD IN ON EACH OTHER...
...AND SHATTER...
I SEE THINGS I FORGOT HAPPENED...
LIKE A DOOR UNLOCKING IN MY MIND...

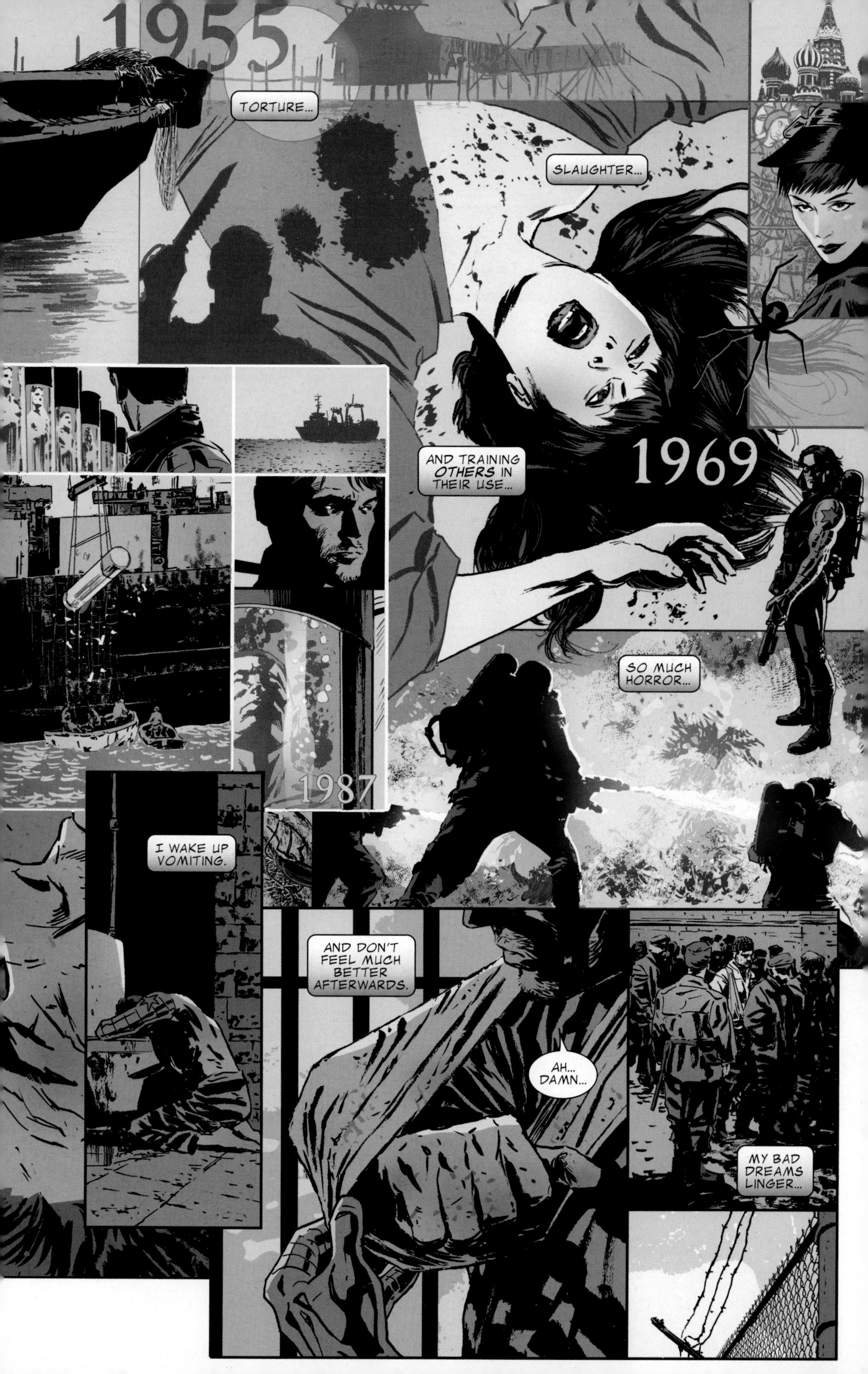
1955
TORTURE...
SLAUGHTER...
AND TRAINING OTHERS IN THEIR USE...
1969
SO MUCH HORROR...
1987
I WAKE UP VOMITING.
AND DON'T FEEL MUCH BETTER AFTERWARDS.
AH... DAMN...
MY BAD DREAMS LINGER...

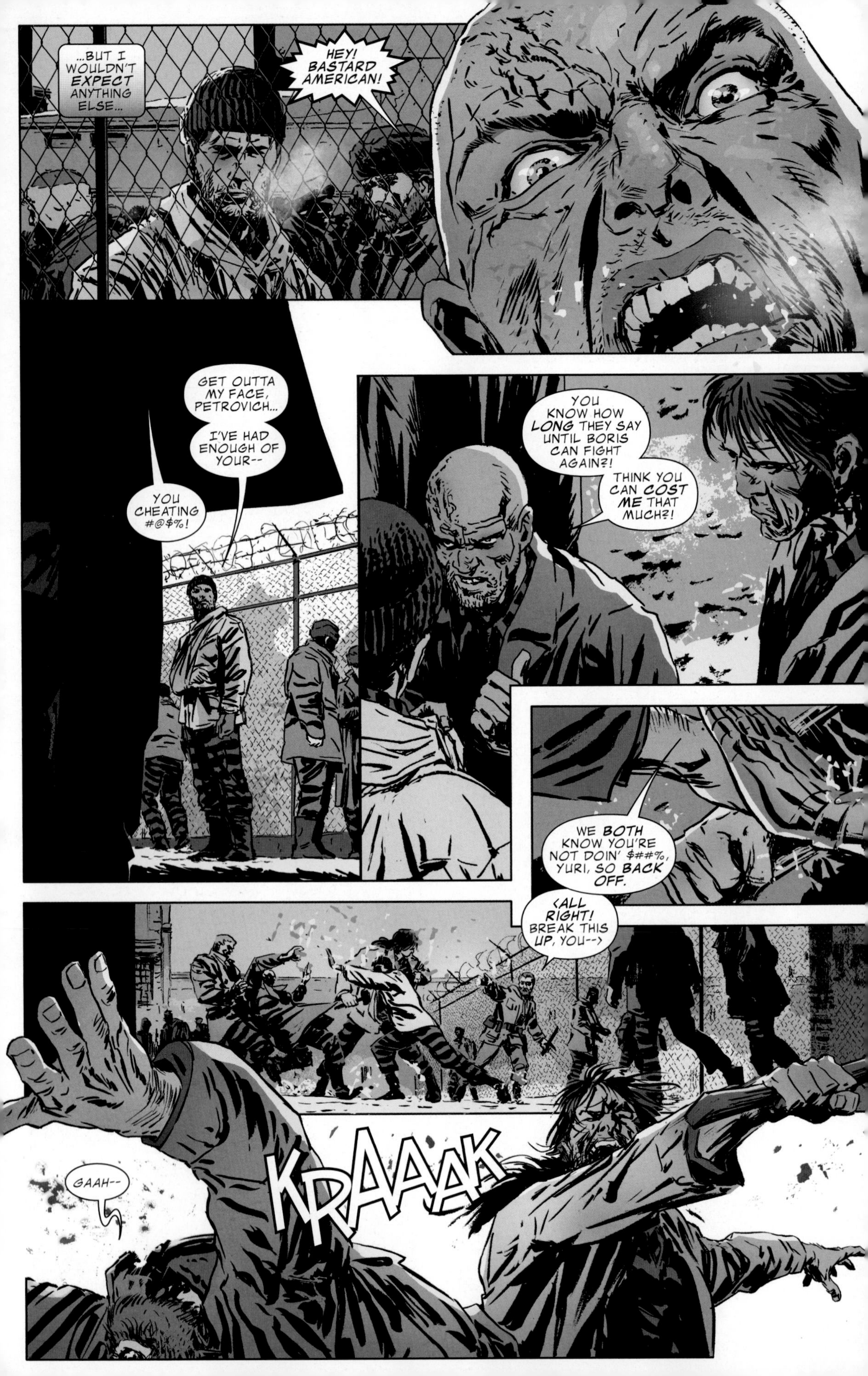
...BUT I WOULDN'T EXPECT ANYTHING ELSE...
HEY! BASTARD AMERICAN!
GET OUTTA MY FACE, PETROVICH...
I'VE HAD ENOUGH OF YOUR--
YOU CHEATING #@$%!
YOU KNOW HOW LONG THEY SAY UNTIL BORIS CAN FIGHT AGAIN?!
THINK YOU CAN COST ME THAT MUCH?!
WE BOTH KNOW YOU'RE NOT DOIN' $##%, YURI, SO BACK OFF.
<ALL RIGHT! BREAK THIS UP, YOU-->
KRAAAK
GAAH--

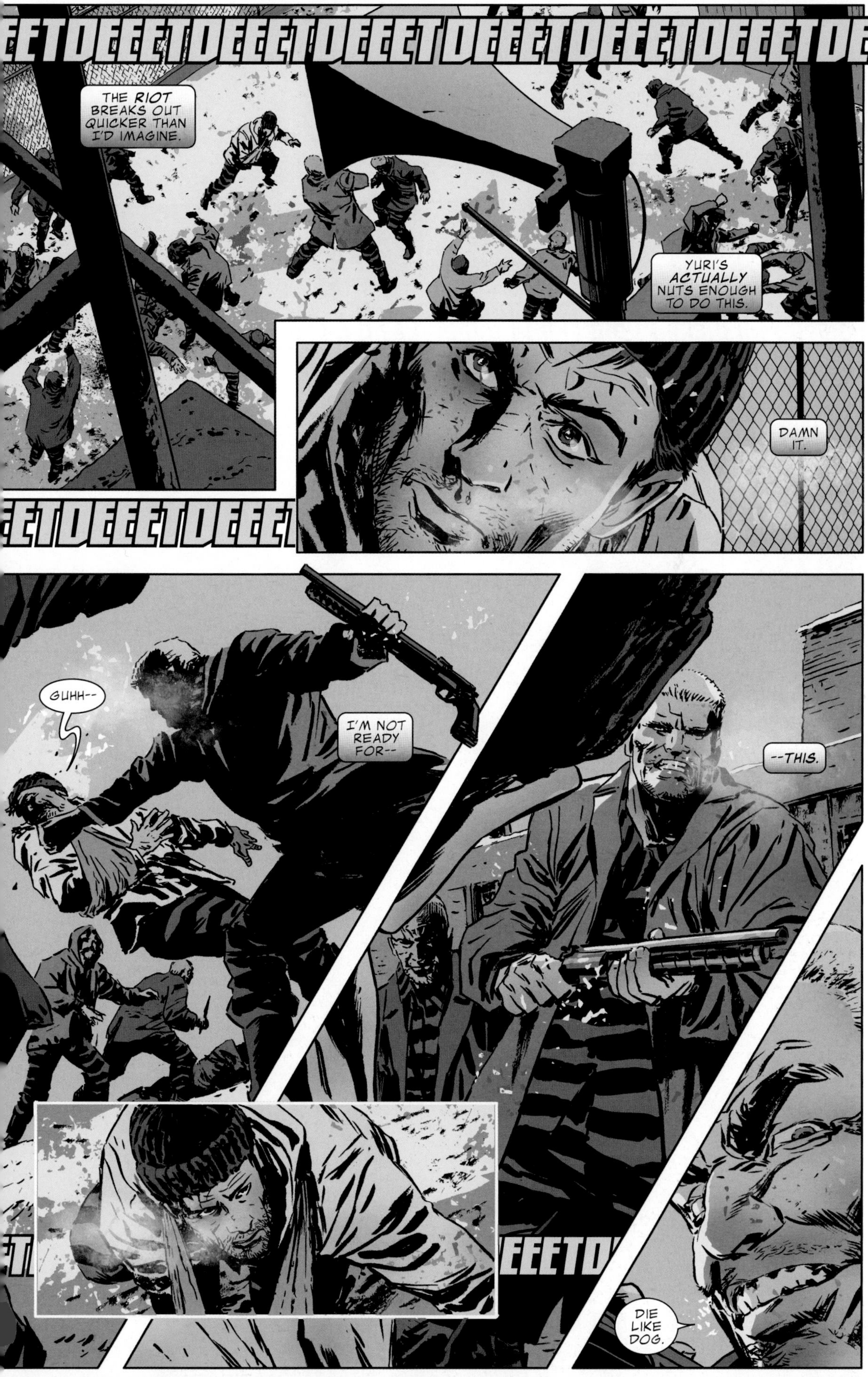
ETDEEETDEEETDEEETDEEETDEEETDEEETDEEETDE
THE RIOT BREAKS OUT QUICKER THAN I'D IMAGINE.
YURI'S ACTUALLY NUTS ENOUGH TO DO THIS.
DAMN IT.
ETDEEETDEEET
GUHH--
I'M NOT READY FOR--
--THIS.
ET
EEETD
DIE LIKE DOG.

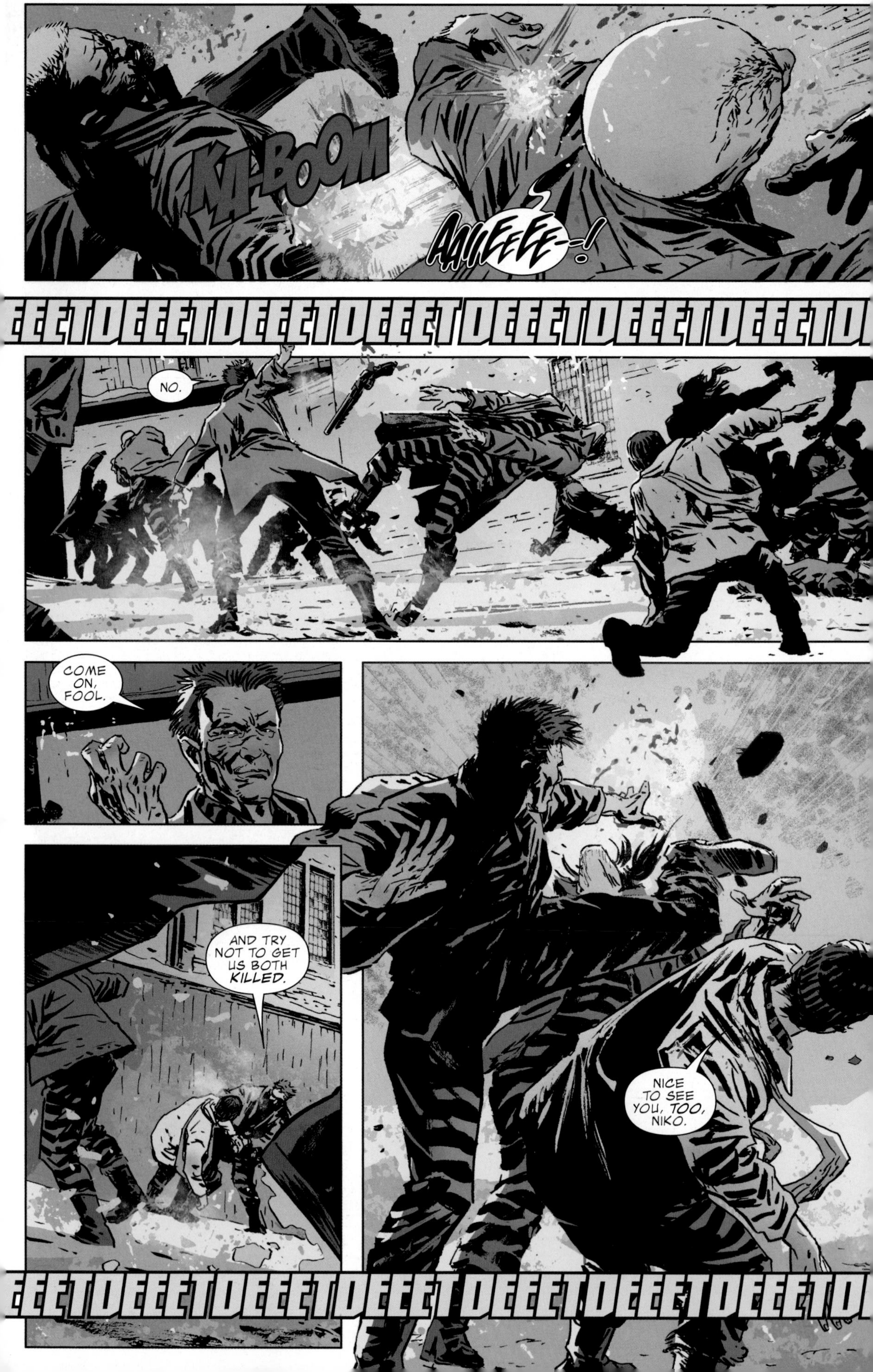
KA-BOOM
AAIIEEEE--!
EEETDEEETDEEETDEEETDEEETDEEETDEEETD
NO.
COME ON, FOOL.
AND TRY NOT TO GET US BOTH KILLED.
NICE TO SEE YOU, TOO, NIKO.
EEETDEEETDEEETDEEETDEEETDEEETDEEETD

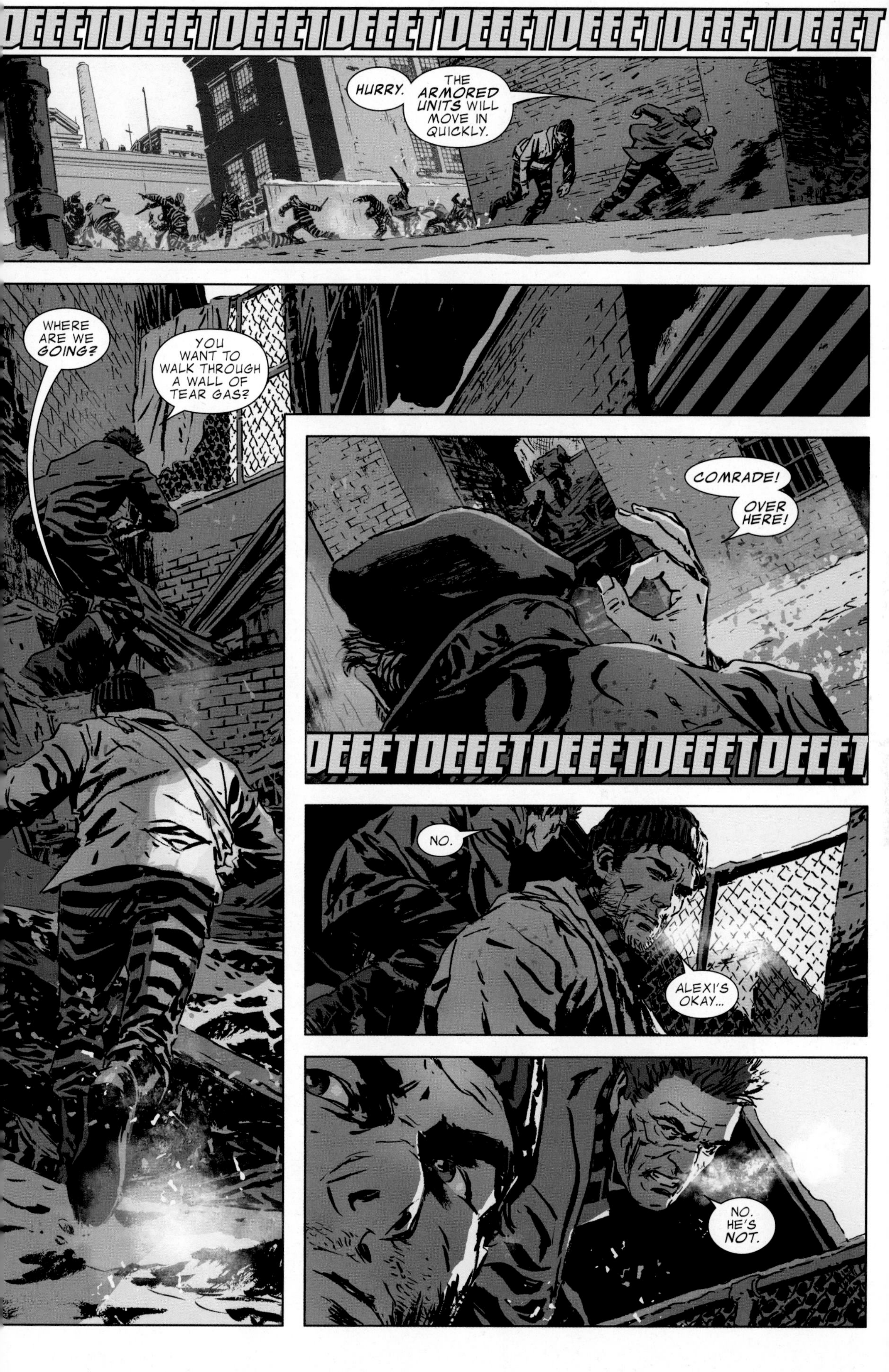
DEEETDEEETDEEETDEEETDEEETDEEETDEEETDEEET
HURRY.
THE ARMORED UNITS WILL MOVE IN QUICKLY.
WHERE ARE WE GOING?
YOU WANT TO WALK THROUGH A WALL OF TEAR GAS?
COMRADE!
OVER HERE!
DEEETDEEETDEEETDEEETDEEET
NO.
ALEXI'S OKAY...
NO. HE'S NOT.

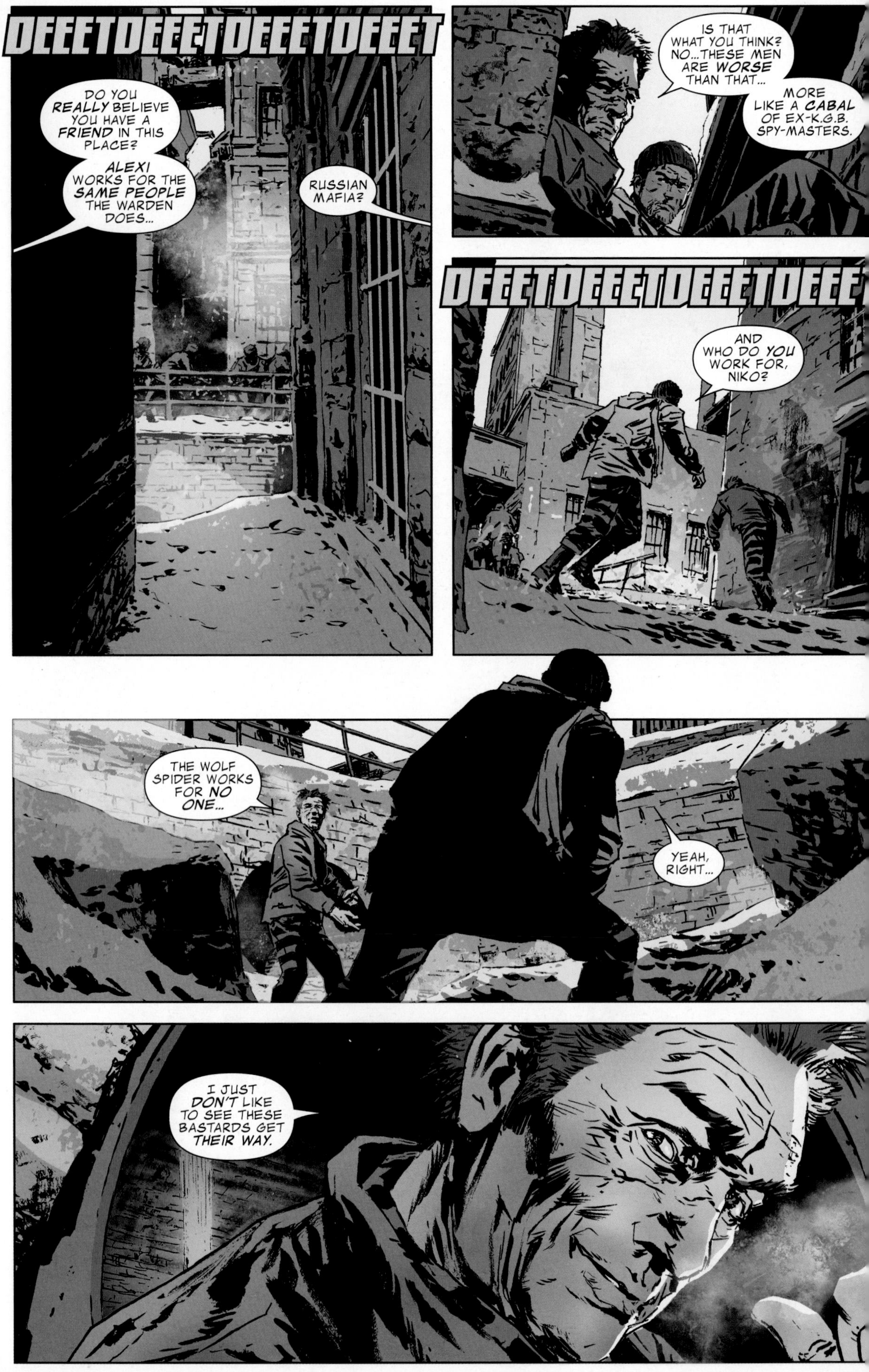
DEEETDEEETDEEETDEEET
DO YOU REALLY BELIEVE YOU HAVE A FRIEND IN THIS PLACE?
ALEXI WORKS FOR THE SAME PEOPLE THE WARDEN DOES...
RUSSIAN MAFIA?
IS THAT WHAT YOU THINK? NO...THESE MEN ARE WORSE THAN THAT...
MORE LIKE A CABAL OF EX-K.G.B. SPY-MASTERS.
DEEETDEEETDEEETDEEE
AND WHO DO YOU WORK FOR, NIKO?
THE WOLF SPIDER WORKS FOR NO ONE...
YEAH, RIGHT...
I JUST DON'T LIKE TO SEE THESE BASTARDS GET THEIR WAY.

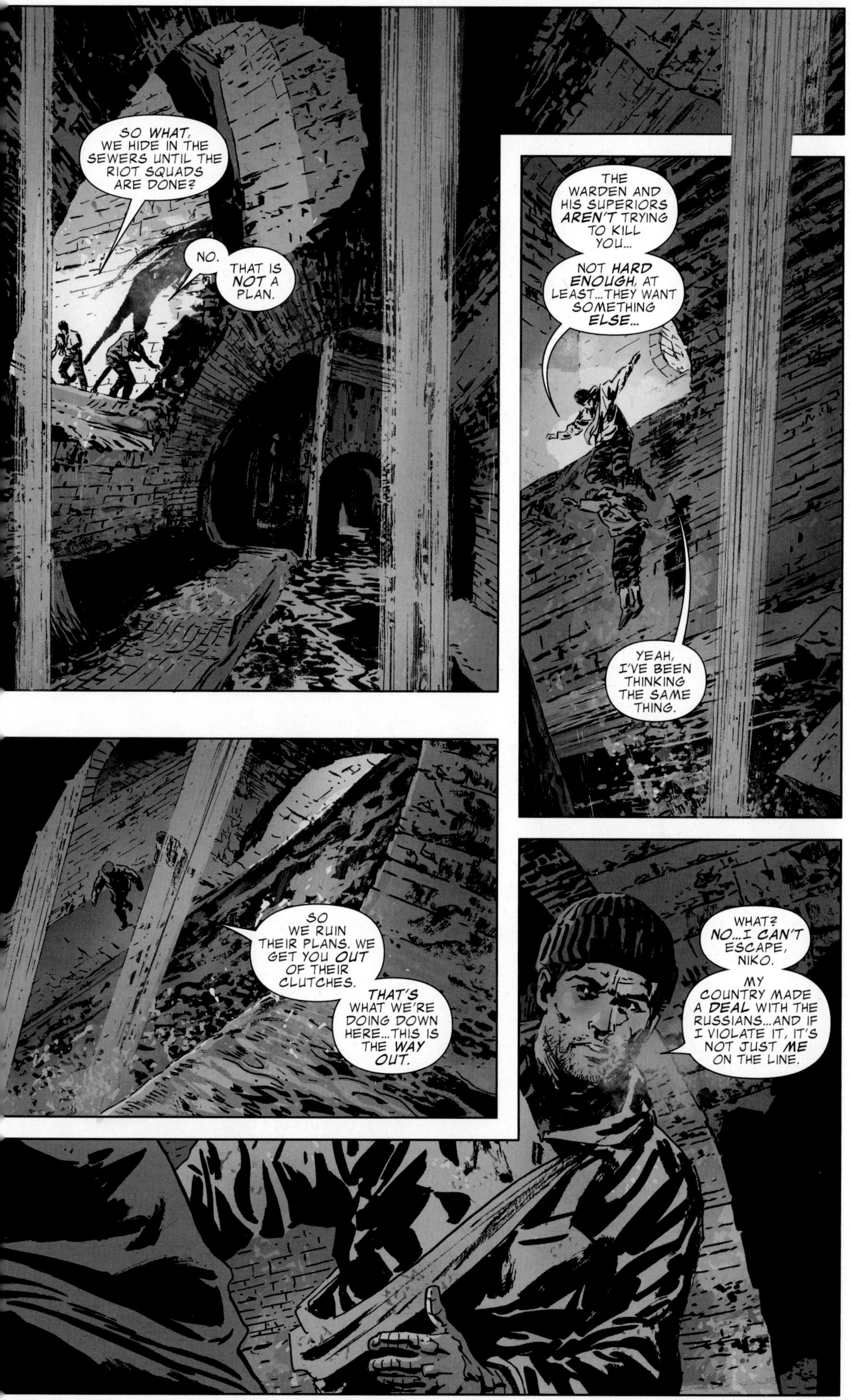
SO WHAT, WE HIDE IN THE SEWERS UNTIL THE RIOT SQUADS ARE DONE?
NO.
THAT IS NOT A PLAN.
THE WARDEN AND HIS SUPERIORS AREN'T TRYING TO KILL YOU...
NOT HARD ENOUGH, AT LEAST...THEY WANT SOMETHING ELSE...
YEAH, I'VE BEEN THINKING THE SAME THING.
SO WE RUIN THEIR PLANS. WE GET YOU OUT OF THEIR CLUTCHES.
THAT'S WHAT WE'RE DOING DOWN HERE...THIS IS THE WAY OUT.
WHAT? NO...I CAN'T ESCAPE, NIKO.
MY COUNTRY MADE A DEAL WITH THE RUSSIANS...AND IF I VIOLATE IT, IT'S NOT JUST ME ON THE LINE.

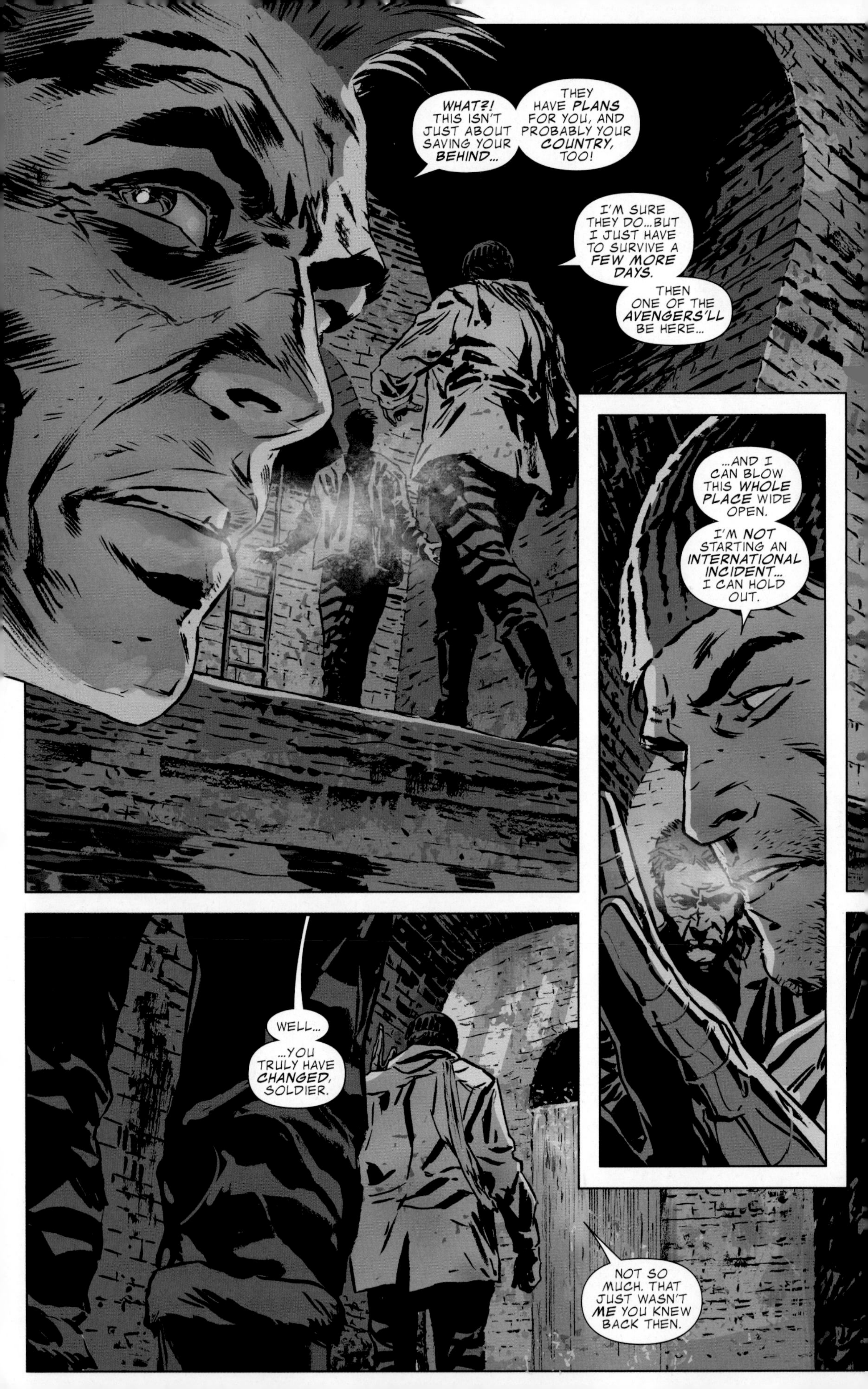
WHAT?! THIS ISN'T JUST ABOUT SAVING YOUR BEHIND...
THEY HAVE PLANS FOR YOU, AND PROBABLY YOUR COUNTRY, TOO!
I'M SURE THEY DO...BUT I JUST HAVE TO SURVIVE A FEW MORE DAYS.
THEN ONE OF THE AVENGERS'LL BE HERE...
...AND I CAN BLOW THIS WHOLE PLACE WIDE OPEN.
I'M NOT STARTING AN INTERNATIONAL INCIDENT... I CAN HOLD OUT.
WELL...
...YOU TRULY HAVE CHANGED, SOLDIER.
NOT SO MUCH. THAT JUST WASN'T ME YOU KNEW BACK THEN.

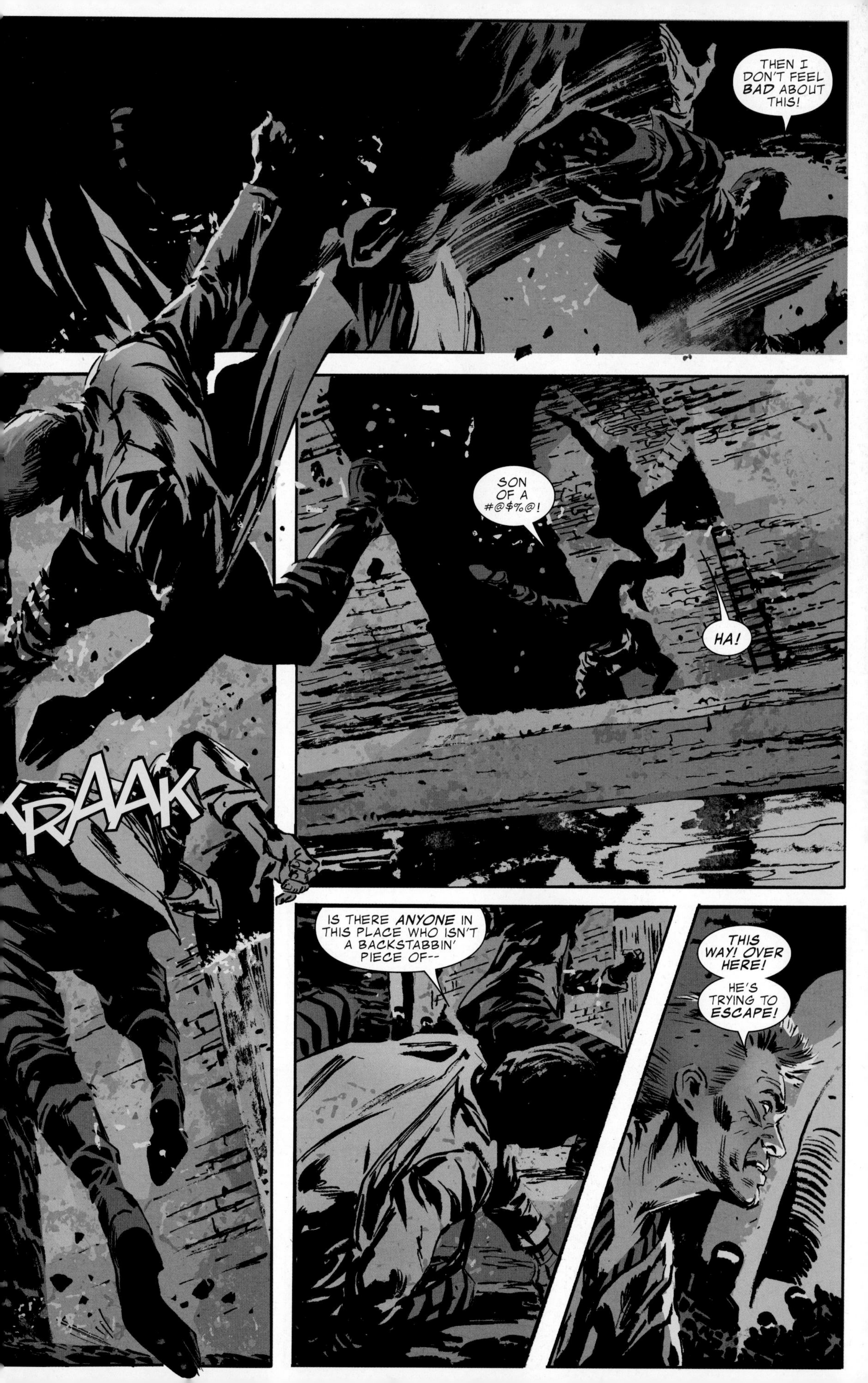
THEN I DON'T FEEL BAD ABOUT THIS!
KRAAK
SON OF A #@$%@!
HA!
IS THERE ANYONE IN THIS PLACE WHO ISN'T A BACKSTABBIN' PIECE OF--
THIS WAY! OVER HERE!
HE'S TRYING TO ESCAPE!

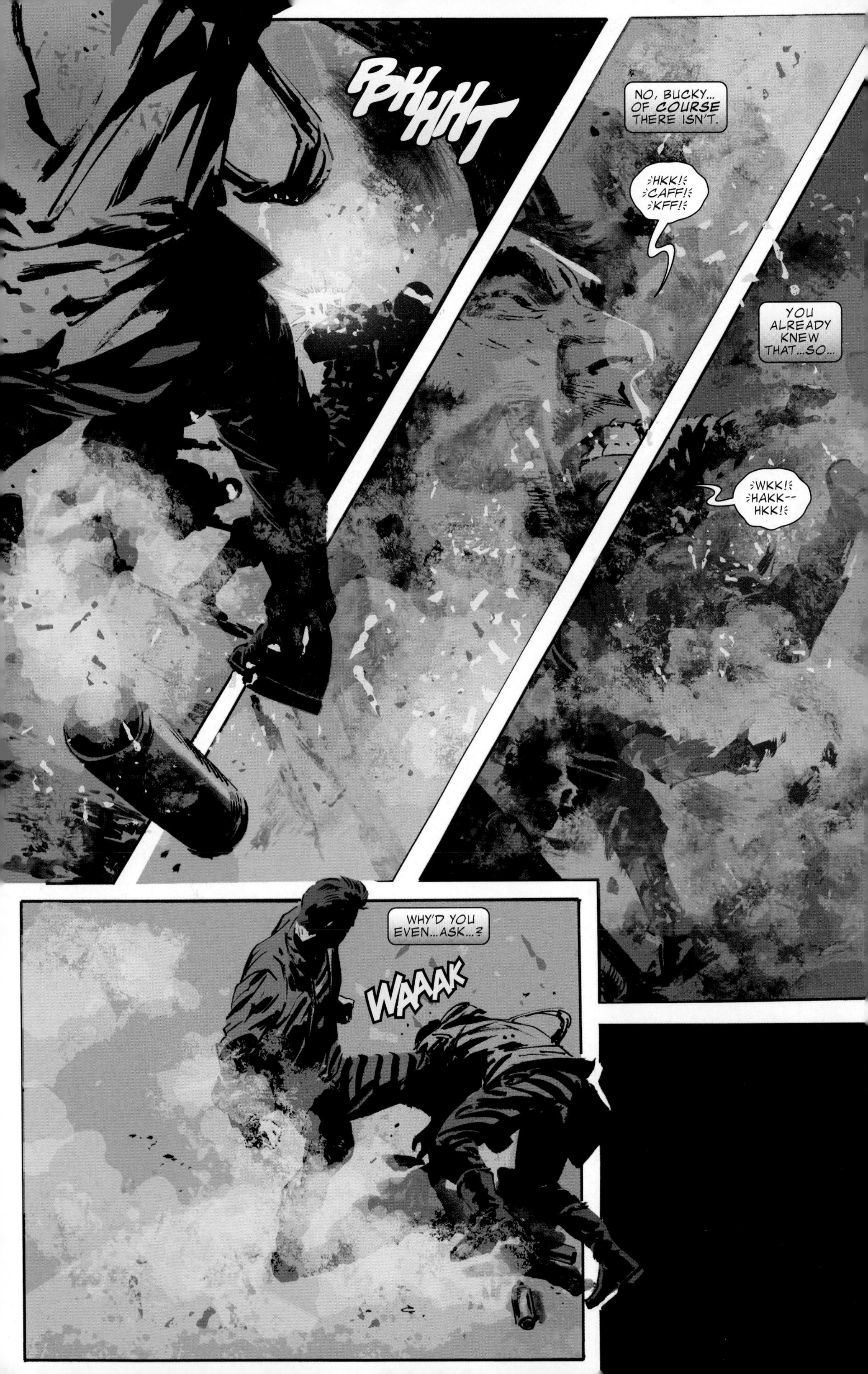
PPHHHT
NO, BUCKY... OF COURSE THERE ISN'T.
HKK! CAFF! KFF!
YOU ALREADY KNEW THAT...SO...
WKK! HAKK-- HKK!
WHY'D YOU EVEN...ASK...?
WAAAK

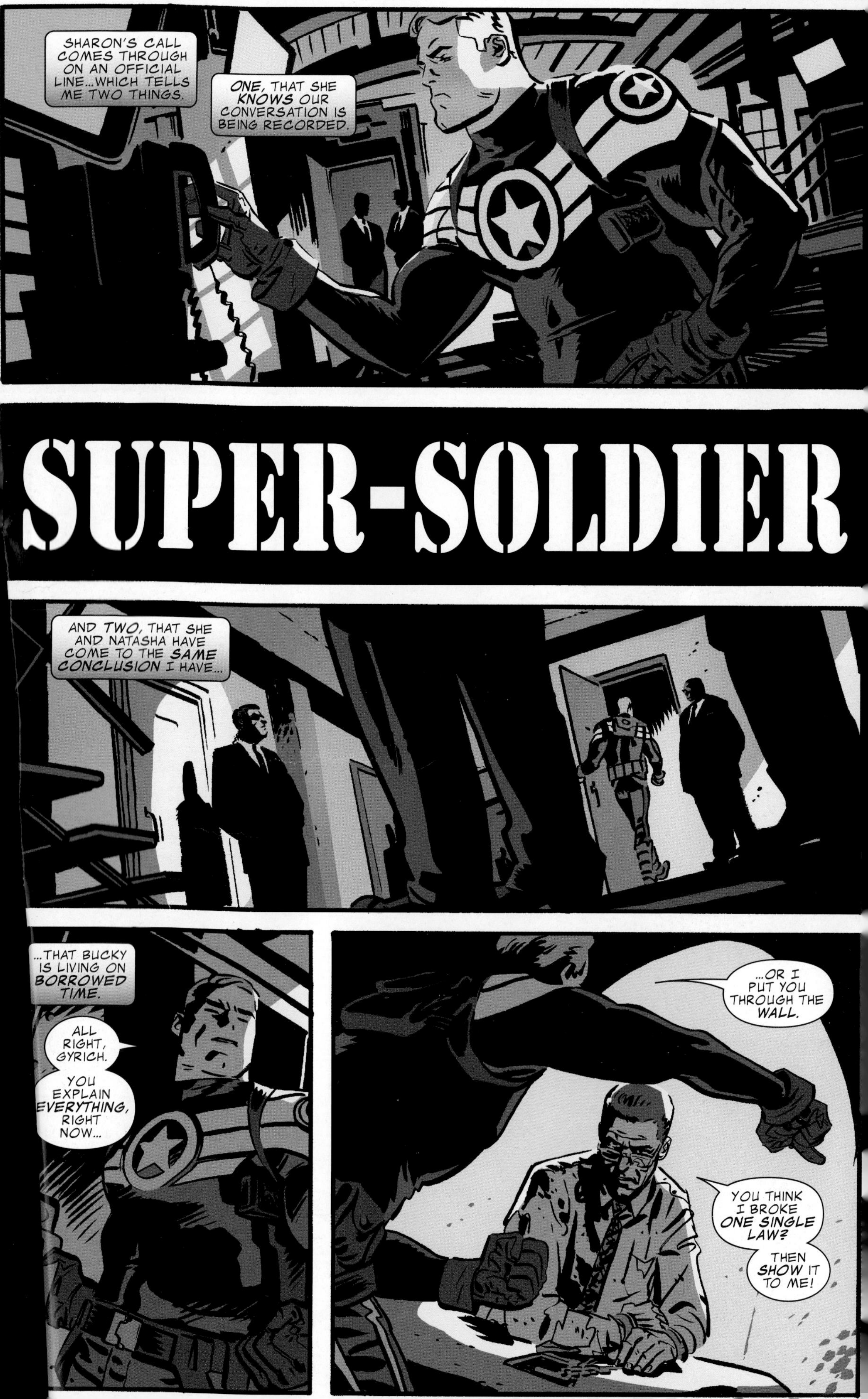
SHARON'S CALL COMES THROUGH ON AN OFFICIAL LINE...WHICH TELLS ME TWO THINGS.
ONE, THAT SHE KNOWS OUR CONVERSATION IS BEING RECORDED.
SUPER-SOLDIER
AND TWO, THAT SHE AND NATASHA HAVE COME TO THE SAME CONCLUSION I HAVE...
...THAT BUCKY IS LIVING ON BORROWED TIME.
ALL RIGHT, GYRICH.
YOU EXPLAIN EVERYTHING, RIGHT NOW...
...OR I PUT YOU THROUGH THE WALL.
YOU THINK I BROKE ONE SINGLE LAW?
THEN SHOW IT TO ME!

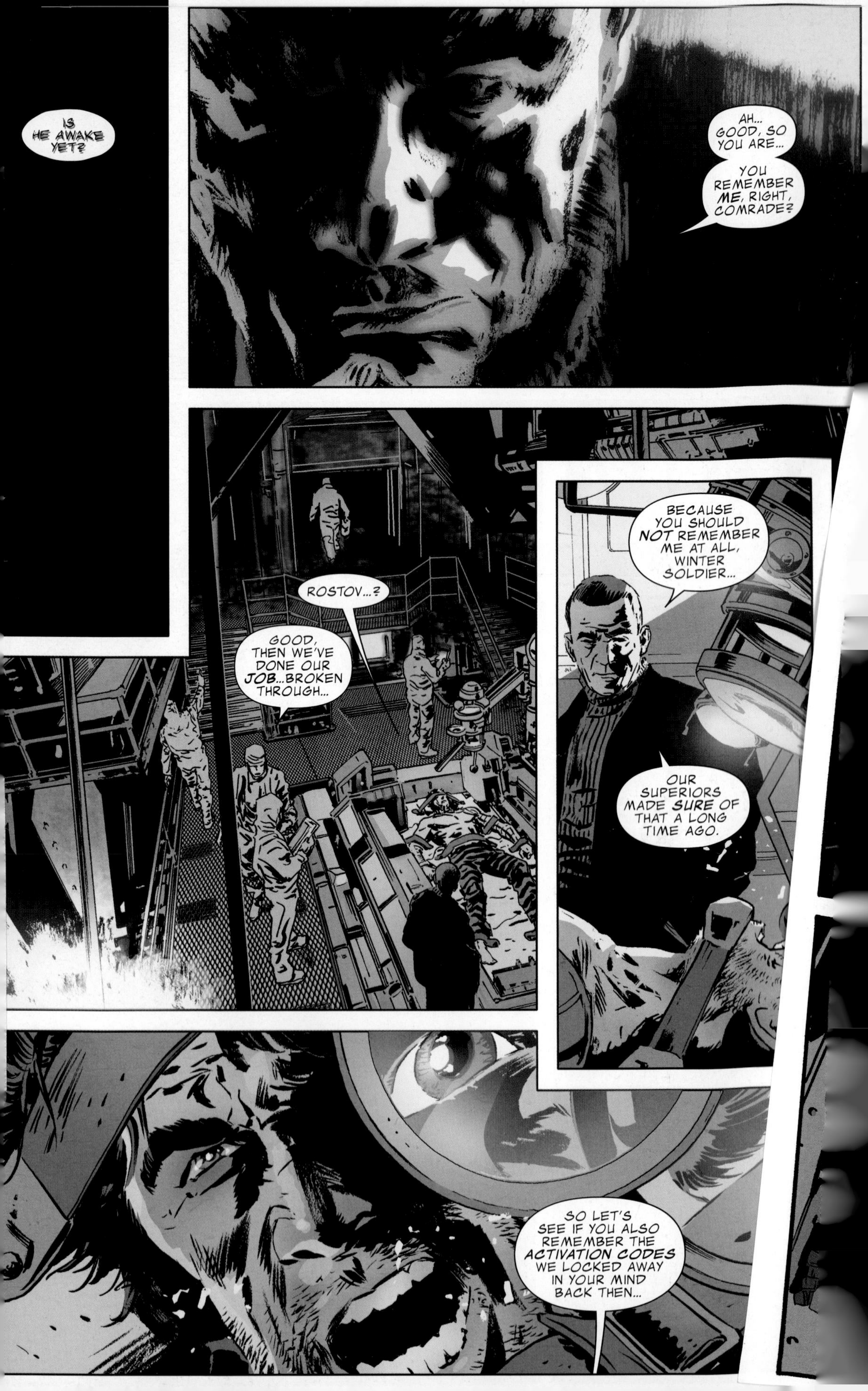
IS HE AWAKE YET?
AH... GOOD, SO YOU ARE...
YOU REMEMBER ME, RIGHT, COMRADE?
ROSTOV...?
GOOD, THEN WE'VE DONE OUR JOB...BROKEN THROUGH...
BECAUSE YOU SHOULD NOT REMEMBER ME AT ALL, WINTER SOLDIER...
OUR SUPERIORS MADE SURE OF THAT A LONG TIME AGO.
SO LET'S SEE IF YOU ALSO REMEMBER THE ACTIVATION CODES WE LOCKED AWAY IN YOUR MIND BACK THEN...

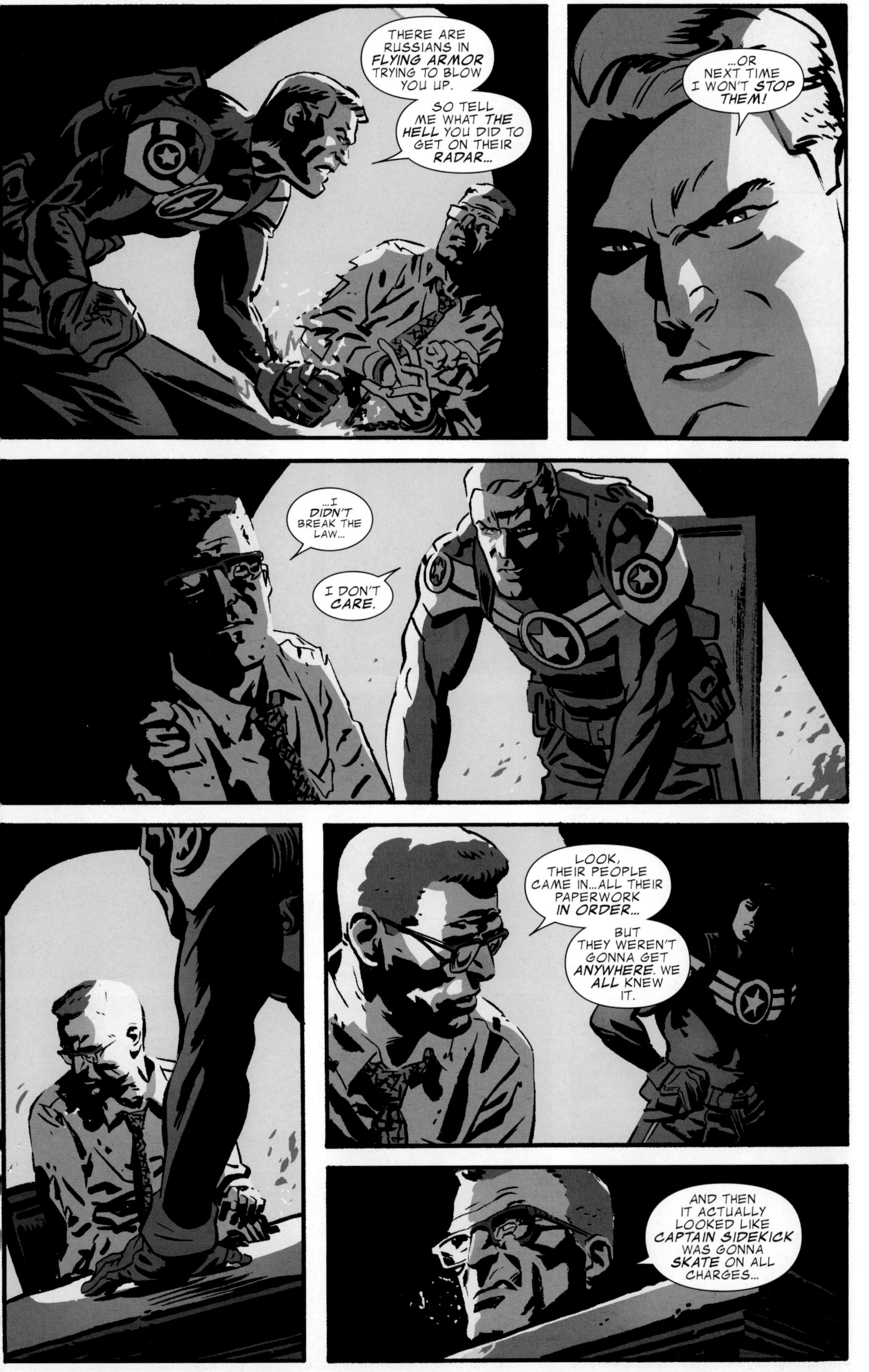
THERE ARE RUSSIANS IN FLYING ARMOR TRYING TO BLOW YOU UP.
SO TELL ME WHAT THE HELL YOU DID TO GET ON THEIR RADAR...
...OR NEXT TIME I WON'T STOP THEM!
...I DIDN'T BREAK THE LAW...
I DON'T CARE.
LOOK, THEIR PEOPLE CAME IN...ALL THEIR PAPERWORK IN ORDER...
BUT THEY WEREN'T GONNA GET ANYWHERE. WE ALL KNEW IT.
AND THEN IT ACTUALLY LOOKED LIKE CAPTAIN SIDEKICK WAS GONNA SKATE ON ALL CHARGES...

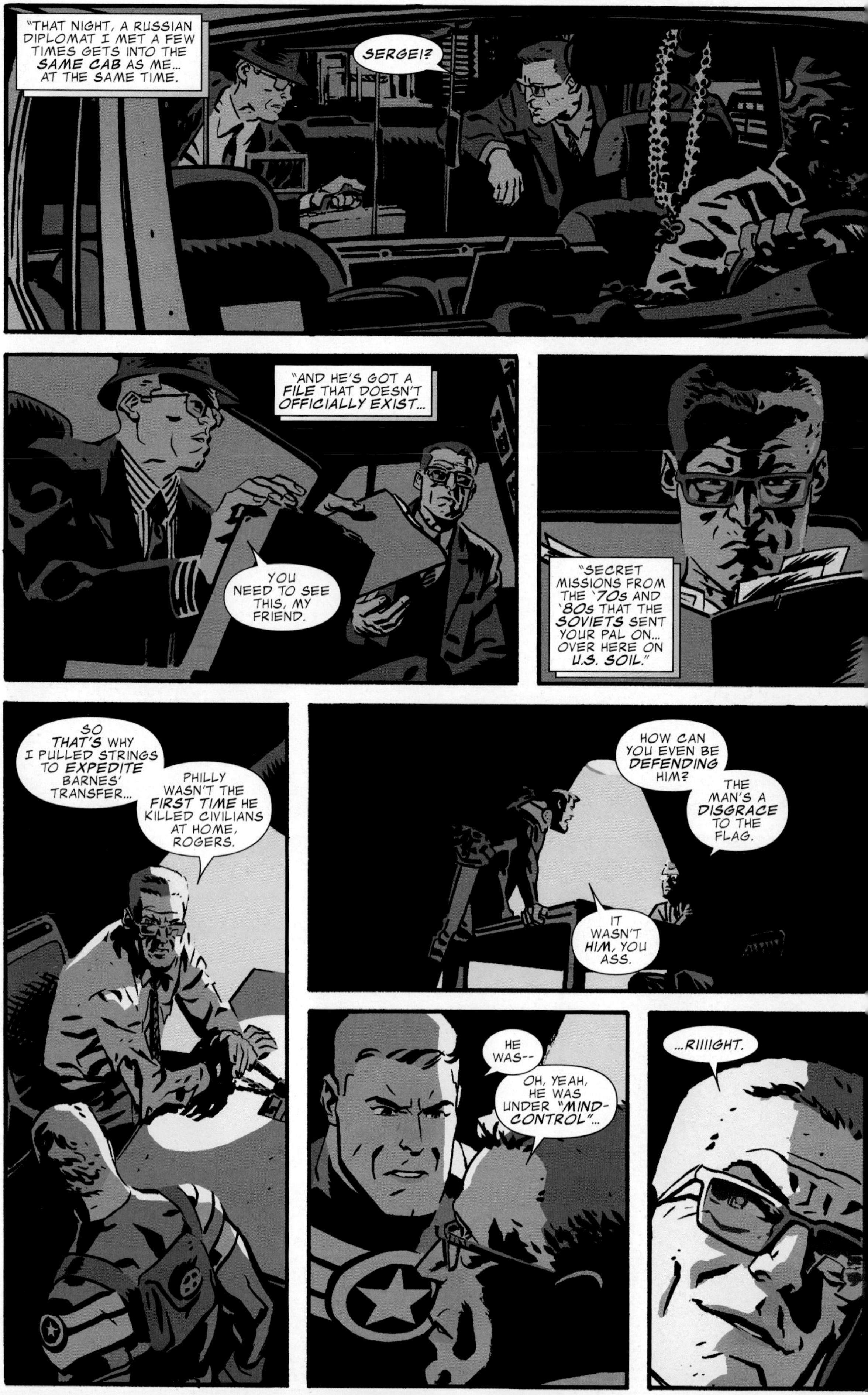
"THAT NIGHT, A RUSSIAN DIPLOMAT I MET A FEW TIMES GETS INTO THE SAME CAB AS ME... AT THE SAME TIME.
SERGEI?
"AND HE'S GOT A FILE THAT DOESN'T OFFICIALLY EXIST...
YOU NEED TO SEE THIS, MY FRIEND.
"SECRET MISSIONS FROM THE '70s AND '80s THAT THE SOVIETS SENT YOUR PAL ON... OVER HERE ON U.S. SOIL."
SO THAT'S WHY I PULLED STRINGS TO EXPEDITE BARNES' TRANSFER...
PHILLY WASN'T THE FIRST TIME HE KILLED CIVILIANS AT HOME, ROGERS.
HOW CAN YOU EVEN BE DEFENDING HIM?
THE MAN'S A DISGRACE TO THE FLAG.
IT WASN'T HIM, YOU ASS.
HE WAS--
OH, YEAH, HE WAS UNDER "MIND-CONTROL"...
...RIIIIGHT.

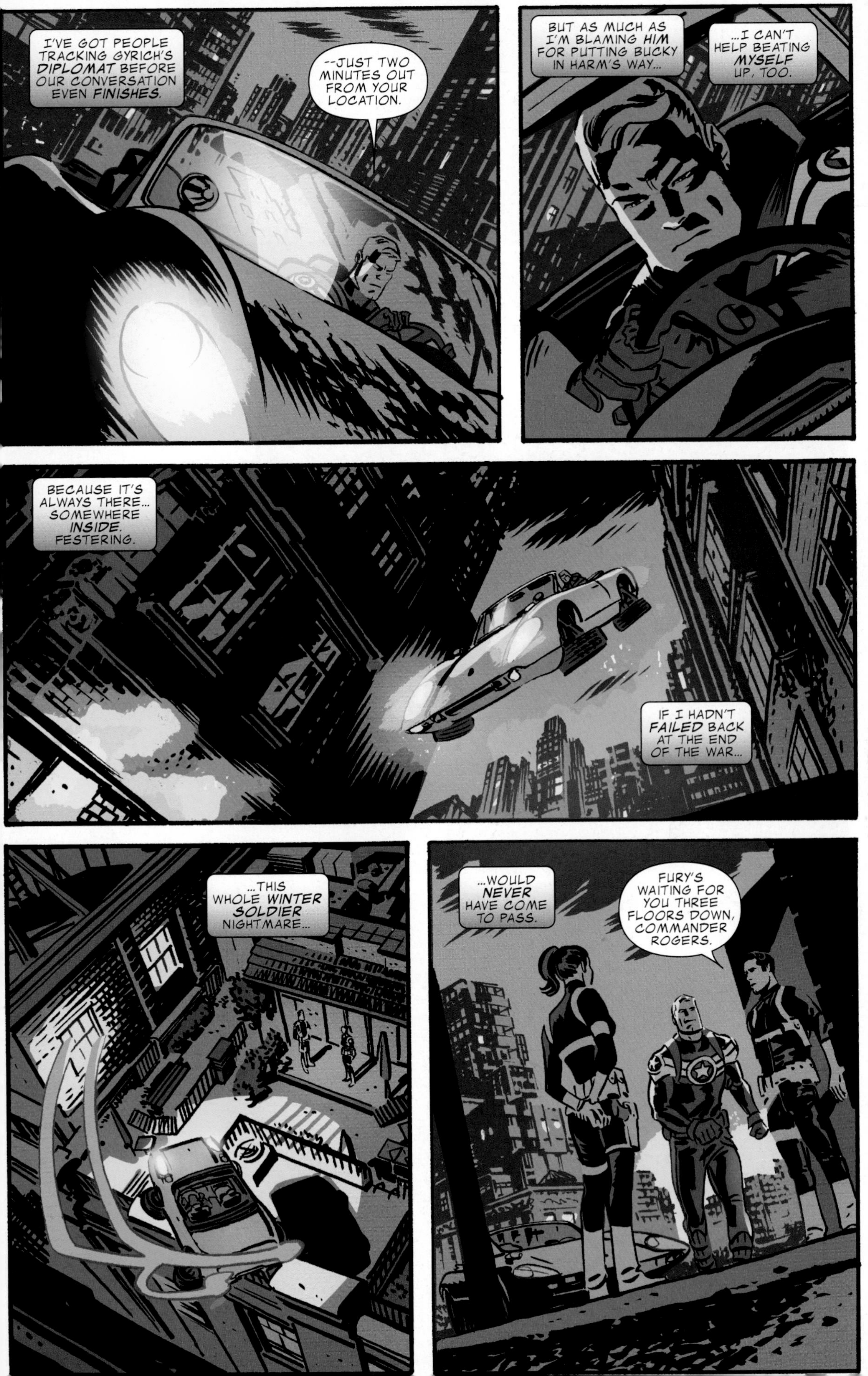
I'VE GOT PEOPLE TRACKING GYRICH'S DIPLOMAT BEFORE OUR CONVERSATION EVEN FINISHES.
--JUST TWO MINUTES OUT FROM YOUR LOCATION.
BUT AS MUCH AS I'M BLAMING HIM FOR PUTTING BUCKY IN HARM'S WAY...
...I CAN'T HELP BEATING MYSELF UP, TOO.
BECAUSE IT'S ALWAYS THERE... SOMEWHERE INSIDE. FESTERING.
IF I HADN'T FAILED BACK AT THE END OF THE WAR...
...THIS WHOLE WINTER SOLDIER NIGHTMARE...
...WOULD NEVER HAVE COME TO PASS.
FURY'S WAITING FOR YOU THREE FLOORS DOWN, COMMANDER ROGERS.

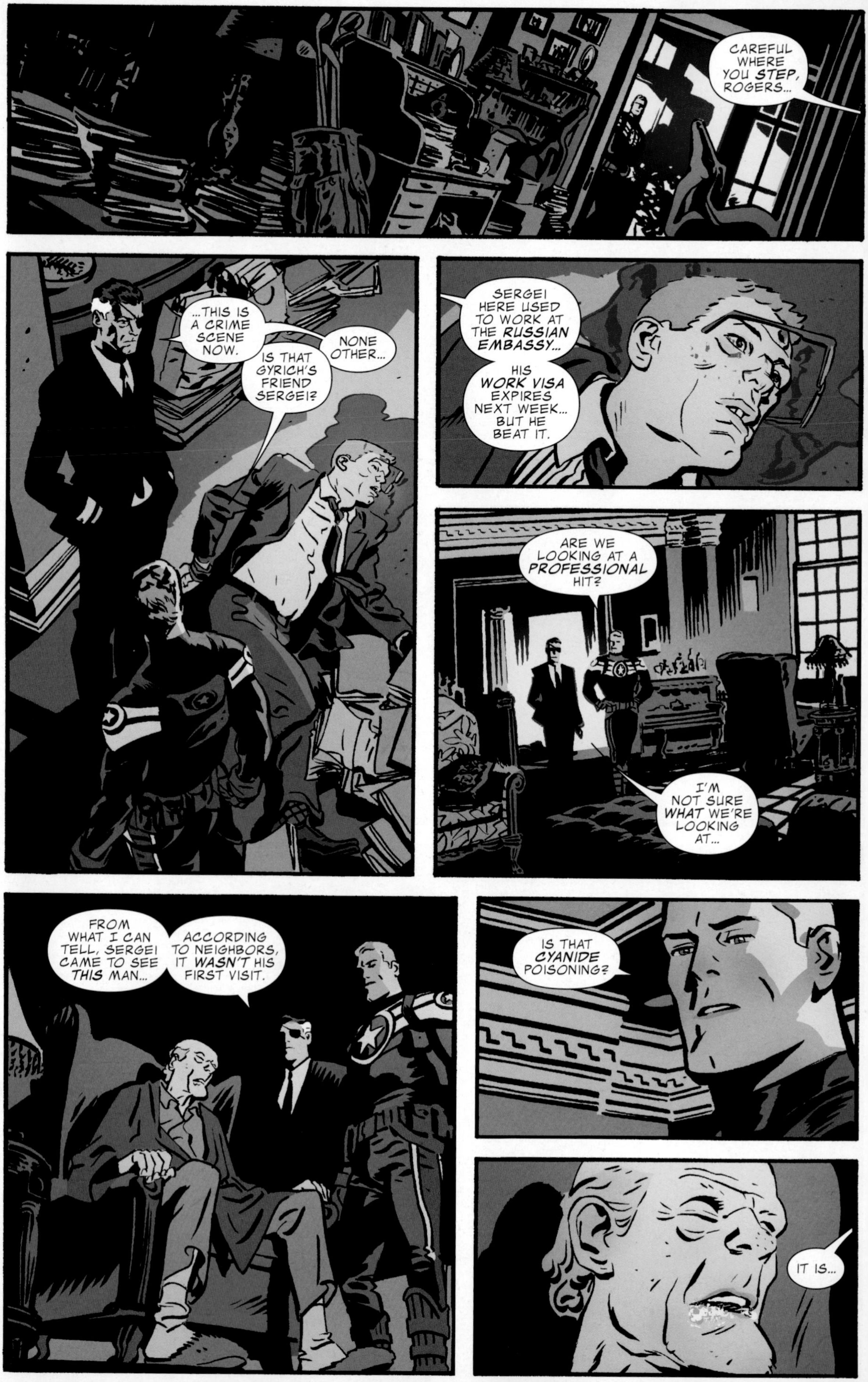
CAREFUL WHERE YOU STEP, ROGERS...
...THIS IS A CRIME SCENE NOW.
IS THAT GYRICH'S FRIEND SERGEI?
NONE OTHER...
SERGEI HERE USED TO WORK AT THE RUSSIAN EMBASSY...
HIS WORK VISA EXPIRES NEXT WEEK... BUT HE BEAT IT.
ARE WE LOOKING AT A PROFESSIONAL HIT?
I'M NOT SURE WHAT WE'RE LOOKING AT...
FROM WHAT I CAN TELL, SERGEI CAME TO SEE THIS MAN...
ACCORDING TO NEIGHBORS, IT WASN'T HIS FIRST VISIT.
IS THAT CYANIDE POISONING?
IT IS...

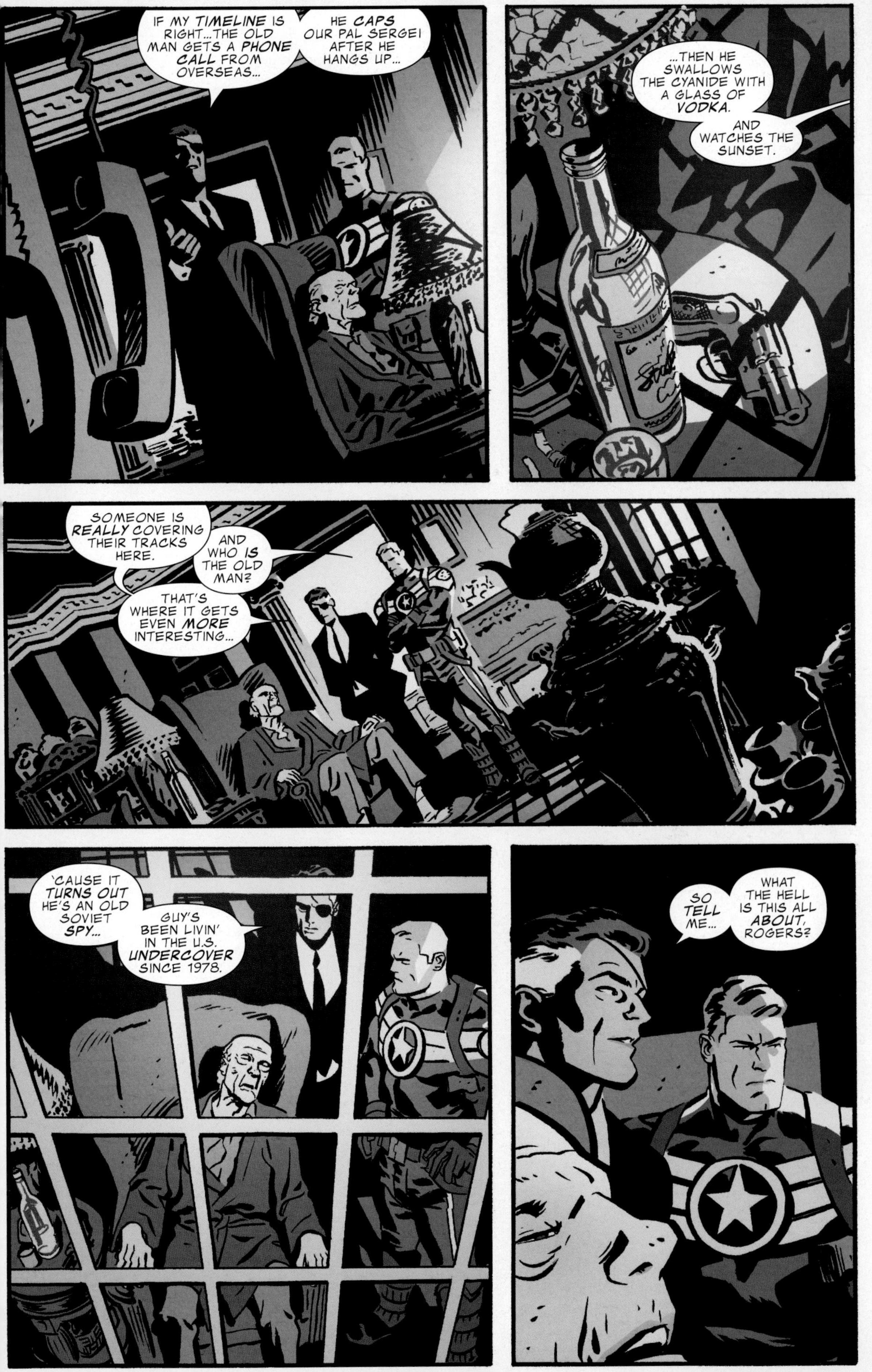
IF MY TIMELINE IS RIGHT...THE OLD MAN GETS A PHONE CALL FROM OVERSEAS...
HE CAPS OUR PAL SERGEI AFTER HE HANGS UP...
...THEN HE SWALLOWS THE CYANIDE WITH A GLASS OF VODKA.
AND WATCHES THE SUNSET.
SOMEONE IS REALLY COVERING THEIR TRACKS HERE.
AND WHO IS THE OLD MAN?
THAT'S WHERE IT GETS EVEN MORE INTERESTING...
'CAUSE IT TURNS OUT HE'S AN OLD SOVIET SPY...
GUY'S BEEN LIVIN' IN THE U.S. UNDERCOVER SINCE 1978.
SO TELL ME...
WHAT THE HELL IS THIS ALL ABOUT, ROGERS?

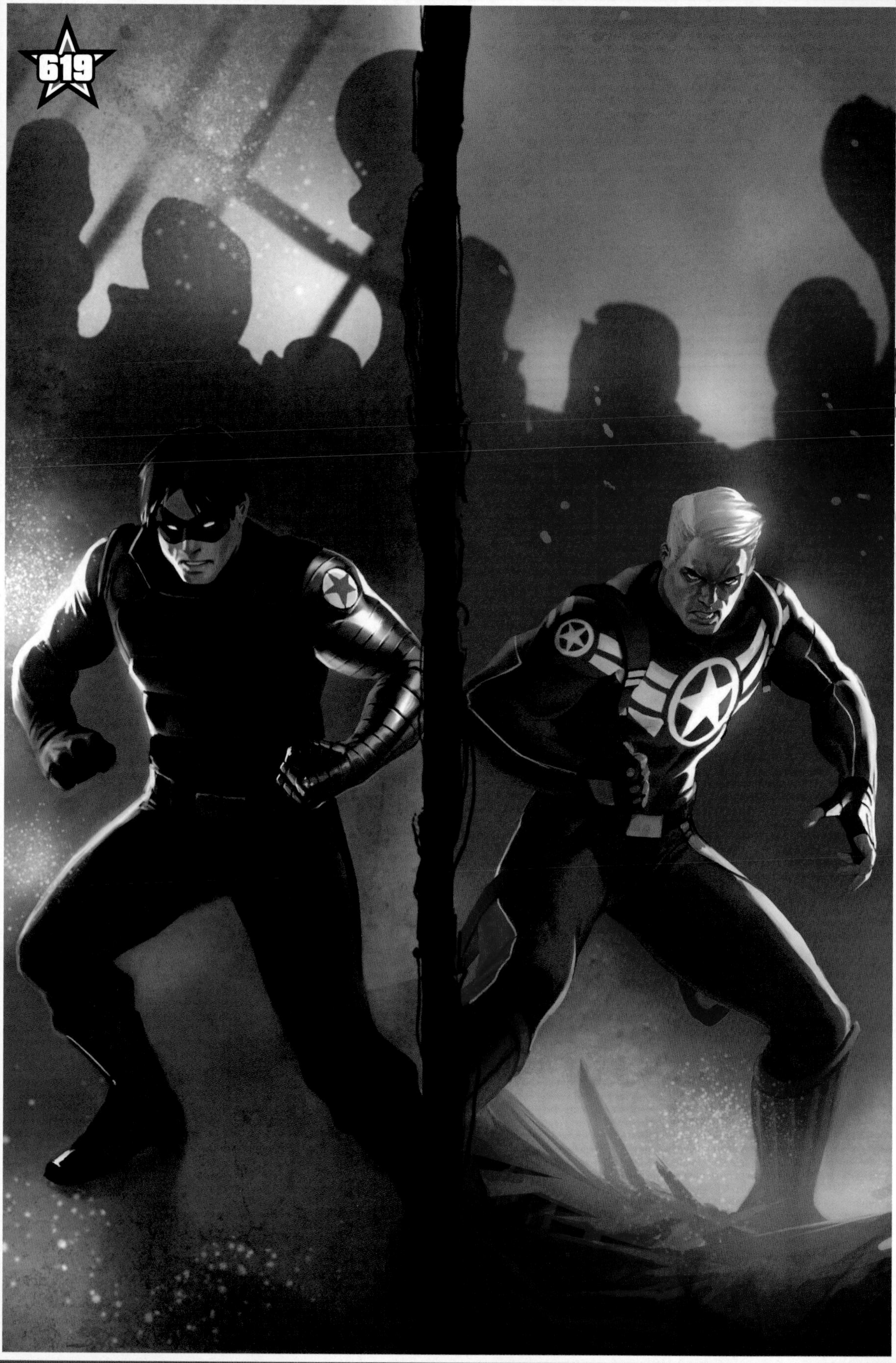
619

GULAG PART 4

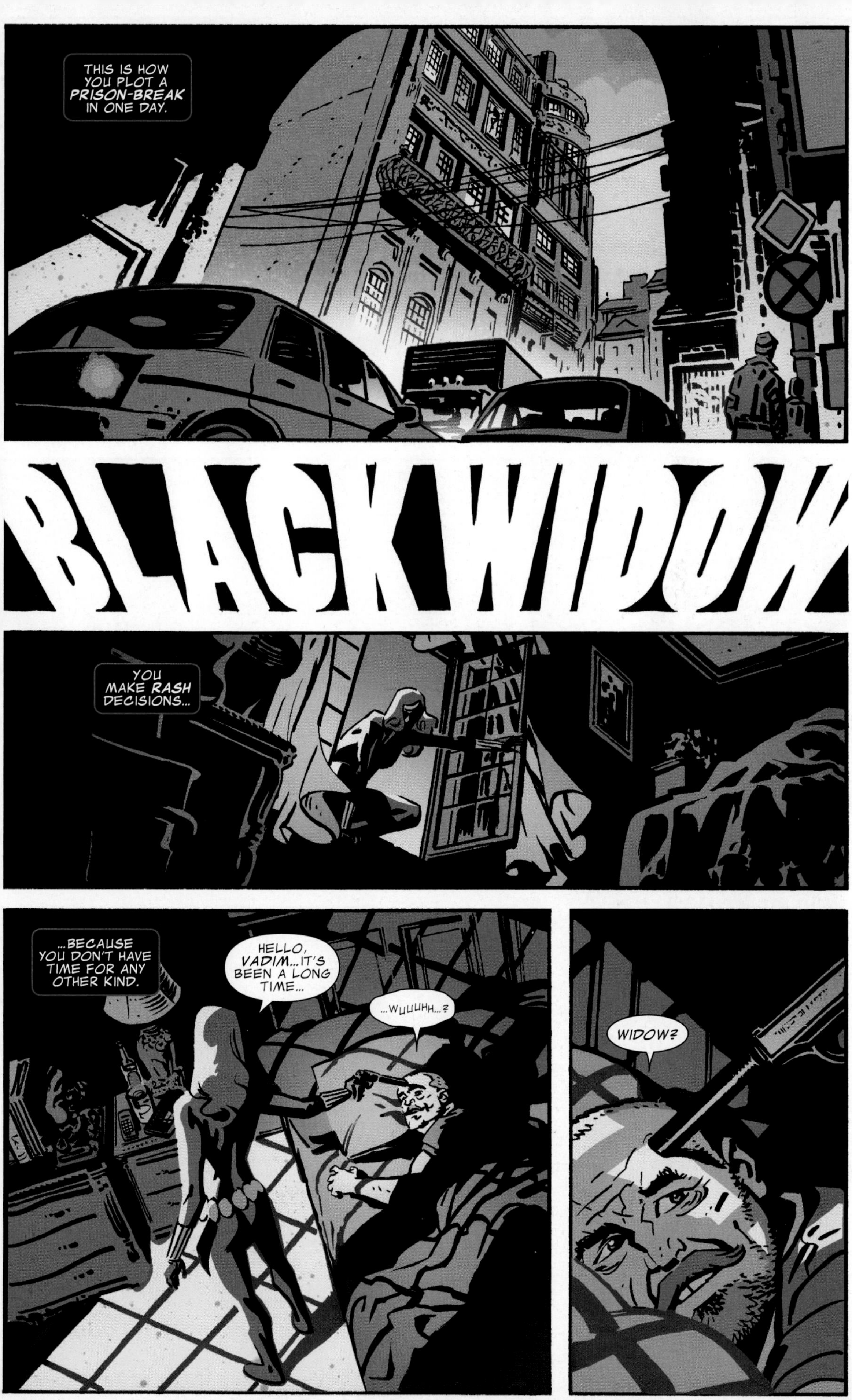
THIS IS HOW YOU PLOT A PRISON-BREAK IN ONE DAY.
BLACK WIDOW
YOU MAKE RASH DECISIONS...
...BECAUSE YOU DON'T HAVE TIME FOR ANY OTHER KIND.
HELLO, VADIM...IT'S BEEN A LONG TIME...
...WUUUHH...?
WIDOW?

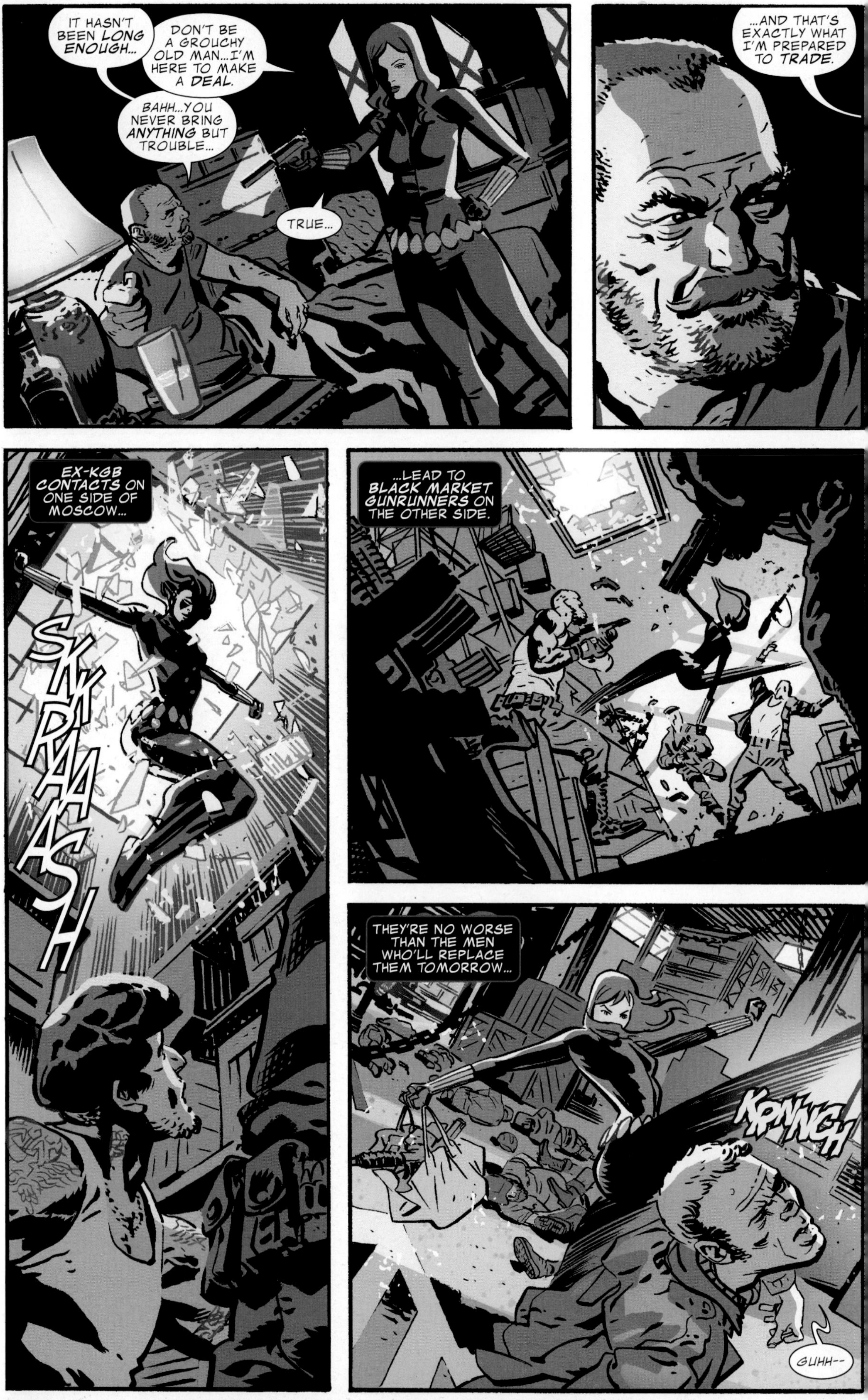
IT HASN'T BEEN LONG ENOUGH...
DON'T BE A GROUCHY OLD MAN...I'M HERE TO MAKE A DEAL.
BAHH...YOU NEVER BRING ANYTHING BUT TROUBLE...
TRUE...
...AND THAT'S EXACTLY WHAT I'M PREPARED TO TRADE.
EX-KGB CONTACTS ON ONE SIDE OF MOSCOW...
SKKRAAAASH
...LEAD TO BLACK MARKET GUNRUNNERS ON THE OTHER SIDE.
THEY'RE NO WORSE THAN THE MEN WHO'LL REPLACE THEM TOMORROW...
KRNNCH
GUHH--

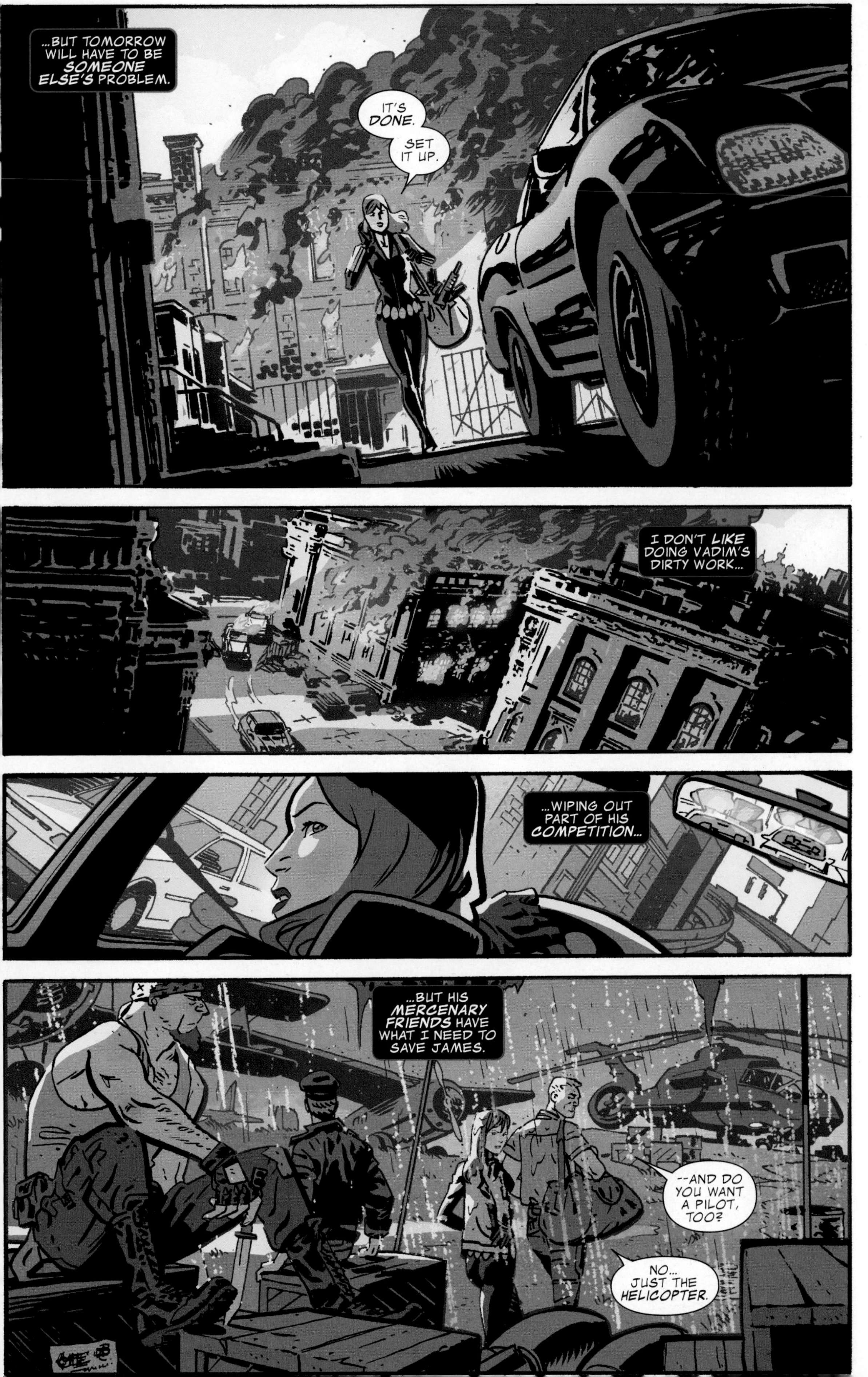
...BUT TOMORROW WILL HAVE TO BE SOMEONE ELSE'S PROBLEM.
IT'S DONE.
SET IT UP.
I DON'T LIKE DOING VADIM'S DIRTY WORK...
...WIPING OUT PART OF HIS COMPETITION...
...BUT HIS MERCENARY FRIENDS HAVE WHAT I NEED TO SAVE JAMES.
--AND DO YOU WANT A PILOT, TOO?
NO... JUST THE HELICOPTER.

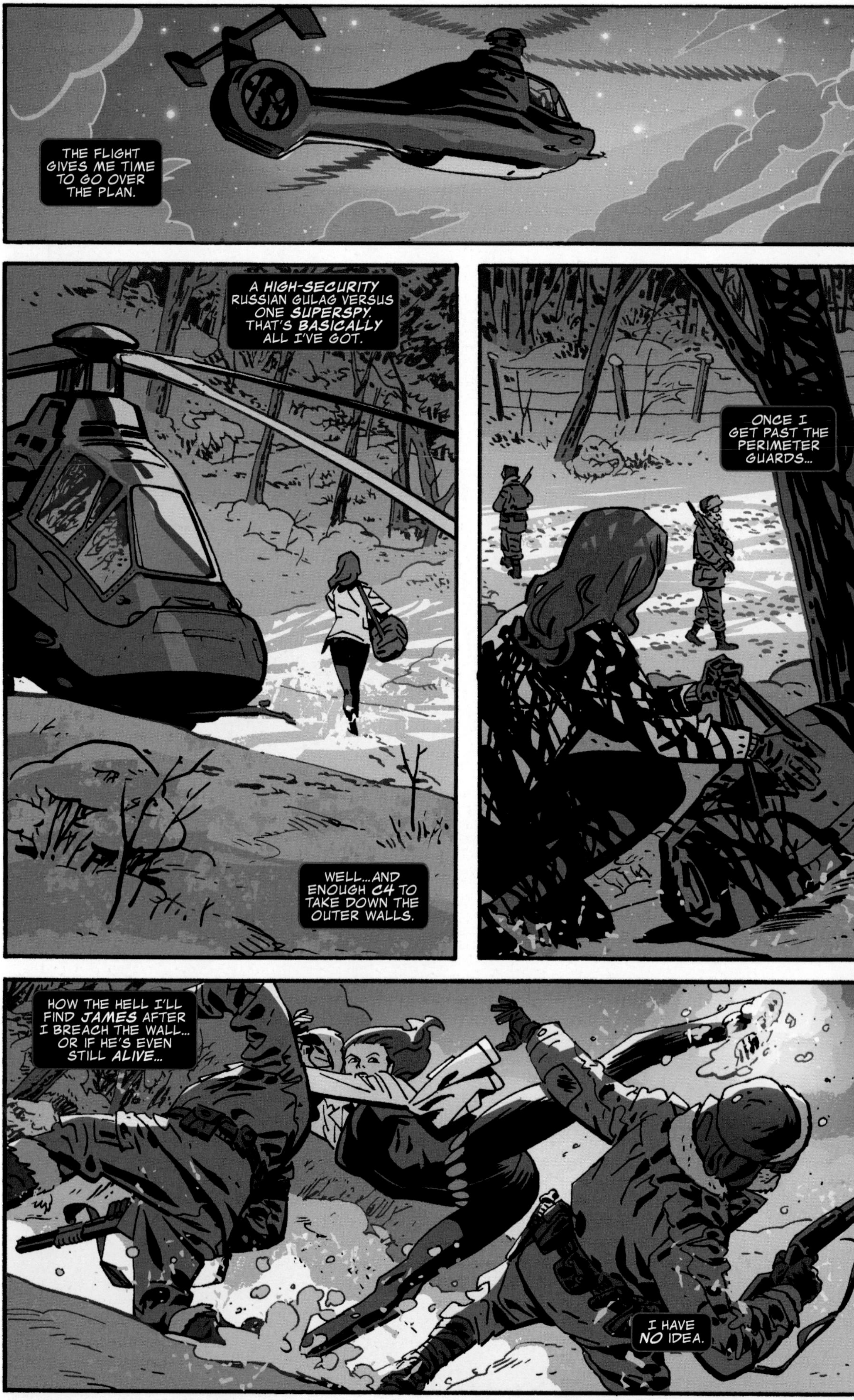

THE FLIGHT GIVES ME TIME TO GO OVER THE PLAN.
A HIGH-SECURITY RUSSIAN GULAG VERSUS ONE SUPERSPY. THAT'S BASICALLY ALL I'VE GOT.
WELL...AND ENOUGH C4 TO TAKE DOWN THE OUTER WALLS.
ONCE I GET PAST THE PERIMETER GUARDS...
HOW THE HELL I'LL FIND JAMES AFTER I BREACH THE WALL... OR IF HE'S EVEN STILL ALIVE...
I HAVE NO IDEA.

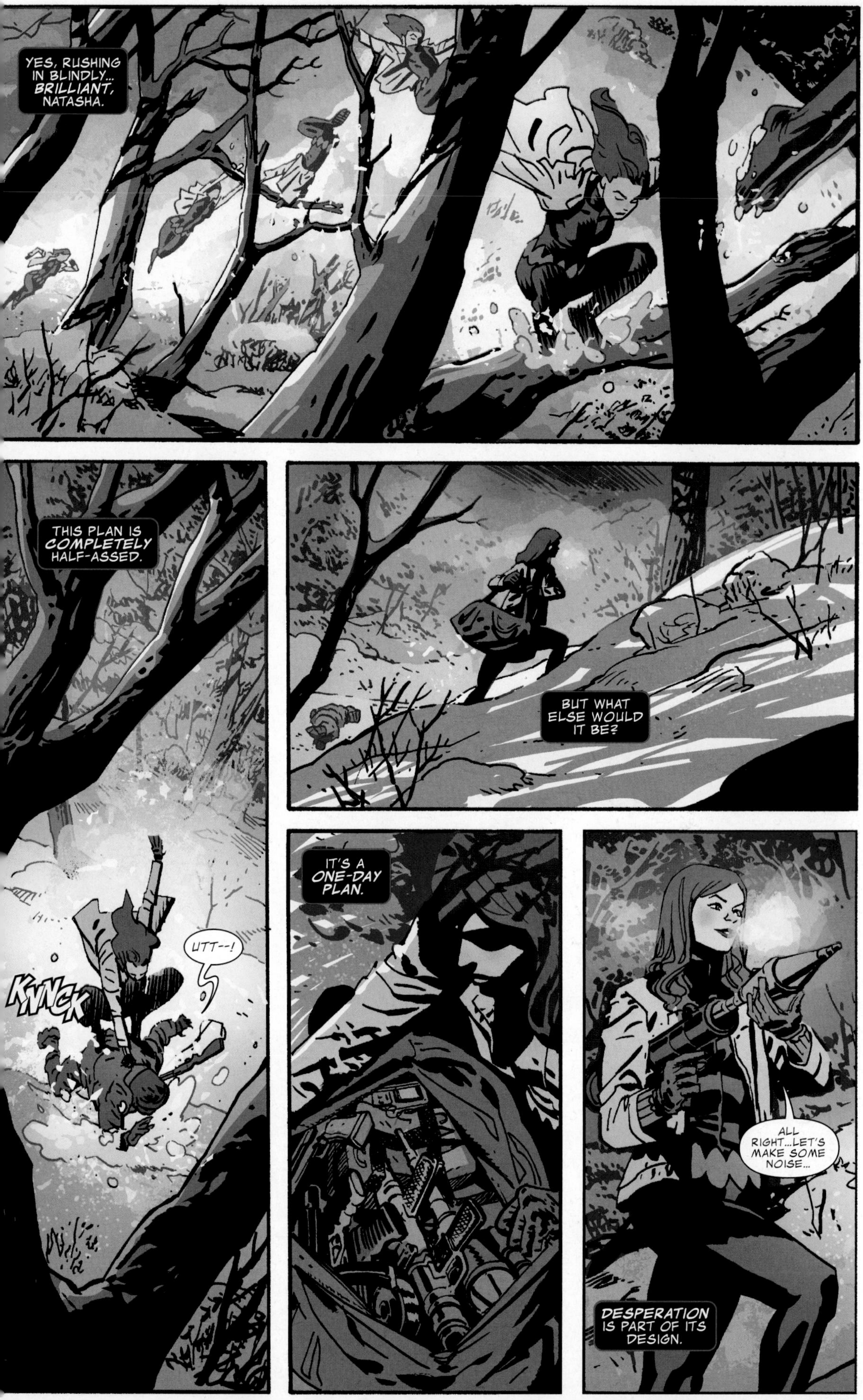
YES, RUSHING IN BLINDLY... BRILLIANT, NATASHA.
THIS PLAN IS COMPLETELY HALF-ASSED.
KVNCK
UTT--!
BUT WHAT ELSE WOULD IT BE?
IT'S A ONE-DAY PLAN.
ALL RIGHT...LET'S MAKE SOME NOISE...
DESPERATION IS PART OF ITS DESIGN.

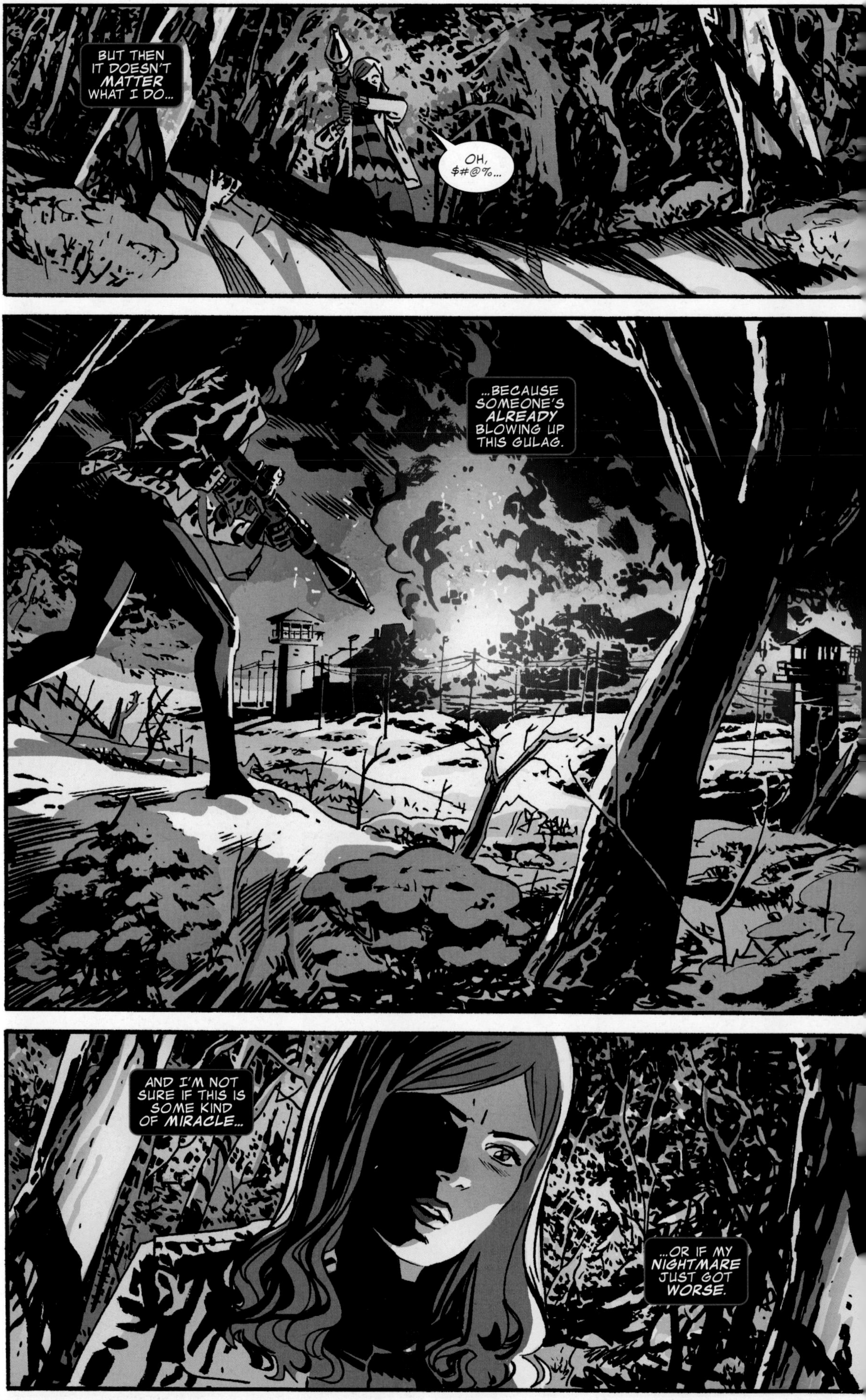
BUT THEN IT DOESN'T MATTER WHAT I DO...
OH, $#@%...
...BECAUSE SOMEONE'S ALREADY BLOWING UP THIS GULAG.
AND I'M NOT SURE IF THIS IS SOME KIND OF MIRACLE...
...OR IF MY NIGHTMARE JUST GOT WORSE.

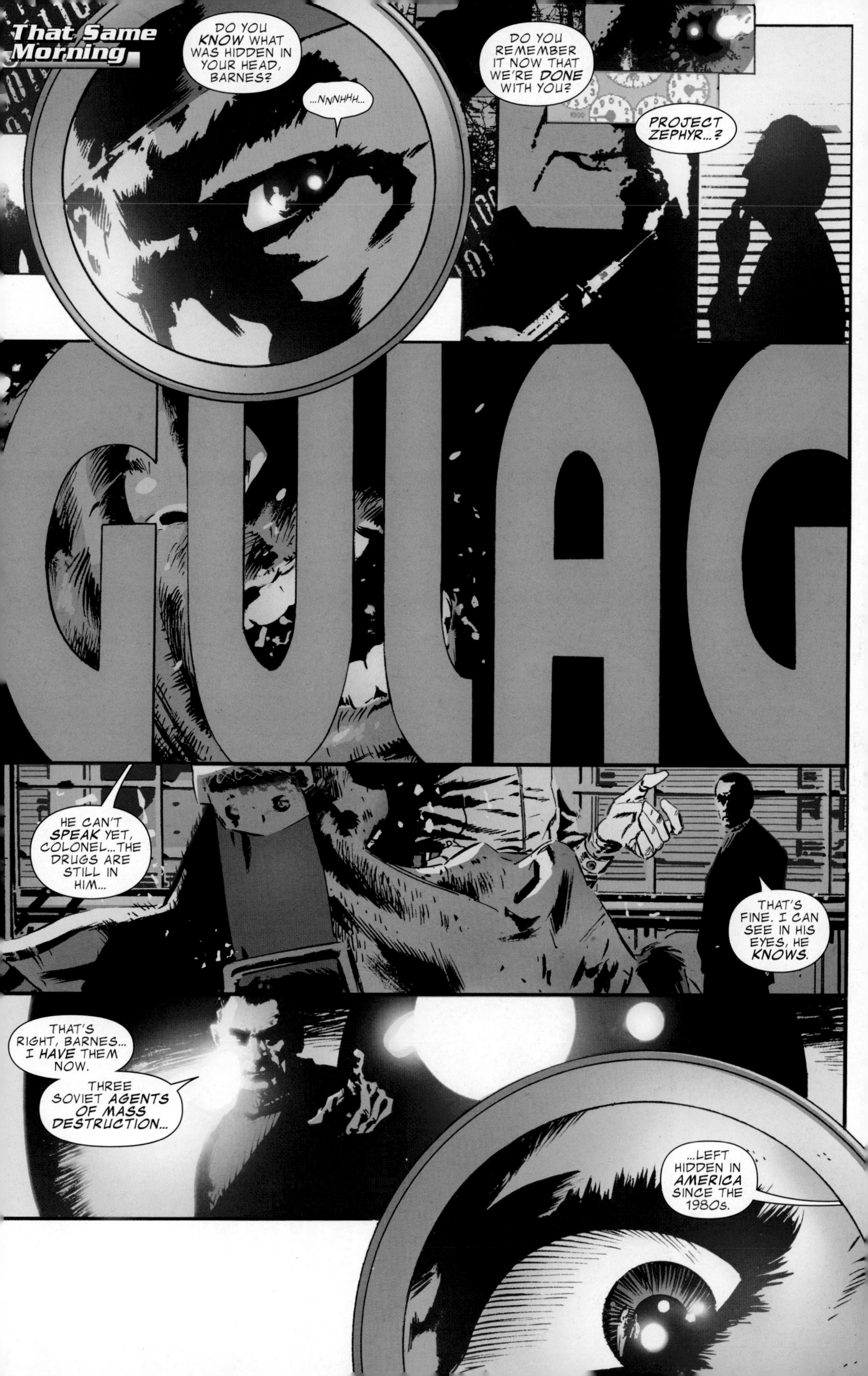
That Same Morning
DO YOU KNOW WHAT WAS HIDDEN IN YOUR HEAD, BARNES?
...NNNHHH...
DO YOU REMEMBER IT NOW THAT WE'RE DONE WITH YOU?
PROJECT ZEPHYR...?
GULAG
HE CAN'T SPEAK YET, COLONEL...THE DRUGS ARE STILL IN HIM...
THAT'S FINE. I CAN SEE IN HIS EYES, HE KNOWS.
THAT'S RIGHT, BARNES... I HAVE THEM NOW.
THREE SOVIET AGENTS OF MASS DESTRUCTION...
...LEFT HIDDEN IN AMERICA SINCE THE 1980s.

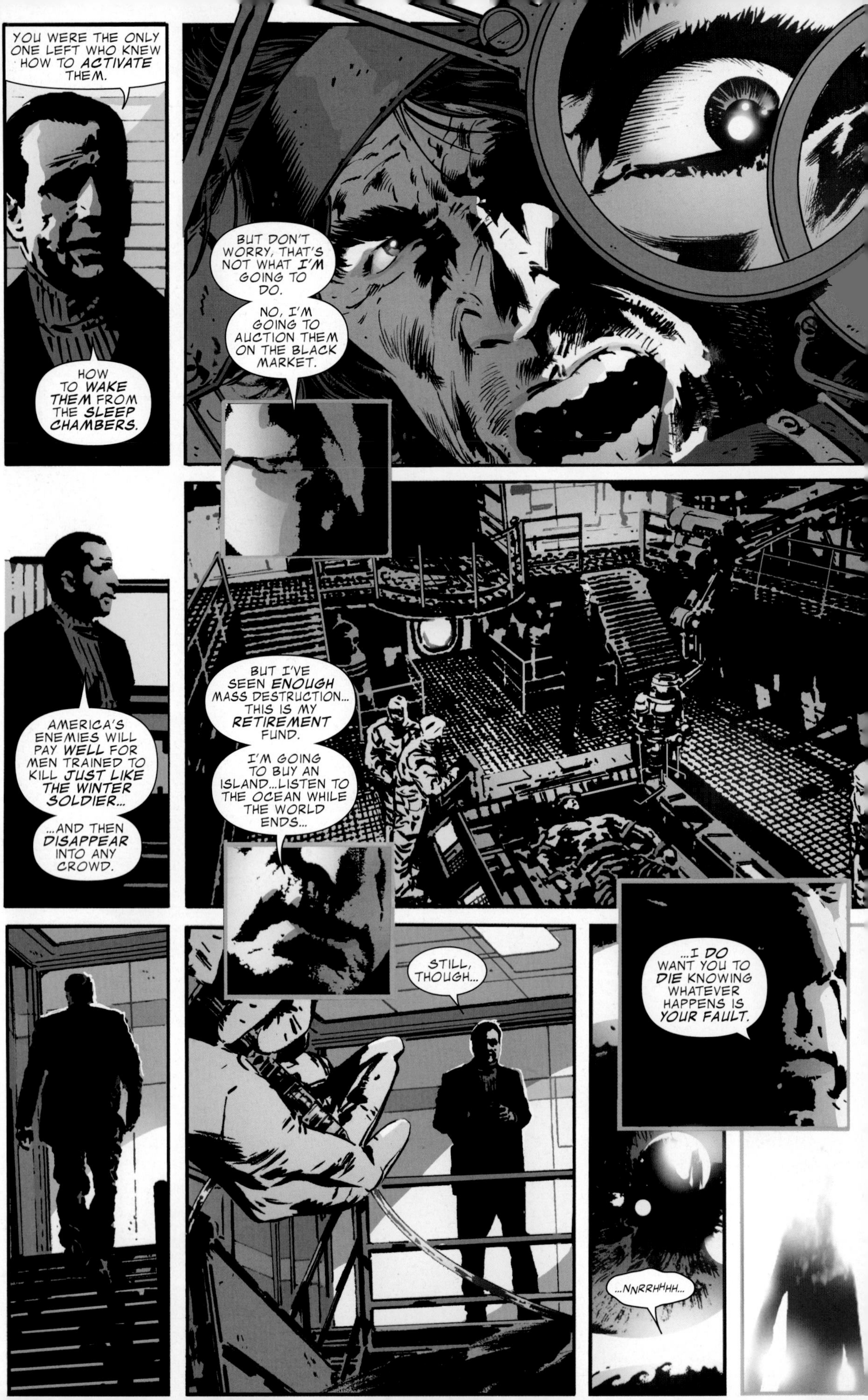

YOU WERE THE ONLY ONE LEFT WHO KNEW HOW TO ACTIVATE THEM.
HOW TO WAKE THEM FROM THE SLEEP CHAMBERS.
BUT DON'T WORRY, THAT'S NOT WHAT I'M GOING TO DO.
NO, I'M GOING TO AUCTION THEM ON THE BLACK MARKET.
AMERICA'S ENEMIES WILL PAY WELL FOR MEN TRAINED TO KILL JUST LIKE THE WINTER SOLDIER...
...AND THEN DISAPPEAR INTO ANY CROWD.
BUT I'VE SEEN ENOUGH MASS DESTRUCTION... THIS IS MY RETIREMENT FUND.
I'M GOING TO BUY AN ISLAND...LISTEN TO THE OCEAN WHILE THE WORLD ENDS...
STILL, THOUGH...
...I DO WANT YOU TO DIE KNOWING WHATEVER HAPPENS IS YOUR FAULT.
...NNRRHHHH...

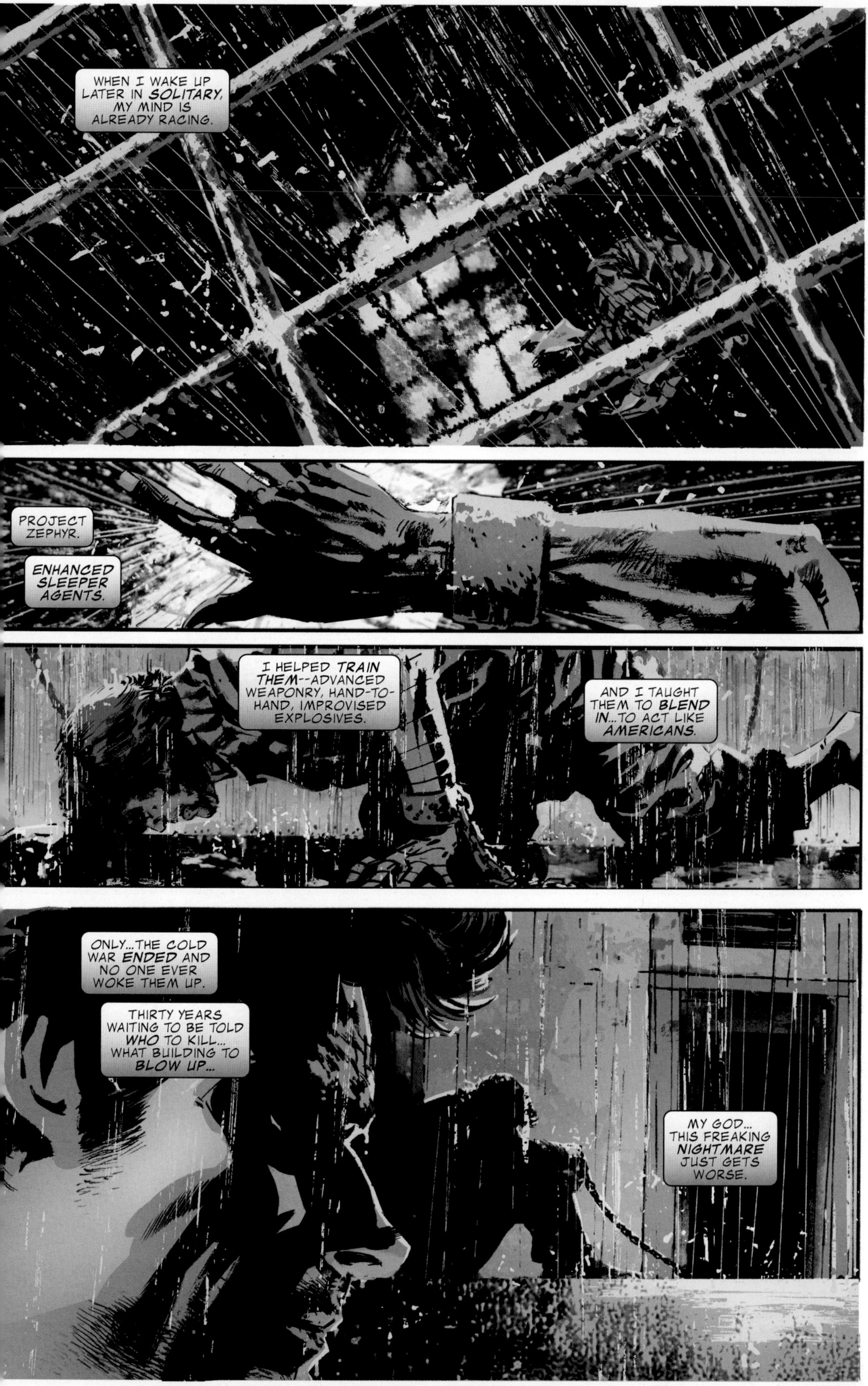
WHEN I WAKE UP LATER IN SOLITARY, MY MIND IS ALREADY RACING.
PROJECT ZEPHYR.
ENHANCED SLEEPER AGENTS.
I HELPED TRAIN THEM--ADVANCED WEAPONRY, HAND-TO-HAND, IMPROVISED EXPLOSIVES.
AND I TAUGHT THEM TO BLEND IN...TO ACT LIKE AMERICANS.
ONLY...THE COLD WAR ENDED AND NO ONE EVER WOKE THEM UP.
THIRTY YEARS WAITING TO BE TOLD WHO TO KILL... WHAT BUILDING TO BLOW UP...
MY GOD... THIS FREAKING NIGHTMARE JUST GETS WORSE.

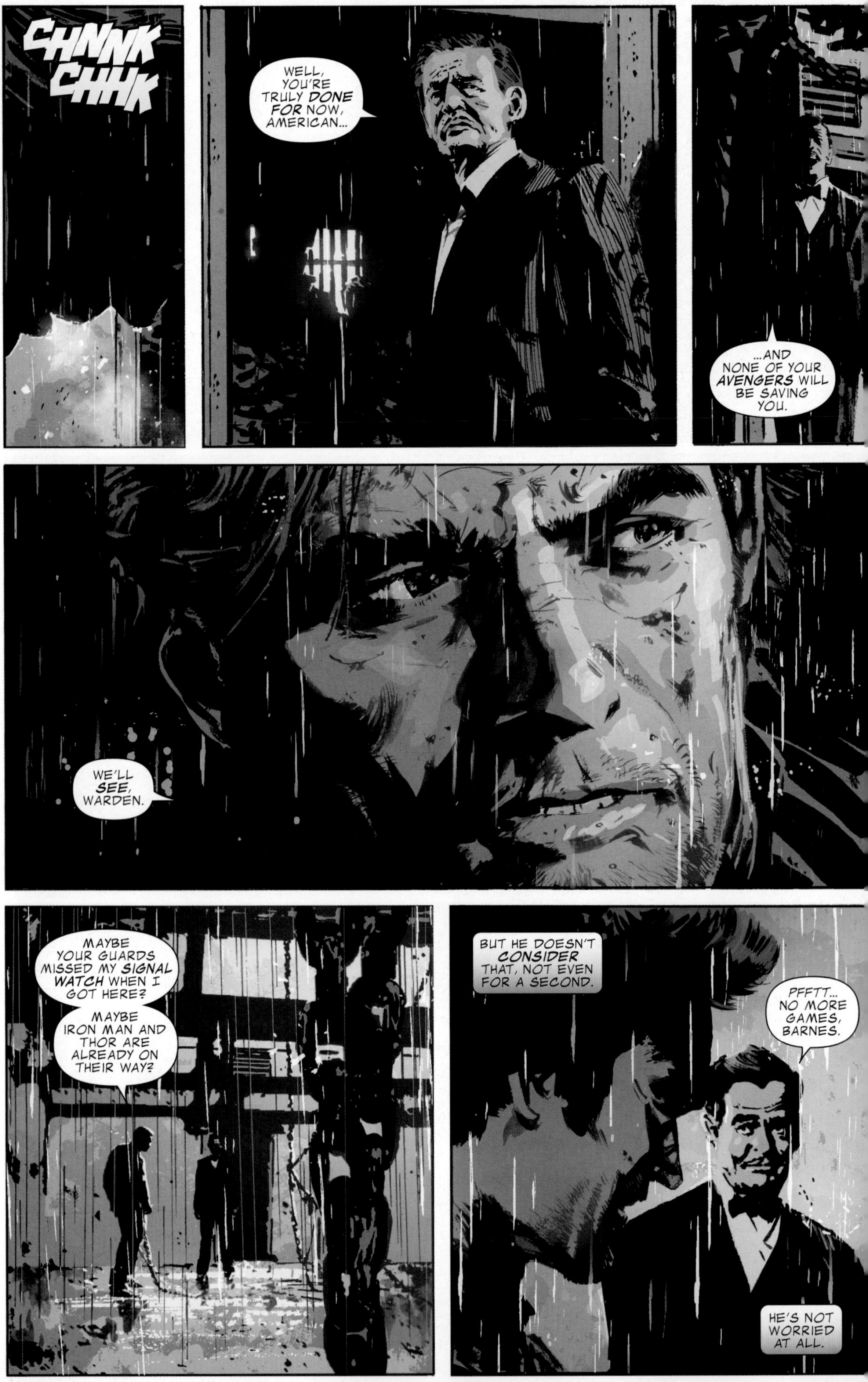
CHNNK CHHK
WELL, YOU'RE TRULY DONE FOR NOW, AMERICAN...
...AND NONE OF YOUR AVENGERS WILL BE SAVING YOU.
WE'LL SEE, WARDEN.
MAYBE YOUR GUARDS MISSED MY SIGNAL WATCH WHEN I GOT HERE?
MAYBE IRON MAN AND THOR ARE ALREADY ON THEIR WAY?
BUT HE DOESN'T CONSIDER THAT, NOT EVEN FOR A SECOND.
PFFTT... NO MORE GAMES, BARNES.
HE'S NOT WORRIED AT ALL.

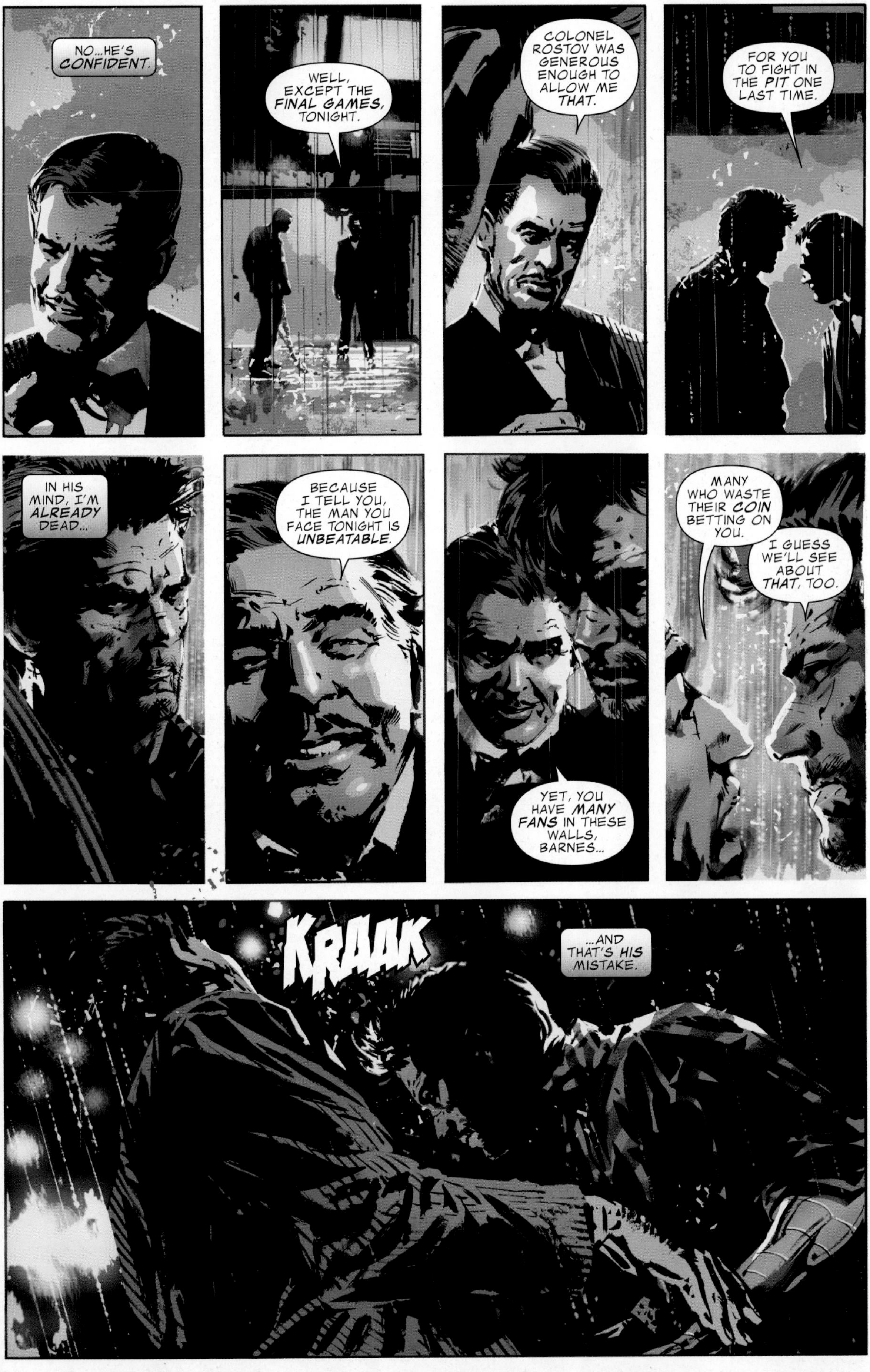
NO...HE'S CONFIDENT.
WELL, EXCEPT THE FINAL GAMES, TONIGHT.
COLONEL ROSTOV WAS GENEROUS ENOUGH TO ALLOW ME THAT.
FOR YOU TO FIGHT IN THE PIT ONE LAST TIME.
IN HIS MIND, I'M ALREADY DEAD...
BECAUSE I TELL YOU, THE MAN YOU FACE TONIGHT IS UNBEATABLE.
YET, YOU HAVE MANY FANS IN THESE WALLS, BARNES...
MANY WHO WASTE THEIR COIN BETTING ON YOU.
I GUESS WE'LL SEE ABOUT THAT, TOO.
KRAAK
...AND THAT'S HIS MISTAKE.

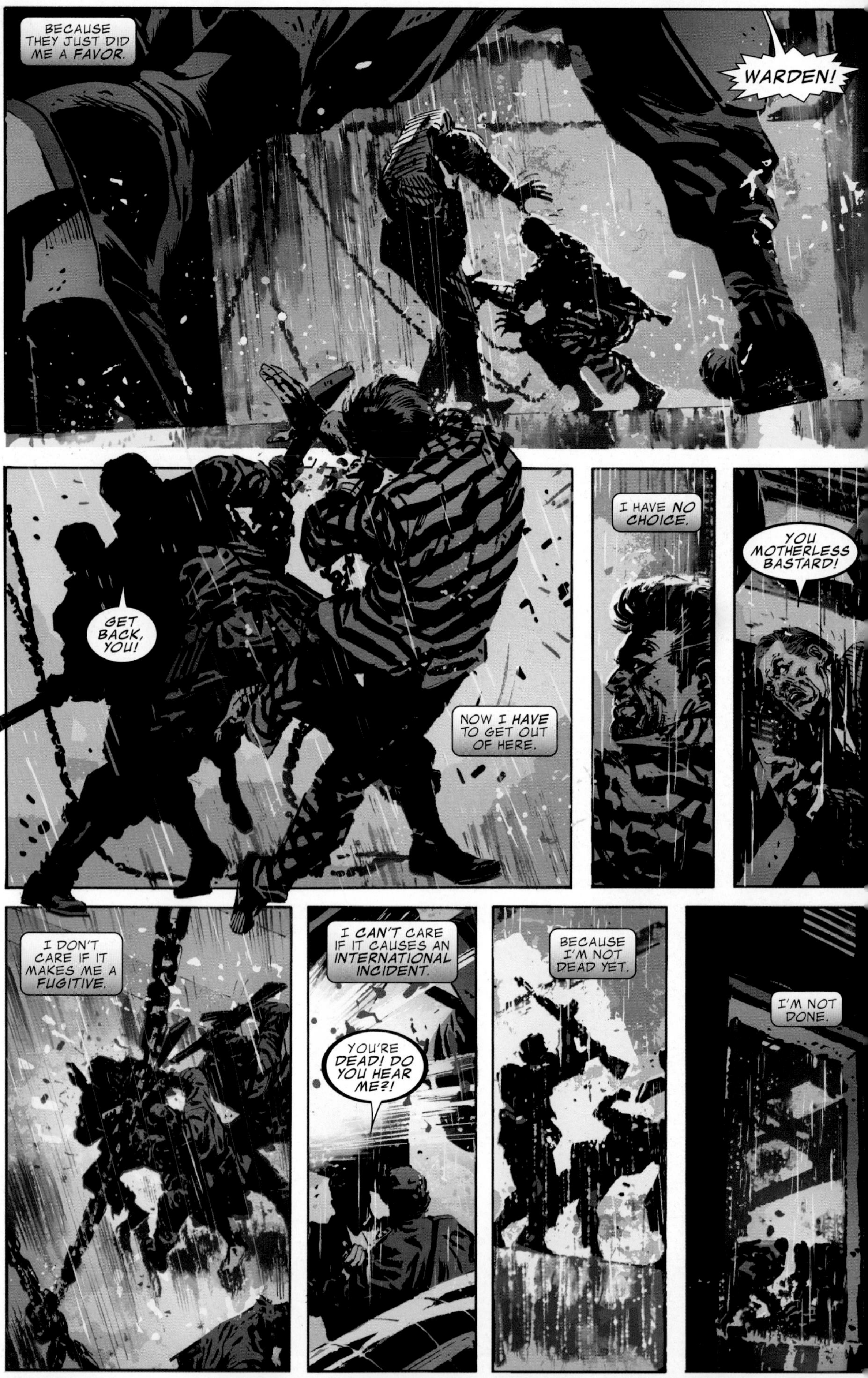
BECAUSE THEY JUST DID ME A FAVOR.
WARDEN!
GET BACK, YOU!
NOW I HAVE TO GET OUT OF HERE.
I HAVE NO CHOICE.
YOU MOTHERLESS BASTARD!
I DON'T CARE IF IT MAKES ME A FUGITIVE.
I CAN'T CARE IF IT CAUSES AN INTERNATIONAL INCIDENT.
YOU'RE DEAD! DO YOU HEAR ME?!
BECAUSE I'M NOT DEAD YET.
I'M NOT DONE.

THE GUARDS THINK THEY BEAT THE FIGHT OUT OF ME...

...AND I LET THEM GO AHEAD AND BELIEVE IT.

BUT I'M FEELING NO PAIN.

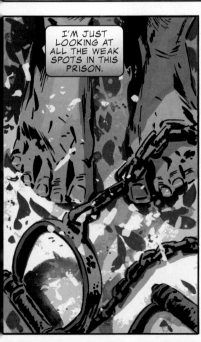

I'M JUST LOOKING AT ALL THE WEAK SPOTS IN THIS PRISON.

PLANNING.

I'M NOT STAYING HERE ANOTHER NIGHT.

I DON'T CARE WHAT THEY THROW AT ME.

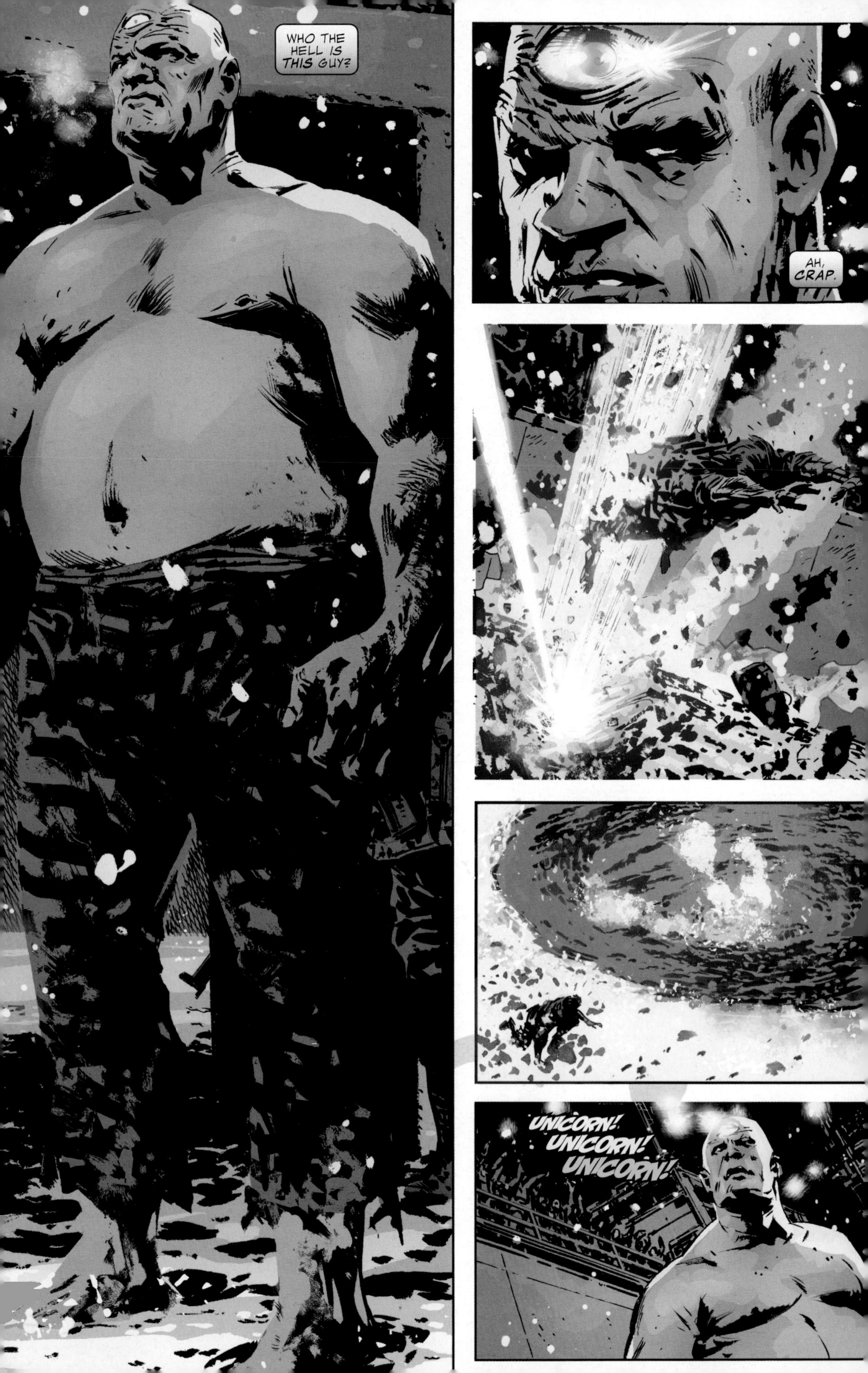
WHO THE HELL IS THIS GUY?
AH, CRAP.
UNICORN! UNICORN! UNICORN!

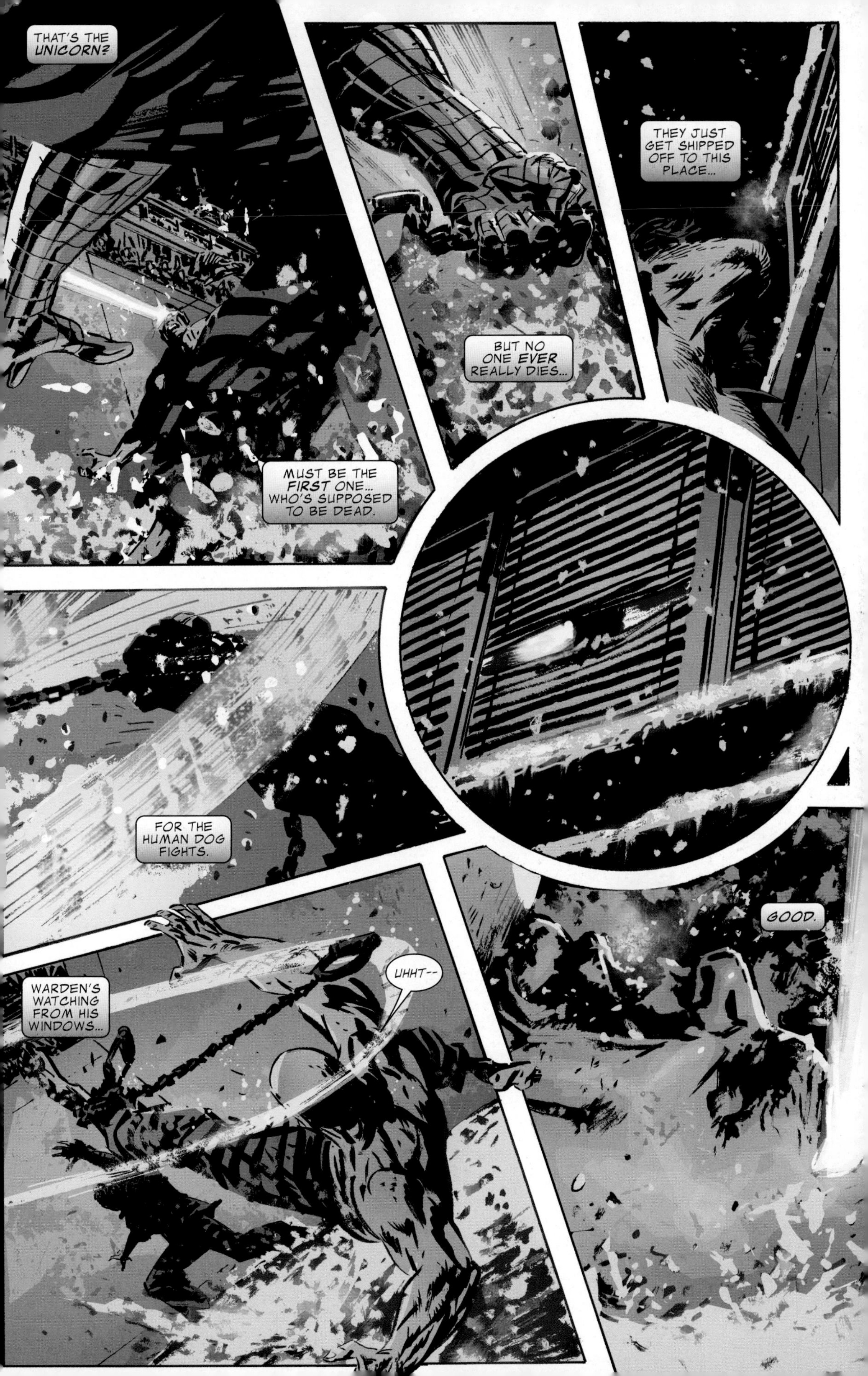
THAT'S THE UNICORN?
MUST BE THE FIRST ONE... WHO'S SUPPOSED TO BE DEAD.
BUT NO ONE EVER REALLY DIES...
THEY JUST GET SHIPPED OFF TO THIS PLACE...
FOR THE HUMAN DOG FIGHTS.
WARDEN'S WATCHING FROM HIS WINDOWS...
UHHT--
GOOD.

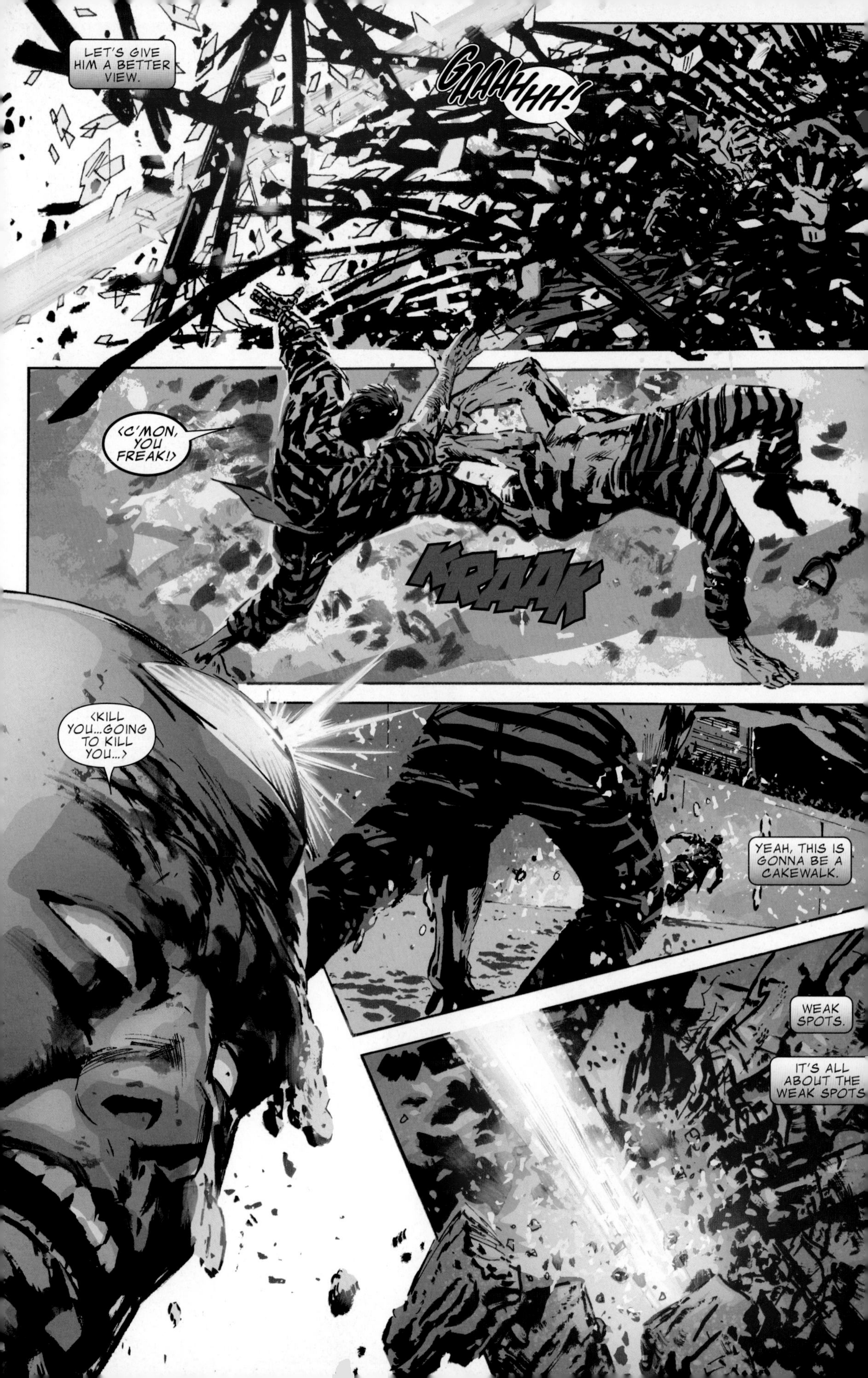
LET'S GIVE HIM A BETTER VIEW.
GAAAHHH!
<C'MON, YOU FREAK!>
KRAAK
<KILL YOU...GOING TO KILL YOU...>
YEAH, THIS IS GONNA BE A CAKEWALK.
WEAK SPOTS.
IT'S ALL ABOUT THE WEAK SPOTS

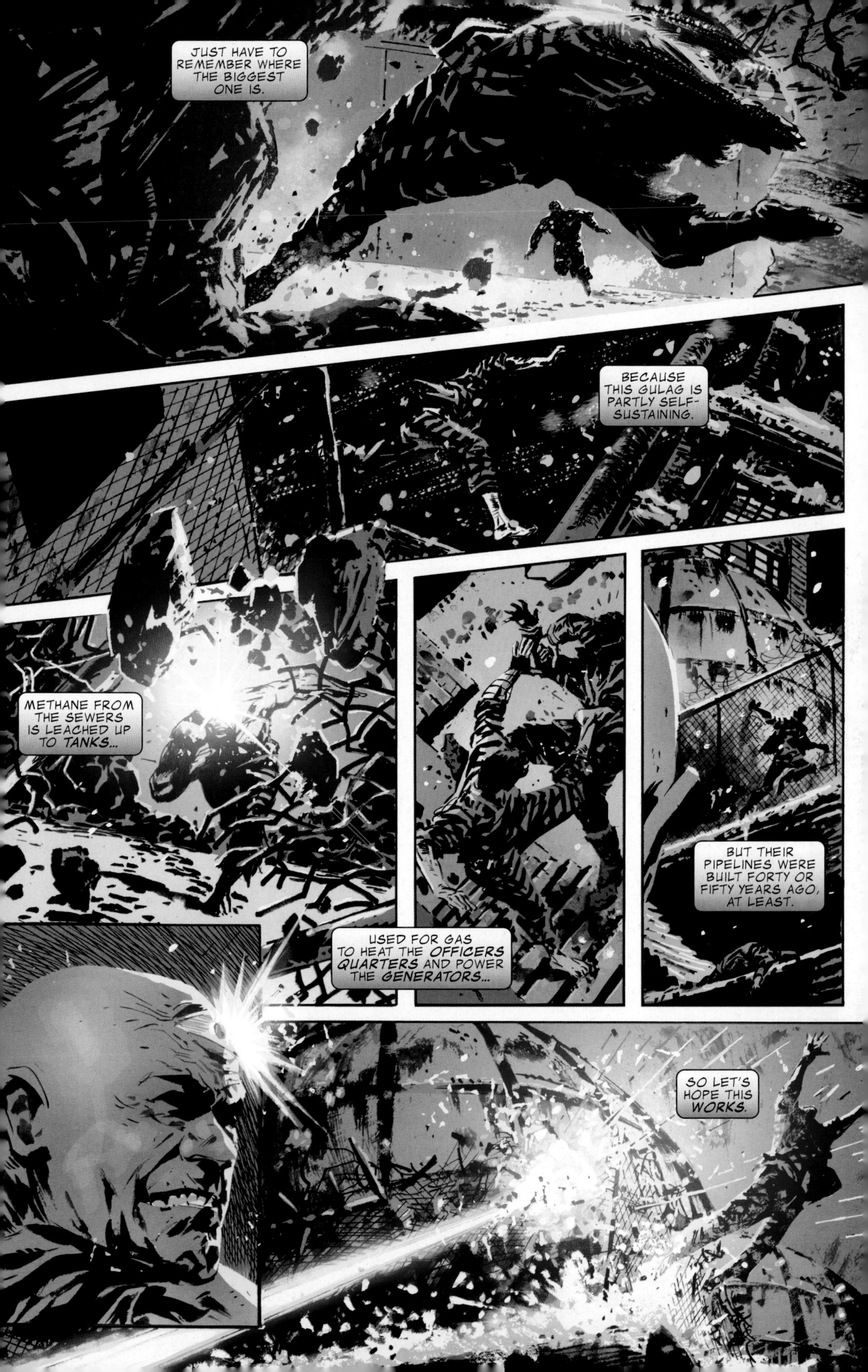
JUST HAVE TO REMEMBER WHERE THE BIGGEST ONE IS.
BECAUSE THIS GULAG IS PARTLY SELF-SUSTAINING.
METHANE FROM THE SEWERS IS LEACHED UP TO TANKS...
USED FOR GAS TO HEAT THE OFFICERS QUARTERS AND POWER THE GENERATORS...
BUT THEIR PIPELINES WERE BUILT FORTY OR FIFTY YEARS AGO, AT LEAST.
SO LET'S HOPE THIS WORKS.

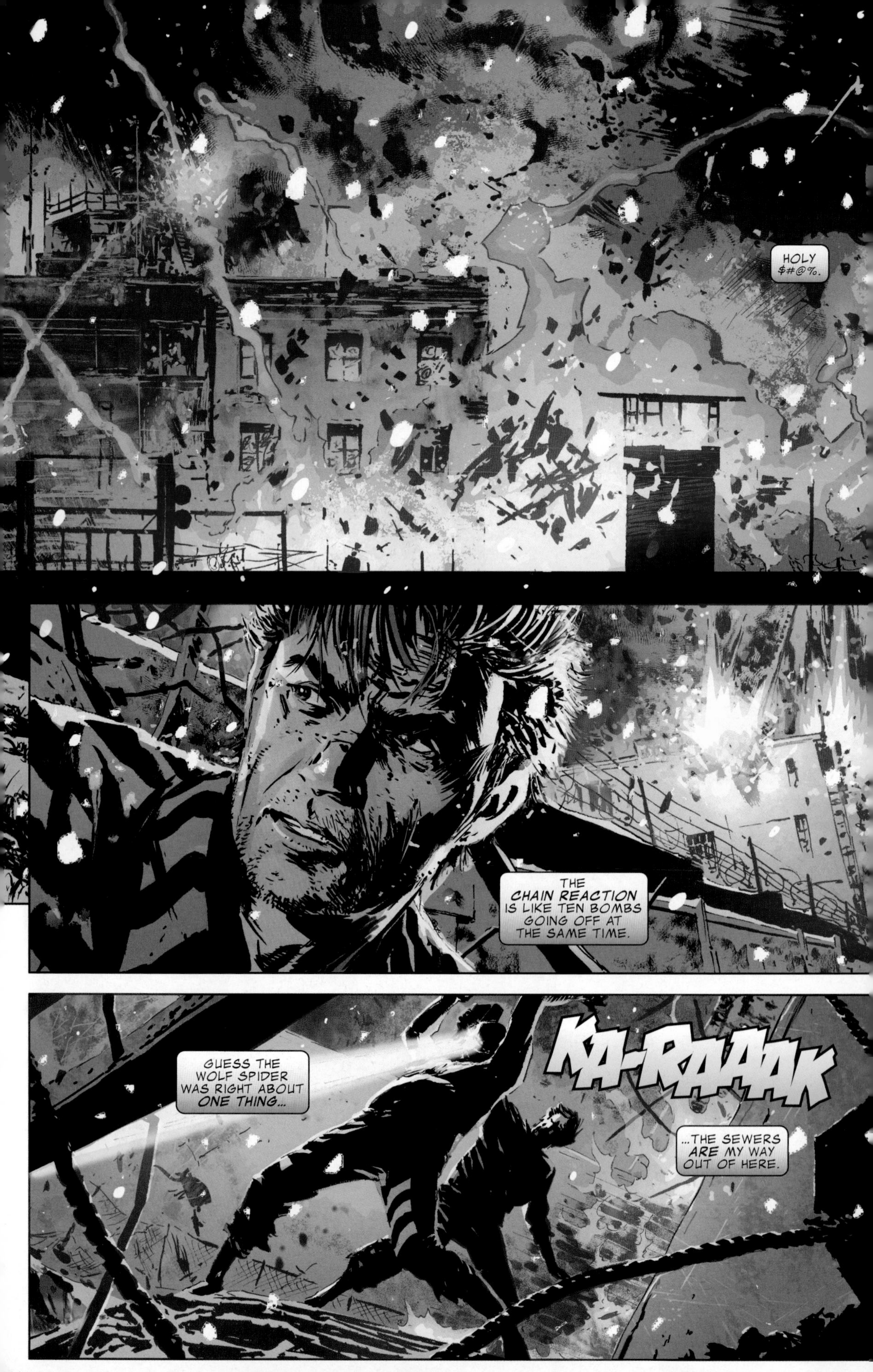
HOLY $#@%.
THE CHAIN REACTION IS LIKE TEN BOMBS GOING OFF AT THE SAME TIME.
GUESS THE WOLF SPIDER WAS RIGHT ABOUT ONE THING...
KA-RAAAK
...THE SEWERS ARE MY WAY OUT OF HERE.

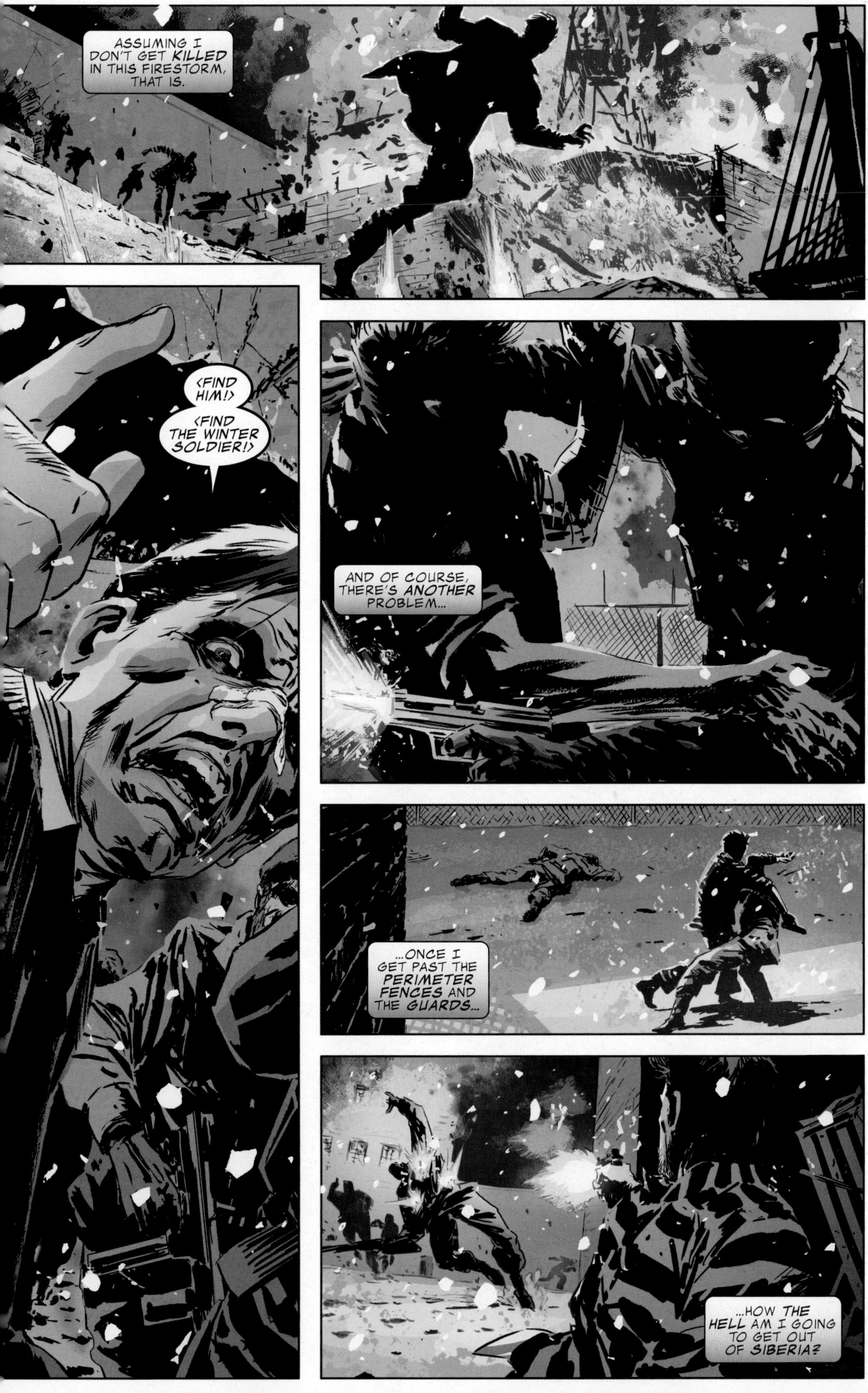
ASSUMING I DON'T GET KILLED IN THIS FIRESTORM, THAT IS.
<FIND HIM!>
<FIND THE WINTER SOLDIER!>
AND OF COURSE, THERE'S ANOTHER PROBLEM...
...ONCE I GET PAST THE PERIMETER FENCES AND THE GUARDS...
...HOW THE HELL AM I GOING TO GET OUT OF SIBERIA?

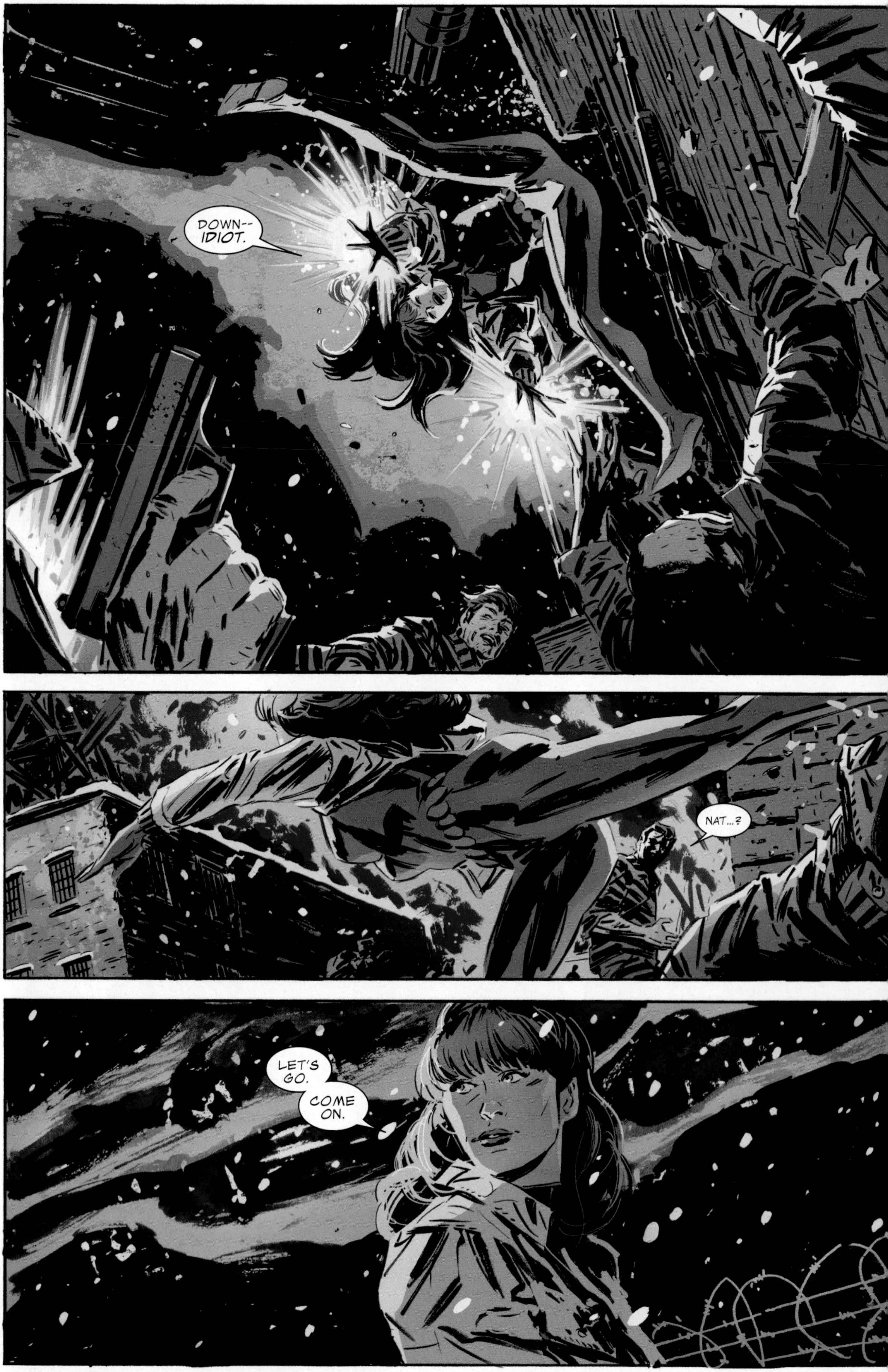
DOWN--
IDIOT.
NAT...?
LET'S GO.
COME ON.

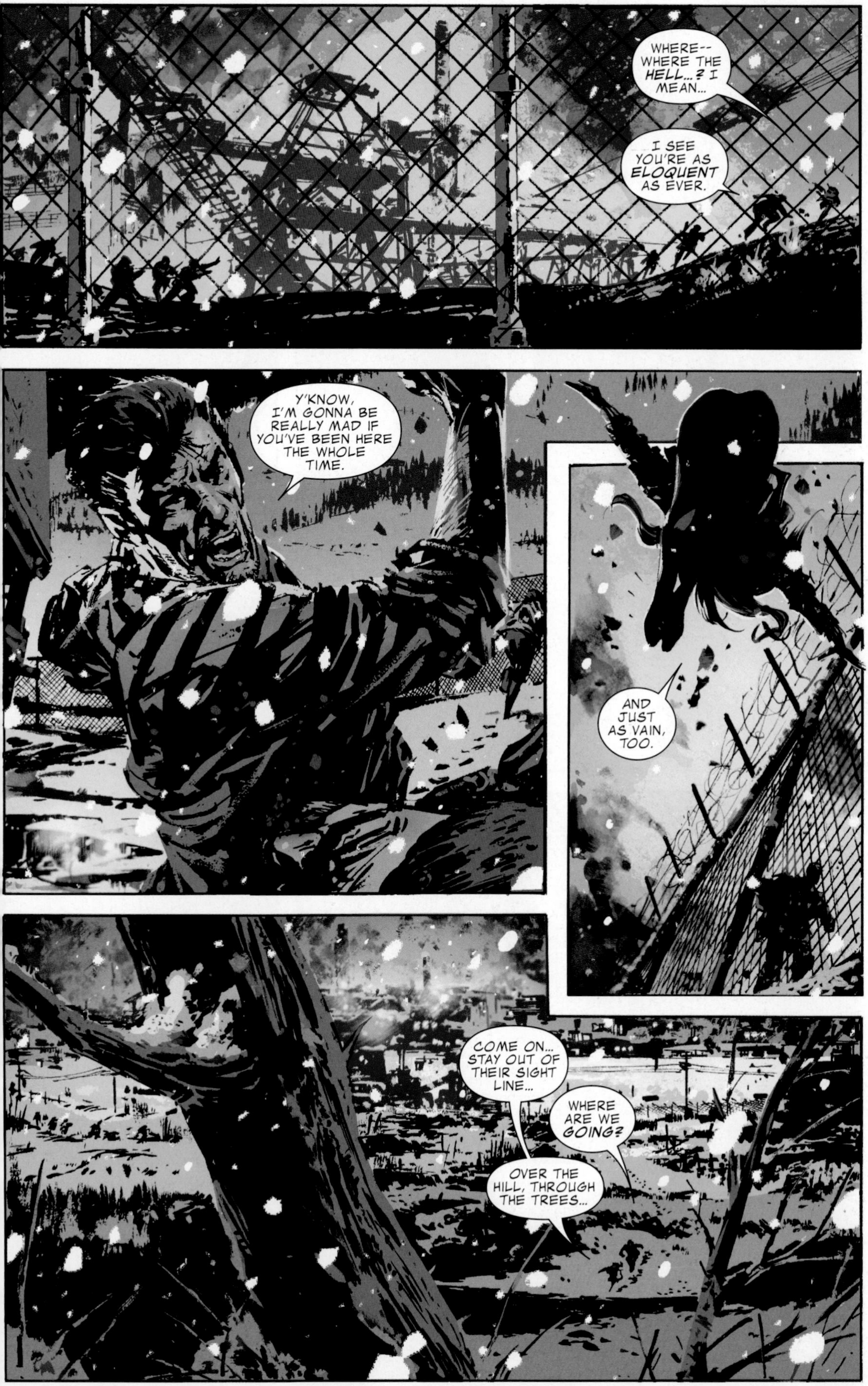

WHERE-- WHERE THE HELL...? I MEAN...
I SEE YOU'RE AS ELOQUENT AS EVER.
Y'KNOW, I'M GONNA BE REALLY MAD IF YOU'VE BEEN HERE THE WHOLE TIME.
AND JUST AS VAIN, TOO.
COME ON... STAY OUT OF THEIR SIGHT LINE...
WHERE ARE WE GOING?
OVER THE HILL, THROUGH THE TREES...

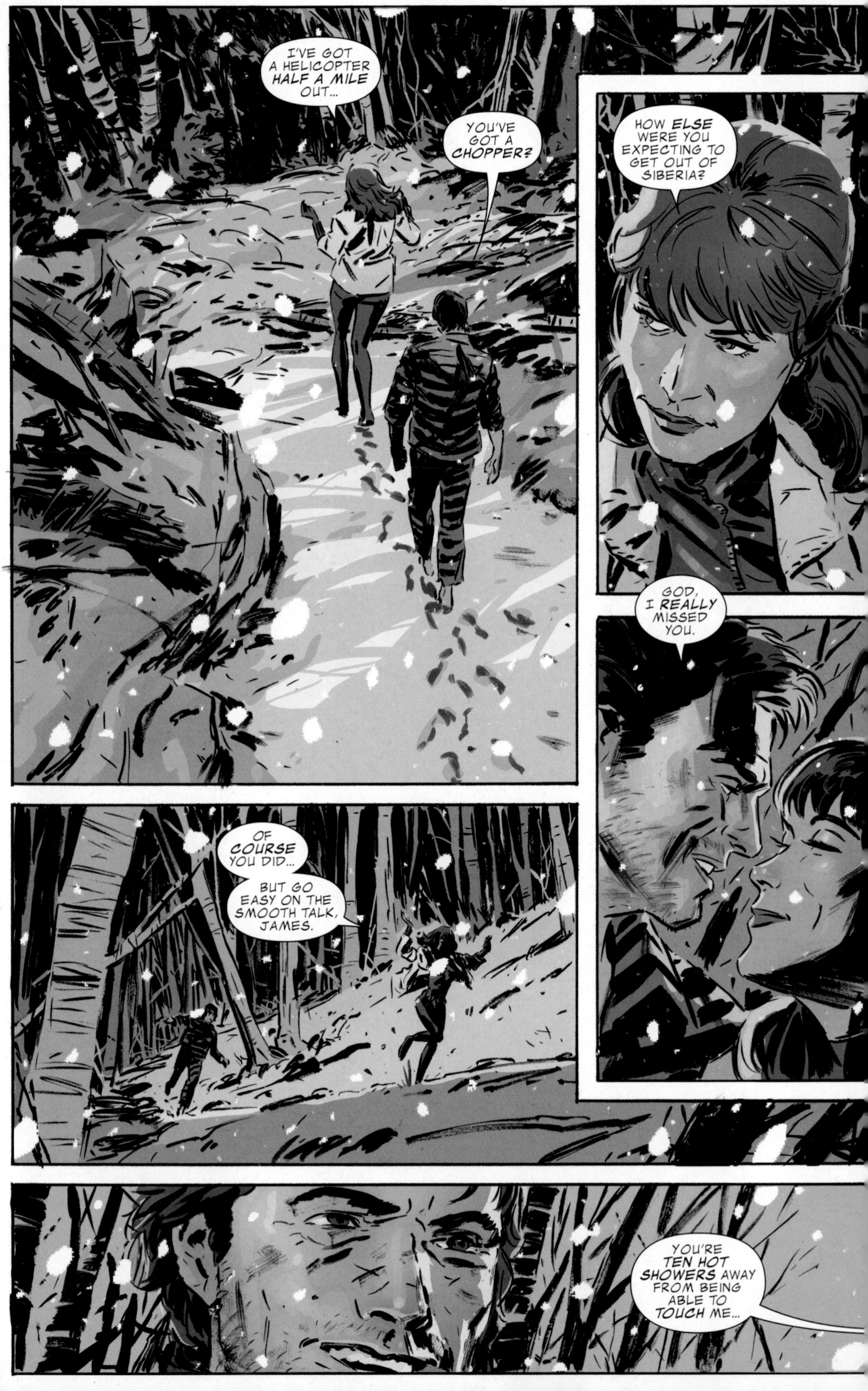
I'VE GOT A HELICOPTER HALF A MILE OUT...
YOU'VE GOT A CHOPPER?
HOW ELSE WERE YOU EXPECTING TO GET OUT OF SIBERIA?
GOD, I REALLY MISSED YOU.
OF COURSE YOU DID...
BUT GO EASY ON THE SMOOTH TALK, JAMES.
YOU'RE TEN HOT SHOWERS AWAY FROM BEING ABLE TO TOUCH ME...

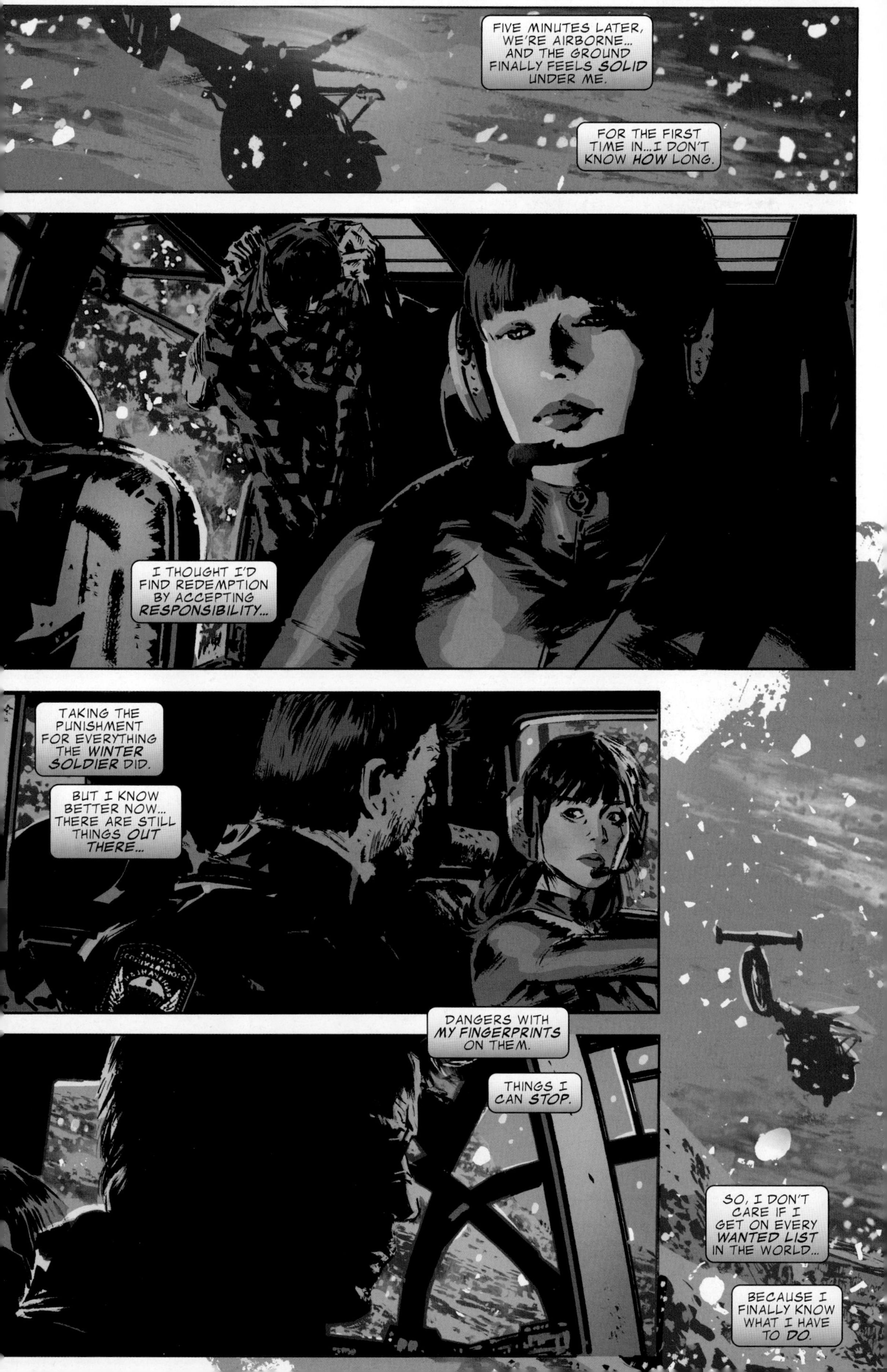

FIVE MINUTES LATER, WE'RE AIRBORNE... AND THE GROUND FINALLY FEELS SOLID UNDER ME.
FOR THE FIRST TIME IN...I DON'T KNOW HOW LONG.
I THOUGHT I'D FIND REDEMPTION BY ACCEPTING RESPONSIBILITY...
TAKING THE PUNISHMENT FOR EVERYTHING THE WINTER SOLDIER DID.
BUT I KNOW BETTER NOW... THERE ARE STILL THINGS OUT THERE...
DANGERS WITH MY FINGERPRINTS ON THEM.
THINGS I CAN STOP.
SO, I DON'T CARE IF I GET ON EVERY WANTED LIST IN THE WORLD...
BECAUSE I FINALLY KNOW WHAT I HAVE TO DO.

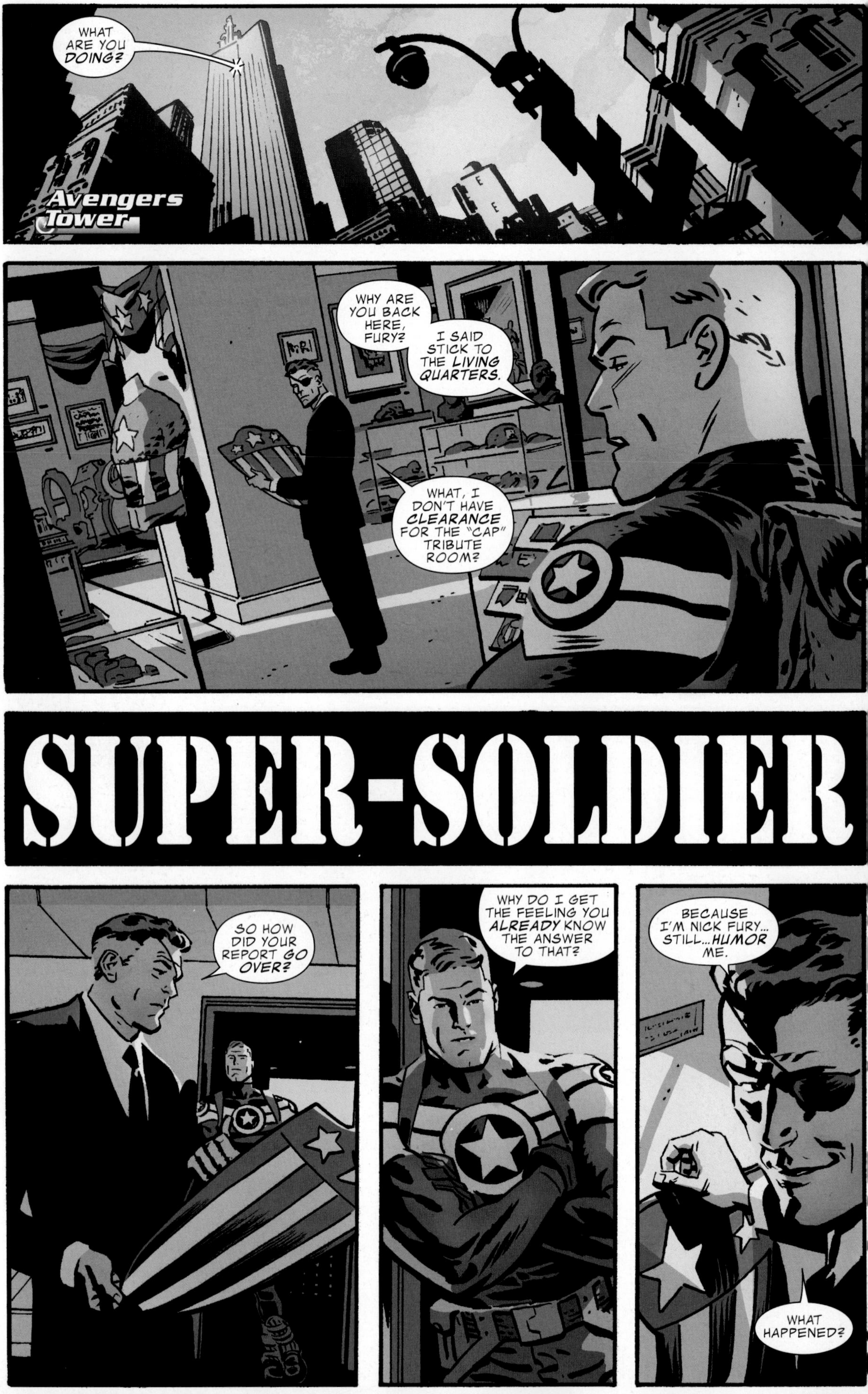
WHAT ARE YOU DOING?
Avengers Tower
WHY ARE YOU BACK HERE, FURY?
I SAID STICK TO THE LIVING QUARTERS.
WHAT, I DON'T HAVE CLEARANCE FOR THE "CAP" TRIBUTE ROOM?
SUPER-SOLDIER
SO HOW DID YOUR REPORT GO OVER?
WHY DO I GET THE FEELING YOU ALREADY KNOW THE ANSWER TO THAT?
BECAUSE I'M NICK FURY... STILL... HUMOR ME.
WHAT HAPPENED?

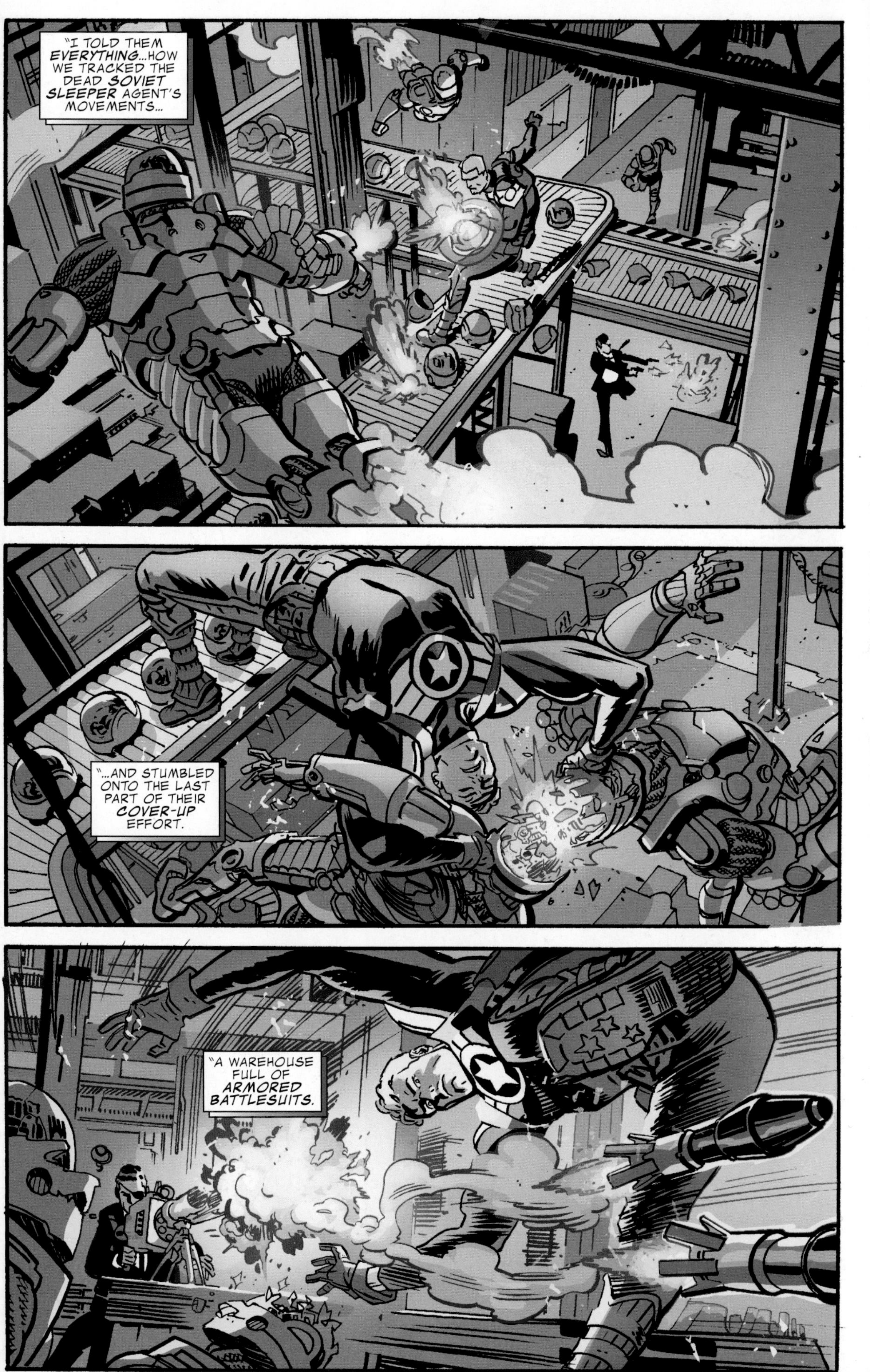
"I TOLD THEM EVERYTHING...HOW WE TRACKED THE DEAD SOVIET SLEEPER AGENT'S MOVEMENTS...
"...AND STUMBLED ONTO THE LAST PART OF THEIR COVER-UP EFFORT.
"A WAREHOUSE FULL OF ARMORED BATTLESUITS.

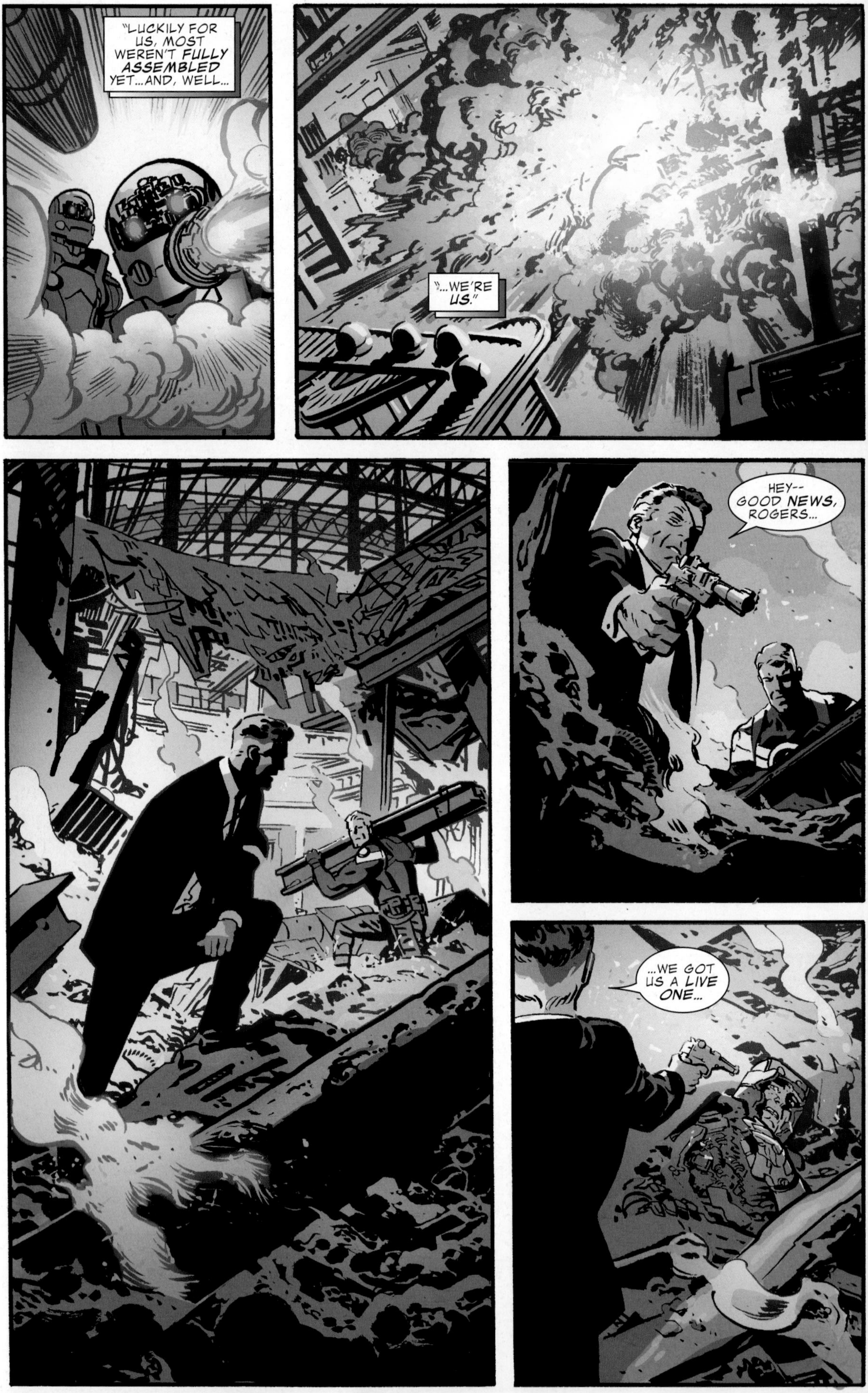
"LUCKILY FOR US, MOST WEREN'T FULLY ASSEMBLED YET...AND, WELL...
"...WE'RE US."
HEY-- GOOD NEWS, ROGERS...
...WE GOT US A LIVE ONE...

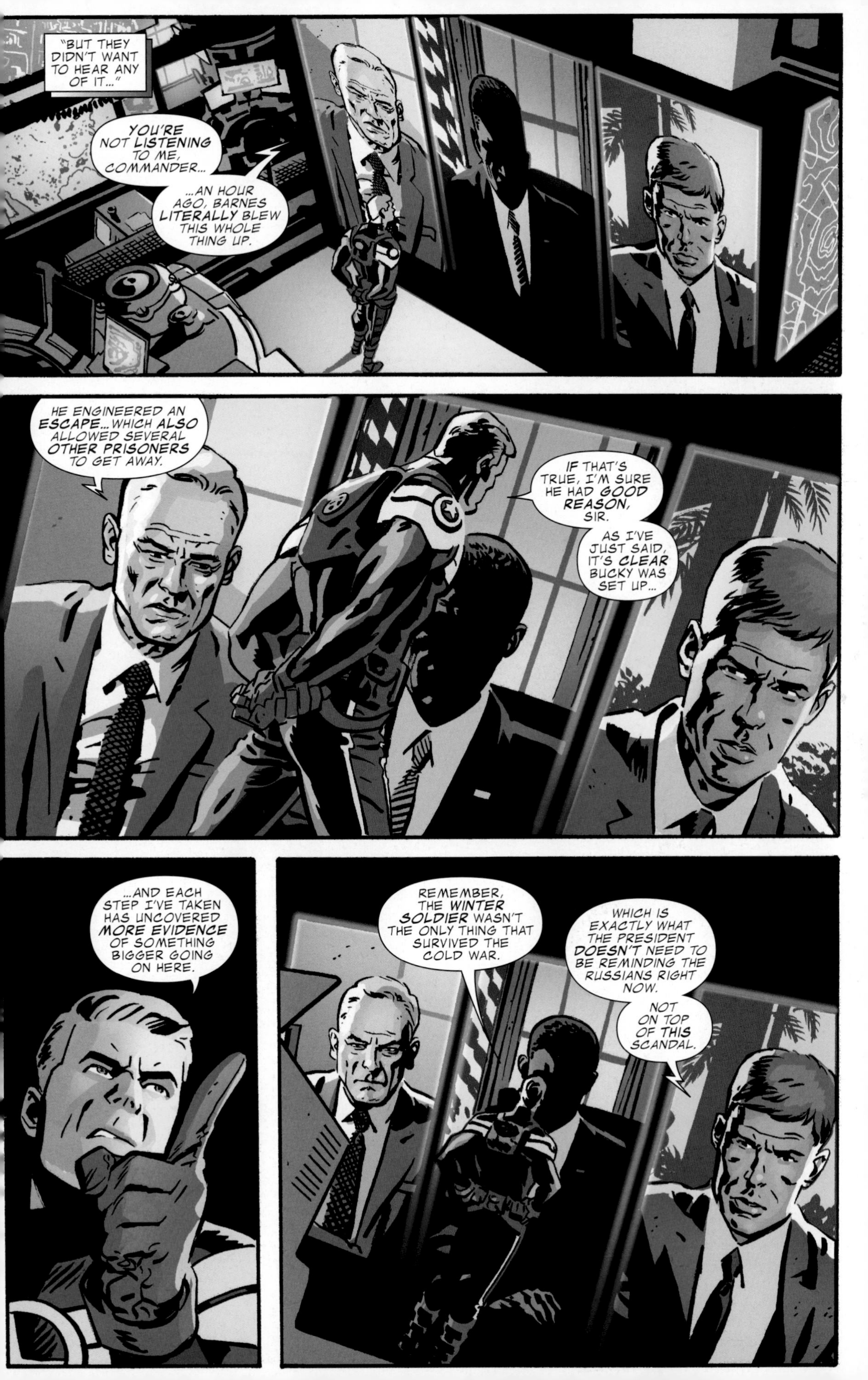
"BUT THEY DIDN'T WANT TO HEAR ANY OF IT..."
YOU'RE NOT LISTENING TO ME, COMMANDER...
...AN HOUR AGO, BARNES LITERALLY BLEW THIS WHOLE THING UP.
HE ENGINEERED AN ESCAPE... WHICH ALSO ALLOWED SEVERAL OTHER PRISONERS TO GET AWAY.
IF THAT'S TRUE, I'M SURE HE HAD GOOD REASON, SIR.
AS I'VE JUST SAID, IT'S CLEAR BUCKY WAS SET UP...
...AND EACH STEP I'VE TAKEN HAS UNCOVERED MORE EVIDENCE OF SOMETHING BIGGER GOING ON HERE.
REMEMBER, THE WINTER SOLDIER WASN'T THE ONLY THING THAT SURVIVED THE COLD WAR.
WHICH IS EXACTLY WHAT THE PRESIDENT DOESN'T NEED TO BE REMINDING THE RUSSIANS RIGHT NOW.
NOT ON TOP OF THIS SCANDAL.

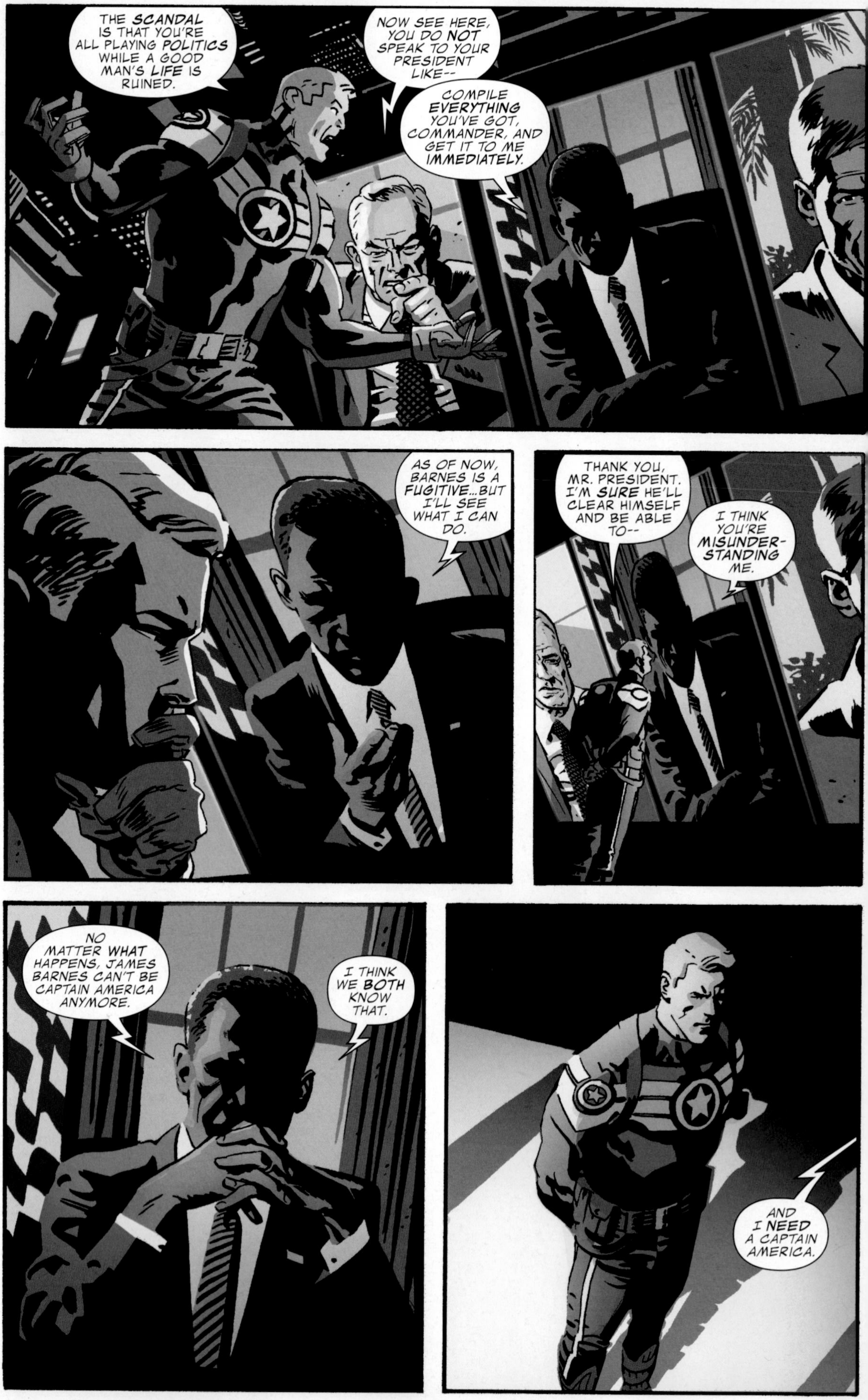
THE SCANDAL IS THAT YOU'RE ALL PLAYING POLITICS WHILE A GOOD MAN'S LIFE IS RUINED.
NOW SEE HERE, YOU DO NOT SPEAK TO YOUR PRESIDENT LIKE--
COMPILE EVERYTHING YOU'VE GOT, COMMANDER, AND GET IT TO ME IMMEDIATELY.
AS OF NOW, BARNES IS A FUGITIVE...BUT I'LL SEE WHAT I CAN DO.
THANK YOU, MR. PRESIDENT. I'M SURE HE'LL CLEAR HIMSELF AND BE ABLE TO--
I THINK YOU'RE MISUNDER-STANDING ME.
NO MATTER WHAT HAPPENS, JAMES BARNES CAN'T BE CAPTAIN AMERICA ANYMORE.
I THINK WE BOTH KNOW THAT.
AND I NEED A CAPTAIN AMERICA.

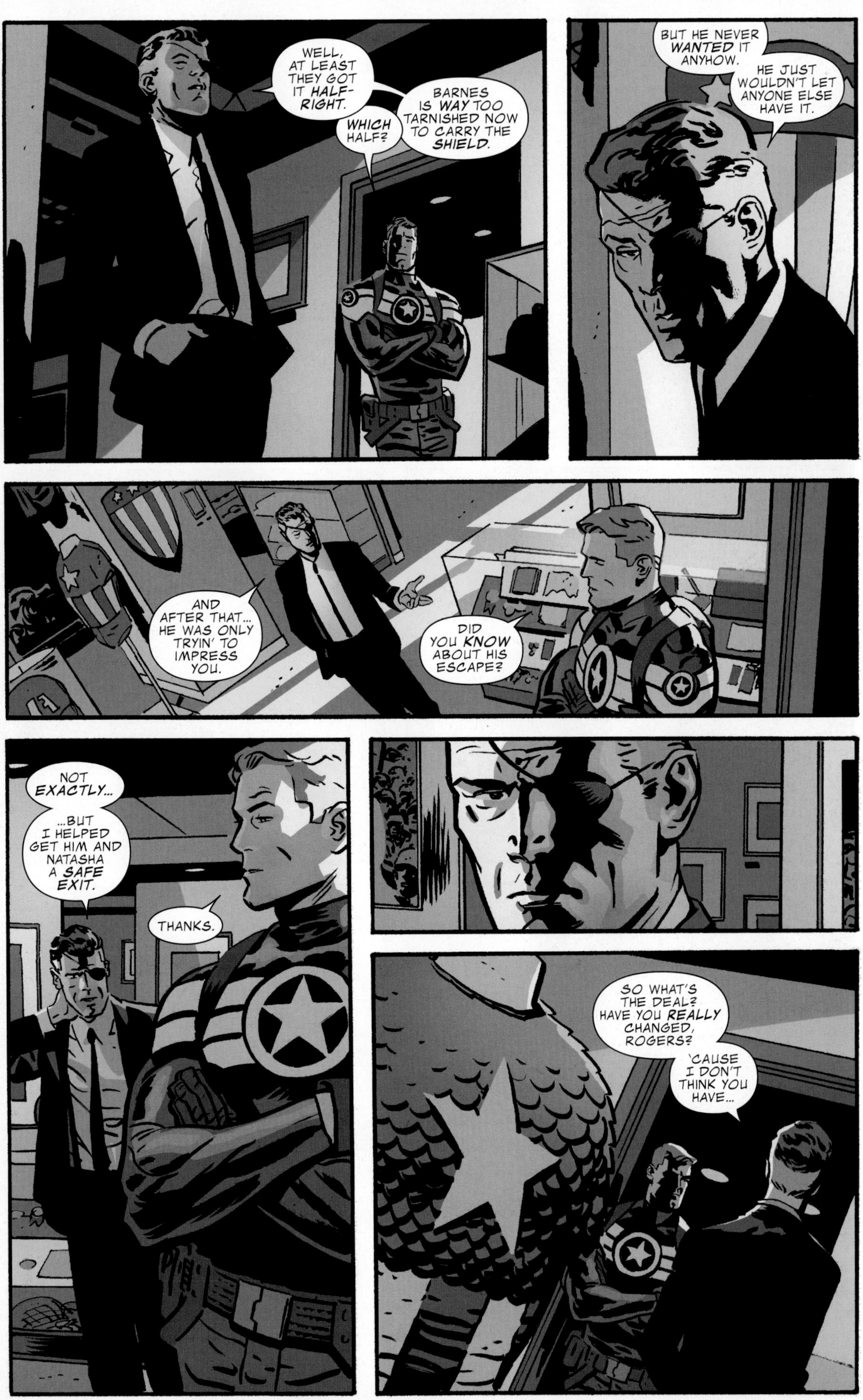
WELL, AT LEAST THEY GOT IT HALF-RIGHT.
WHICH HALF?
BARNES IS WAY TOO TARNISHED NOW TO CARRY THE SHIELD.
BUT HE NEVER WANTED IT ANYHOW.
HE JUST WOULDN'T LET ANYONE ELSE HAVE IT.
AND AFTER THAT... HE WAS ONLY TRYIN' TO IMPRESS YOU.
DID YOU KNOW ABOUT HIS ESCAPE?
NOT EXACTLY...
...BUT I HELPED GET HIM AND NATASHA A SAFE EXIT.
THANKS.
SO WHAT'S THE DEAL? HAVE YOU REALLY CHANGED, ROGERS?
'CAUSE I DON'T THINK YOU HAVE...

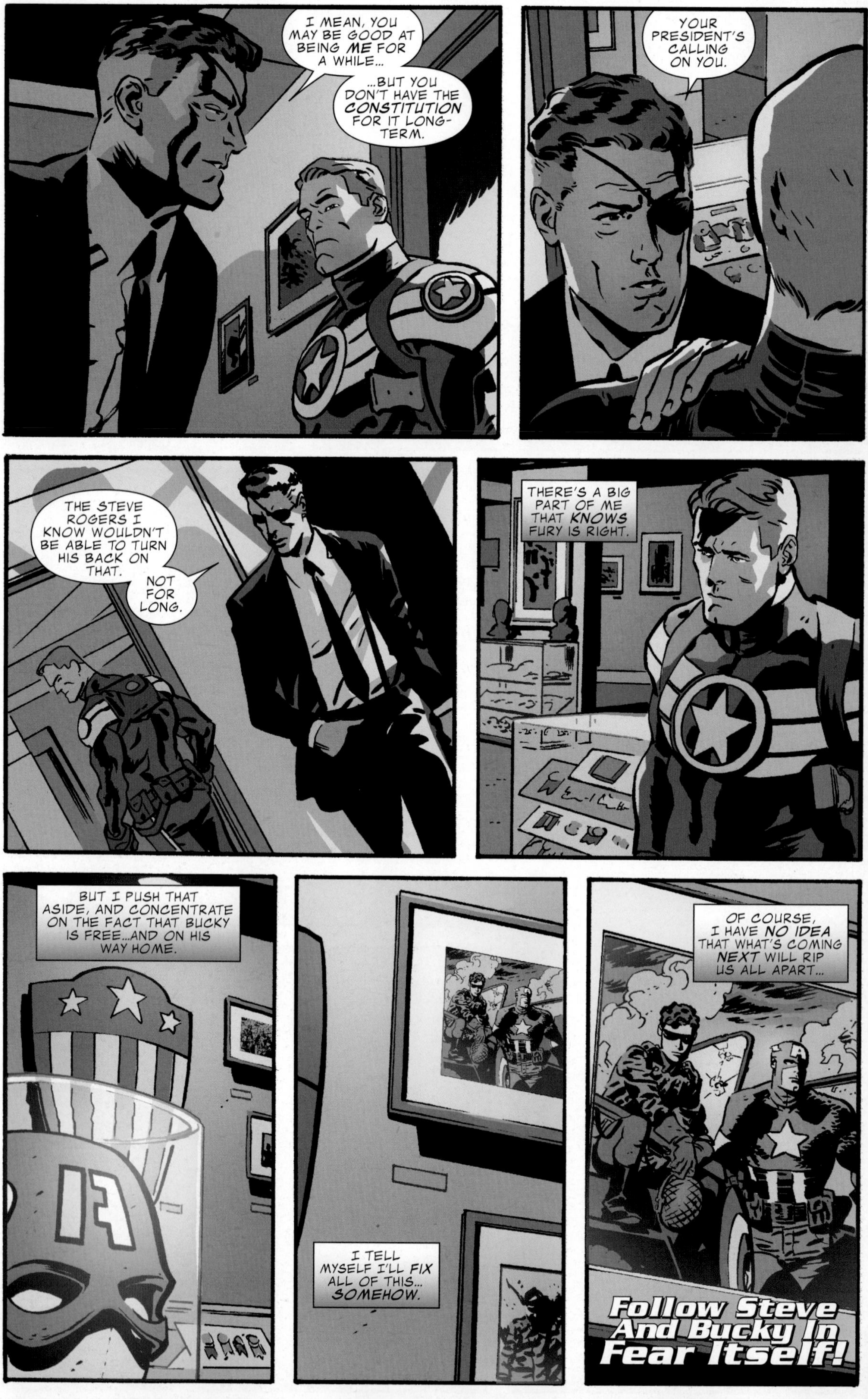
I MEAN, YOU MAY BE GOOD AT BEING ME FOR A WHILE...
...BUT YOU DON'T HAVE THE CONSTITUTION FOR IT LONG-TERM.
YOUR PRESIDENT'S CALLING ON YOU.
THE STEVE ROGERS I KNOW WOULDN'T BE ABLE TO TURN HIS BACK ON THAT.
NOT FOR LONG.
THERE'S A BIG PART OF ME THAT KNOWS FURY IS RIGHT.
BUT I PUSH THAT ASIDE, AND CONCENTRATE ON THE FACT THAT BUCKY IS FREE...AND ON HIS WAY HOME.
I TELL MYSELF I'LL FIX ALL OF THIS... SOMEHOW.
OF COURSE, I HAVE NO IDEA THAT WHAT'S COMING NEXT WILL RIP US ALL APART...
Follow Steve And Bucky In Fear Itself!

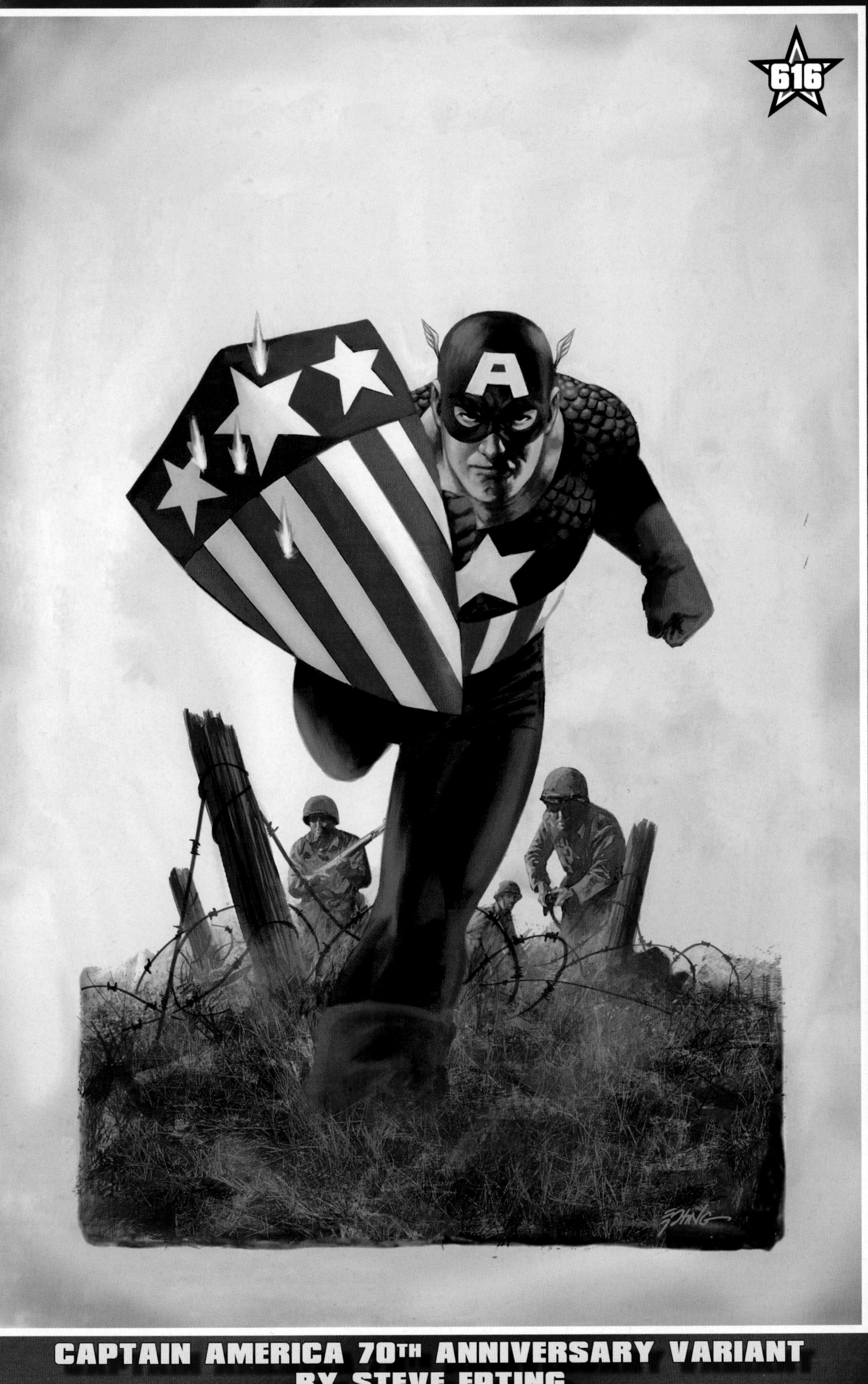
616

CAPTAIN AMERICA 70TH ANNIVERSARY VARIANT
BY STEVE EPTING

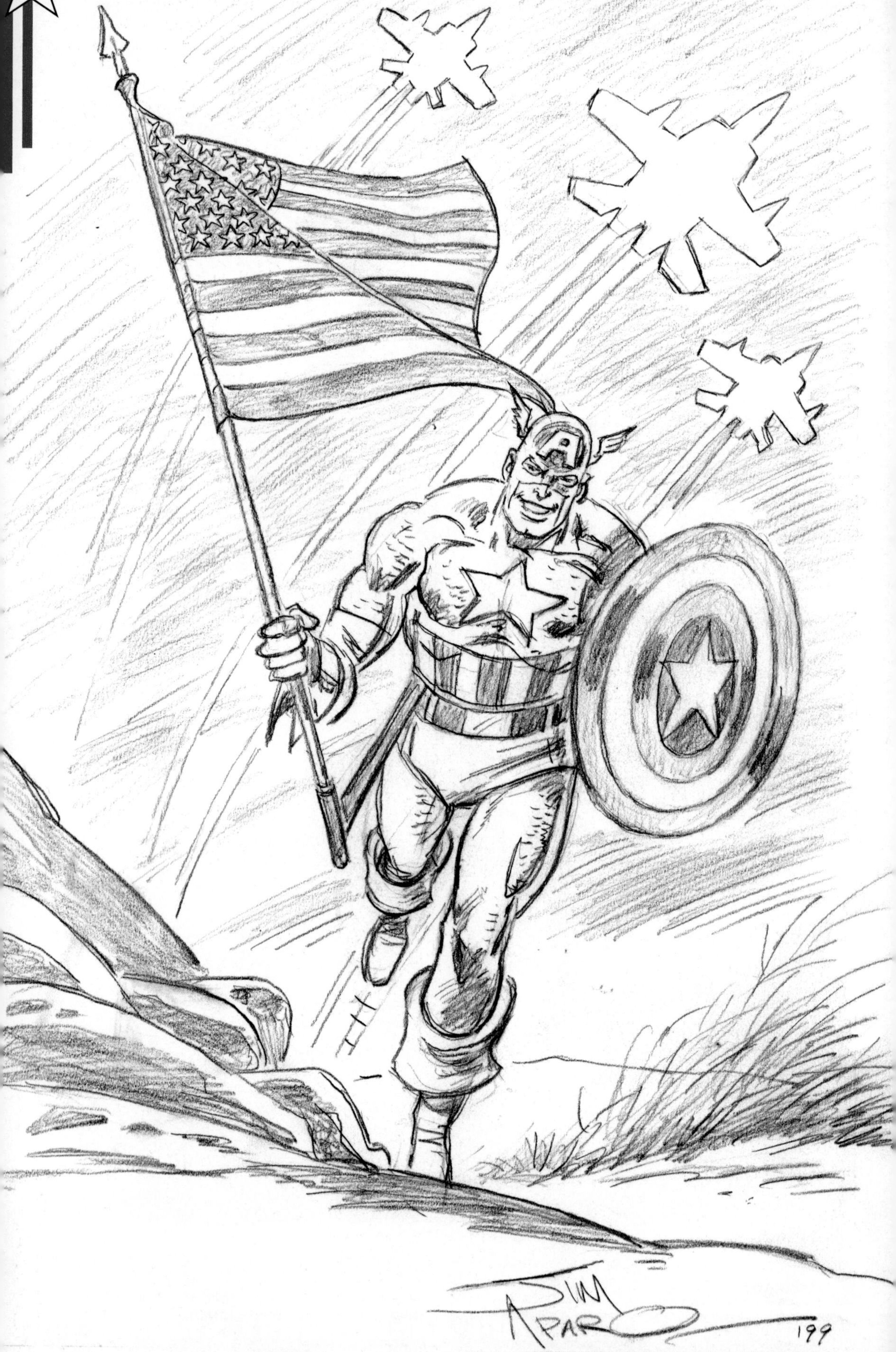
JIM APARO
'99

Seventy years ago, a red, white and blue icon first delivered a sock to the jaw of a real-life would-be world conqueror and entered the pantheon of truly great comic book super heroes. Captain America carries the singular honor of being the first Marvel character to have been launched in his own title (as opposed to having proven his mettle beforehand in a then-common anthology series.) He was, from the very first, an important character, one who reflected the very real concerns and love of country as his readers. He was as much a symbol as he was a man.

Over those seventy years, a veritable who's who of the greatest names the comic book industry has to offer worked to add to his legend, in ways both large and small. But even after seven decades, not everybody has gotten a chance to play, a chance to illustrate how the concept of Captain America speaks to them. So we thought it might be fun to enlist the services of a number of creators who haven't really worked on Cap (save for a small appearance here or there) and ask them to tell a story that in some way sums up what Captain America means to them.

Additionally, thanks to the efforts of art representative extraordinaire Spencer Beck, we've got a pair of pieces penciled as commissions by two legends of the industry who are no longer with us, Curt Swan and Jim Aparo, neither of whom ever worked on Captain America as far as we can recall. But it is an honor to have them represented here as well, for all that Captain America has meant to entire generations of readers and creators.

CURT SWAN 3/94

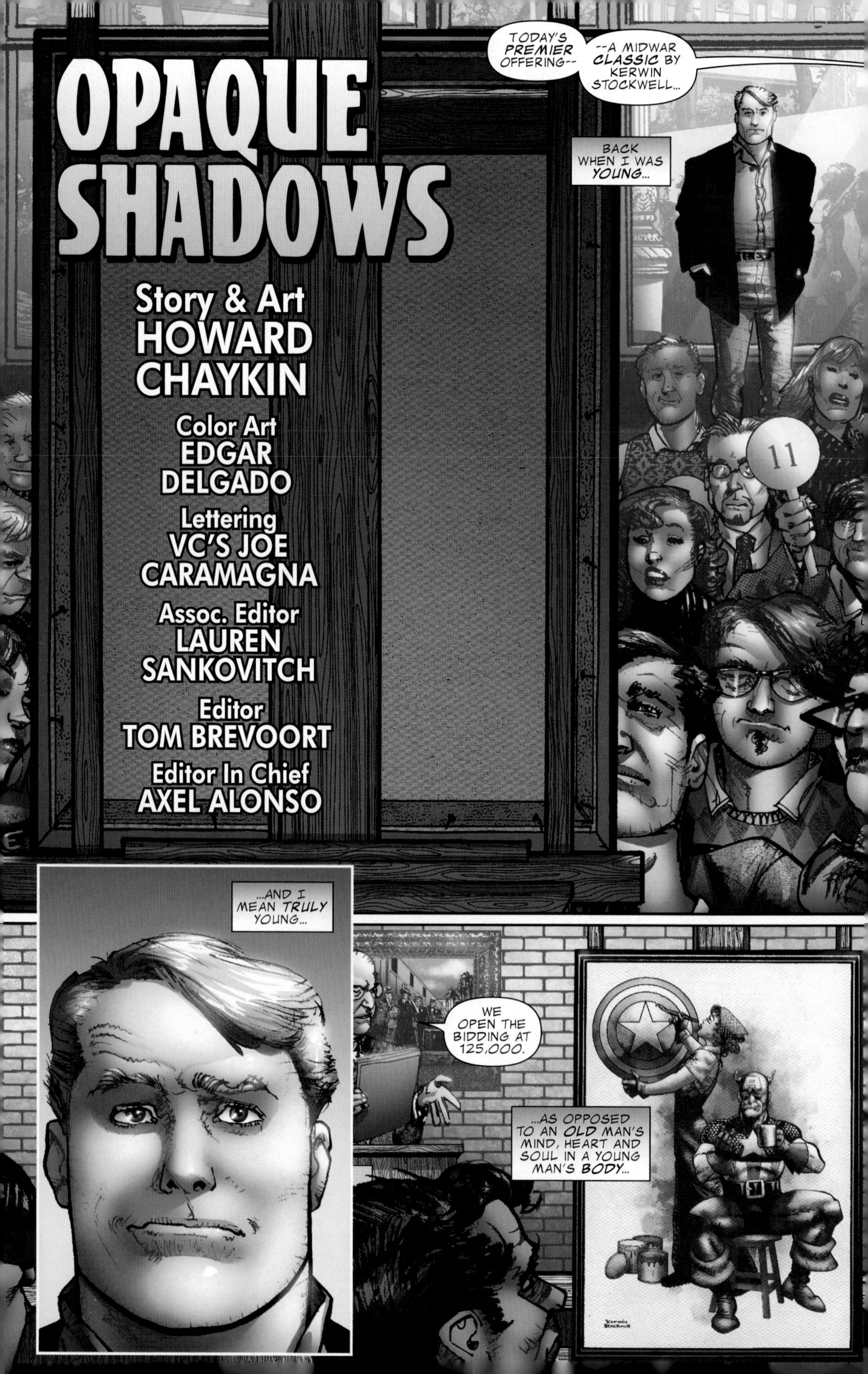
OPAQUE SHADOWS
Story & Art HOWARD CHAYKIN
Color Art EDGAR DELGADO
Lettering VC'S JOE CARAMAGNA
Assoc. Editor LAUREN SANKOVITCH
Editor TOM BREVOORT
Editor In Chief AXEL ALONSO
TODAY'S PREMIER OFFERING--
--A MIDWAR CLASSIC BY KERWIN STOCKWELL...
BACK WHEN I WAS YOUNG...
11
...AND I MEAN TRULY YOUNG...
WE OPEN THE BIDDING AT 125,000.
...AS OPPOSED TO AN OLD MAN'S MIND, HEART AND SOUL IN A YOUNG MAN'S BODY...

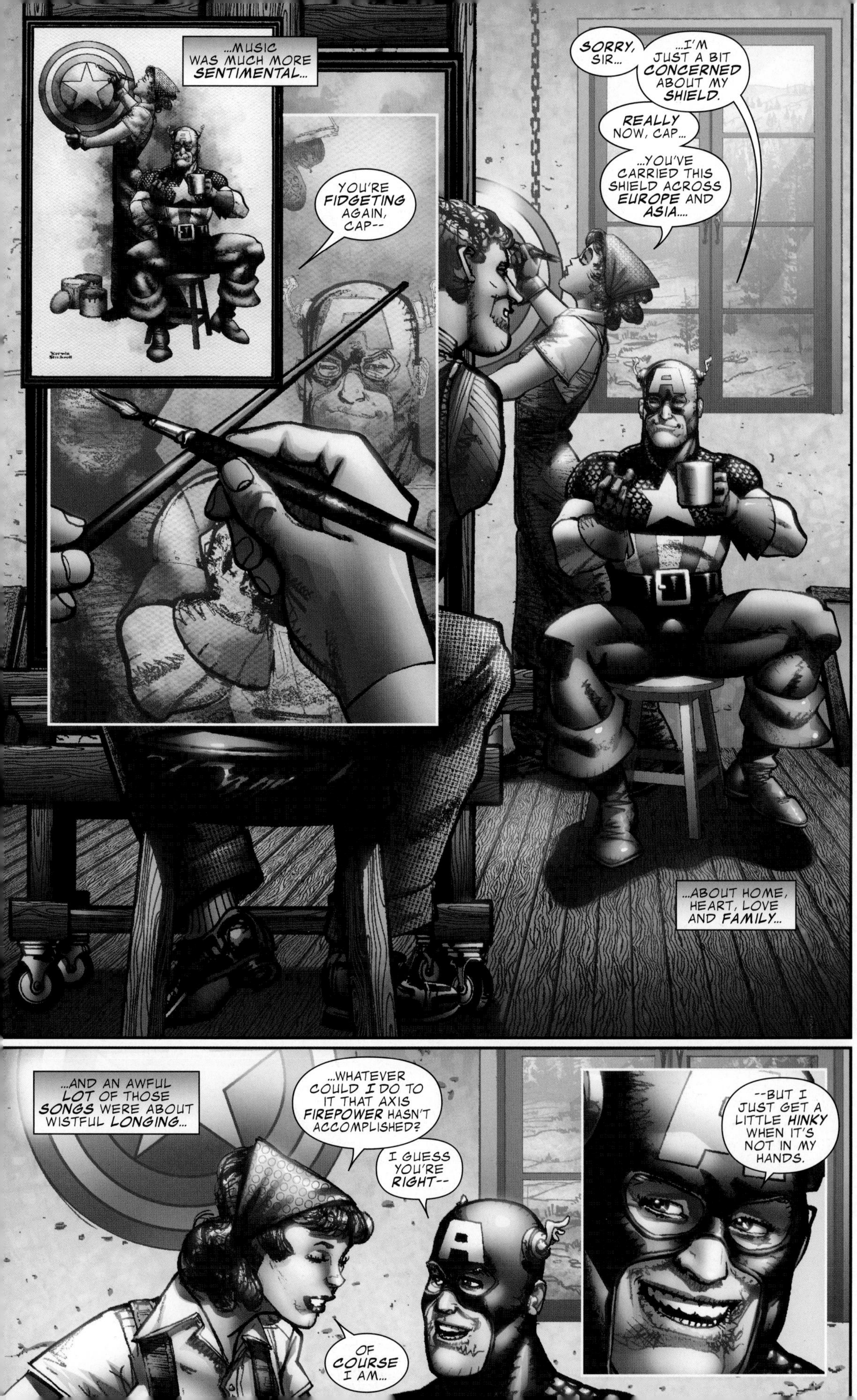

...MUSIC WAS MUCH MORE SENTIMENTAL...
YOU'RE FIDGETING AGAIN, CAP--
SORRY, SIR...
...I'M JUST A BIT CONCERNED ABOUT MY SHIELD.
REALLY NOW, CAP...
...YOU'VE CARRIED THIS SHIELD ACROSS EUROPE AND ASIA....
...ABOUT HOME, HEART, LOVE AND FAMILY...
...AND AN AWFUL LOT OF THOSE SONGS WERE ABOUT WISTFUL LONGING...
...WHATEVER COULD I DO TO IT THAT AXIS FIREPOWER HASN'T ACCOMPLISHED?
I GUESS YOU'RE RIGHT--
OF COURSE I AM...
--BUT I JUST GET A LITTLE HINKY WHEN IT'S NOT IN MY HANDS.

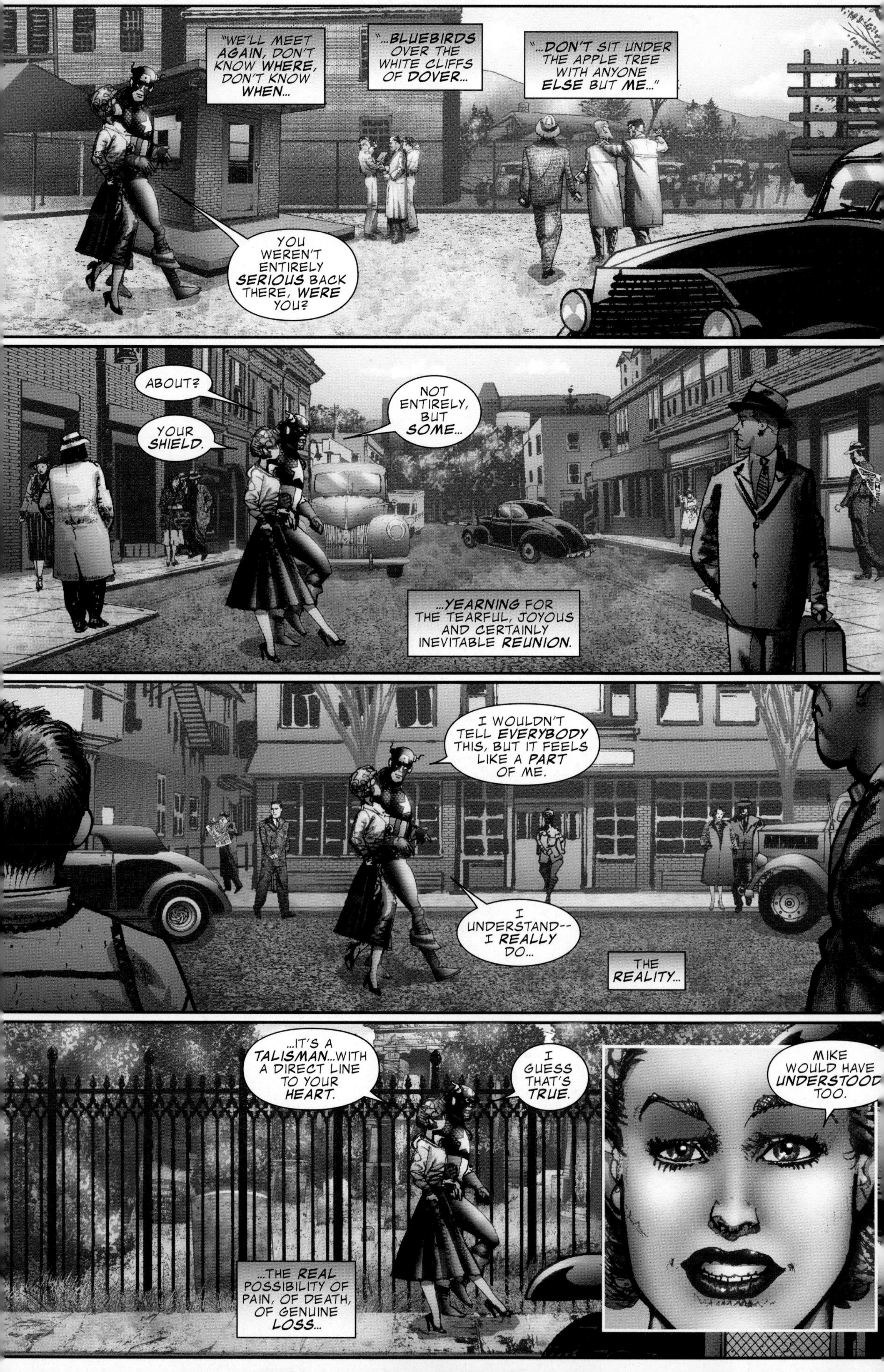
"WE'LL MEET AGAIN, DON'T KNOW WHERE, DON'T KNOW WHEN...
"...BLUEBIRDS OVER THE WHITE CLIFFS OF DOVER...
"...DON'T SIT UNDER THE APPLE TREE WITH ANYONE ELSE BUT ME..."
YOU WEREN'T ENTIRELY SERIOUS BACK THERE, WERE YOU?
ABOUT?
YOUR SHIELD.
NOT ENTIRELY, BUT SOME...
...YEARNING FOR THE TEARFUL, JOYOUS AND CERTAINLY INEVITABLE REUNION.
I WOULDN'T TELL EVERYBODY THIS, BUT IT FEELS LIKE A PART OF ME.
I UNDERSTAND-- I REALLY DO...
THE REALITY...
...IT'S A TALISMAN...WITH A DIRECT LINE TO YOUR HEART.
I GUESS THAT'S TRUE.
...THE REAL POSSIBILITY OF PAIN, OF DEATH, OF GENUINE LOSS...
MIKE WOULD HAVE UNDERSTOOD TOO.

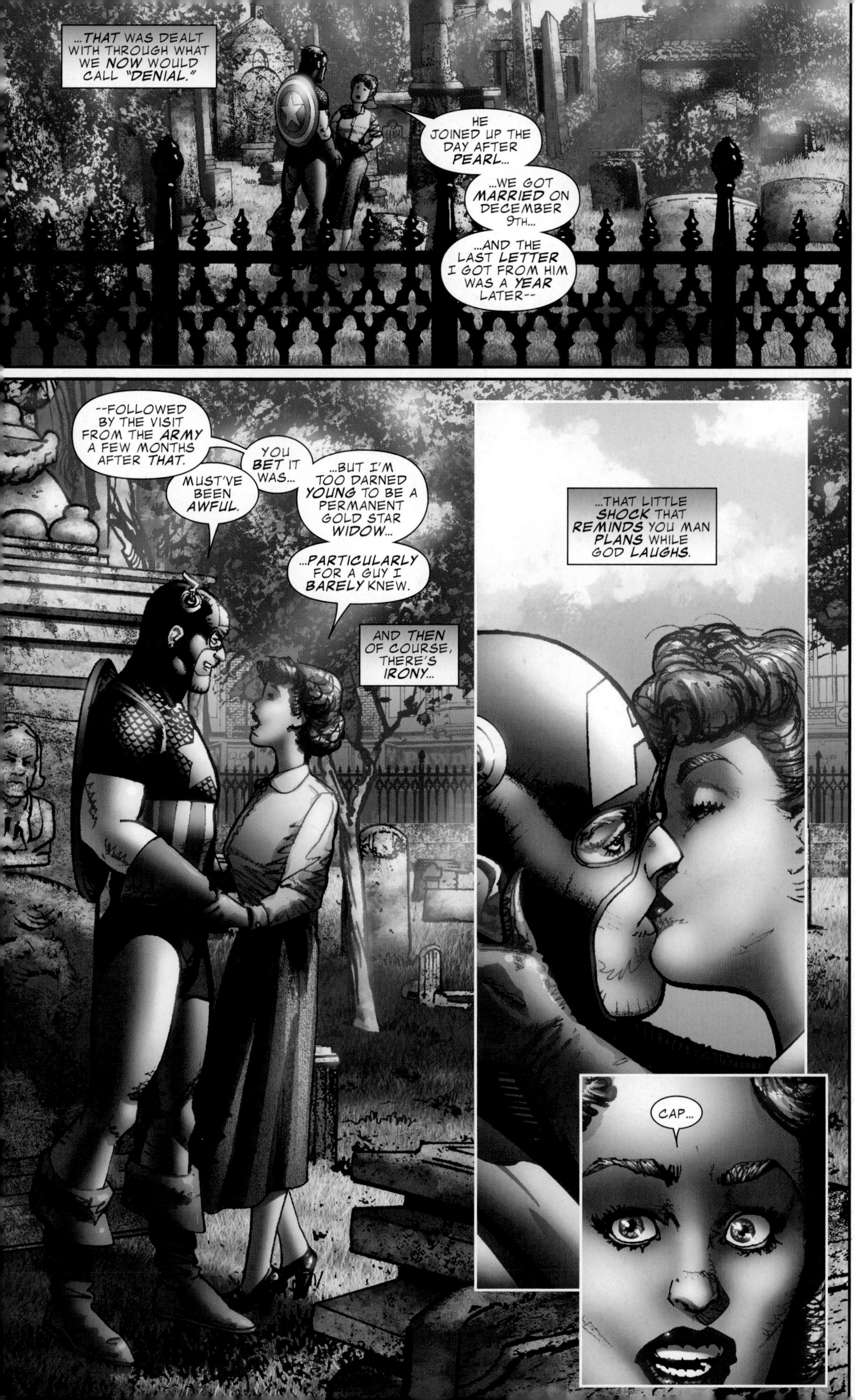
...THAT WAS DEALT WITH THROUGH WHAT WE NOW WOULD CALL "DENIAL."
HE JOINED UP THE DAY AFTER PEARL...
...WE GOT MARRIED ON DECEMBER 9TH...
...AND THE LAST LETTER I GOT FROM HIM WAS A YEAR LATER--
--FOLLOWED BY THE VISIT FROM THE ARMY A FEW MONTHS AFTER THAT.
MUST'VE BEEN AWFUL.
YOU BET IT WAS...
...BUT I'M TOO DARNED YOUNG TO BE A PERMANENT GOLD STAR WIDOW...
...PARTICULARLY FOR A GUY I BARELY KNEW.
AND THEN OF COURSE, THERE'S IRONY...
...THAT LITTLE SHOCK THAT REMINDS YOU MAN PLANS WHILE GOD LAUGHS.
CAP...

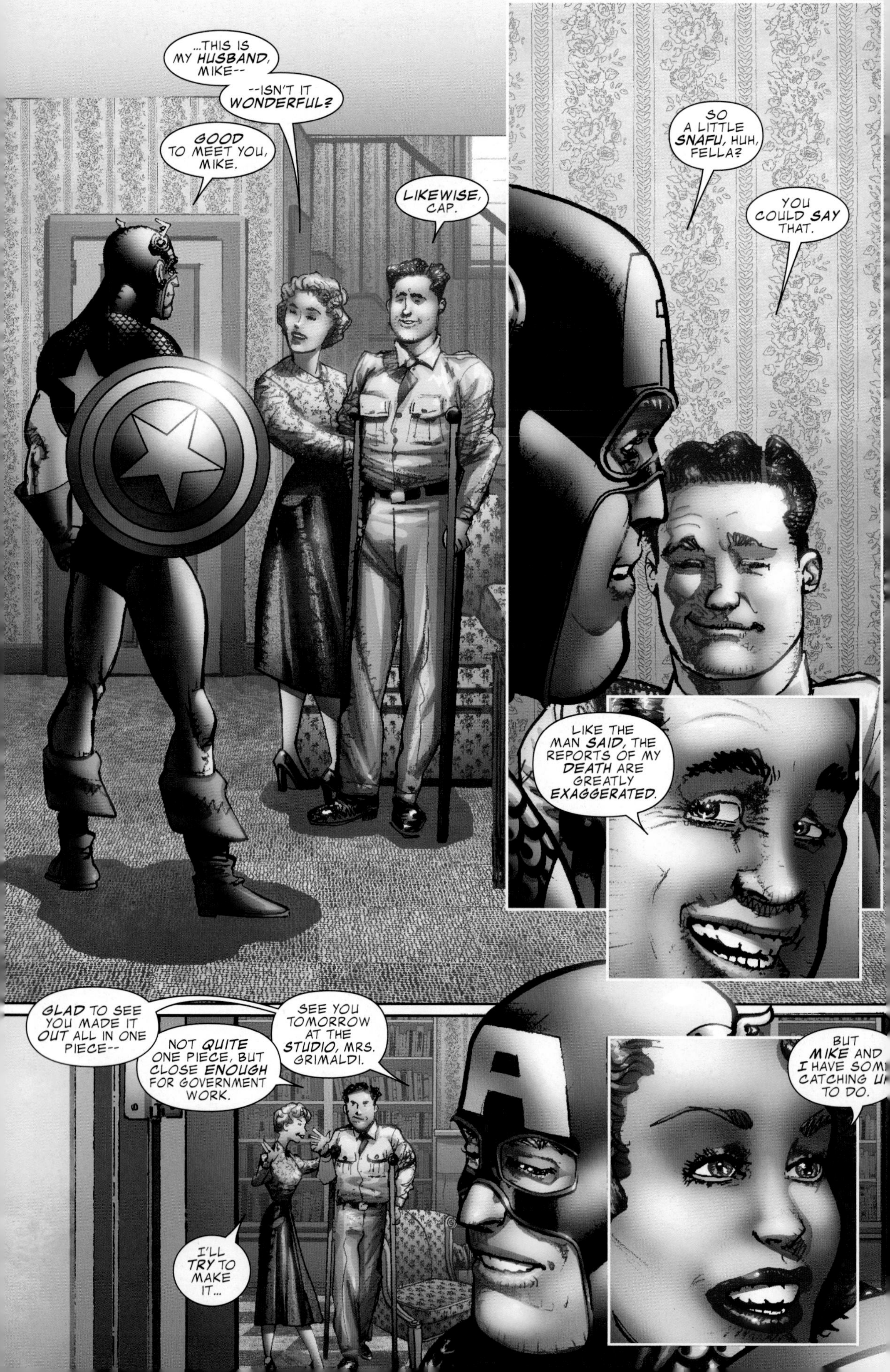
...THIS IS MY HUSBAND, MIKE--
--ISN'T IT WONDERFUL?
GOOD TO MEET YOU, MIKE.
LIKEWISE, CAP.
SO A LITTLE SNAFU, HUH, FELLA?
YOU COULD SAY THAT.
LIKE THE MAN SAID, THE REPORTS OF MY DEATH ARE GREATLY EXAGGERATED.
GLAD TO SEE YOU MADE IT OUT ALL IN ONE PIECE--
NOT QUITE ONE PIECE, BUT CLOSE ENOUGH FOR GOVERNMENT WORK.
SEE YOU TOMORROW AT THE STUDIO, MRS. GRIMALDI.
I'LL TRY TO MAKE IT...
BUT MIKE AND I HAVE SOM
CATCHING U
TO DO.

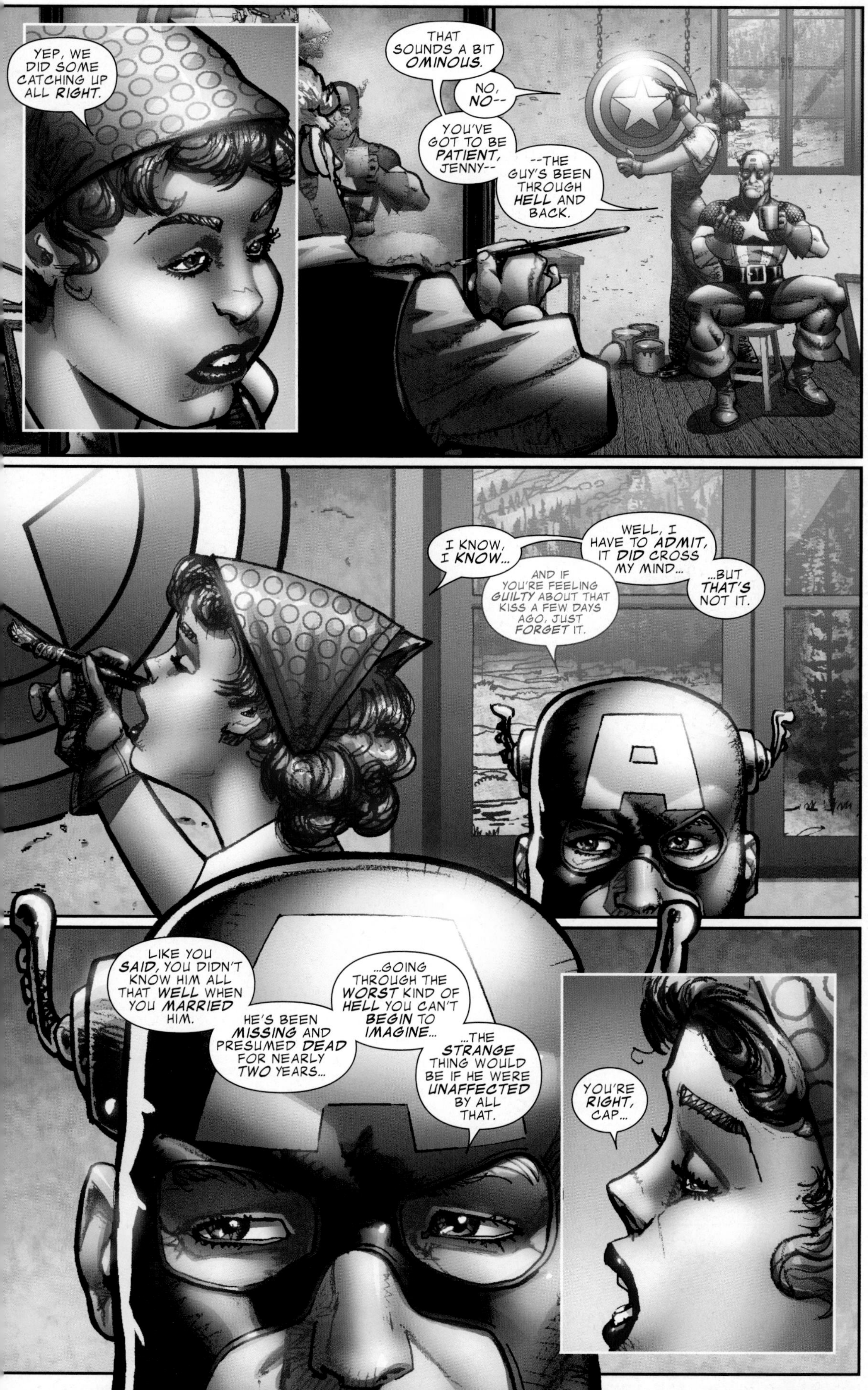
YEP, WE DID SOME CATCHING UP ALL RIGHT.
THAT SOUNDS A BIT OMINOUS.
NO, NO--
YOU'VE GOT TO BE PATIENT, JENNY--
--THE GUY'S BEEN THROUGH HELL AND BACK.
I KNOW, I KNOW...
AND IF YOU'RE FEELING GUILTY ABOUT THAT KISS A FEW DAYS AGO, JUST FORGET IT.
WELL, I HAVE TO ADMIT, IT DID CROSS MY MIND...
...BUT THAT'S NOT IT.
LIKE YOU SAID, YOU DIDN'T KNOW HIM ALL THAT WELL WHEN YOU MARRIED HIM.
HE'S BEEN MISSING AND PRESUMED DEAD FOR NEARLY TWO YEARS...
...GOING THROUGH THE WORST KIND OF HELL YOU CAN'T BEGIN TO IMAGINE...
...THE STRANGE THING WOULD BE IF HE WERE UNAFFECTED BY ALL THAT.
YOU'RE RIGHT, CAP...

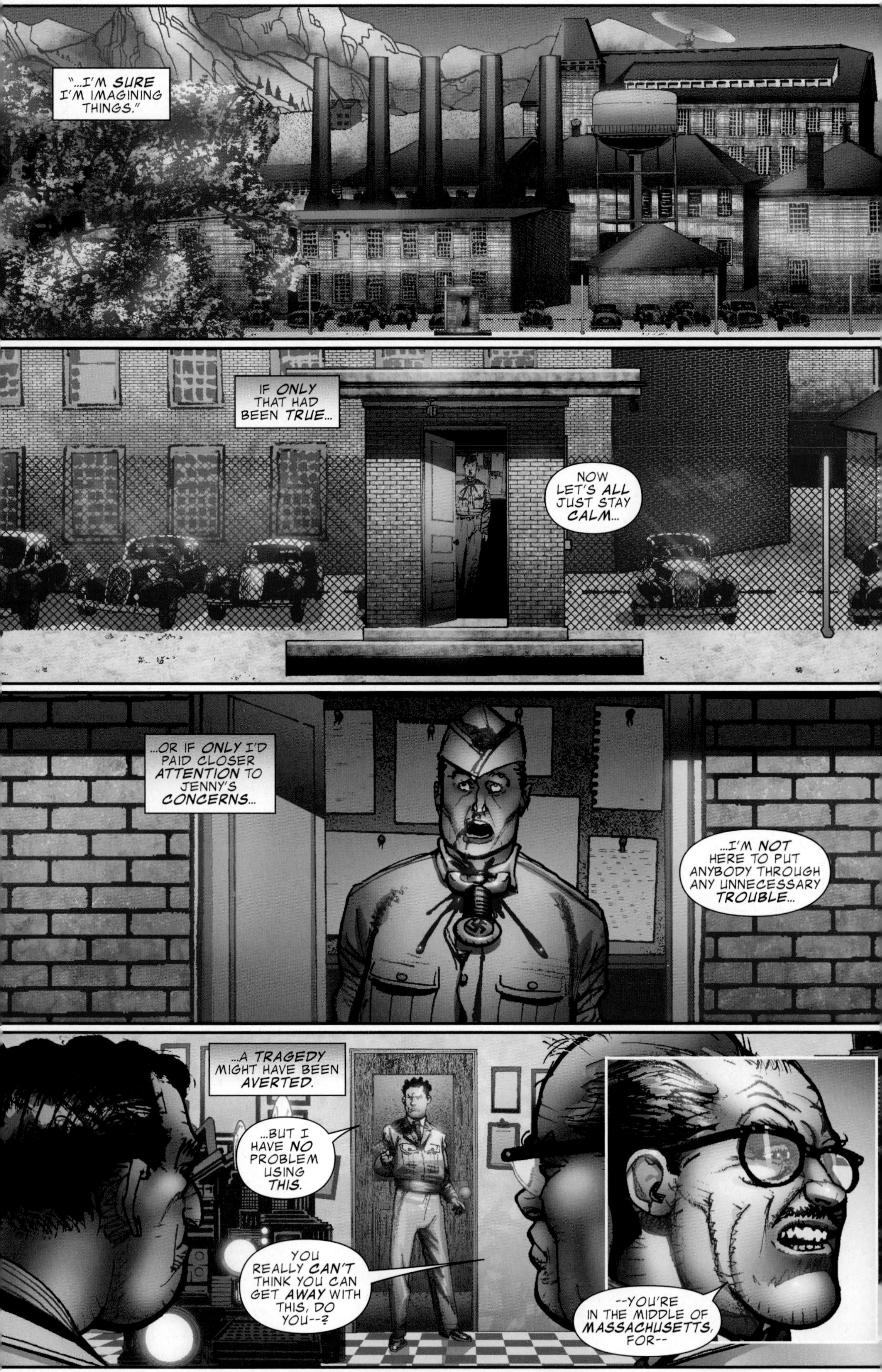
"...I'M SURE I'M IMAGINING THINGS."
IF ONLY THAT HAD BEEN TRUE...
NOW LET'S ALL JUST STAY CALM...
...OR IF ONLY I'D PAID CLOSER ATTENTION TO JENNY'S CONCERNS...
...I'M NOT HERE TO PUT ANYBODY THROUGH ANY UNNECESSARY TROUBLE...
...A TRAGEDY MIGHT HAVE BEEN AVERTED.
...BUT I HAVE NO PROBLEM USING THIS.
YOU REALLY CAN'T THINK YOU CAN GET AWAY WITH THIS, DO YOU--?
--YOU'RE IN THE MIDDLE OF MASSACHUSETTS, FOR--

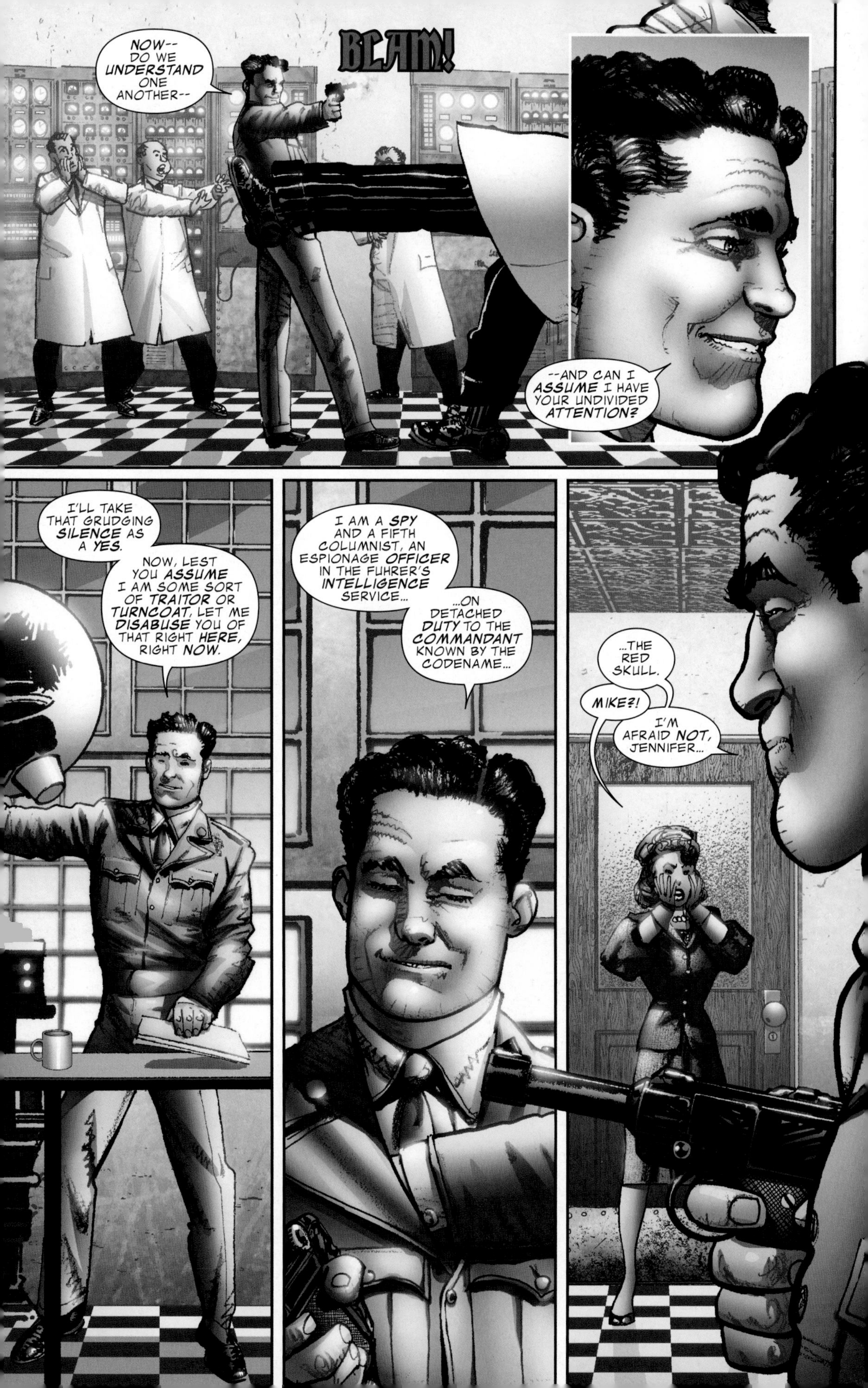
NOW-- DO WE UNDERSTAND ONE ANOTHER--
BLAM!
--AND CAN I ASSUME I HAVE YOUR UNDIVIDED ATTENTION?
I'LL TAKE THAT GRUDGING SILENCE AS A YES.
NOW, LEST YOU ASSUME I AM SOME SORT OF TRAITOR OR TURNCOAT, LET ME DISABUSE YOU OF THAT RIGHT HERE, RIGHT NOW.
I AM A SPY AND A FIFTH COLUMNIST, AN ESPIONAGE OFFICER IN THE FUHRER'S INTELLIGENCE SERVICE...
...ON DETACHED DUTY TO THE COMMANDANT KNOWN BY THE CODENAME...
...THE RED SKULL.
MIKE?!
I'M AFRAID NOT, JENNIFER...

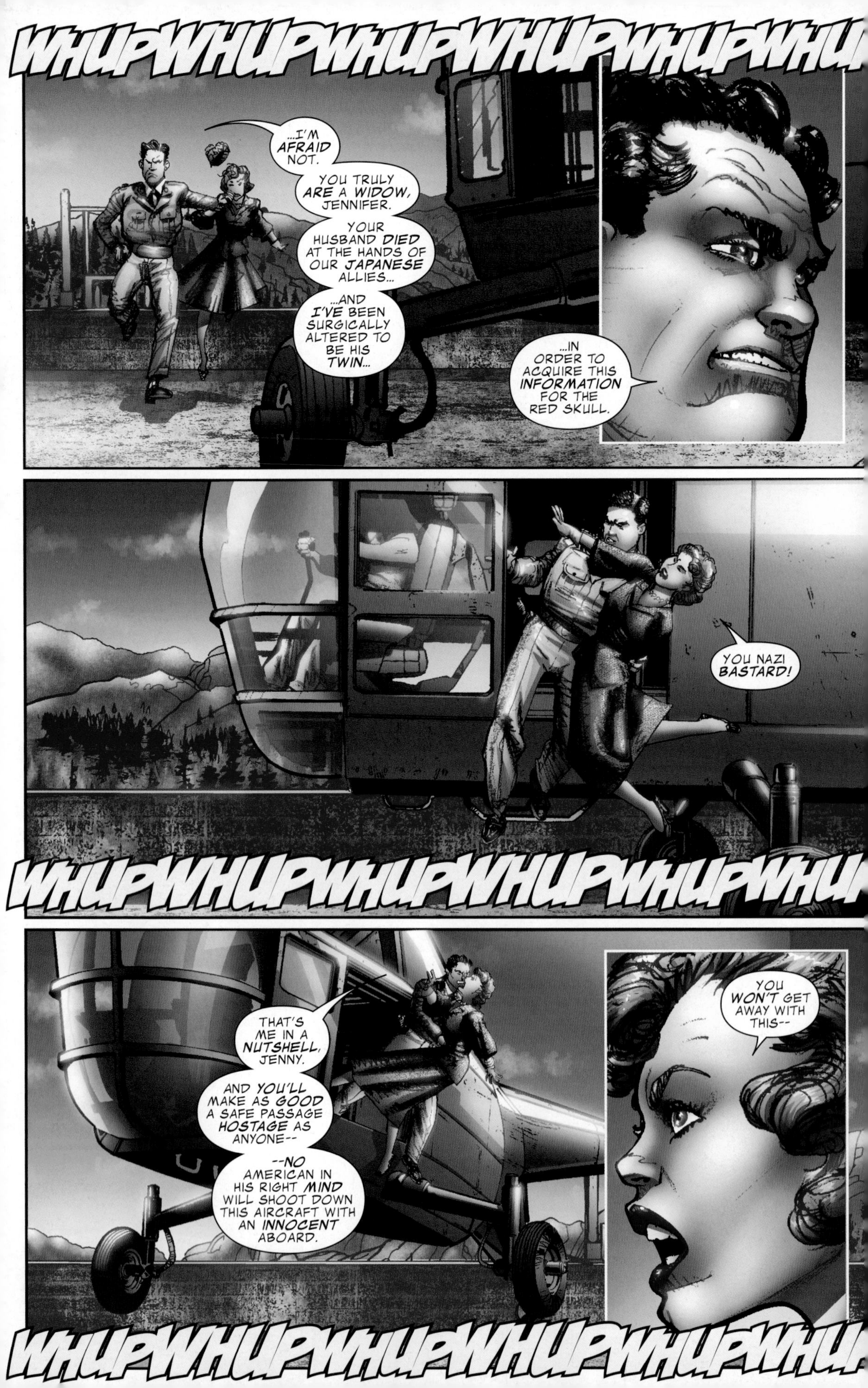
WHUPWHUPWHUPWHUPWHUPWHU
...I'M AFRAID NOT.
YOU TRULY ARE A WIDOW, JENNIFER.
YOUR HUSBAND DIED AT THE HANDS OF OUR JAPANESE ALLIES...
...AND I'VE BEEN SURGICALLY ALTERED TO BE HIS TWIN...
...IN ORDER TO ACQUIRE THIS INFORMATION FOR THE RED SKULL.
YOU NAZI BASTARD!
WHUPWHUPWHUPWHUPWHUPWHU
THAT'S ME IN A NUTSHELL, JENNY.
AND YOU'LL MAKE AS GOOD A SAFE PASSAGE HOSTAGE AS ANYONE--
--NO AMERICAN IN HIS RIGHT MIND WILL SHOOT DOWN THIS AIRCRAFT WITH AN INNOCENT ABOARD.
YOU WON'T GET AWAY WITH THIS--
WHUPWHUPWHUPWHUPWHUPWHU

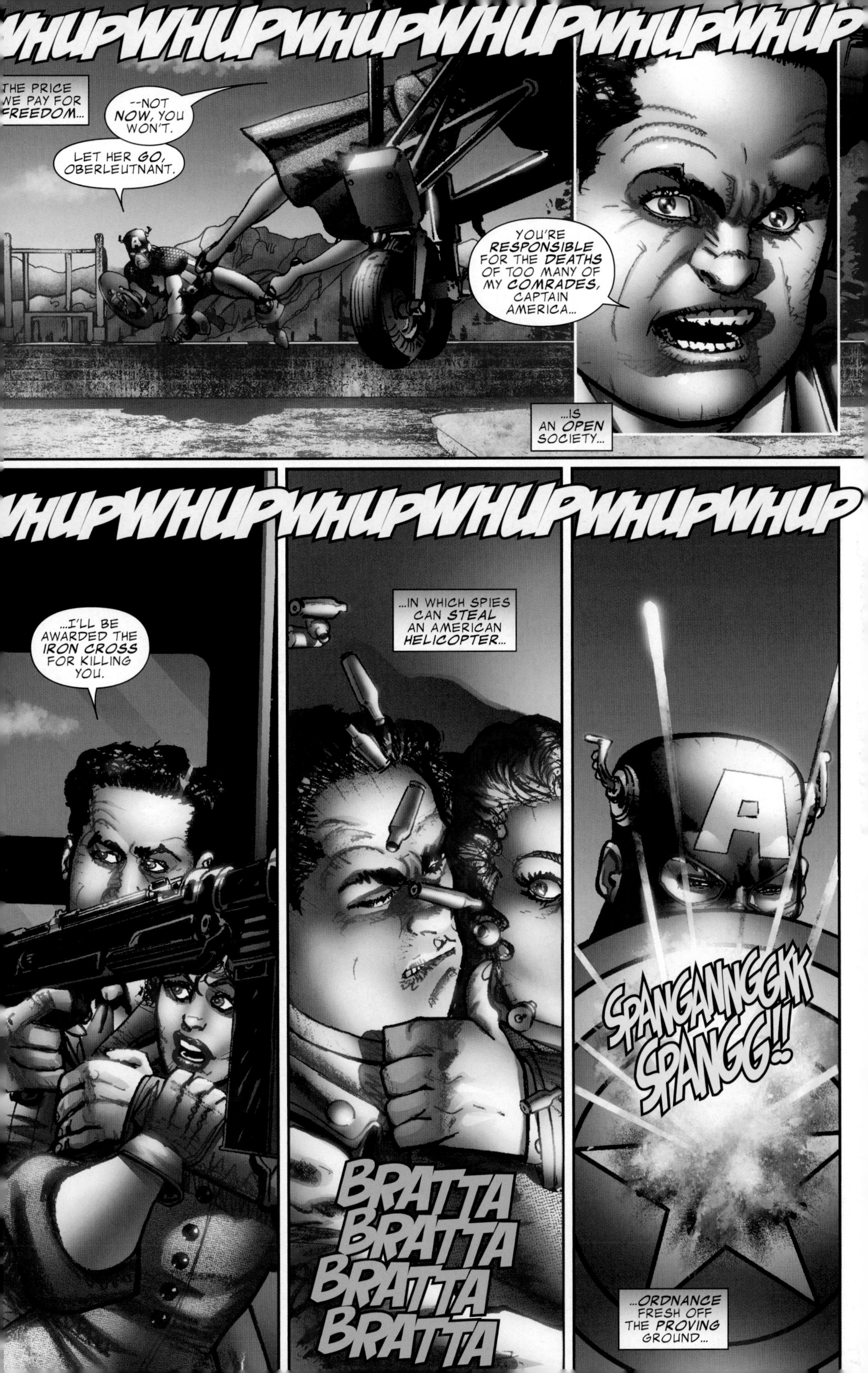
WHUPWHUPWHUPWHUPWHUPWHUP
THE PRICE WE PAY FOR FREEDOM...
LET HER GO, OBERLEUTNANT.
--NOT NOW, YOU WON'T.
YOU'RE RESPONSIBLE FOR THE DEATHS OF TOO MANY OF MY COMRADES, CAPTAIN AMERICA...
...IS AN OPEN SOCIETY...
WHUPWHUPWHUPWHUPWHUPWHUP
...I'LL BE AWARDED THE IRON CROSS FOR KILLING YOU.
...IN WHICH SPIES CAN STEAL AN AMERICAN HELICOPTER...
BRATTA BRATTA BRATTA BRATTA
SPANGANNGGKK SPANGG!!
...ORDNANCE FRESH OFF THE PROVING GROUND...

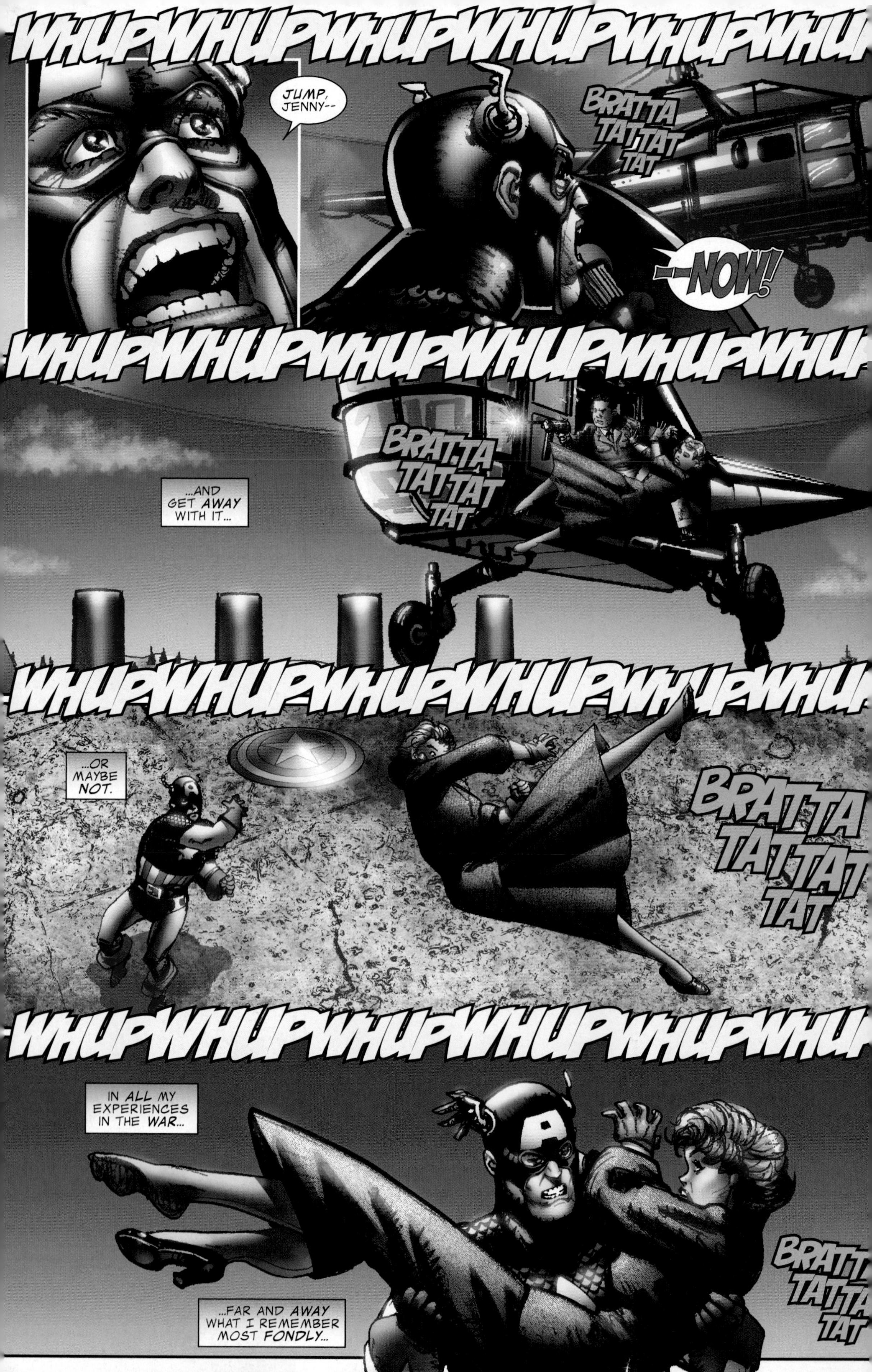
WHUPWHUPWHUPWHUPWHUPWHU
JUMP, JENNY--
BRATTA TATTAT TAT
--NOW!
WHUPWHUPWHUPWHUPWHUPWHU
...AND GET AWAY WITH IT...
BRAT-TA TATTAT TAT
WHUPWHUPWHUPWHUPWHUPWHU
...OR MAYBE NOT.
BRATTA TATTAT TAT
WHUPWHUPWHUPWHUPWHUPWHU
IN ALL MY EXPERIENCES IN THE WAR...
...FAR AND AWAY WHAT I REMEMBER MOST FONDLY...
BRATT TATTA TAT

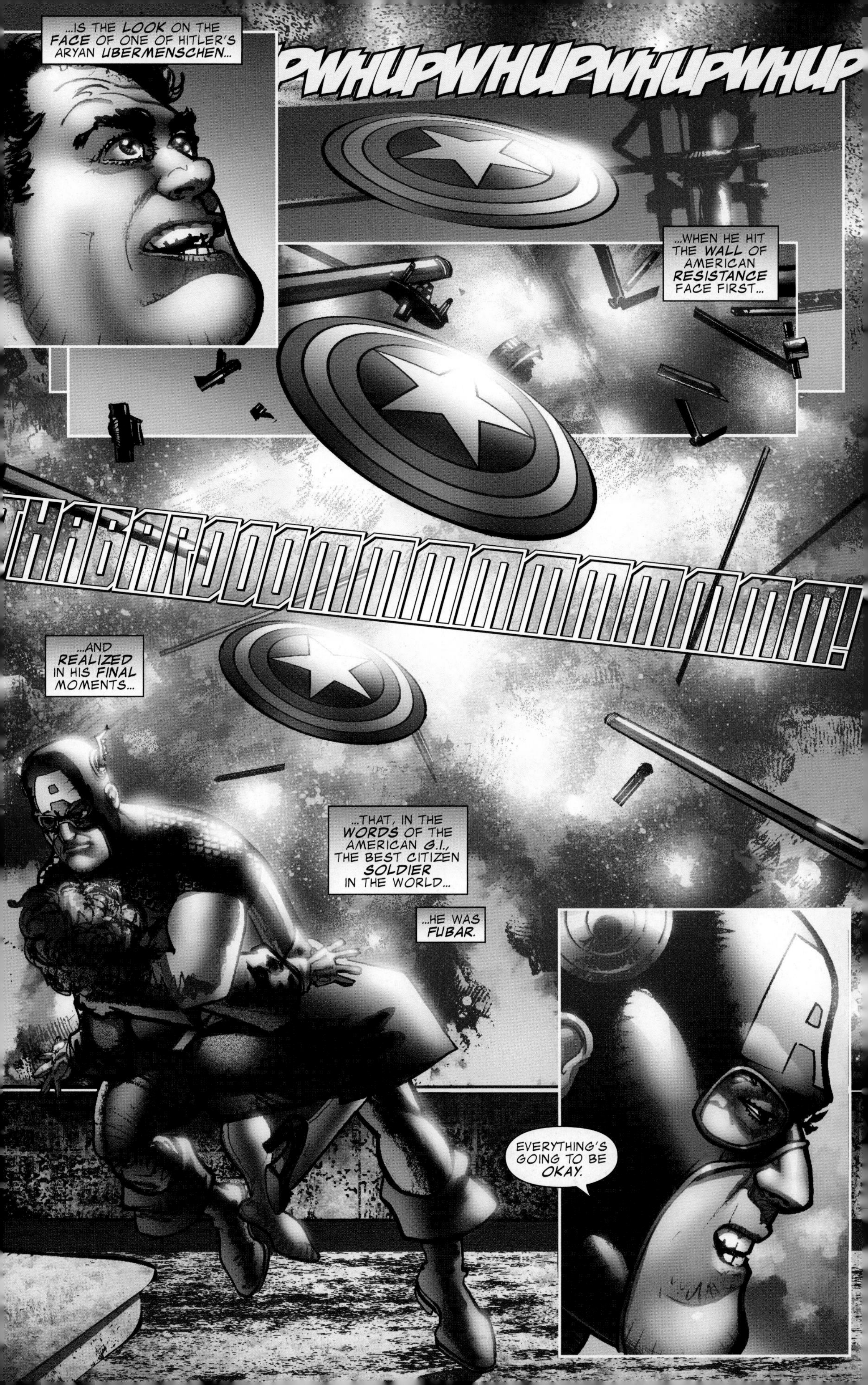
...IS THE LOOK ON THE FACE OF ONE OF HITLER'S ARYAN UBERMENSCHEN...
PWHUPWHUPWHUPWHUP
...WHEN HE HIT THE WALL OF AMERICAN RESISTANCE FACE FIRST...
THABAROOOOMMMMMMMMMMMMMM!
...AND REALIZED IN HIS FINAL MOMENTS...
...THAT, IN THE WORDS OF THE AMERICAN G.I., THE BEST CITIZEN SOLDIER IN THE WORLD...
...HE WAS FUBAR.
EVERYTHING'S GOING TO BE OKAY.

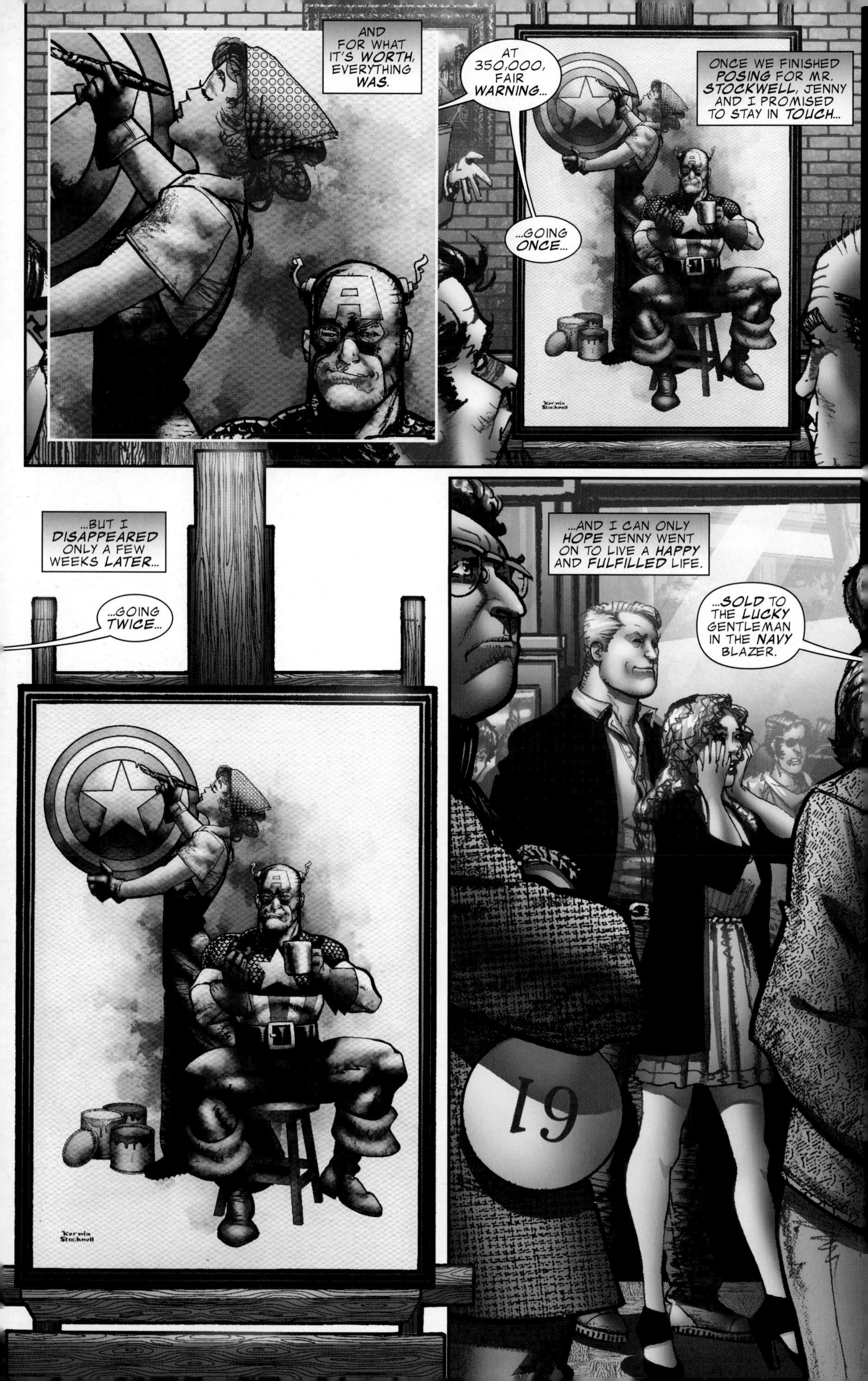

AND FOR WHAT IT'S WORTH, EVERYTHING WAS.
AT 350,000, FAIR WARNING...
ONCE WE FINISHED POSING FOR MR. STOCKWELL, JENNY AND I PROMISED TO STAY IN TOUCH...
...GOING ONCE...
Kerwin Stockwell
...BUT I DISAPPEARED ONLY A FEW WEEKS LATER...
...GOING TWICE...
...AND I CAN ONLY HOPE JENNY WENT ON TO LIVE A HAPPY AND FULFILLED LIFE.
...SOLD TO THE LUCKY GENTLEMAN IN THE NAVY BLAZER.
Kerwin Stockwell
19

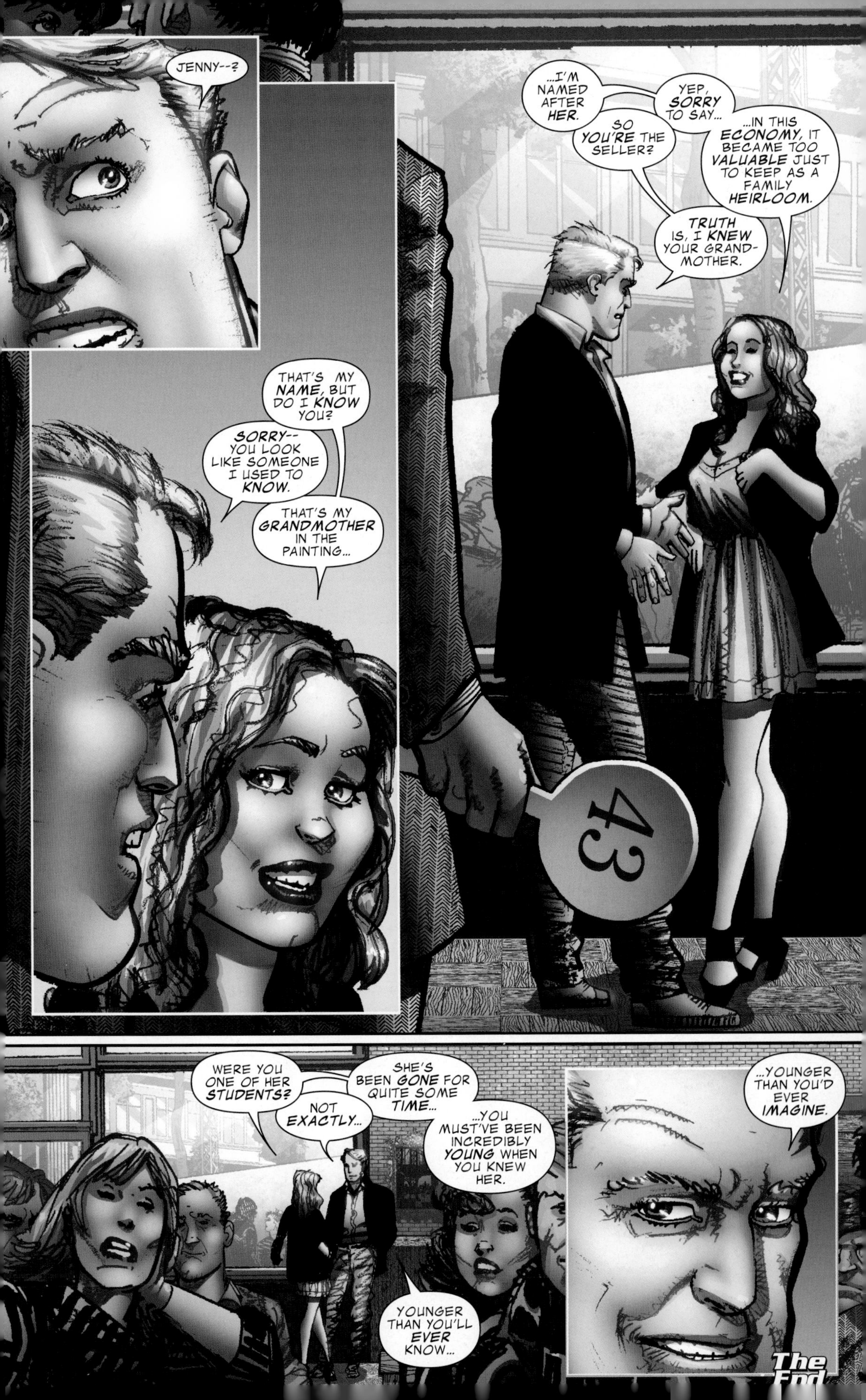
JENNY--?
THAT'S MY NAME, BUT DO I KNOW YOU?
SORRY-- YOU LOOK LIKE SOMEONE I USED TO KNOW.
THAT'S MY GRANDMOTHER IN THE PAINTING...
...I'M NAMED AFTER HER.
SO YOU'RE THE SELLER?
YEP, SORRY TO SAY...
...IN THIS ECONOMY, IT BECAME TOO VALUABLE JUST TO KEEP AS A FAMILY HEIRLOOM.
TRUTH IS, I KNEW YOUR GRAND-MOTHER.
43
WERE YOU ONE OF HER STUDENTS?
NOT EXACTLY...
SHE'S BEEN GONE FOR QUITE SOME TIME...
...YOU MUST'VE BEEN INCREDIBLY YOUNG WHEN YOU KNEW HER.
YOUNGER THAN YOU'LL EVER KNOW...
...YOUNGER THAN YOU'D EVER IMAGINE.
The End

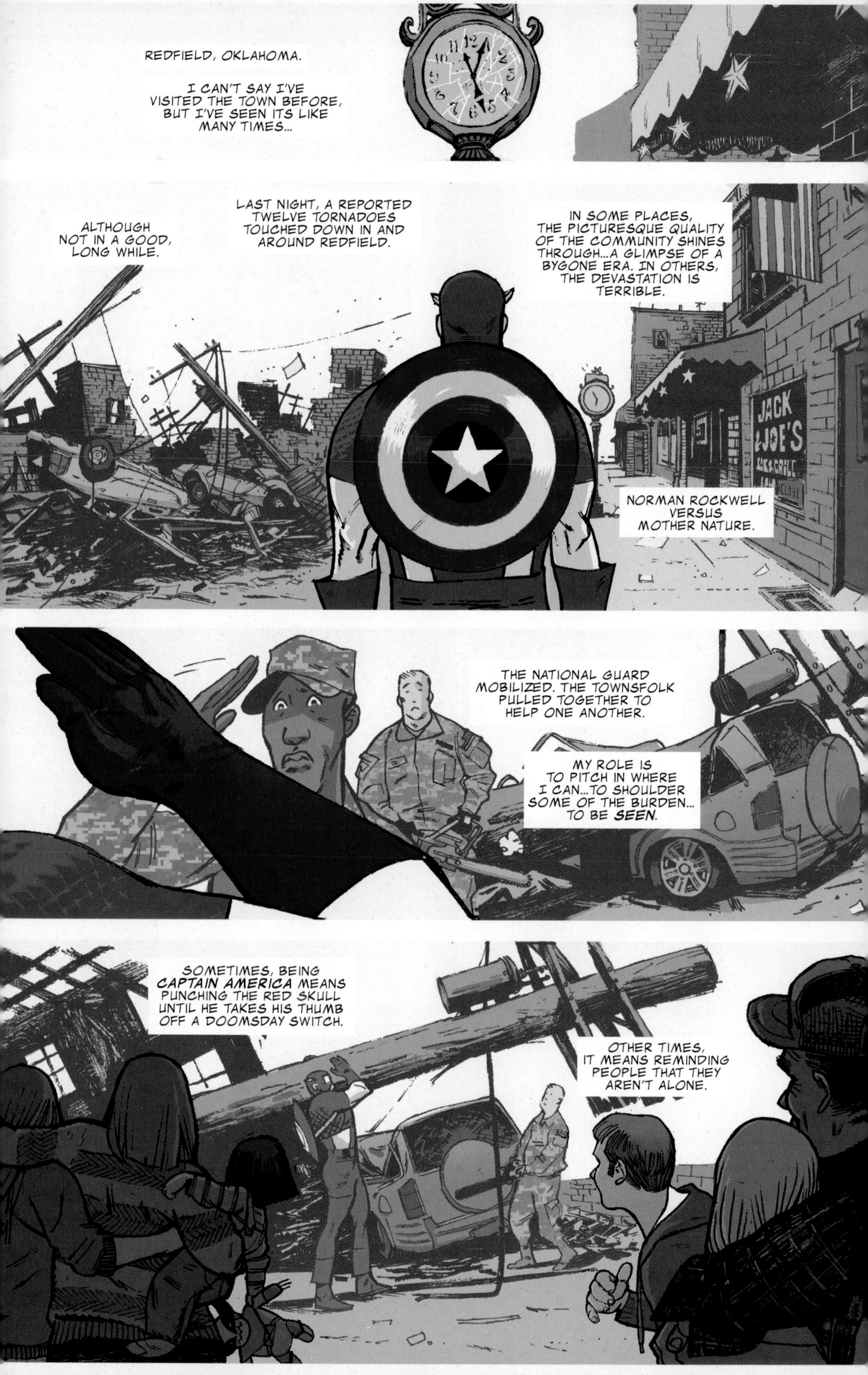
REDFIELD, OKLAHOMA.
I CAN'T SAY I'VE VISITED THE TOWN BEFORE, BUT I'VE SEEN ITS LIKE MANY TIMES...
ALTHOUGH NOT IN A GOOD, LONG WHILE.
LAST NIGHT, A REPORTED TWELVE TORNADOES TOUCHED DOWN IN AND AROUND REDFIELD.
IN SOME PLACES, THE PICTURESQUE QUALITY OF THE COMMUNITY SHINES THROUGH...A GLIMPSE OF A BYGONE ERA. IN OTHERS, THE DEVASTATION IS TERRIBLE.
JACK &JOE'S
NORMAN ROCKWELL VERSUS MOTHER NATURE.
THE NATIONAL GUARD MOBILIZED. THE TOWNSFOLK PULLED TOGETHER TO HELP ONE ANOTHER.
MY ROLE IS TO PITCH IN WHERE I CAN...TO SHOULDER SOME OF THE BURDEN... TO BE *SEEN*.
SOMETIMES, BEING *CAPTAIN AMERICA* MEANS PUNCHING THE RED SKULL UNTIL HE TAKES HIS THUMB OFF A DOOMSDAY SWITCH.
OTHER TIMES, IT MEANS REMINDING PEOPLE THAT THEY AREN'T ALONE.

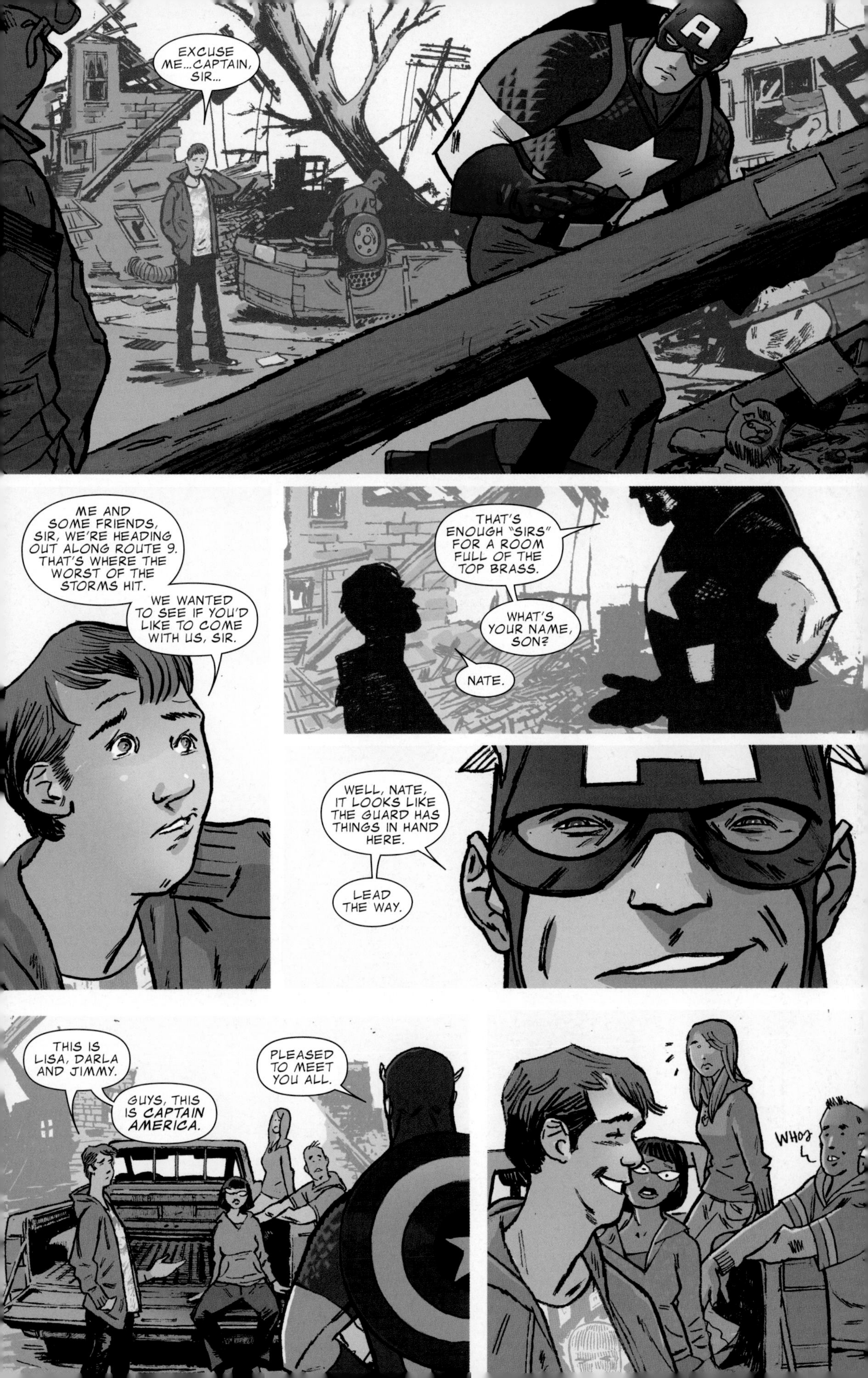
EXCUSE ME...CAPTAIN, SIR...
ME AND SOME FRIENDS, SIR, WE'RE HEADING OUT ALONG ROUTE 9. THAT'S WHERE THE WORST OF THE STORMS HIT.
WE WANTED TO SEE IF YOU'D LIKE TO COME WITH US, SIR.
THAT'S ENOUGH "SIRS" FOR A ROOM FULL OF THE TOP BRASS.
WHAT'S YOUR NAME, SON?
NATE.
WELL, NATE, IT LOOKS LIKE THE GUARD HAS THINGS IN HAND HERE.
LEAD THE WAY.
THIS IS LISA, DARLA AND JIMMY.
GUYS, THIS IS *CAPTAIN AMERICA*.
PLEASED TO MEET YOU ALL.
WHOA

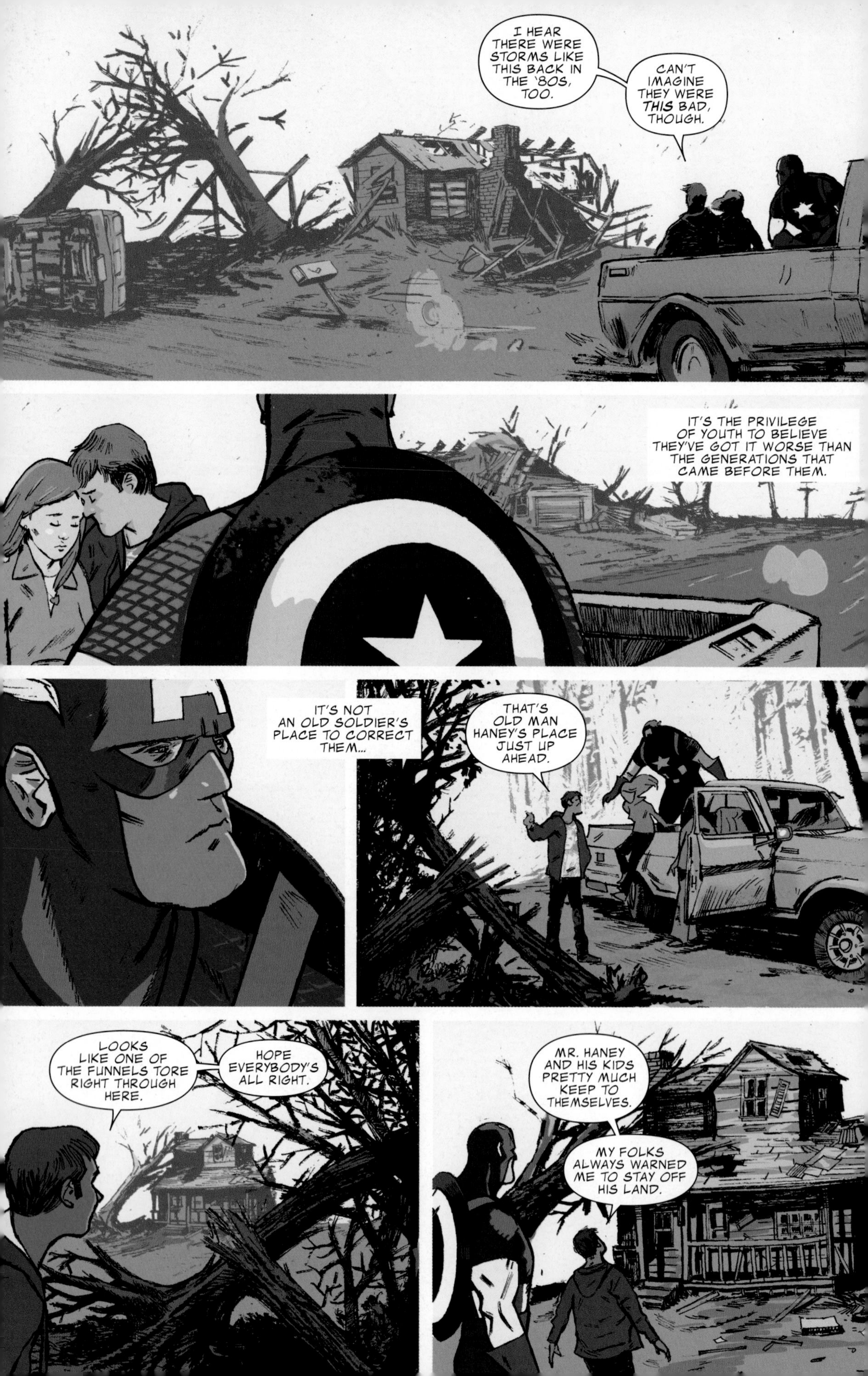
I HEAR THERE WERE STORMS LIKE THIS BACK IN THE '80S, TOO.
CAN'T IMAGINE THEY WERE THIS BAD, THOUGH.
IT'S THE PRIVILEGE OF YOUTH TO BELIEVE THEY'VE GOT IT WORSE THAN THE GENERATIONS THAT CAME BEFORE THEM.
IT'S NOT AN OLD SOLDIER'S PLACE TO CORRECT THEM...
THAT'S OLD MAN HANEY'S PLACE JUST UP AHEAD.
LOOKS LIKE ONE OF THE FUNNELS TORE RIGHT THROUGH HERE.
HOPE EVERYBODY'S ALL RIGHT.
MR. HANEY AND HIS KIDS PRETTY MUCH KEEP TO THEMSELVES.
MY FOLKS ALWAYS WARNED ME TO STAY OFF HIS LAND.

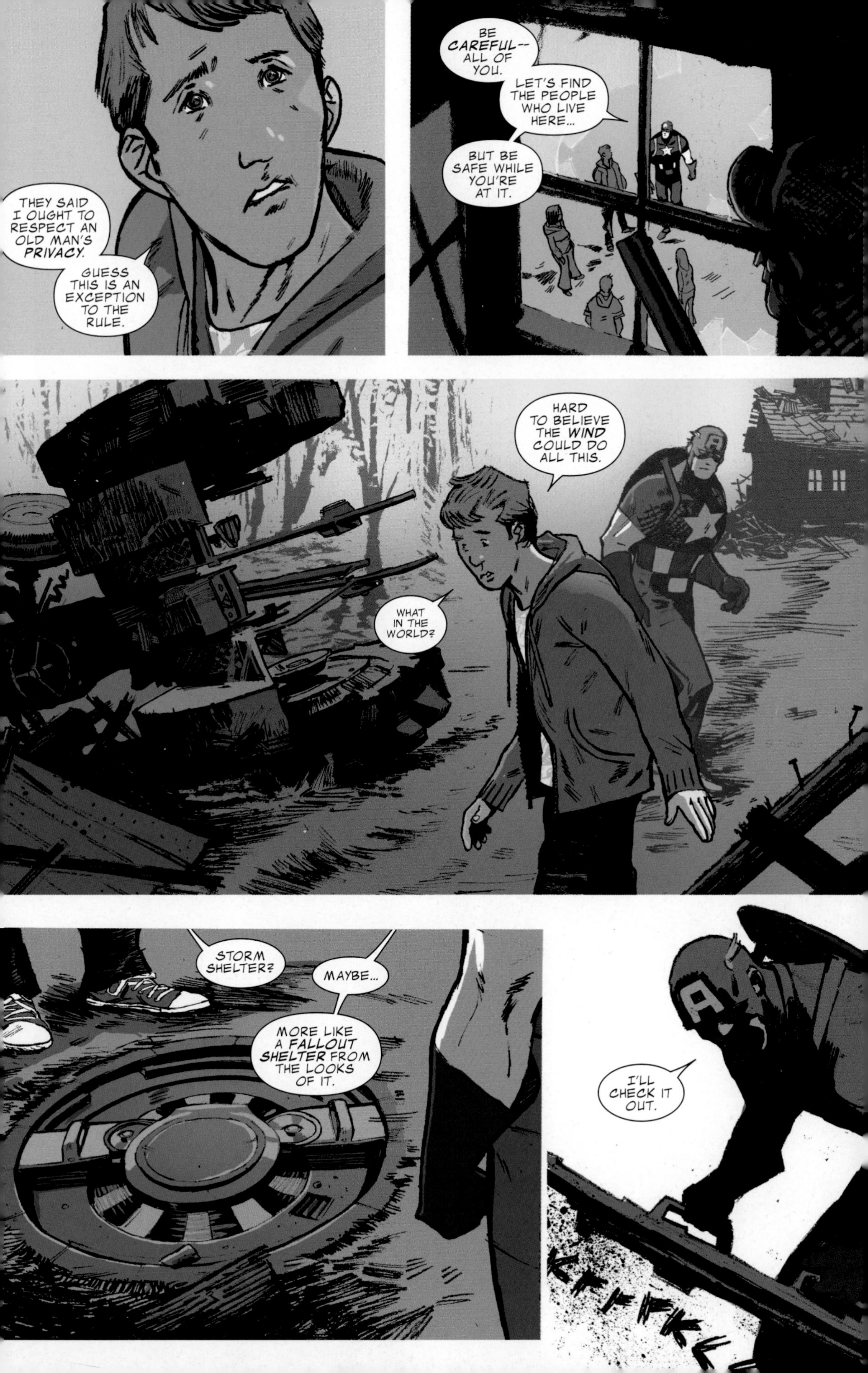
THEY SAID I OUGHT TO RESPECT AN OLD MAN'S PRIVACY.
GUESS THIS IS AN EXCEPTION TO THE RULE.
BE CAREFUL-- ALL OF YOU.
LET'S FIND THE PEOPLE WHO LIVE HERE...
BUT BE SAFE WHILE YOU'RE AT IT.
HARD TO BELIEVE THE WIND COULD DO ALL THIS.
WHAT IN THE WORLD?
STORM SHELTER?
MAYBE...
MORE LIKE A FALLOUT SHELTER FROM THE LOOKS OF IT.
I'LL CHECK IT OUT.

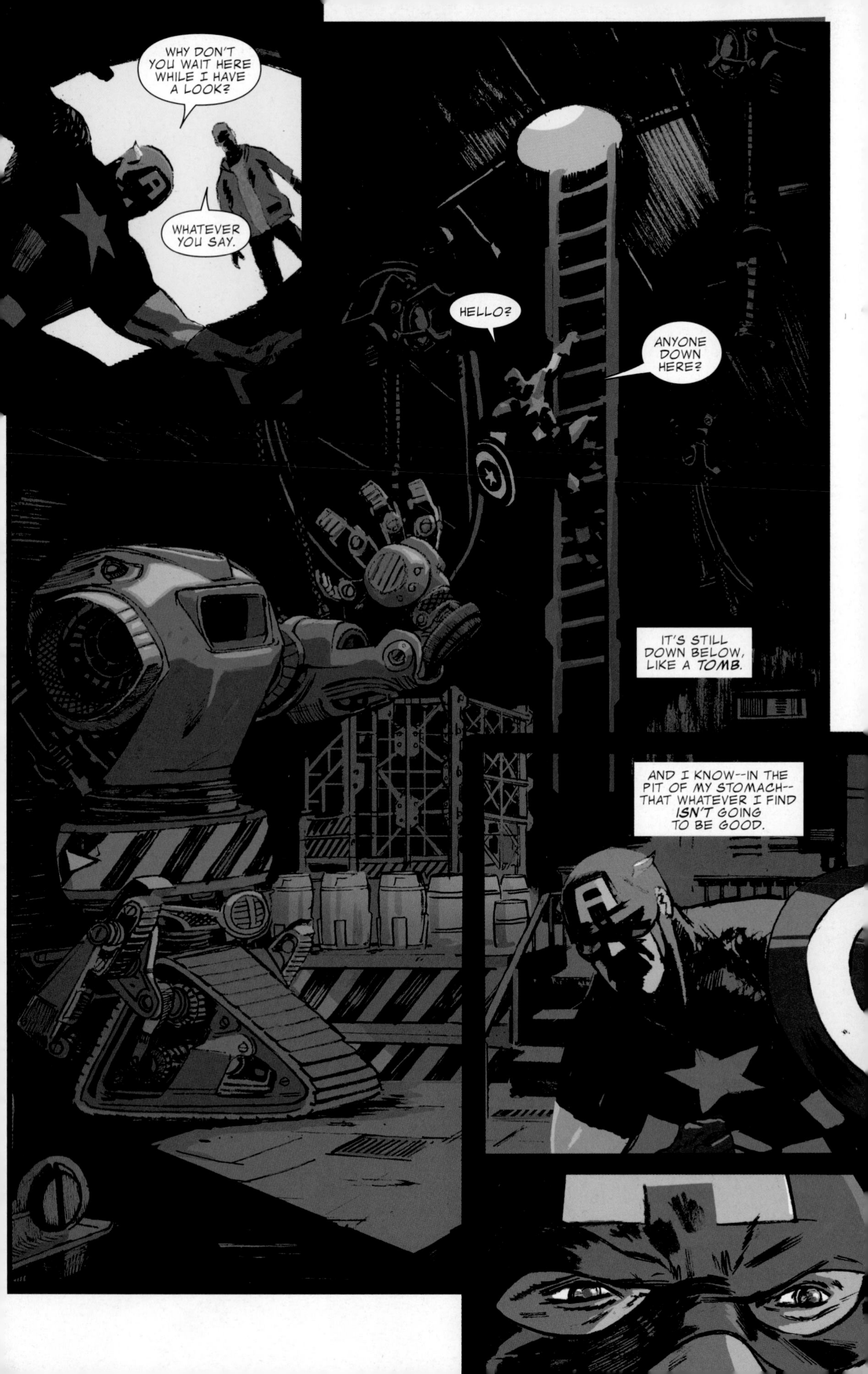

WHY DON'T YOU WAIT HERE WHILE I HAVE A LOOK?
WHATEVER YOU SAY.
HELLO?
ANYONE DOWN HERE?
IT'S STILL DOWN BELOW, LIKE A TOMB.
AND I KNOW--IN THE PIT OF MY STOMACH--THAT WHATEVER I FIND ISN'T GOING TO BE GOOD.

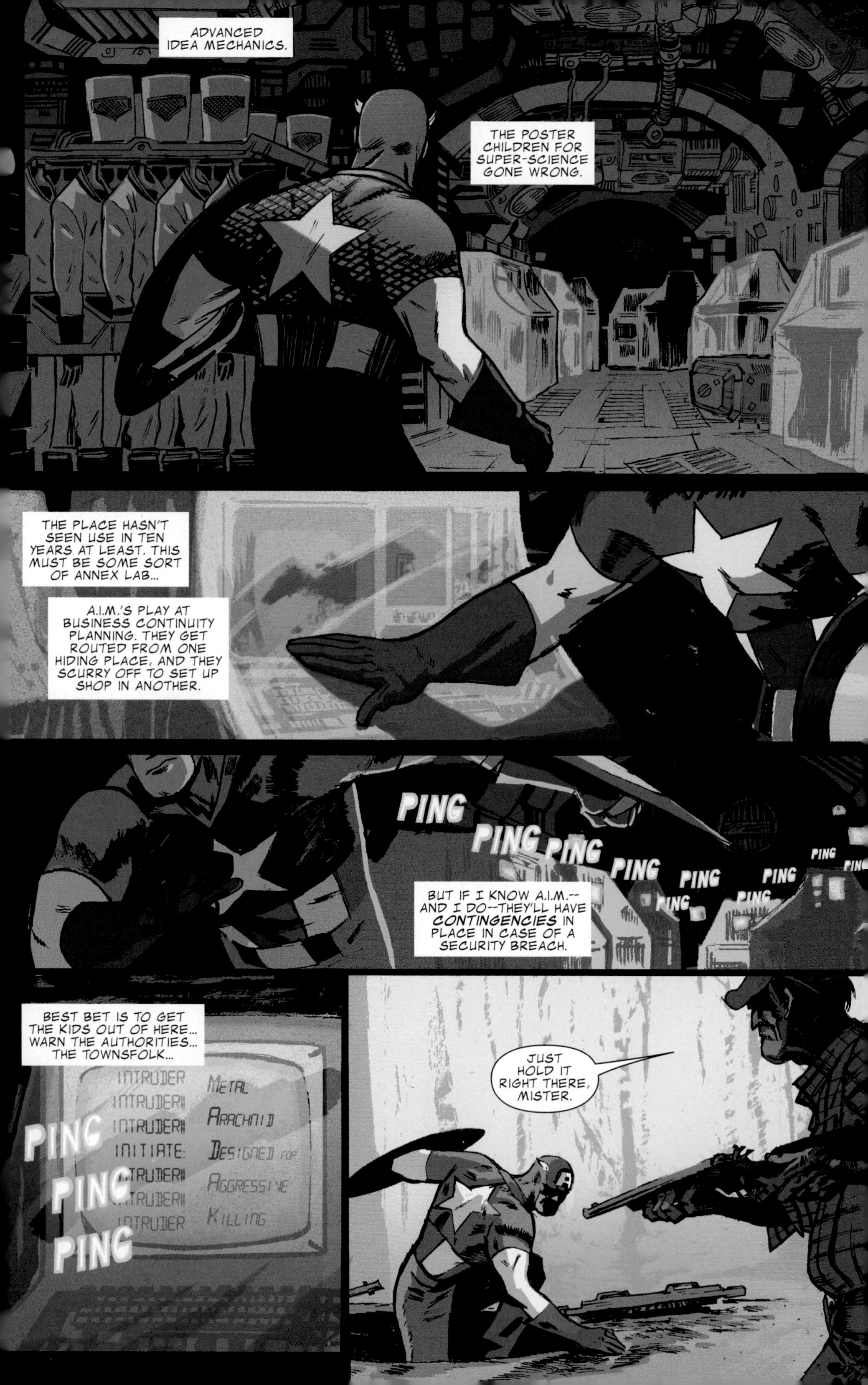
ADVANCED IDEA MECHANICS.
THE POSTER CHILDREN FOR SUPER-SCIENCE GONE WRONG.
THE PLACE HASN'T SEEN USE IN TEN YEARS AT LEAST. THIS MUST BE SOME SORT OF ANNEX LAB...
A.I.M.'S PLAY AT BUSINESS CONTINUITY PLANNING. THEY GET ROUTED FROM ONE HIDING PLACE, AND THEY SCURRY OFF TO SET UP SHOP IN ANOTHER.
PING PING PING PING PING PING PING PING PING
BUT IF I KNOW A.I.M.-- AND I DO--THEY'LL HAVE CONTINGENCIES IN PLACE IN CASE OF A SECURITY BREACH.
BEST BET IS TO GET THE KIDS OUT OF HERE... WARN THE AUTHORITIES... THE TOWNSFOLK...
INTRUDER METAL
INTRUDER!! ARACHNID
INTRUDER!!
INITIATE: DESIGNED FOR
AGGRESSIVE
INTRUDER KILLING
PING PING PING
JUST HOLD IT RIGHT THERE, MISTER.

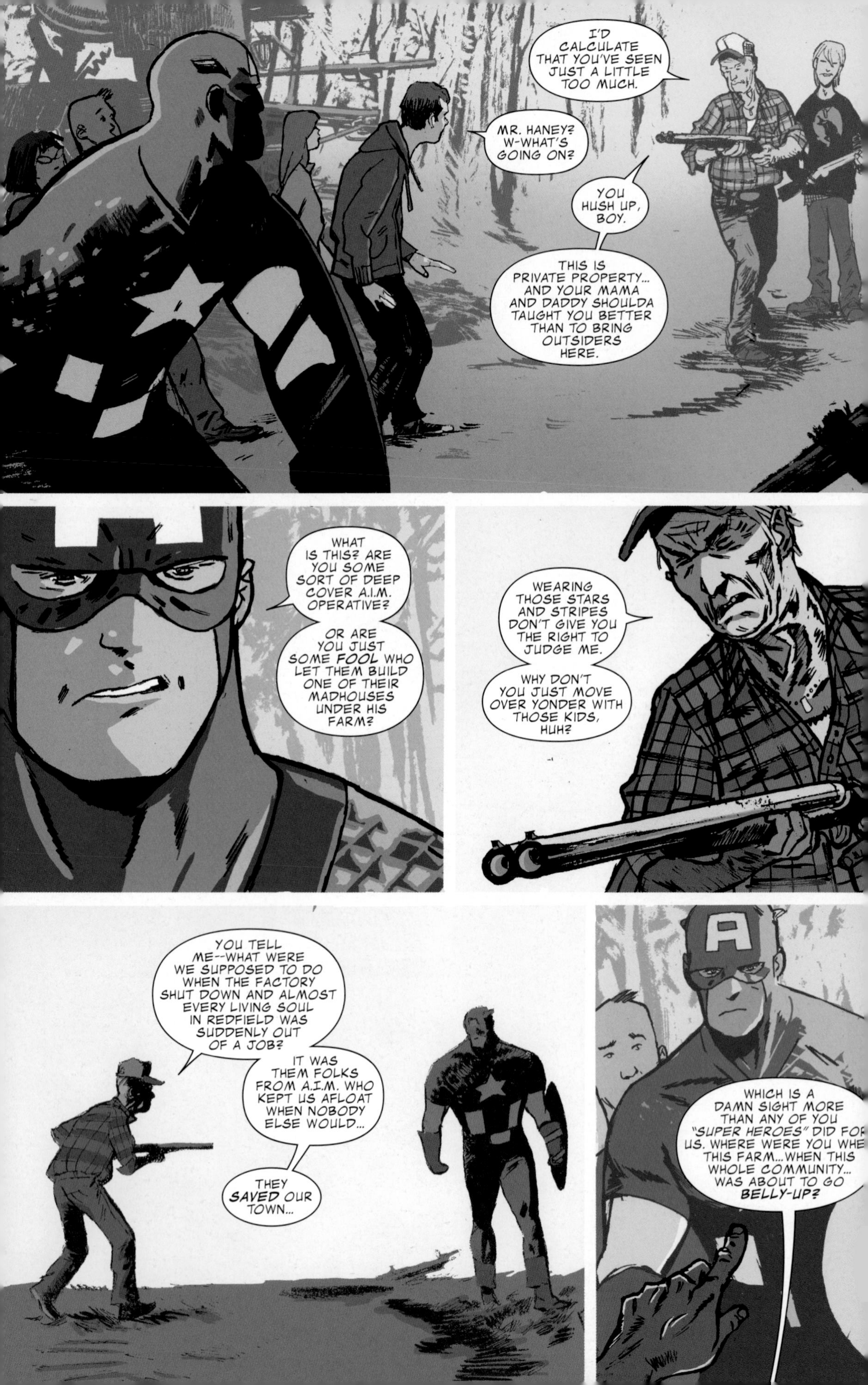
I'D CALCULATE THAT YOU'VE SEEN JUST A LITTLE TOO MUCH.
MR. HANEY? W-WHAT'S GOING ON?
YOU HUSH UP, BOY.
THIS IS PRIVATE PROPERTY... AND YOUR MAMA AND DADDY SHOULDA TAUGHT YOU BETTER THAN TO BRING OUTSIDERS HERE.
WHAT IS THIS? ARE YOU SOME SORT OF DEEP COVER A.I.M. OPERATIVE?
OR ARE YOU JUST SOME FOOL WHO LET THEM BUILD ONE OF THEIR MADHOUSES UNDER HIS FARM?
WEARING THOSE STARS AND STRIPES DON'T GIVE YOU THE RIGHT TO JUDGE ME.
WHY DON'T YOU JUST MOVE OVER YONDER WITH THOSE KIDS, HUH?
YOU TELL ME--WHAT WERE WE SUPPOSED TO DO WHEN THE FACTORY SHUT DOWN AND ALMOST EVERY LIVING SOUL IN REDFIELD WAS SUDDENLY OUT OF A JOB?
IT WAS THEM FOLKS FROM A.I.M. WHO KEPT US AFLOAT WHEN NOBODY ELSE WOULD...
THEY SAVED OUR TOWN...
WHICH IS A DAMN SIGHT MORE THAN ANY OF YOU "SUPER HEROES" DID FOR US. WHERE WERE YOU WHEN THIS FARM...WHEN THIS WHOLE COMMUNITY... WAS ABOUT TO GO BELLY-UP?

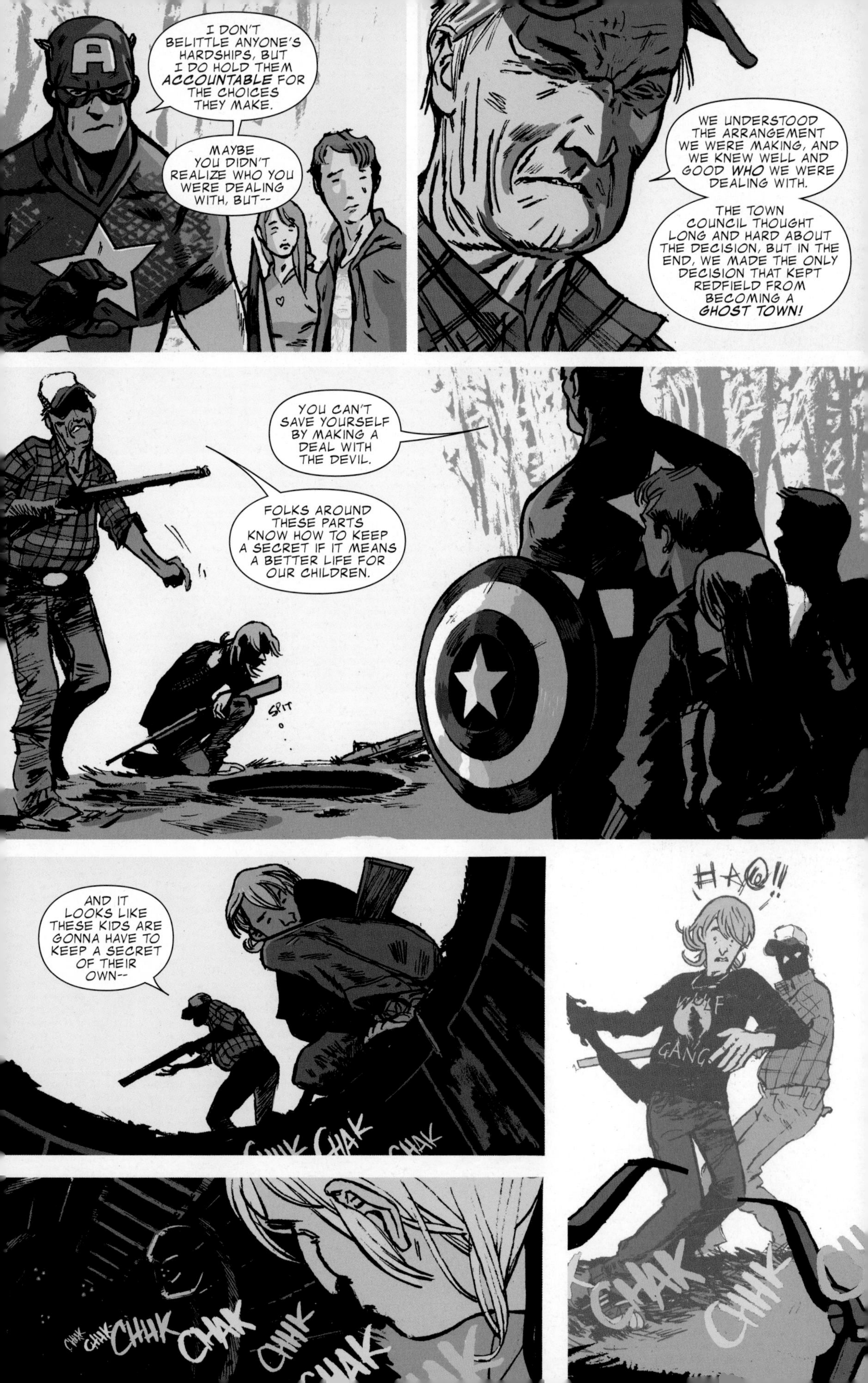
I DON'T BELITTLE ANYONE'S HARDSHIPS, BUT I DO HOLD THEM ACCOUNTABLE FOR THE CHOICES THEY MAKE.
MAYBE YOU DIDN'T REALIZE WHO YOU WERE DEALING WITH, BUT--
WE UNDERSTOOD THE ARRANGEMENT WE WERE MAKING, AND WE KNEW WELL AND GOOD WHO WE WERE DEALING WITH.
THE TOWN COUNCIL THOUGHT LONG AND HARD ABOUT THE DECISION, BUT IN THE END, WE MADE THE ONLY DECISION THAT KEPT REDFIELD FROM BECOMING A GHOST TOWN!
YOU CAN'T SAVE YOURSELF BY MAKING A DEAL WITH THE DEVIL.
FOLKS AROUND THESE PARTS KNOW HOW TO KEEP A SECRET IF IT MEANS A BETTER LIFE FOR OUR CHILDREN.
SPIT
AND IT LOOKS LIKE THESE KIDS ARE GONNA HAVE TO KEEP A SECRET OF THEIR OWN--
CHAK CHAK CHAK
WOLF GANG
CHAK CHAK CHAK CHAK CHAK
CHAK CHAK

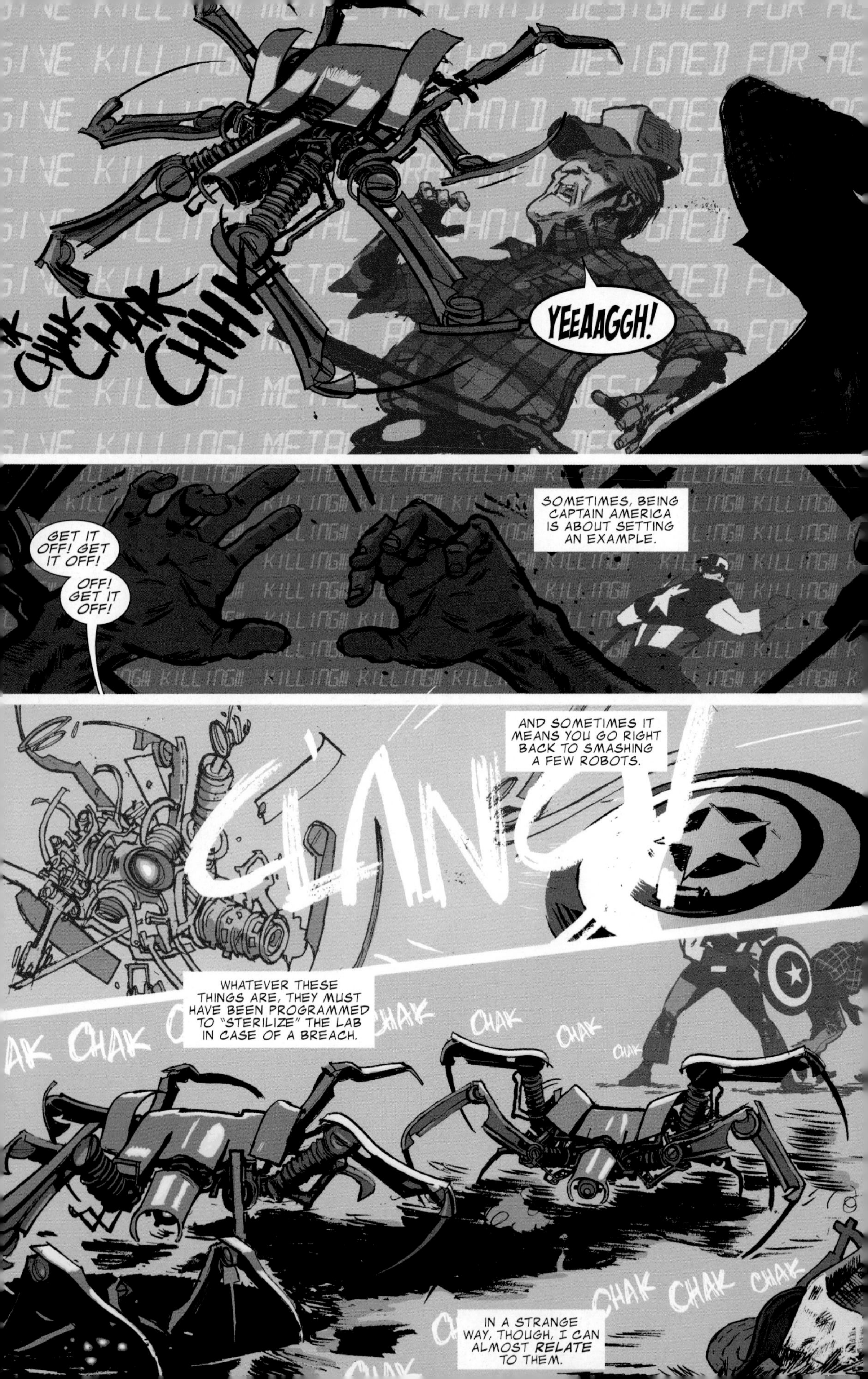
CHUK CHAK CHUK
YEEAAGGH!
GET IT OFF! GET IT OFF!
OFF! GET IT OFF!
SOMETIMES, BEING CAPTAIN AMERICA IS ABOUT SETTING AN EXAMPLE.
AND SOMETIMES IT MEANS YOU GO RIGHT BACK TO SMASHING A FEW ROBOTS.
CLANG!
WHATEVER THESE THINGS ARE, THEY MUST HAVE BEEN PROGRAMMED TO "STERILIZE" THE LAB IN CASE OF A BREACH.
CHAK CHAK CHAK CHAK
IN A STRANGE WAY, THOUGH, I CAN ALMOST *RELATE* TO THEM.
CHAK CHAK CHAK

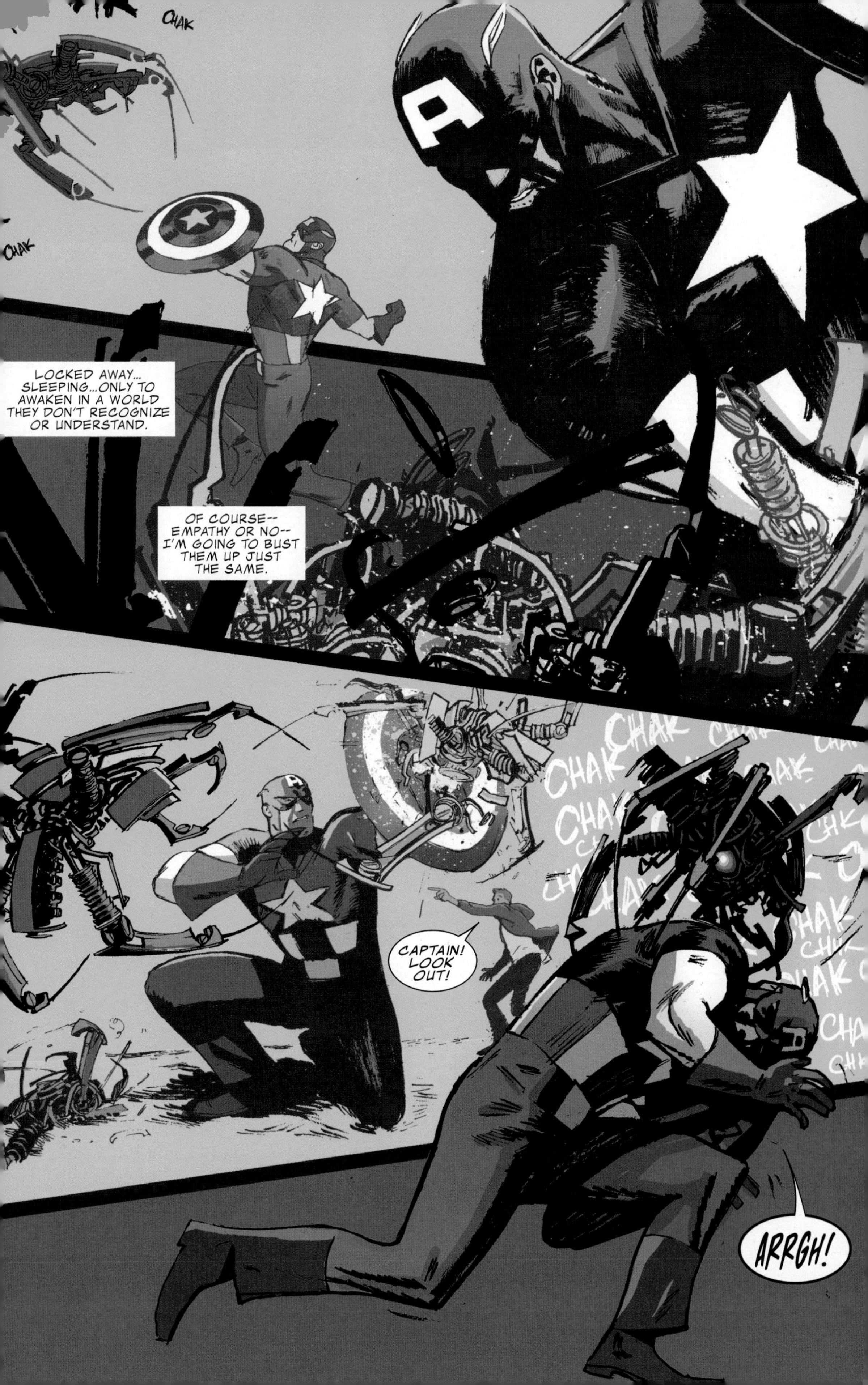
CHAK
CHAK
LOCKED AWAY... SLEEPING...ONLY TO AWAKEN IN A WORLD THEY DON'T RECOGNIZE OR UNDERSTAND.
OF COURSE-- EMPATHY OR NO-- I'M GOING TO BUST THEM UP JUST THE SAME.
CAPTAIN! LOOK OUT!
ARRGH!

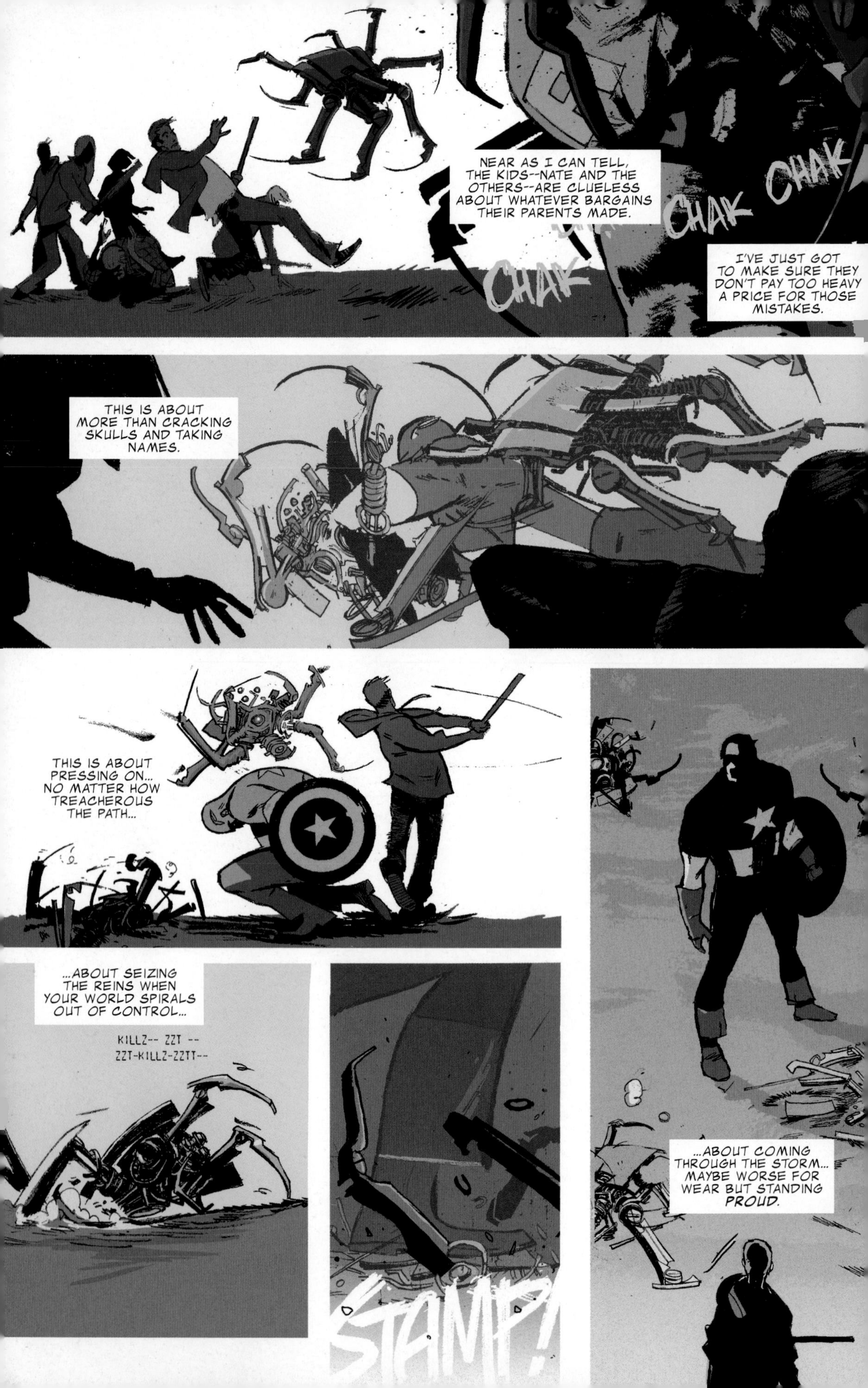
NEAR AS I CAN TELL, THE KIDS--NATE AND THE OTHERS--ARE CLUELESS ABOUT WHATEVER BARGAINS THEIR PARENTS MADE.
CHAK CHAK
CHAK
CHAK
I'VE JUST GOT TO MAKE SURE THEY DON'T PAY TOO HEAVY A PRICE FOR THOSE MISTAKES.
THIS IS ABOUT MORE THAN CRACKING SKULLS AND TAKING NAMES.
THIS IS ABOUT PRESSING ON... NO MATTER HOW TREACHEROUS THE PATH...
...ABOUT SEIZING THE REINS WHEN YOUR WORLD SPIRALS OUT OF CONTROL...
KILLZ-- ZZT --
ZZT-KILLZ-ZZTT--
STAMP!
...ABOUT COMING THROUGH THE STORM... MAYBE WORSE FOR WEAR BUT STANDING *PROUD*.

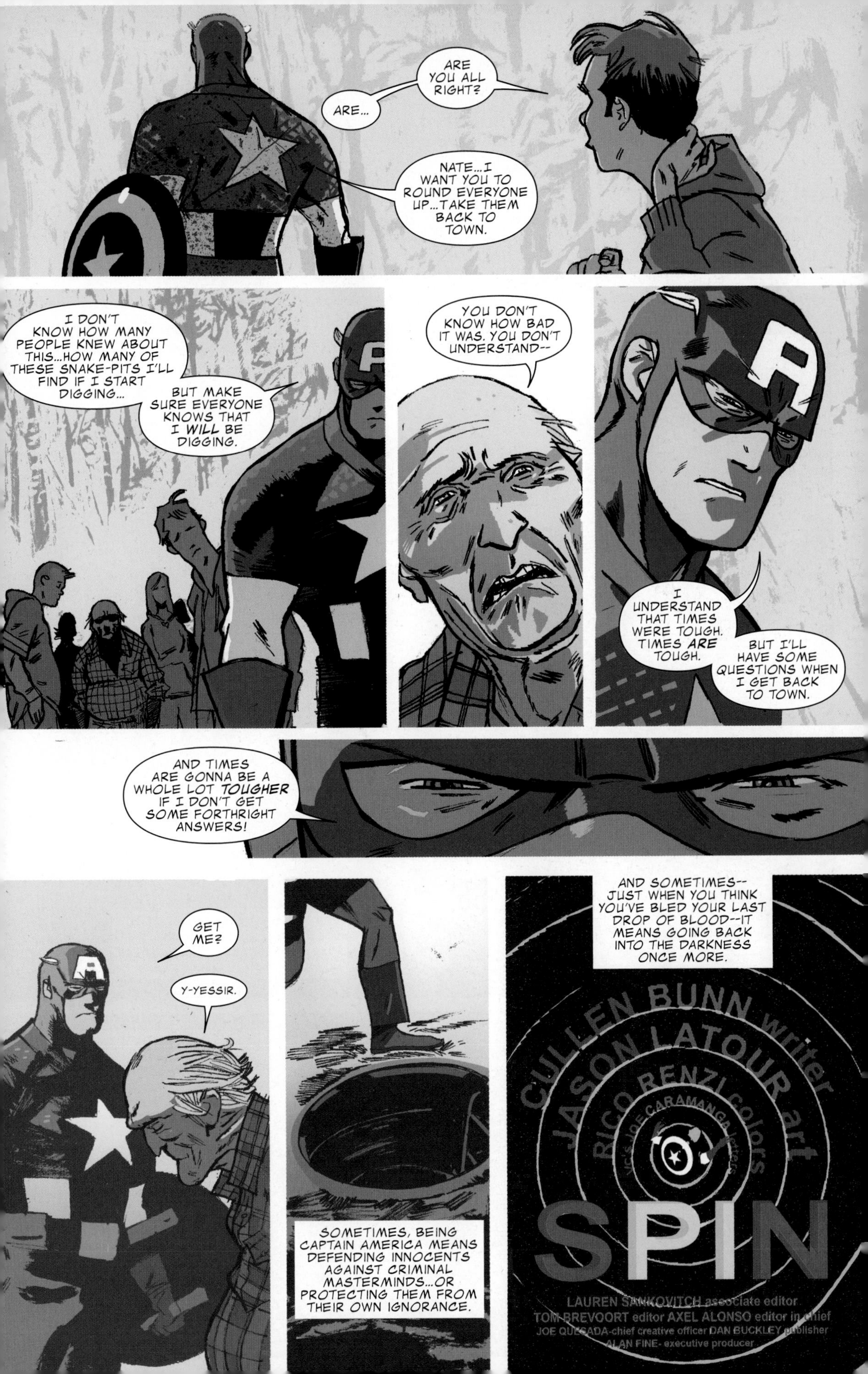
ARE YOU ALL RIGHT?
ARE...
NATE...I WANT YOU TO ROUND EVERYONE UP...TAKE THEM BACK TO TOWN.
I DON'T KNOW HOW MANY PEOPLE KNEW ABOUT THIS...HOW MANY OF THESE SNAKE-PITS I'LL FIND IF I START DIGGING...
BUT MAKE SURE EVERYONE KNOWS THAT I WILL BE DIGGING.
YOU DON'T KNOW HOW BAD IT WAS. YOU DON'T UNDERSTAND--
I UNDERSTAND THAT TIMES WERE TOUGH. TIMES ARE TOUGH.
BUT I'LL HAVE SOME QUESTIONS WHEN I GET BACK TO TOWN.
AND TIMES ARE GONNA BE A WHOLE LOT TOUGHER IF I DON'T GET SOME FORTHRIGHT ANSWERS!
GET ME?
Y-YESSIR.
SOMETIMES, BEING CAPTAIN AMERICA MEANS DEFENDING INNOCENTS AGAINST CRIMINAL MASTERMINDS...OR PROTECTING THEM FROM THEIR OWN IGNORANCE.
AND SOMETIMES--JUST WHEN YOU THINK YOU'VE BLED YOUR LAST DROP OF BLOOD--IT MEANS GOING BACK INTO THE DARKNESS ONCE MORE.
CULLEN BUNN writer
JASON LATOUR art
RICO RENZI colors
VC's JOE CARAMANGA letters
SPIN
LAUREN SANKOVITCH associate editor
TOM BREVOORT editor AXEL ALONSO editor in chief
JOE QUESADA-chief creative officer DAN BUCKLEY publisher
ALAN FINE- executive producer

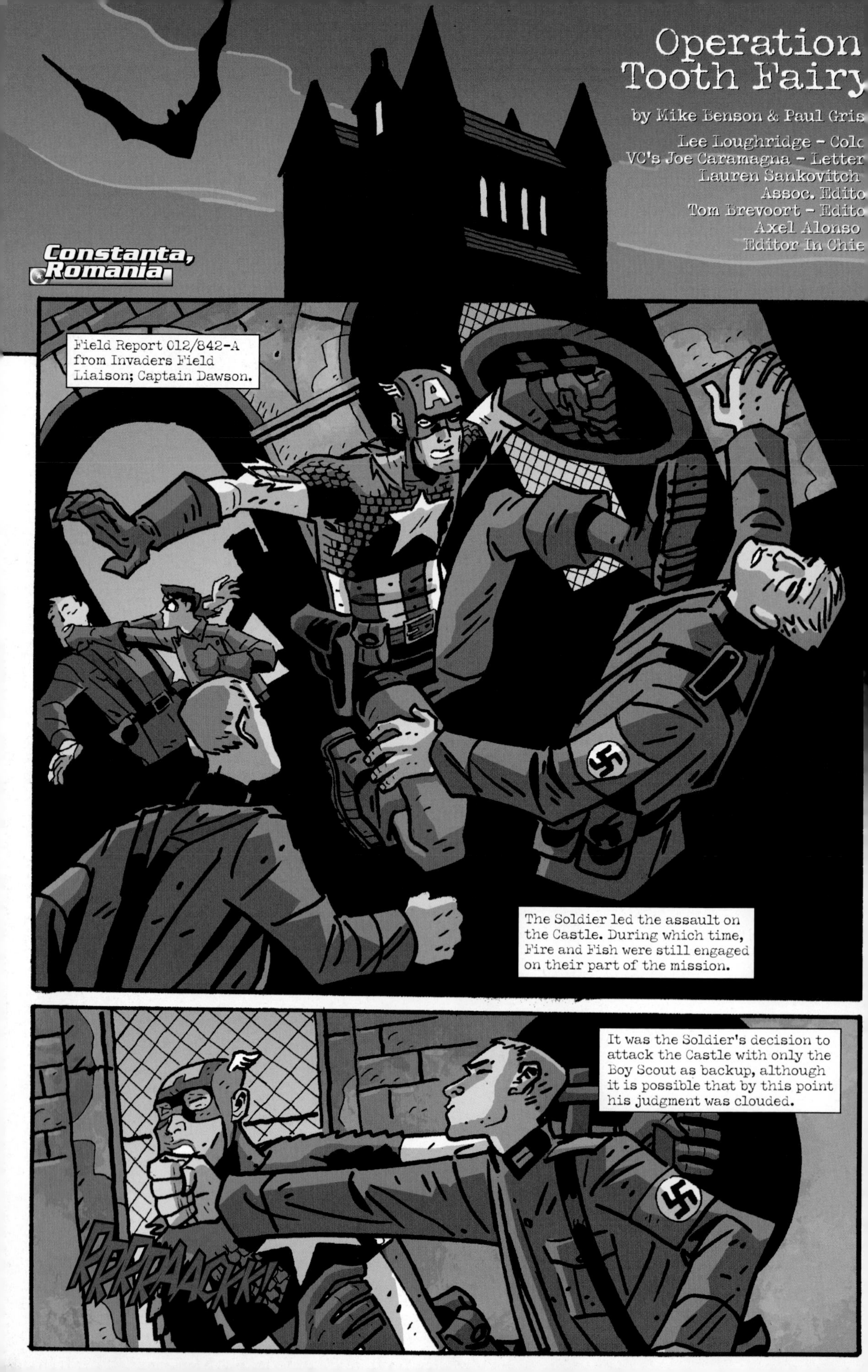

Operation Tooth Fairy
by Mike Benson & Paul Gris
Lee Loughridge - Colc
VC's Joe Caramagna - Letter
Lauren Sankovitch Assoc. Edito
Tom Brevoort - Edito
Axel Alonso Editor In Chie
Constanta, Romania
Field Report 012/842-A from Invaders Field Liaison; Captain Dawson.
The Soldier led the assault on the Castle. During which time, Fire and Fish were still engaged on their part of the mission.
It was the Soldier's decision to attack the Castle with only the Boy Scout as backup, although it is possible that by this point his judgment was clouded.

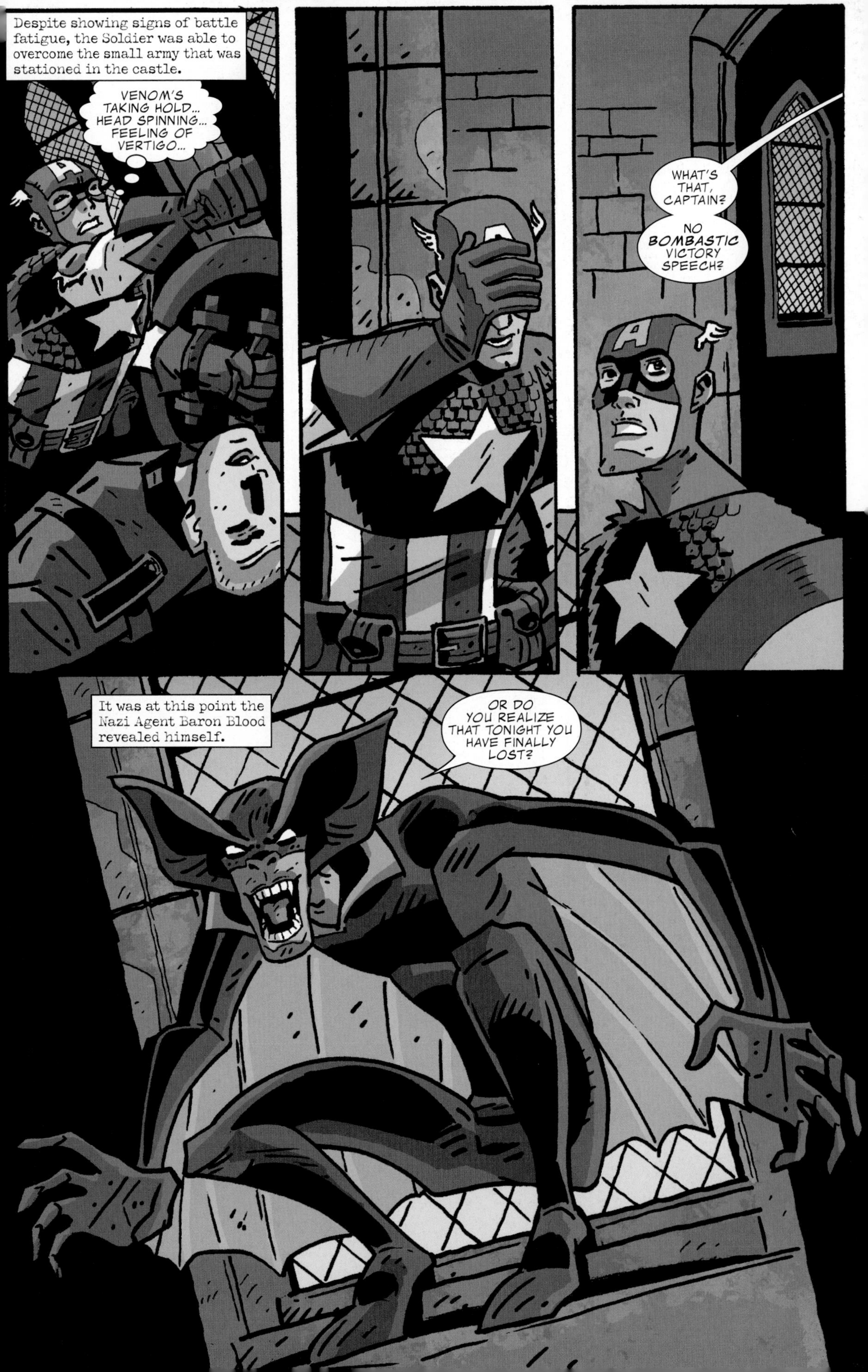
Despite showing signs of battle fatigue, the Soldier was able to overcome the small army that was stationed in the castle.
VENOM'S TAKING HOLD... HEAD SPINNING... FEELING OF VERTIGO...
WHAT'S THAT, CAPTAIN?
NO BOMBASTIC VICTORY SPEECH?
It was at this point the Nazi Agent Baron Blood revealed himself.
OR DO YOU REALIZE THAT TONIGHT YOU HAVE FINALLY LOST?

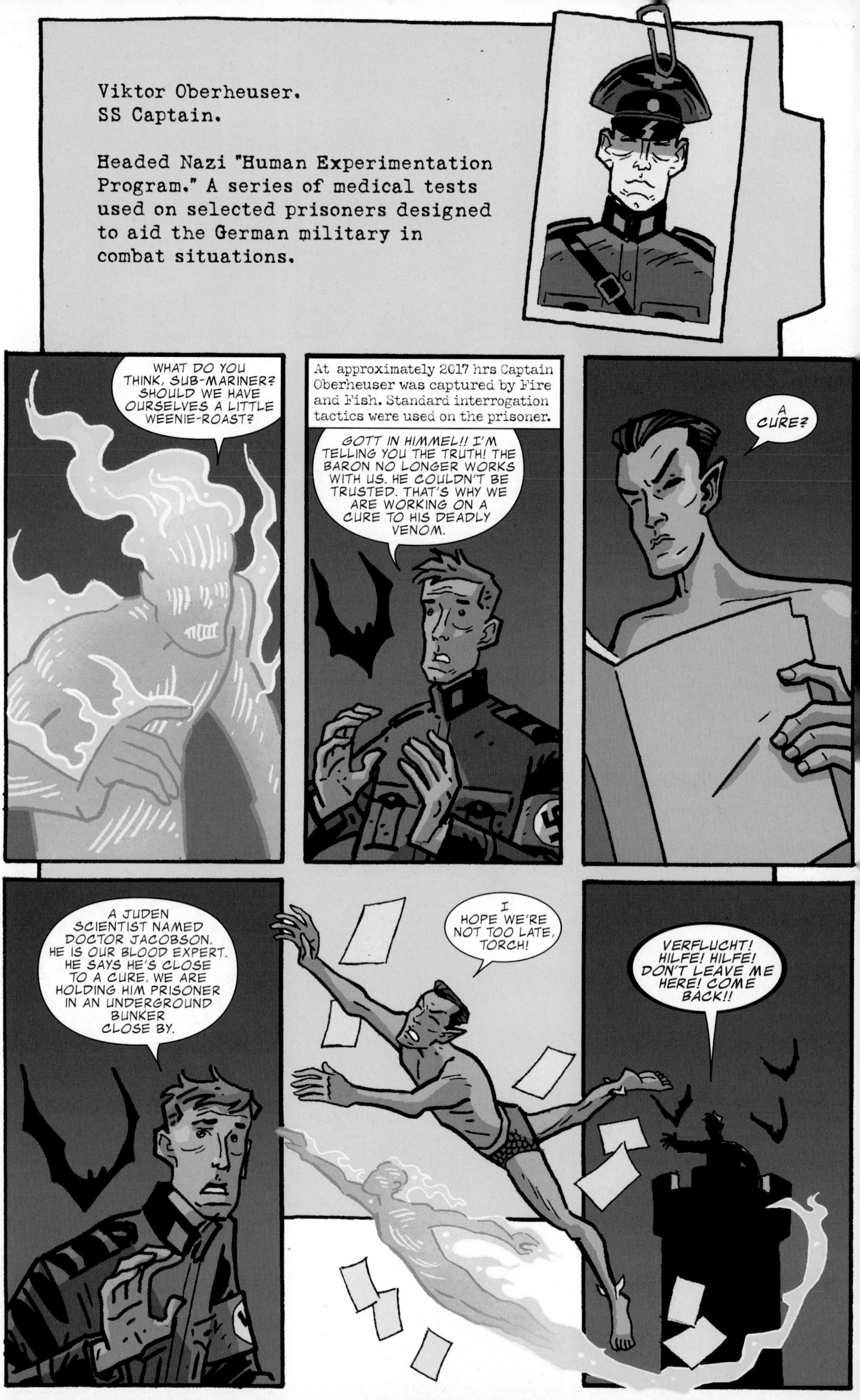

Viktor Oberheuser.
SS Captain.
Headed Nazi "Human Experimentation Program." A series of medical tests used on selected prisoners designed to aid the German military in combat situations.
WHAT DO YOU THINK, SUB-MARINER? SHOULD WE HAVE OURSELVES A LITTLE WEENIE-ROAST?
At approximately 2017 hrs Captain Oberheuser was captured by Fire and Fish. Standard interrogation tactics were used on the prisoner.
GOTT IN HIMMEL!! I'M TELLING YOU THE TRUTH! THE BARON NO LONGER WORKS WITH US. HE COULDN'T BE TRUSTED. THAT'S WHY WE ARE WORKING ON A CURE TO HIS DEADLY VENOM.
A CURE?
A JUDEN SCIENTIST NAMED DOCTOR JACOBSON. HE IS OUR BLOOD EXPERT. HE SAYS HE'S CLOSE TO A CURE. WE ARE HOLDING HIM PRISONER IN AN UNDERGROUND BUNKER CLOSE BY.
I HOPE WE'RE NOT TOO LATE, TORCH!
VERFLUCHT! HILFE! HILFE! DON'T LEAVE ME HERE! COME BACK!!

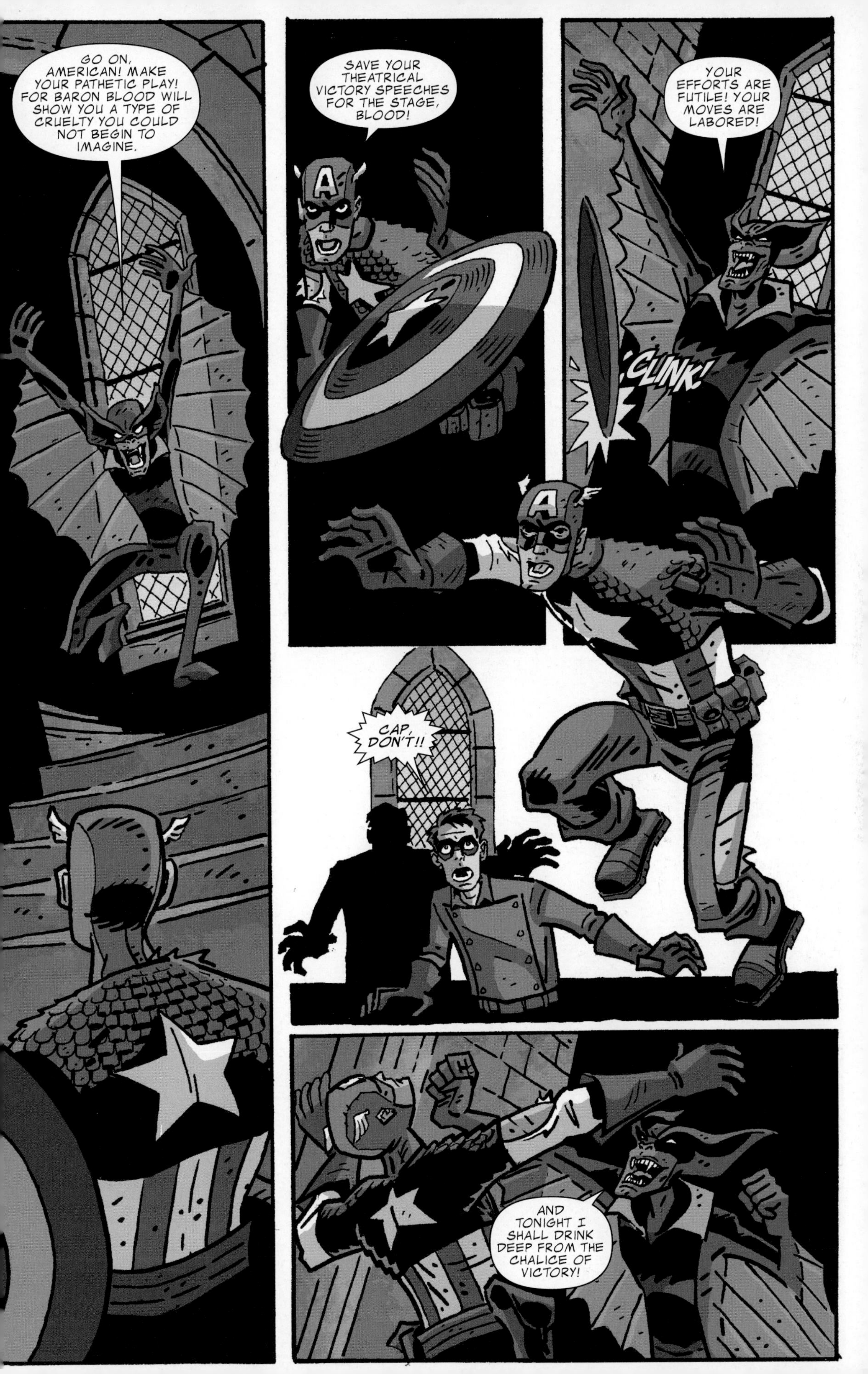
GO ON, AMERICAN! MAKE YOUR PATHETIC PLAY! FOR BARON BLOOD WILL SHOW YOU A TYPE OF CRUELTY YOU COULD NOT BEGIN TO IMAGINE.
SAVE YOUR THEATRICAL VICTORY SPEECHES FOR THE STAGE, BLOOD!
YOUR EFFORTS ARE FUTILE! YOUR MOVES ARE LABORED!
CLINK!
CAP, DON'T!!
AND TONIGHT I SHALL DRINK DEEP FROM THE CHALICE OF VICTORY!

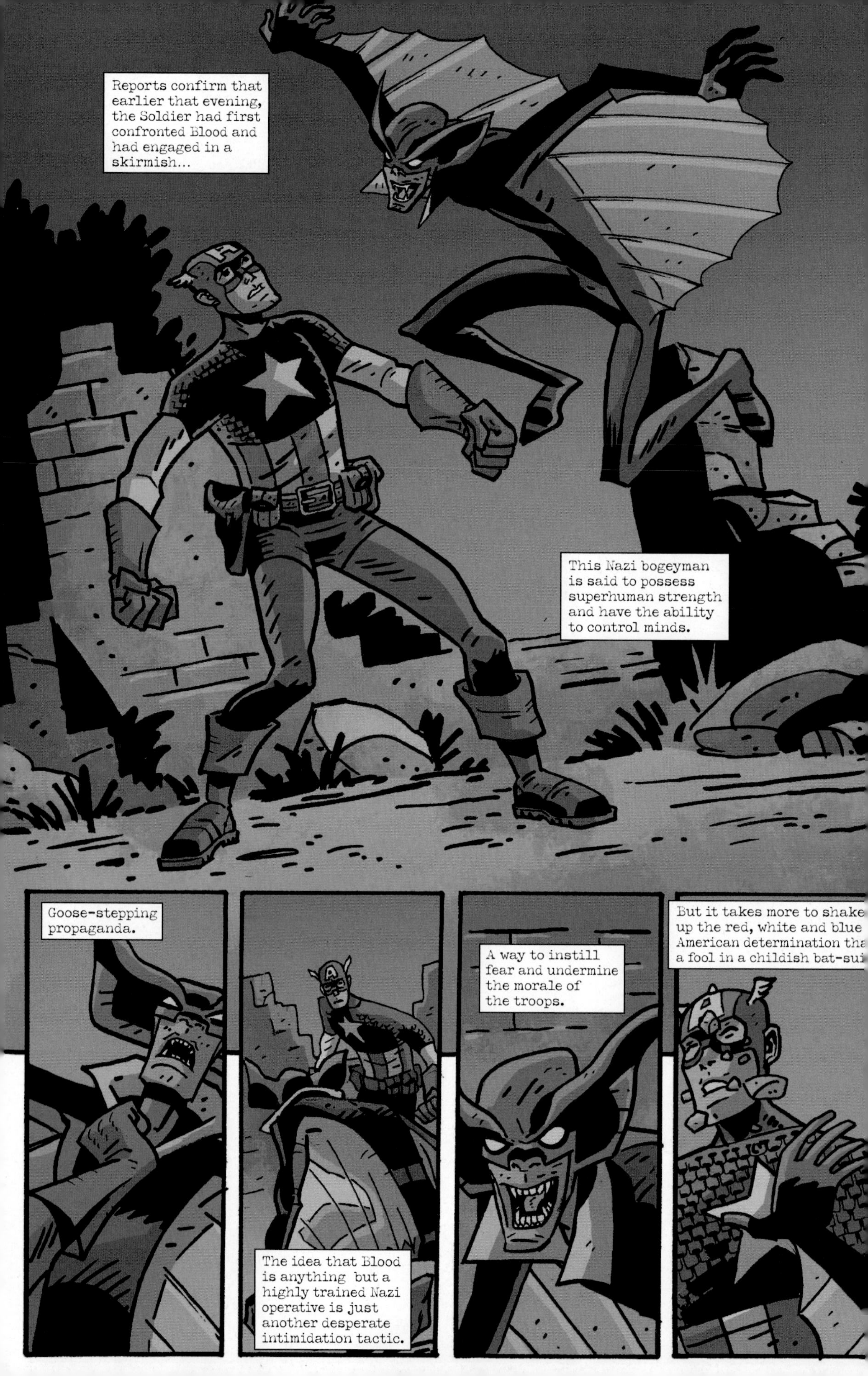
Reports confirm that earlier that evening, the Soldier had first confronted Blood and had engaged in a skirmish...
This Nazi bogeyman is said to possess superhuman strength and have the ability to control minds.
Goose-stepping propaganda.
The idea that Blood is anything but a highly trained Nazi operative is just another desperate intimidation tactic.
A way to instill fear and undermine the morale of the troops.
But it takes more to shake up the red, white and blue American determination tha a fool in a childish bat-sui

Unfortunately, a stray shell caused an explosion before the Soldier was able to apprehend the so-called vampire...

...and he was momentarily rendered unconscious by the blast.

Giving Blood enough time to infect the Soldier with his poison.

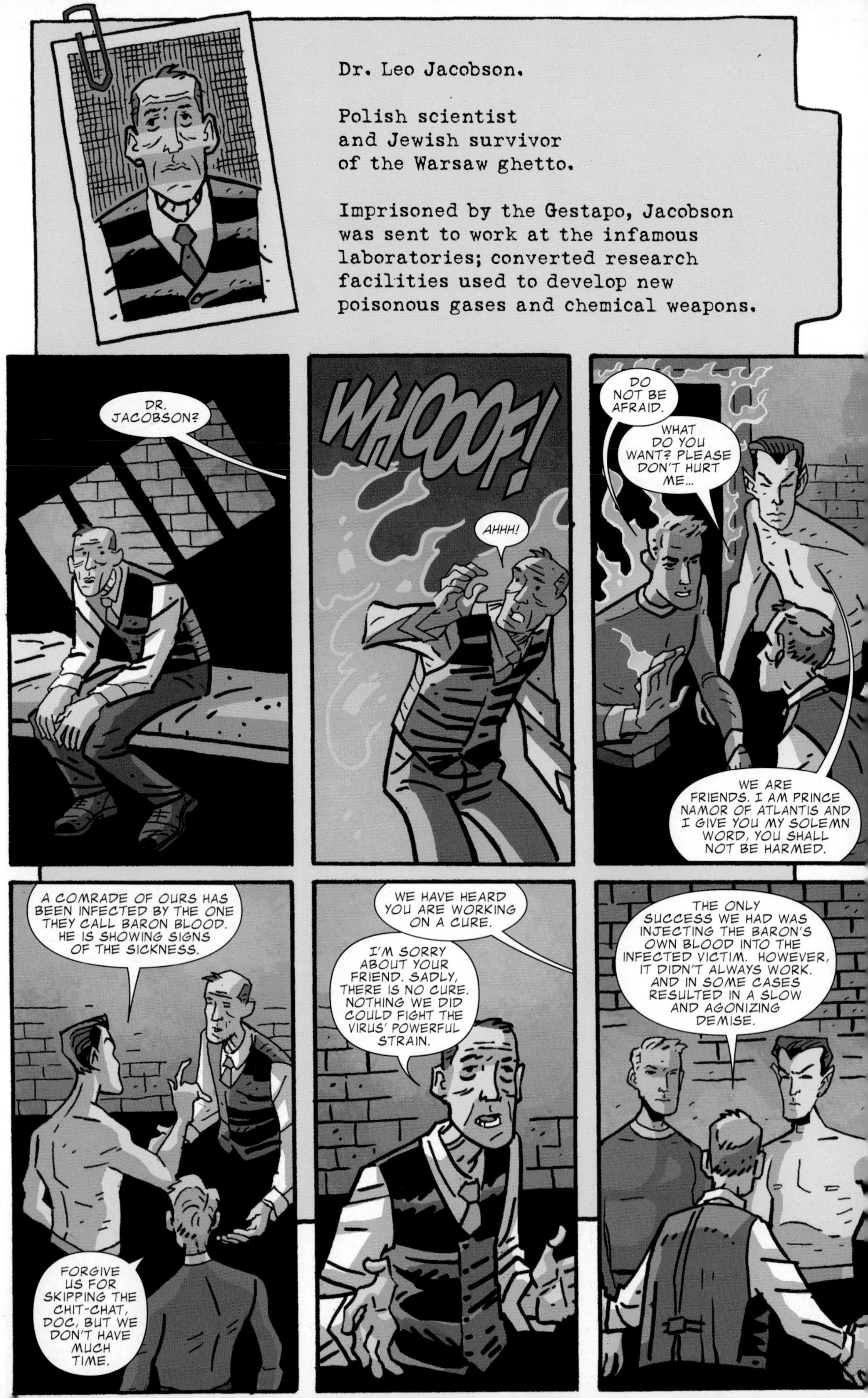
Dr. Leo Jacobson.
Polish scientist and Jewish survivor of the Warsaw ghetto.
Imprisoned by the Gestapo, Jacobson was sent to work at the infamous laboratories; converted research facilities used to develop new poisonous gases and chemical weapons.
DR. JACOBSON?
WHOOOF!
AHHH!
DO NOT BE AFRAID.
WHAT DO YOU WANT? PLEASE DON'T HURT ME...
WE ARE FRIENDS. I AM PRINCE NAMOR OF ATLANTIS AND I GIVE YOU MY SOLEMN WORD, YOU SHALL NOT BE HARMED.
A COMRADE OF OURS HAS BEEN INFECTED BY THE ONE THEY CALL BARON BLOOD. HE IS SHOWING SIGNS OF THE SICKNESS.
FORGIVE US FOR SKIPPING THE CHIT-CHAT, DOC, BUT WE DON'T HAVE MUCH TIME.
WE HAVE HEARD YOU ARE WORKING ON A CURE.
I'M SORRY ABOUT YOUR FRIEND. SADLY, THERE IS NO CURE. NOTHING WE DID COULD FIGHT THE VIRUS' POWERFUL STRAIN.
THE ONLY SUCCESS WE HAD WAS INJECTING THE BARON'S OWN BLOOD INTO THE INFECTED VICTIM. HOWEVER, IT DIDN'T ALWAYS WORK. AND IN SOME CASES RESULTED IN A SLOW AND AGONIZING DEMISE.

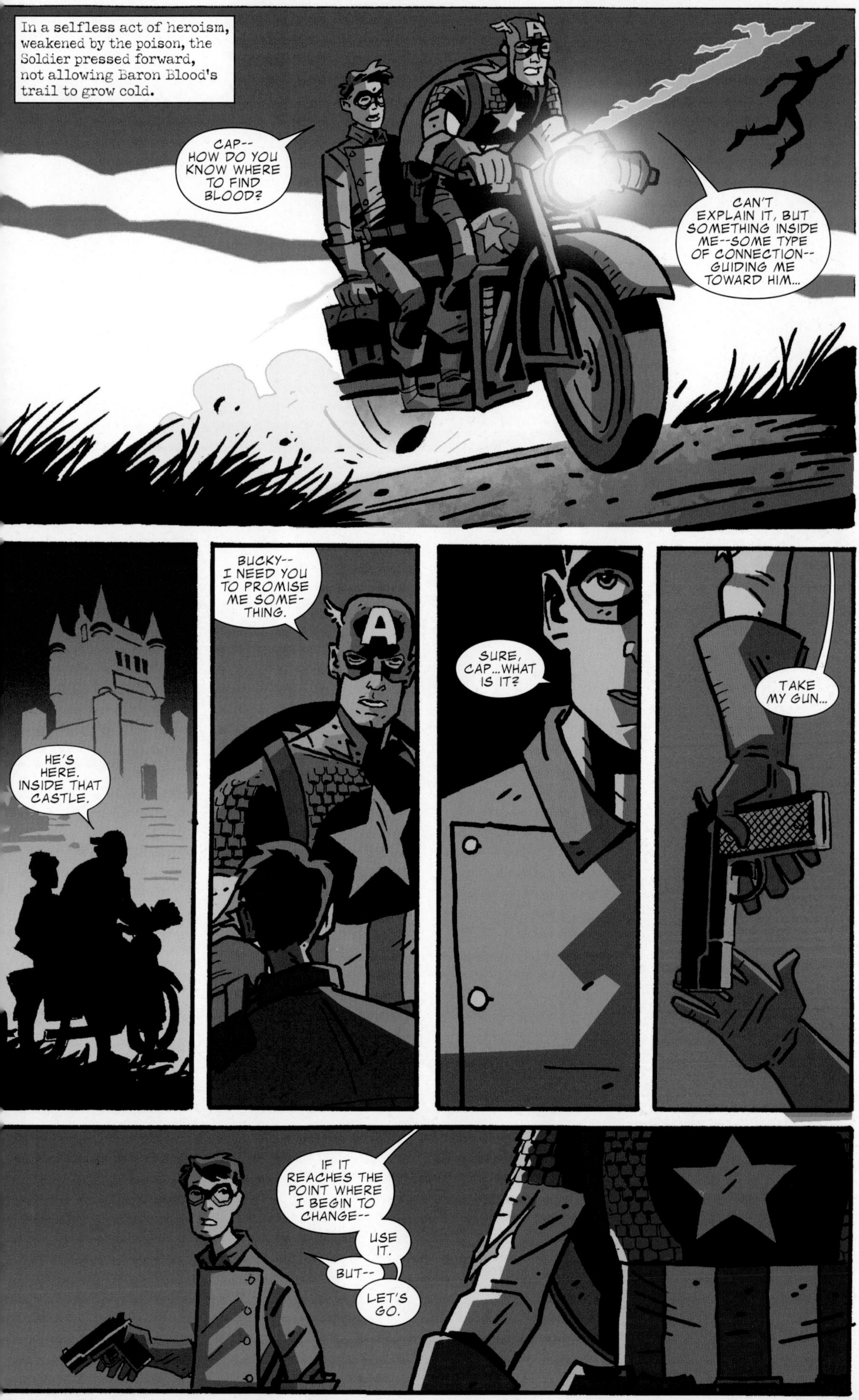
In a selfless act of heroism, weakened by the poison, the Soldier pressed forward, not allowing Baron Blood's trail to grow cold.
CAP-- HOW DO YOU KNOW WHERE TO FIND BLOOD?
CAN'T EXPLAIN IT, BUT SOMETHING INSIDE ME--SOME TYPE OF CONNECTION-- GUIDING ME TOWARD HIM...
HE'S HERE. INSIDE THAT CASTLE.
BUCKY-- I NEED YOU TO PROMISE ME SOME-THING.
SURE, CAP...WHAT IS IT?
TAKE MY GUN...
IF IT REACHES THE POINT WHERE I BEGIN TO CHANGE--
USE IT.
BUT--
LET'S GO.

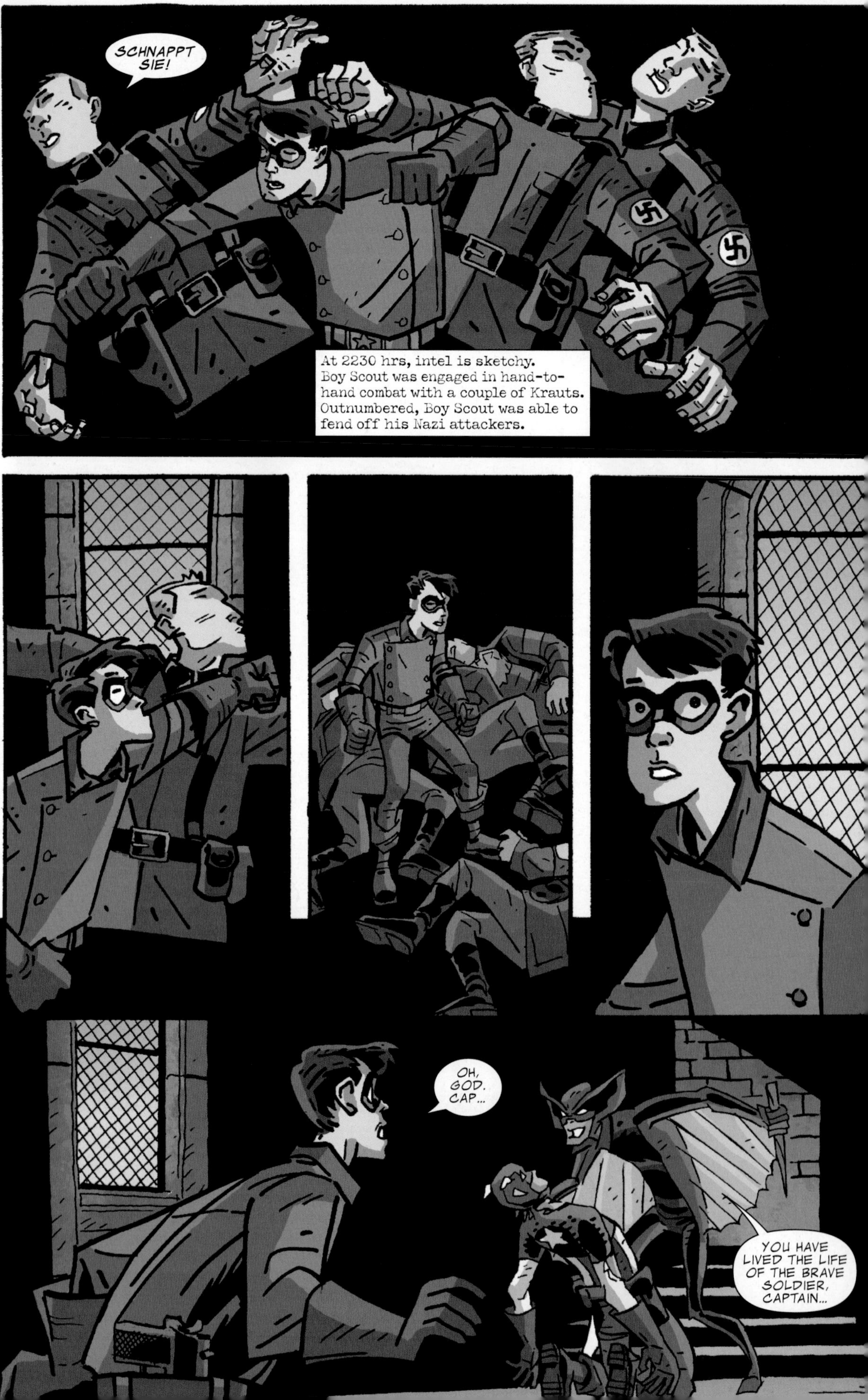

SCHNAPPT SIE!
At 2230 hrs, intel is sketchy. Boy Scout was engaged in hand-to-hand combat with a couple of Krauts. Outnumbered, Boy Scout was able to fend off his Nazi attackers.
OH, GOD. CAP...
YOU HAVE LIVED THE LIFE OF THE BRAVE SOLDIER, CAPTAIN...

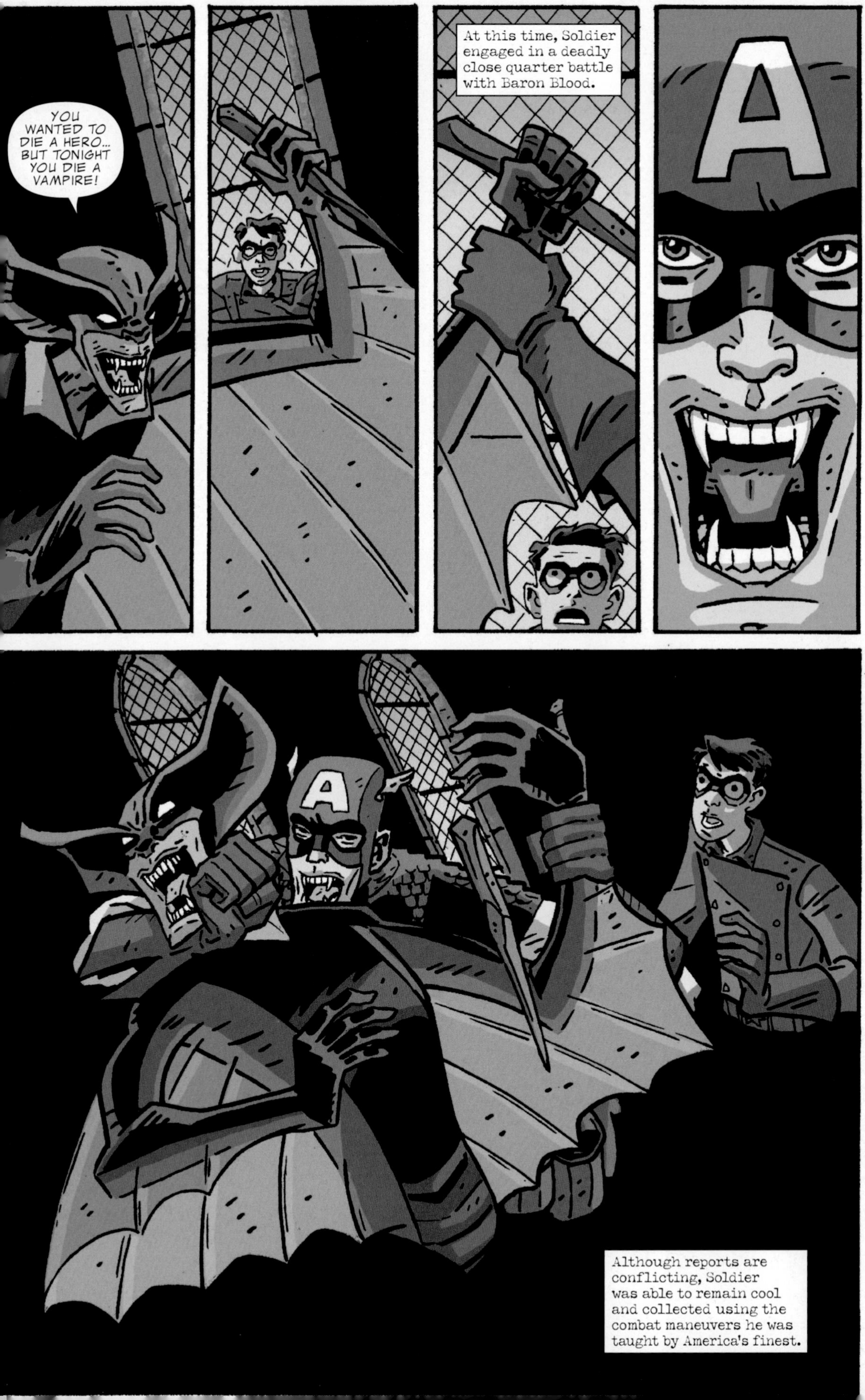
YOU WANTED TO DIE A HERO... BUT TONIGHT YOU DIE A VAMPIRE!
At this time, Soldier engaged in a deadly close quarter battle with Baron Blood.
Although reports are conflicting, Soldier was able to remain cool and collected using the combat maneuvers he was taught by America's finest.

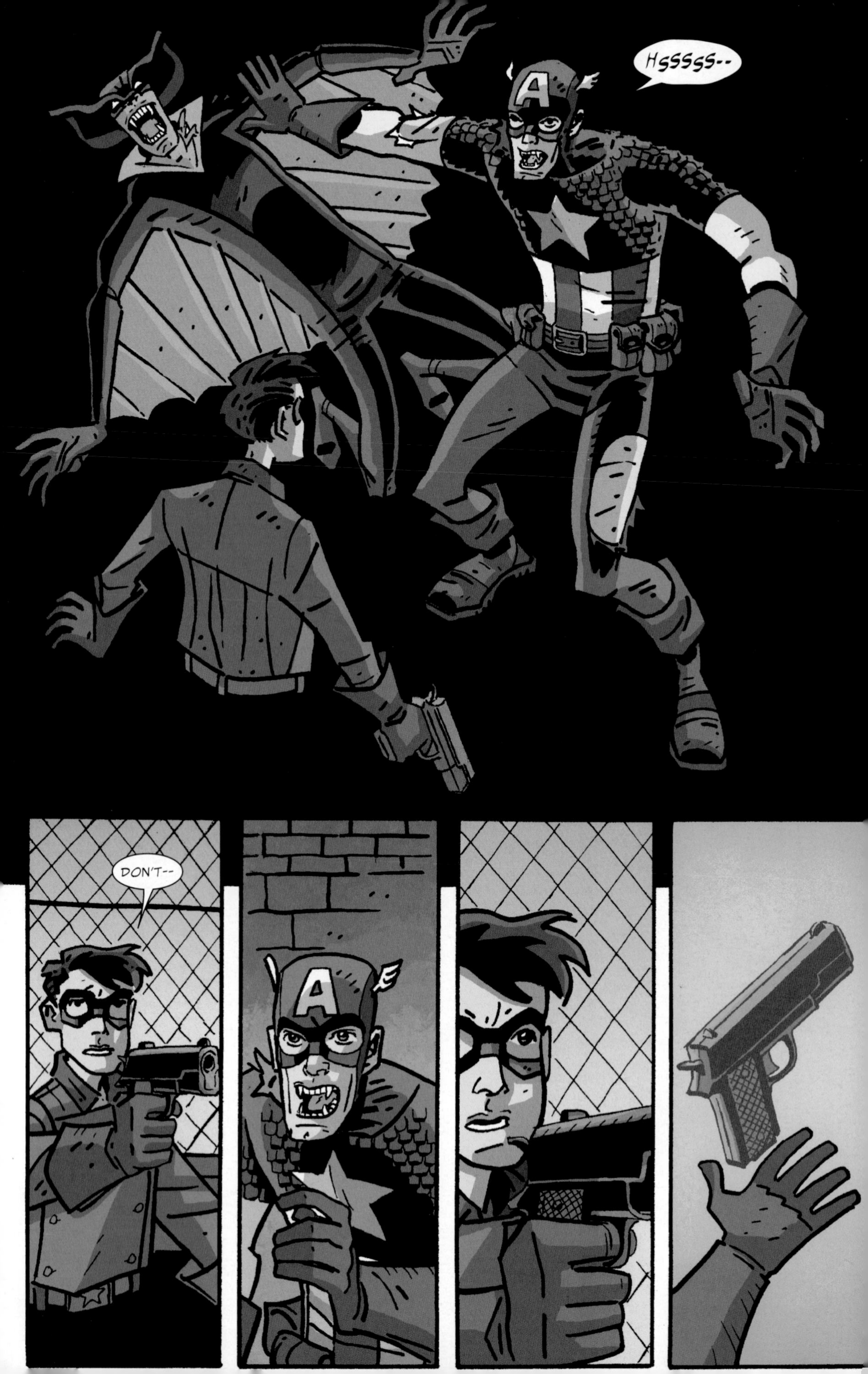
HSSSSS--
DON'T--

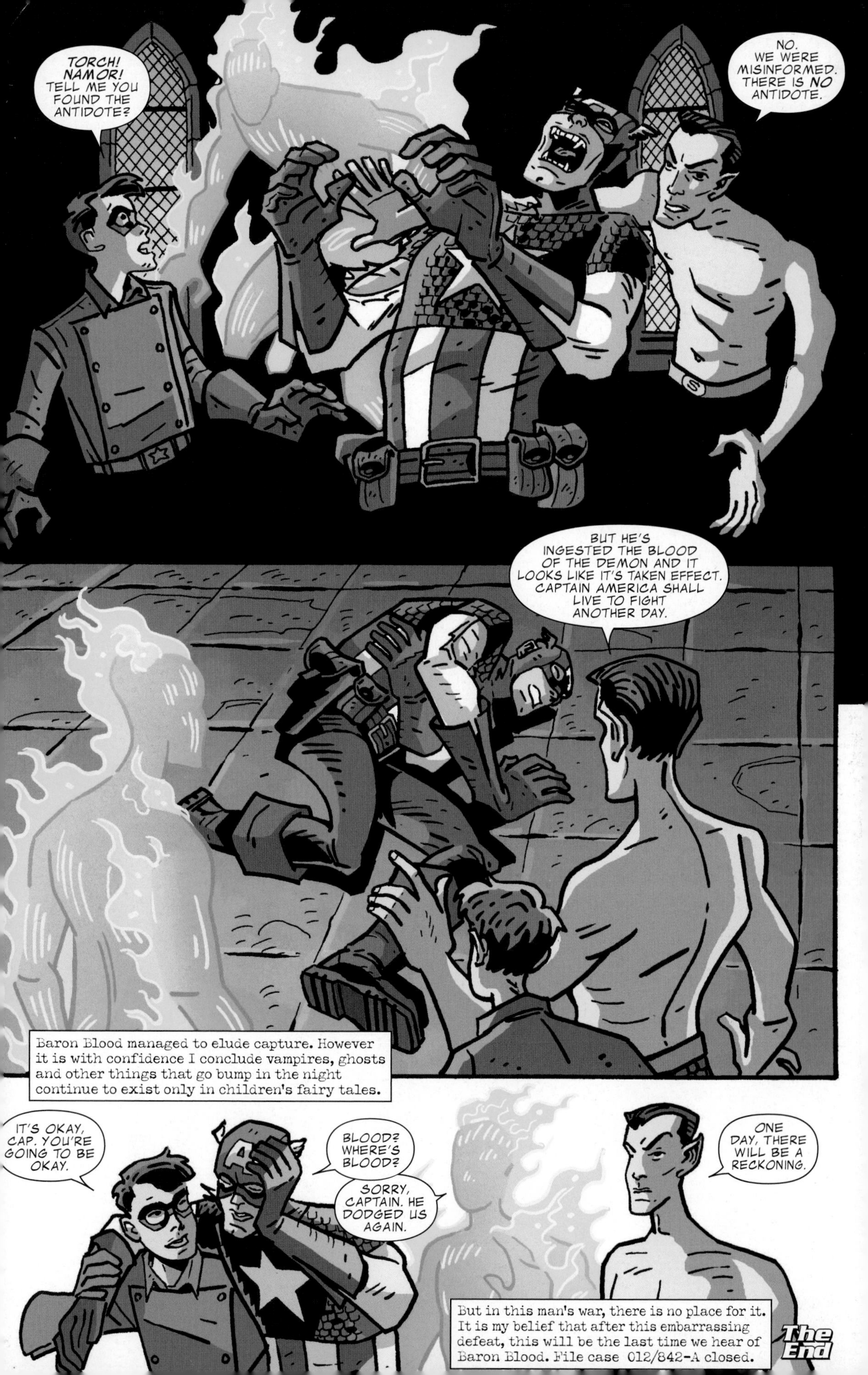
TORCH! NAMOR! TELL ME YOU FOUND THE ANTIDOTE?
NO. WE WERE MISINFORMED. THERE IS NO ANTIDOTE.
BUT HE'S INGESTED THE BLOOD OF THE DEMON AND IT LOOKS LIKE IT'S TAKEN EFFECT. CAPTAIN AMERICA SHALL LIVE TO FIGHT ANOTHER DAY.
Baron Blood managed to elude capture. However it is with confidence I conclude vampires, ghosts and other things that go bump in the night continue to exist only in children's fairy tales.
IT'S OKAY, CAP. YOU'RE GOING TO BE OKAY.
BLOOD? WHERE'S BLOOD?
SORRY, CAPTAIN. HE DODGED US AGAIN.
ONE DAY, THERE WILL BE A RECKONING.
But in this man's war, there is no place for it. It is my belief that after this embarrassing defeat, this will be the last time we hear of Baron Blood. File case 012/842-A closed.
The End

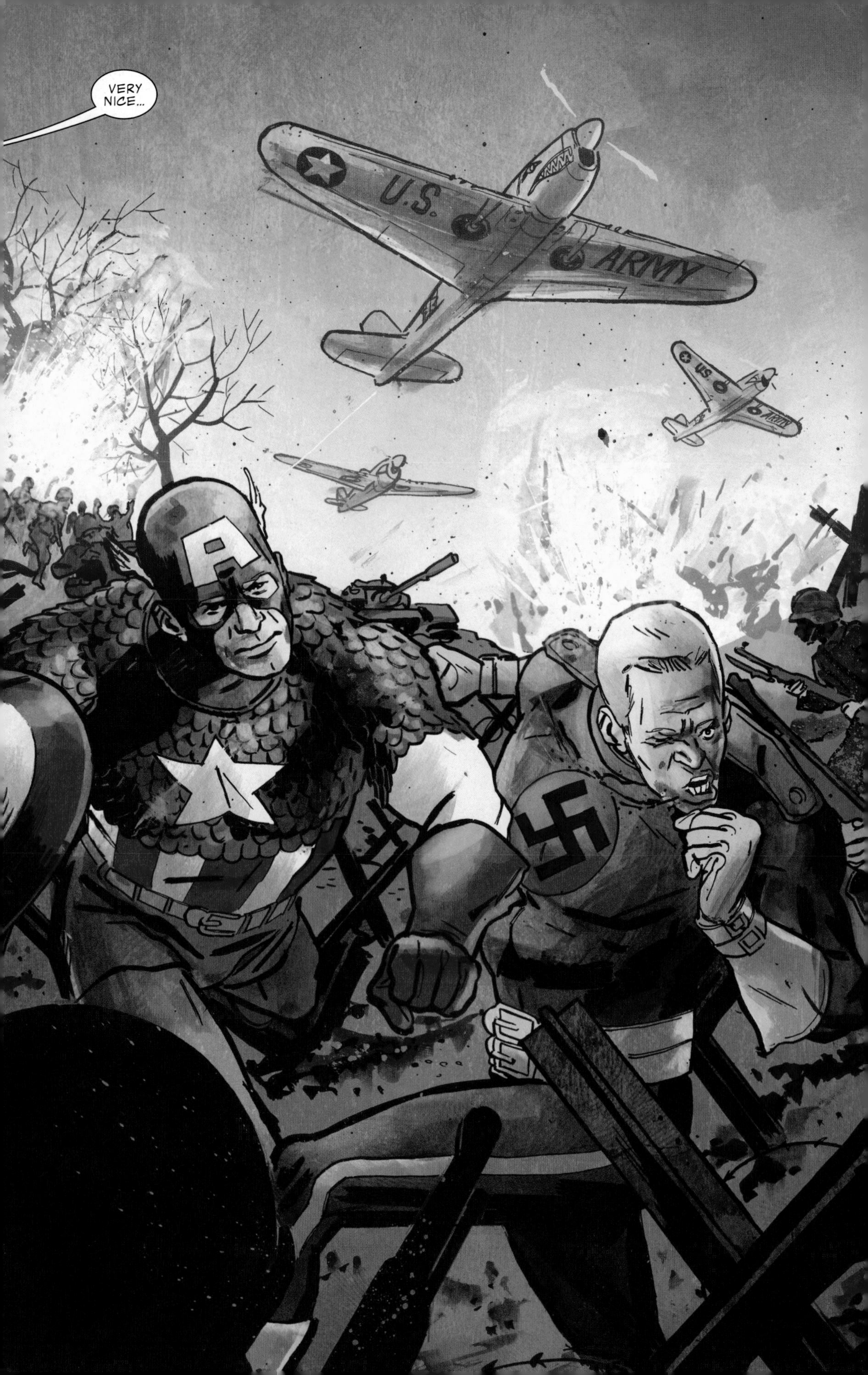
VERY NICE...
U.S.
ARMY

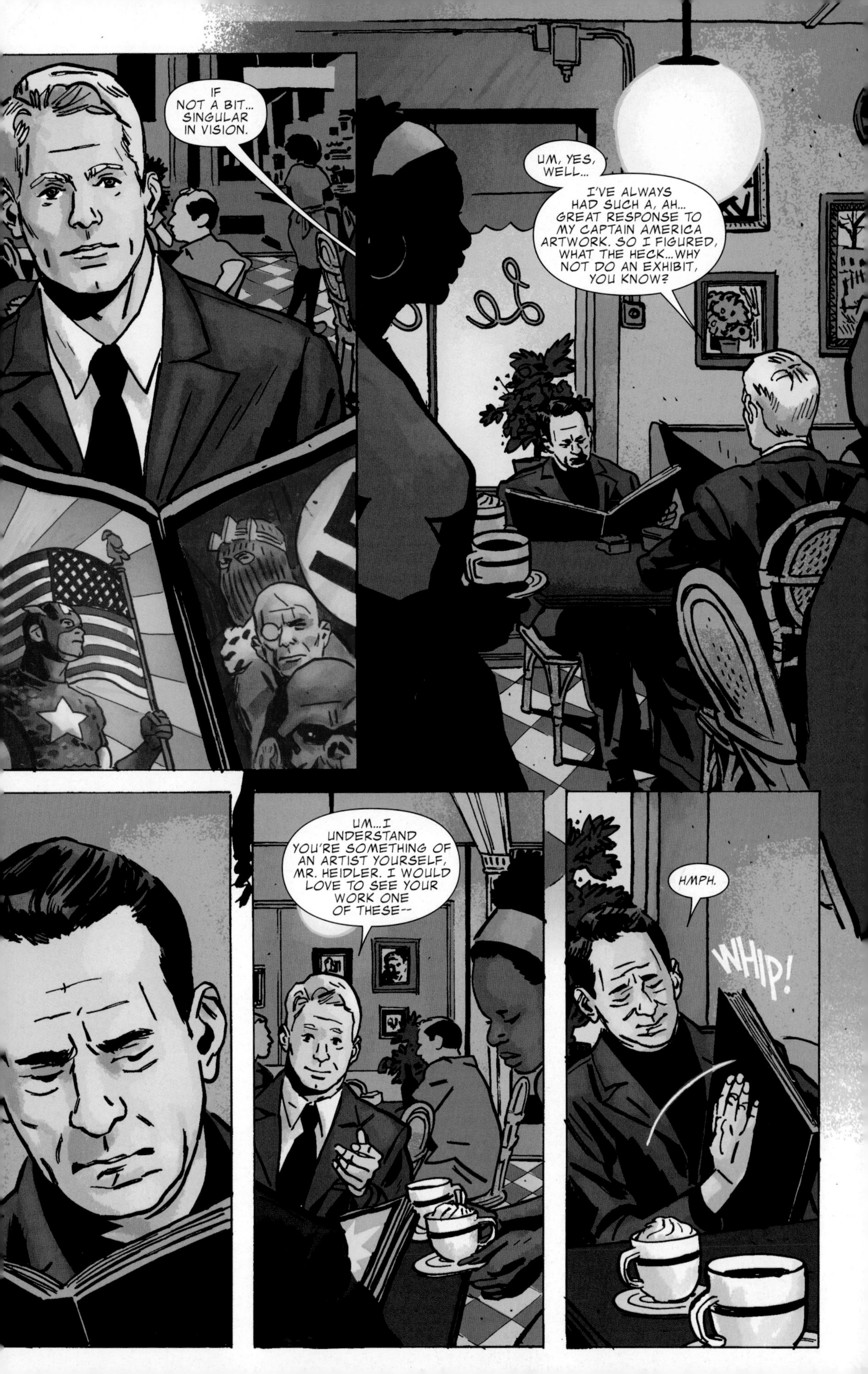
IF NOT A BIT... SINGULAR IN VISION.
UM, YES, WELL...
I'VE ALWAYS HAD SUCH A, AH... GREAT RESPONSE TO MY CAPTAIN AMERICA ARTWORK. SO I FIGURED, WHAT THE HECK...WHY NOT DO AN EXHIBIT, YOU KNOW?
UM...I UNDERSTAND YOU'RE SOMETHING OF AN ARTIST YOURSELF, MR. HEIDLER. I WOULD LOVE TO SEE YOUR WORK ONE OF THESE--
HMPH.
WHIP!

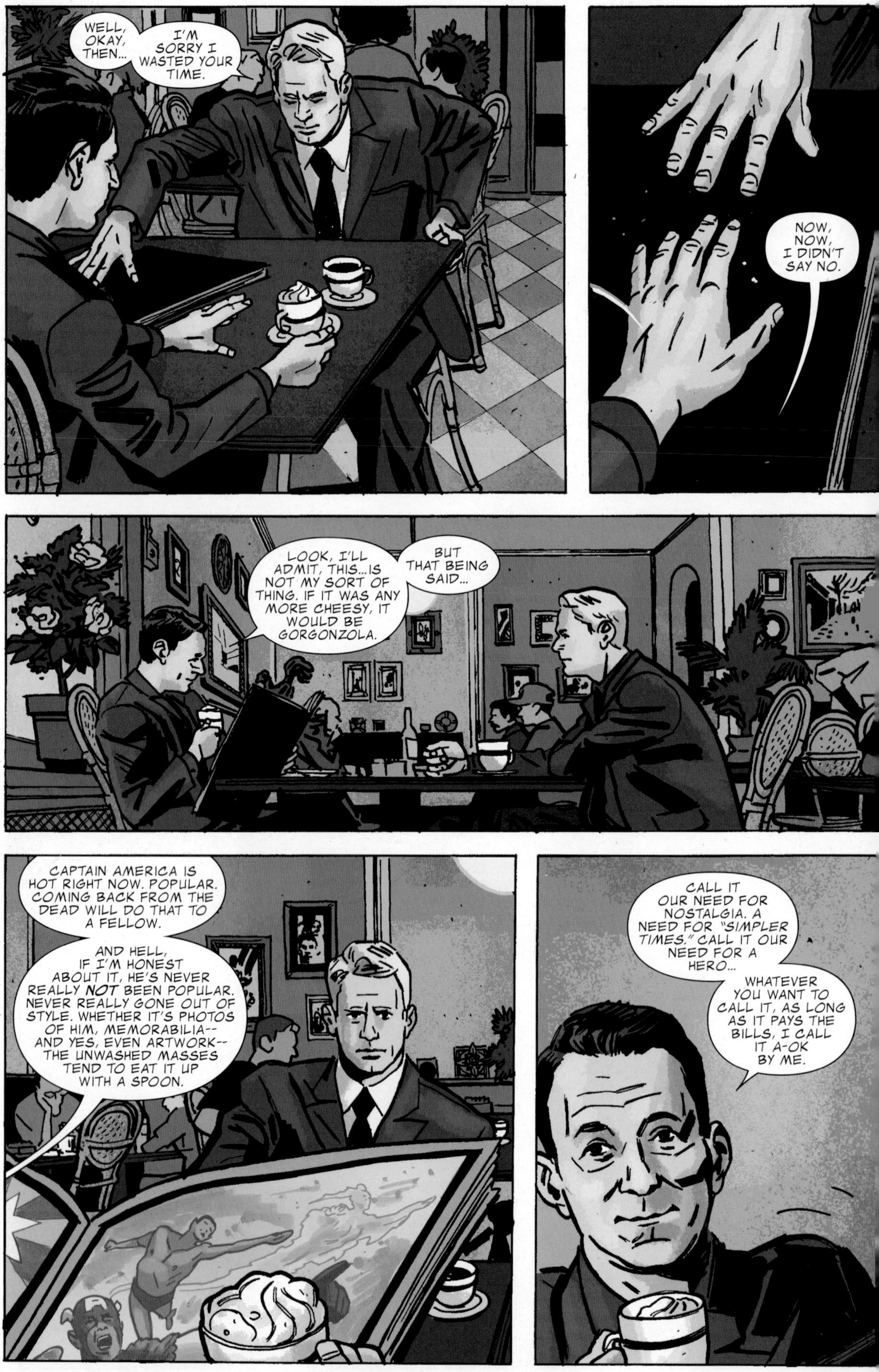
WELL, OKAY, THEN...
I'M SORRY I WASTED YOUR TIME.
NOW, NOW, I DIDN'T SAY NO.
LOOK, I'LL ADMIT, THIS...IS NOT MY SORT OF THING. IF IT WAS ANY MORE CHEESY, IT WOULD BE GORGONZOLA.
BUT THAT BEING SAID...
CAPTAIN AMERICA IS HOT RIGHT NOW. POPULAR. COMING BACK FROM THE DEAD WILL DO THAT TO A FELLOW.
AND HELL, IF I'M HONEST ABOUT IT, HE'S NEVER REALLY NOT BEEN POPULAR. NEVER REALLY GONE OUT OF STYLE. WHETHER IT'S PHOTOS OF HIM, MEMORABILIA-- AND YES, EVEN ARTWORK-- THE UNWASHED MASSES TEND TO EAT IT UP WITH A SPOON.
CALL IT OUR NEED FOR NOSTALGIA. A NEED FOR "SIMPLER TIMES." CALL IT OUR NEED FOR A HERO...
WHATEVER YOU WANT TO CALL IT, AS LONG AS IT PAYS THE BILLS, I CALL IT A-OK BY ME.

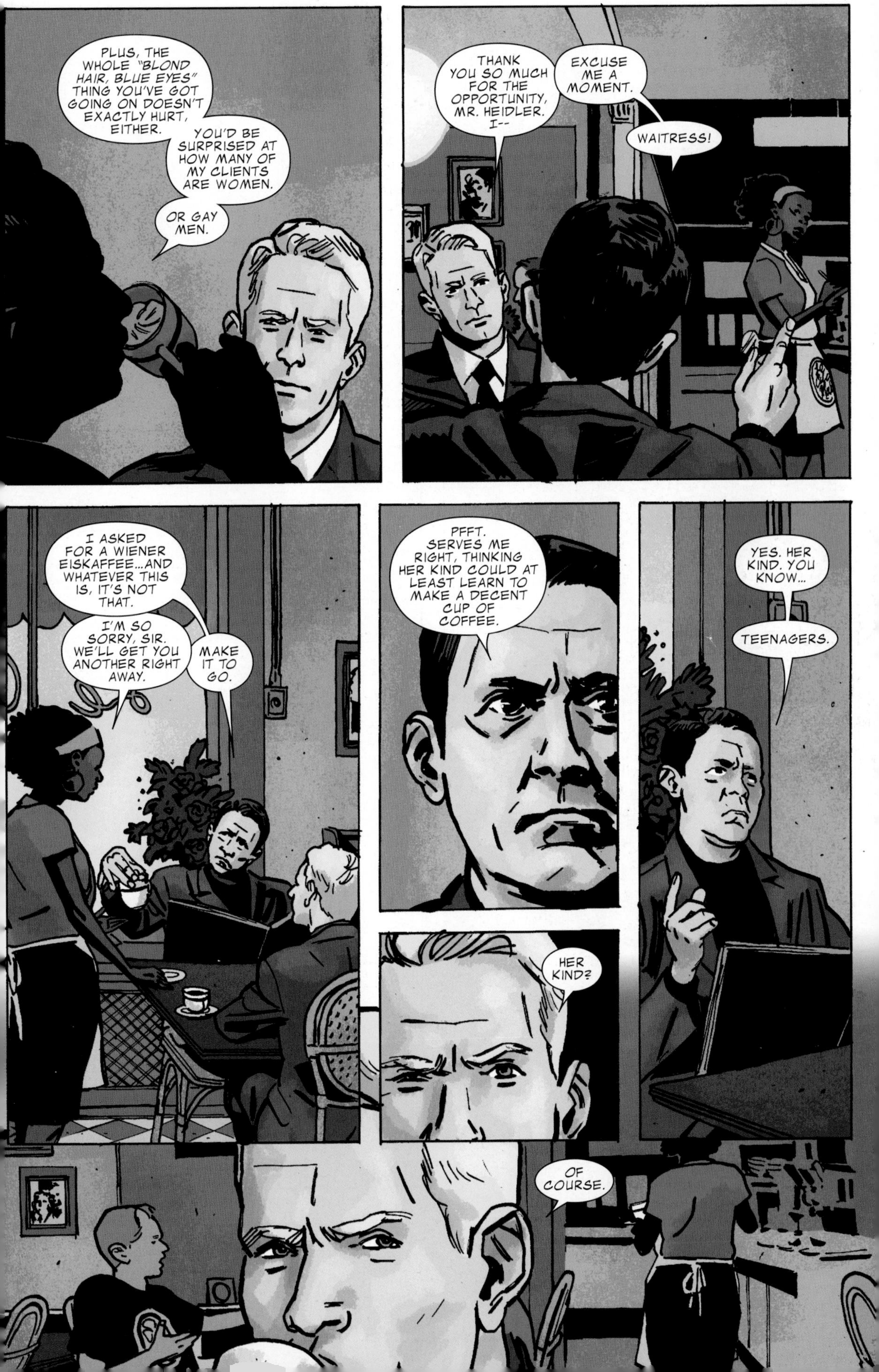
PLUS, THE WHOLE "BLOND HAIR, BLUE EYES" THING YOU'VE GOT GOING ON DOESN'T EXACTLY HURT, EITHER.
YOU'D BE SURPRISED AT HOW MANY OF MY CLIENTS ARE WOMEN.
OR GAY MEN.
THANK YOU SO MUCH FOR THE OPPORTUNITY, MR. HEIDLER. I--
EXCUSE ME A MOMENT.
WAITRESS!
I ASKED FOR A WIENER EISKAFFEE...AND WHATEVER THIS IS, IT'S NOT THAT.
I'M SO SORRY, SIR. WE'LL GET YOU ANOTHER RIGHT AWAY.
MAKE IT TO GO.
PFFT. SERVES ME RIGHT, THINKING HER KIND COULD AT LEAST LEARN TO MAKE A DECENT CUP OF COFFEE.
HER KIND?
YES. HER KIND. YOU KNOW...
TEENAGERS.
OF COURSE.

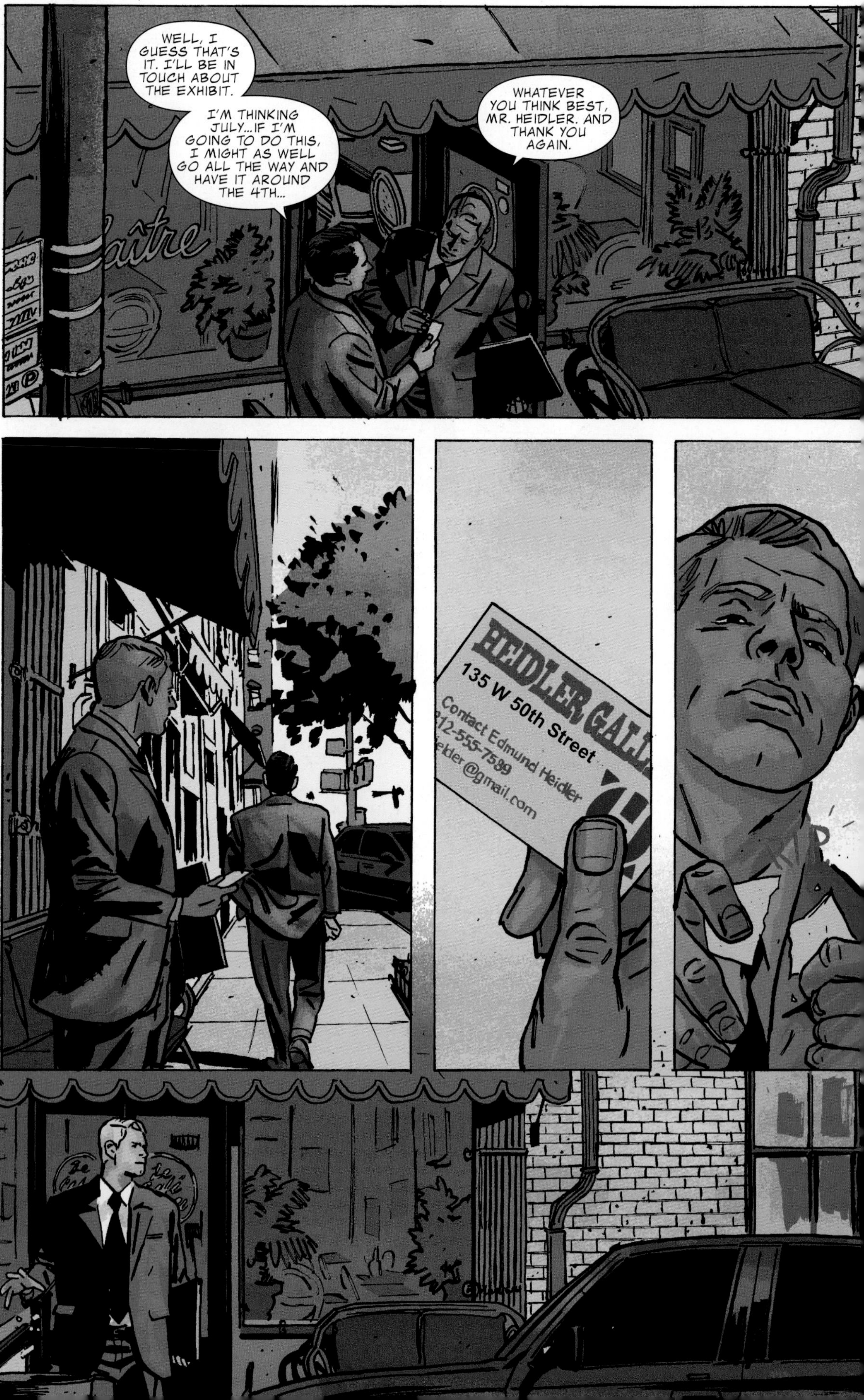
WELL, I GUESS THAT'S IT. I'LL BE IN TOUCH ABOUT THE EXHIBIT.
I'M THINKING JULY...IF I'M GOING TO DO THIS, I MIGHT AS WELL GO ALL THE WAY AND HAVE IT AROUND THE 4TH...
WHATEVER YOU THINK BEST, MR. HEIDLER. AND THANK YOU AGAIN.
HEIDLER GALL
135 W 50th Street
Contact Edmund Heidler
12-555-7589
eidler@gmail.com
RIP

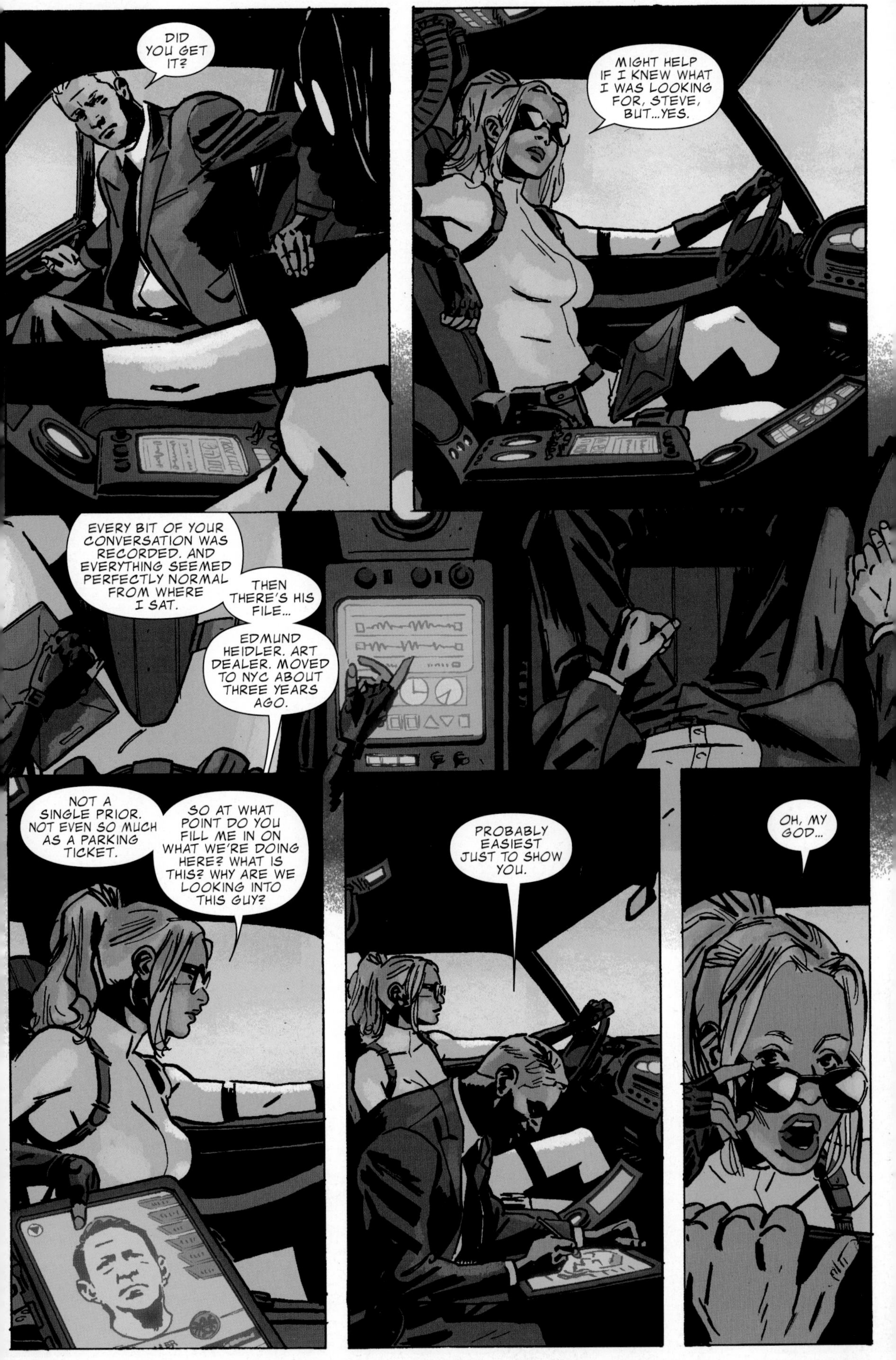
DID YOU GET IT?
MIGHT HELP IF I KNEW WHAT I WAS LOOKING FOR, STEVE, BUT...YES.
EVERY BIT OF YOUR CONVERSATION WAS RECORDED. AND EVERYTHING SEEMED PERFECTLY NORMAL FROM WHERE I SAT.
THEN THERE'S HIS FILE...
EDMUND HEIDLER. ART DEALER. MOVED TO NYC ABOUT THREE YEARS AGO.
NOT A SINGLE PRIOR. NOT EVEN SO MUCH AS A PARKING TICKET.
SO AT WHAT POINT DO YOU FILL ME IN ON WHAT WE'RE DOING HERE? WHAT IS THIS? WHY ARE WE LOOKING INTO THIS GUY?
PROBABLY EASIEST JUST TO SHOW YOU.
OH, MY GOD...

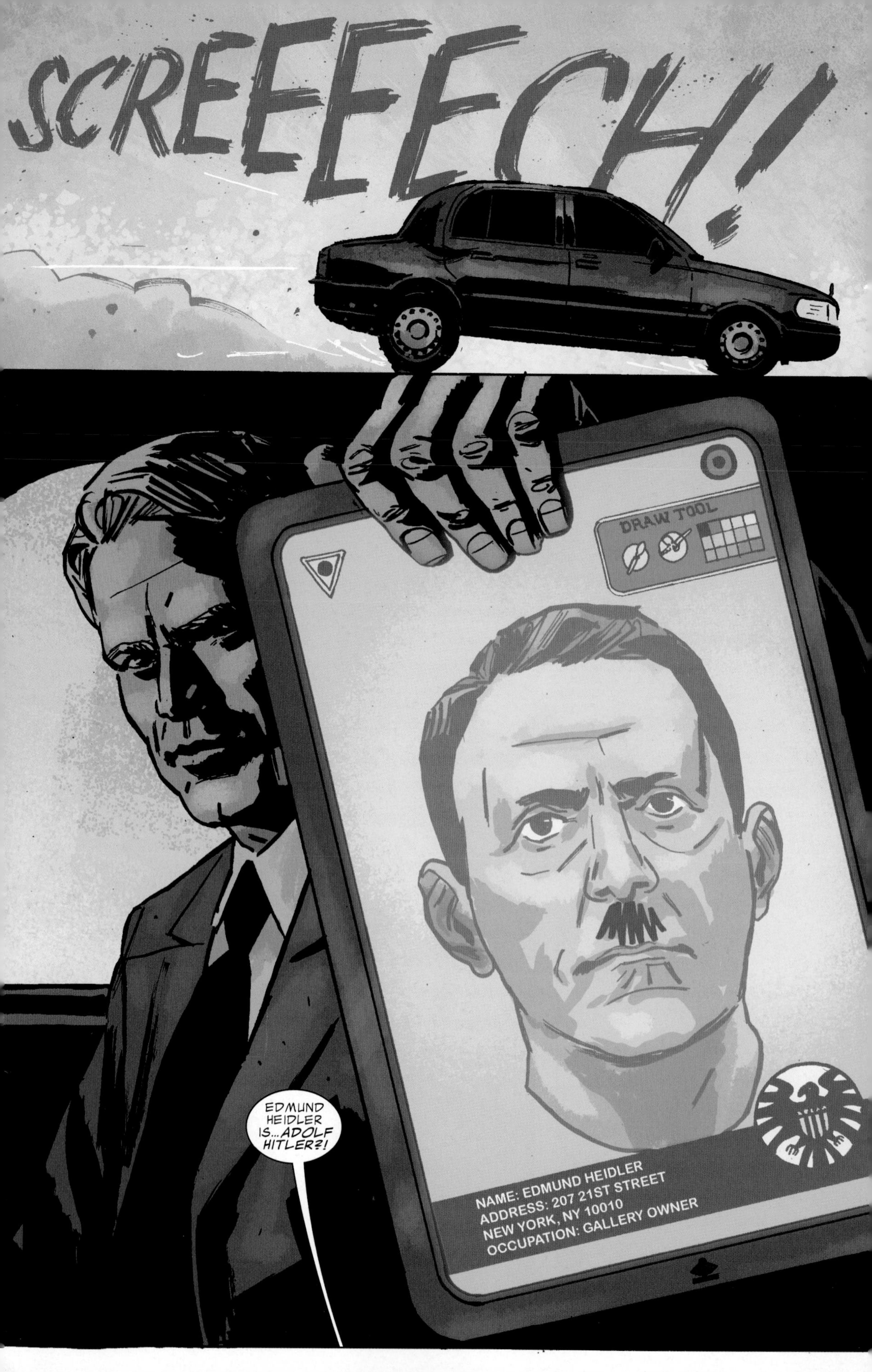
SCREEEECH!
DRAW TOOL
EDMUND HEIDLER IS...ADOLF HITLER?!
NAME: EDMUND HEIDLER
ADDRESS: 207 21ST STREET
NEW YORK, NY 10010
OCCUPATION: GALLERY OWNER

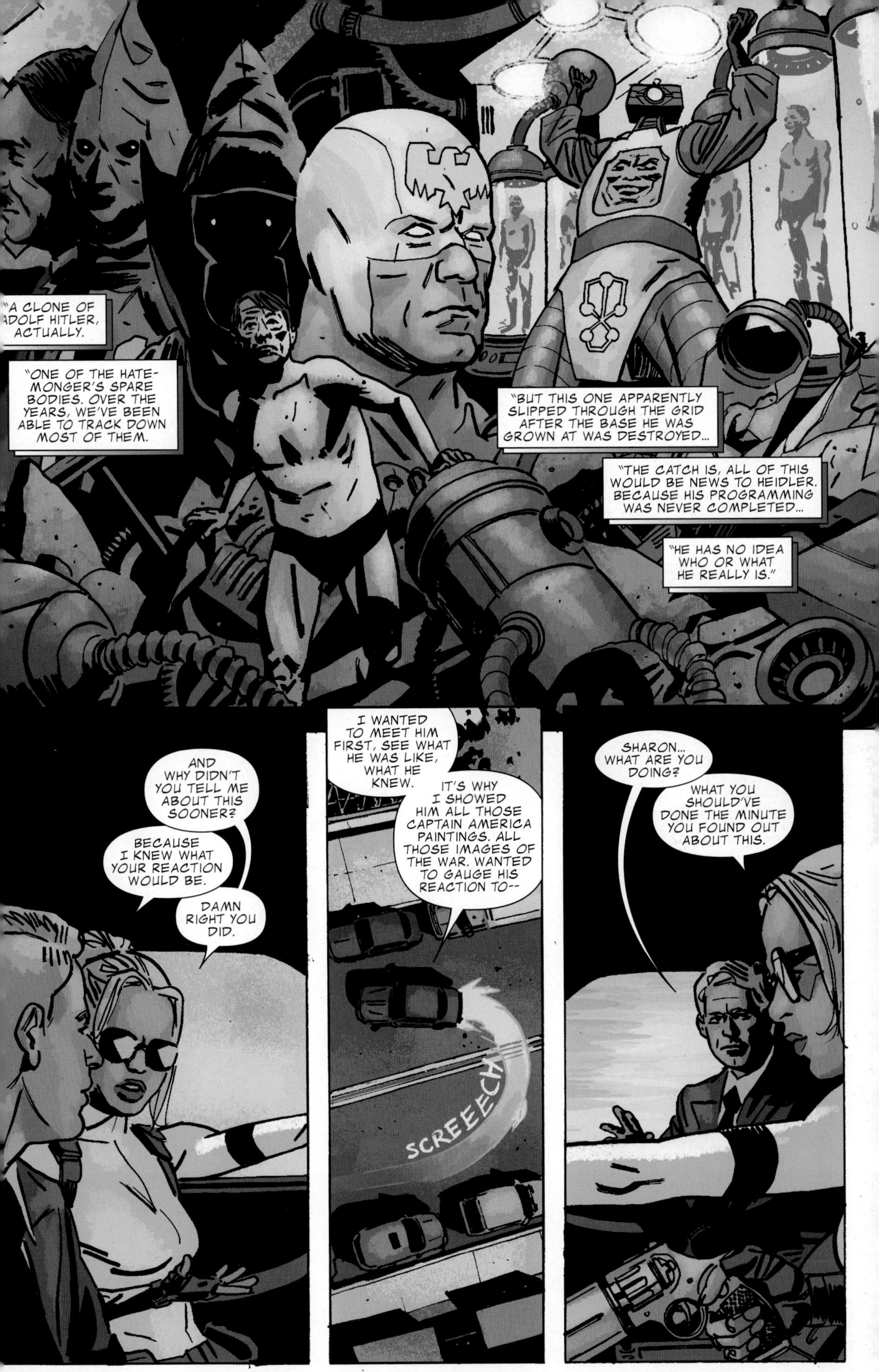
"A CLONE OF ADOLF HITLER, ACTUALLY.
"ONE OF THE HATE-MONGER'S SPARE BODIES. OVER THE YEARS, WE'VE BEEN ABLE TO TRACK DOWN MOST OF THEM.
"BUT THIS ONE APPARENTLY SLIPPED THROUGH THE GRID AFTER THE BASE HE WAS GROWN AT WAS DESTROYED...
"THE CATCH IS, ALL OF THIS WOULD BE NEWS TO HEIDLER. BECAUSE HIS PROGRAMMING WAS NEVER COMPLETED...
"HE HAS NO IDEA WHO OR WHAT HE REALLY IS."
AND WHY DIDN'T YOU TELL ME ABOUT THIS SOONER?
BECAUSE I KNEW WHAT YOUR REACTION WOULD BE.
DAMN RIGHT YOU DID.
I WANTED TO MEET HIM FIRST, SEE WHAT HE WAS LIKE, WHAT HE KNEW.
IT'S WHY I SHOWED HIM ALL THOSE CAPTAIN AMERICA PAINTINGS. ALL THOSE IMAGES OF THE WAR. WANTED TO GAUGE HIS REACTION TO--
SCREEECH
SHARON... WHAT ARE YOU DOING?
WHAT YOU SHOULD'VE DONE THE MINUTE YOU FOUND OUT ABOUT THIS.

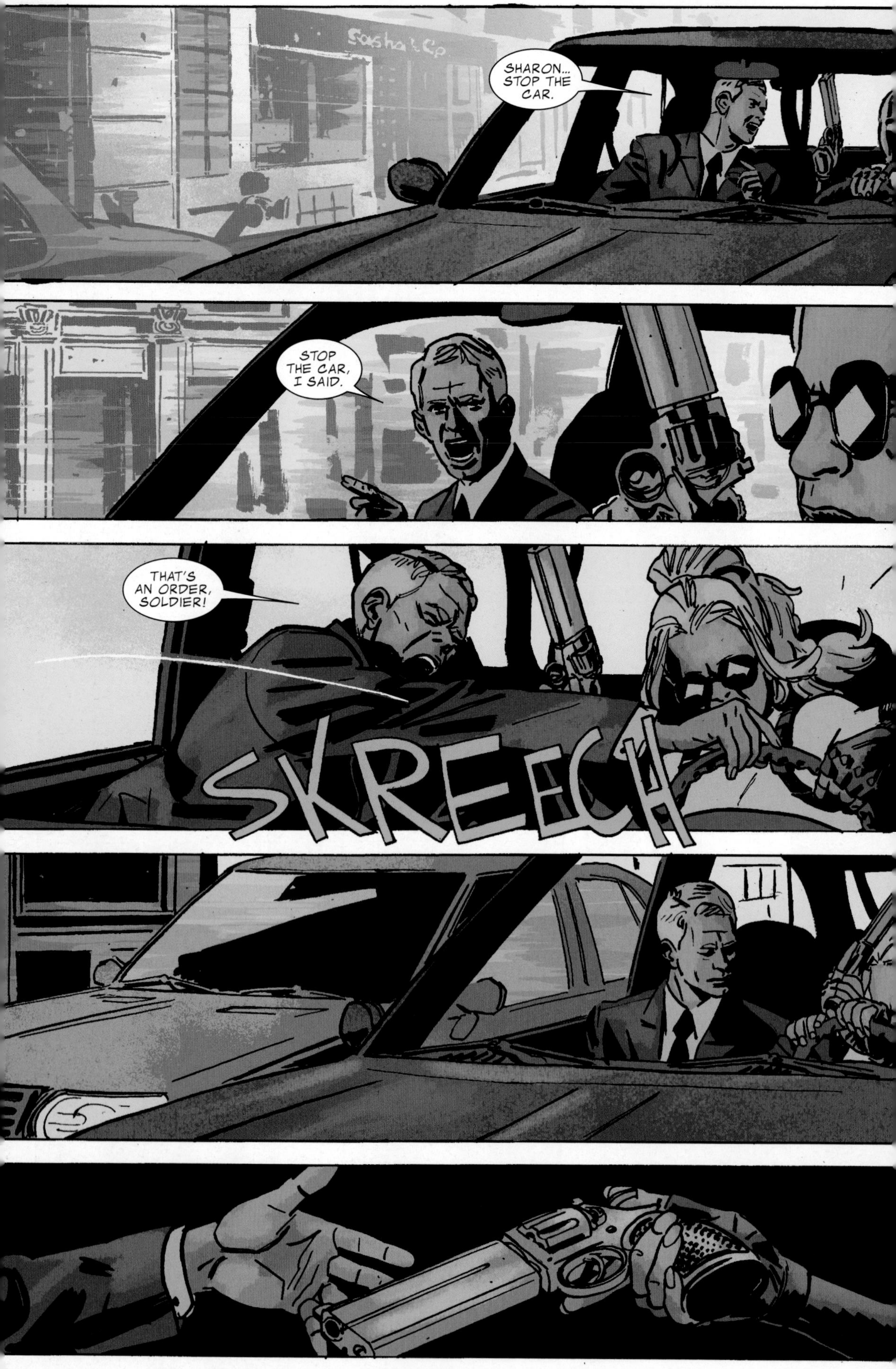
SHARON... STOP THE CAR.
STOP THE CAR, I SAID.
THAT'S AN ORDER, SOLDIER!
SKREECH

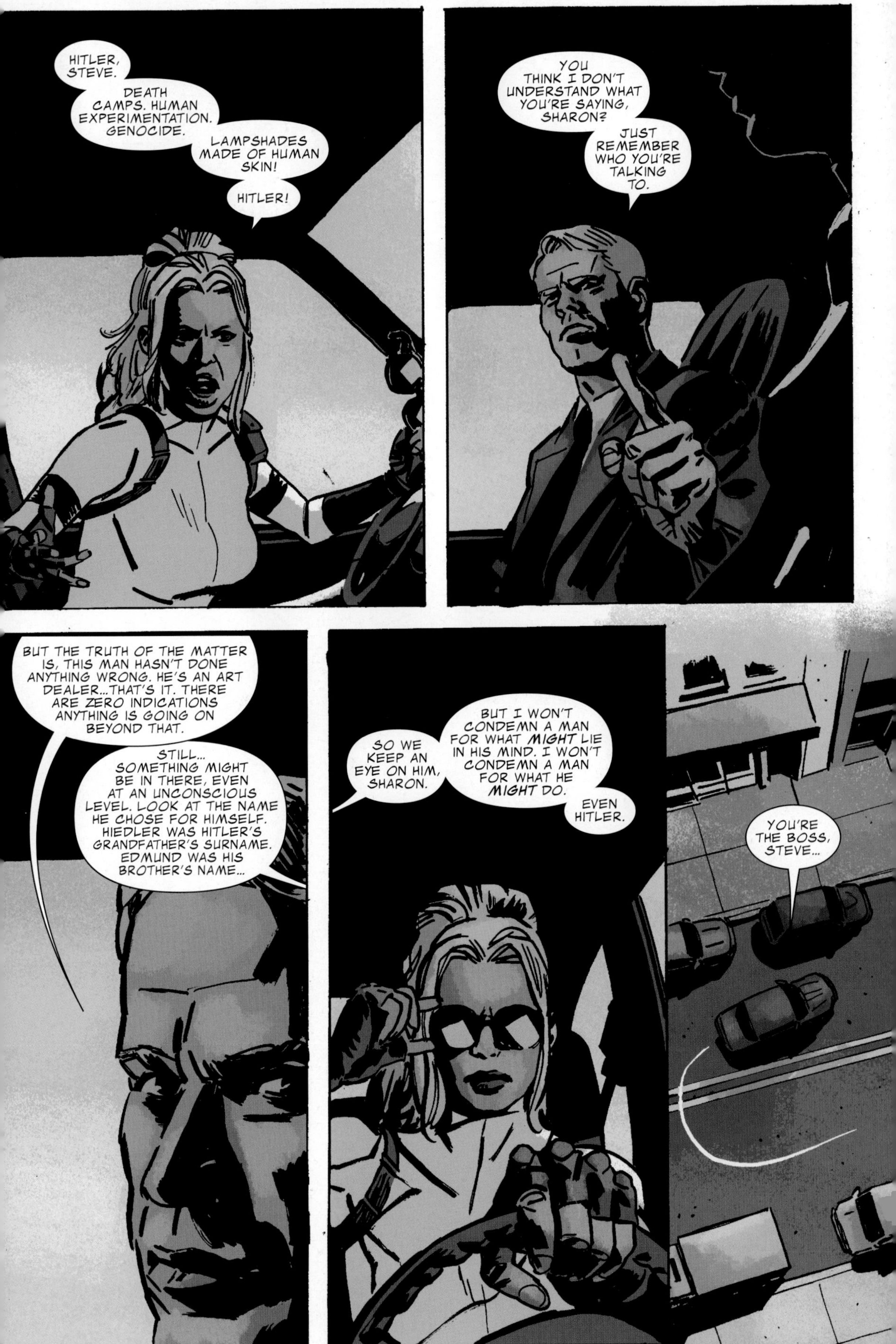
HITLER, STEVE.
DEATH CAMPS. HUMAN EXPERIMENTATION. GENOCIDE.
LAMPSHADES MADE OF HUMAN SKIN!
HITLER!
YOU THINK I DON'T UNDERSTAND WHAT YOU'RE SAYING, SHARON?
JUST REMEMBER WHO YOU'RE TALKING TO.
BUT THE TRUTH OF THE MATTER IS, THIS MAN HASN'T DONE ANYTHING WRONG. HE'S AN ART DEALER...THAT'S IT. THERE ARE ZERO INDICATIONS ANYTHING IS GOING ON BEYOND THAT.
STILL... SOMETHING MIGHT BE IN THERE, EVEN AT AN UNCONSCIOUS LEVEL. LOOK AT THE NAME HE CHOSE FOR HIMSELF. HIEDLER WAS HITLER'S GRANDFATHER'S SURNAME. EDMUND WAS HIS BROTHER'S NAME...
SO WE KEEP AN EYE ON HIM, SHARON.
BUT I WON'T CONDEMN A MAN FOR WHAT MIGHT LIE IN HIS MIND. I WON'T CONDEMN A MAN FOR WHAT HE MIGHT DO.
EVEN HITLER.
YOU'RE THE BOSS, STEVE...

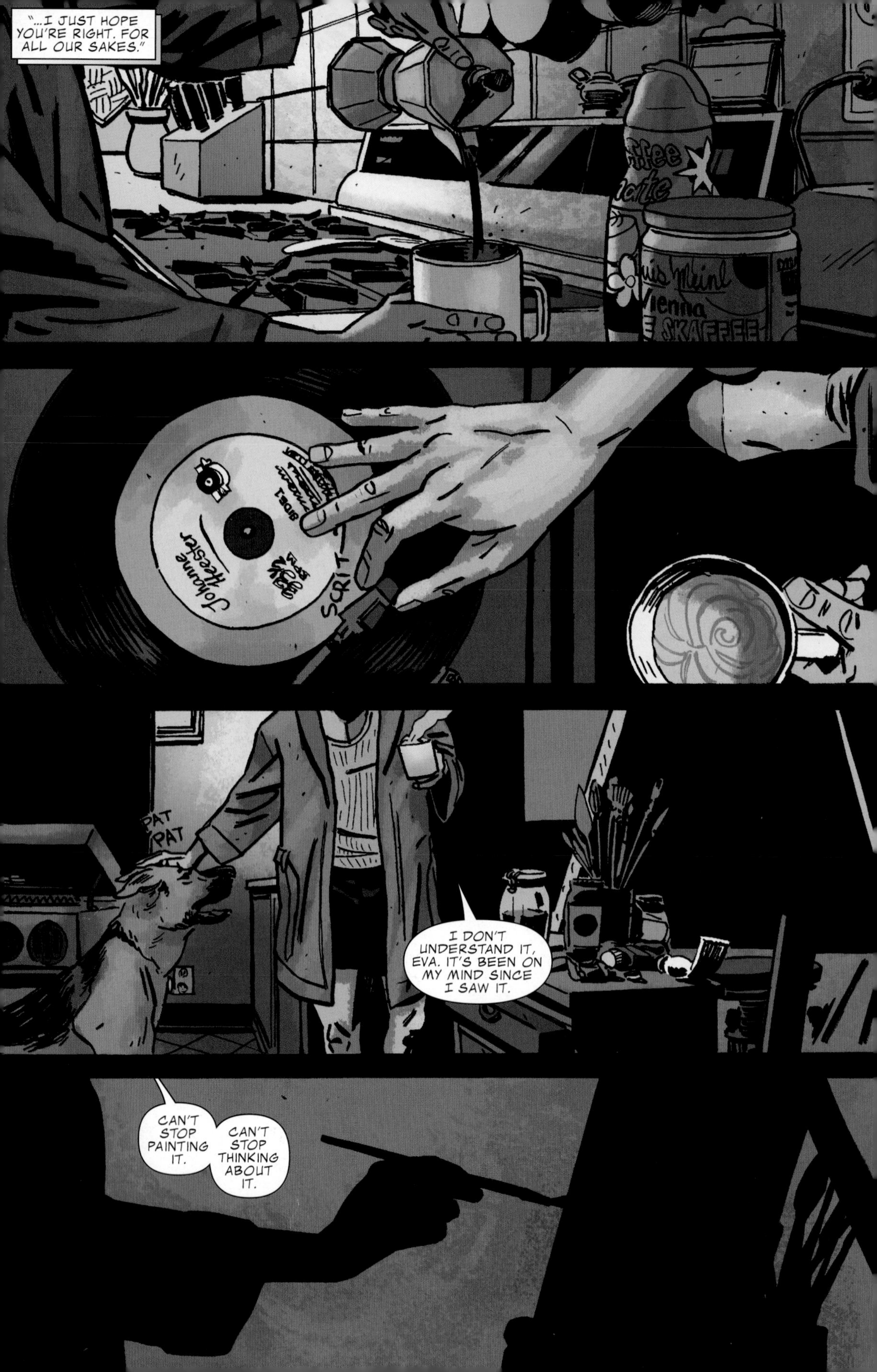
"...I JUST HOPE YOU'RE RIGHT. FOR ALL OUR SAKES."
PAT PAT
I DON'T UNDERSTAND IT, EVA. IT'S BEEN ON MY MIND SINCE I SAW IT.
CAN'T STOP PAINTING IT.
CAN'T STOP THINKING ABOUT IT.

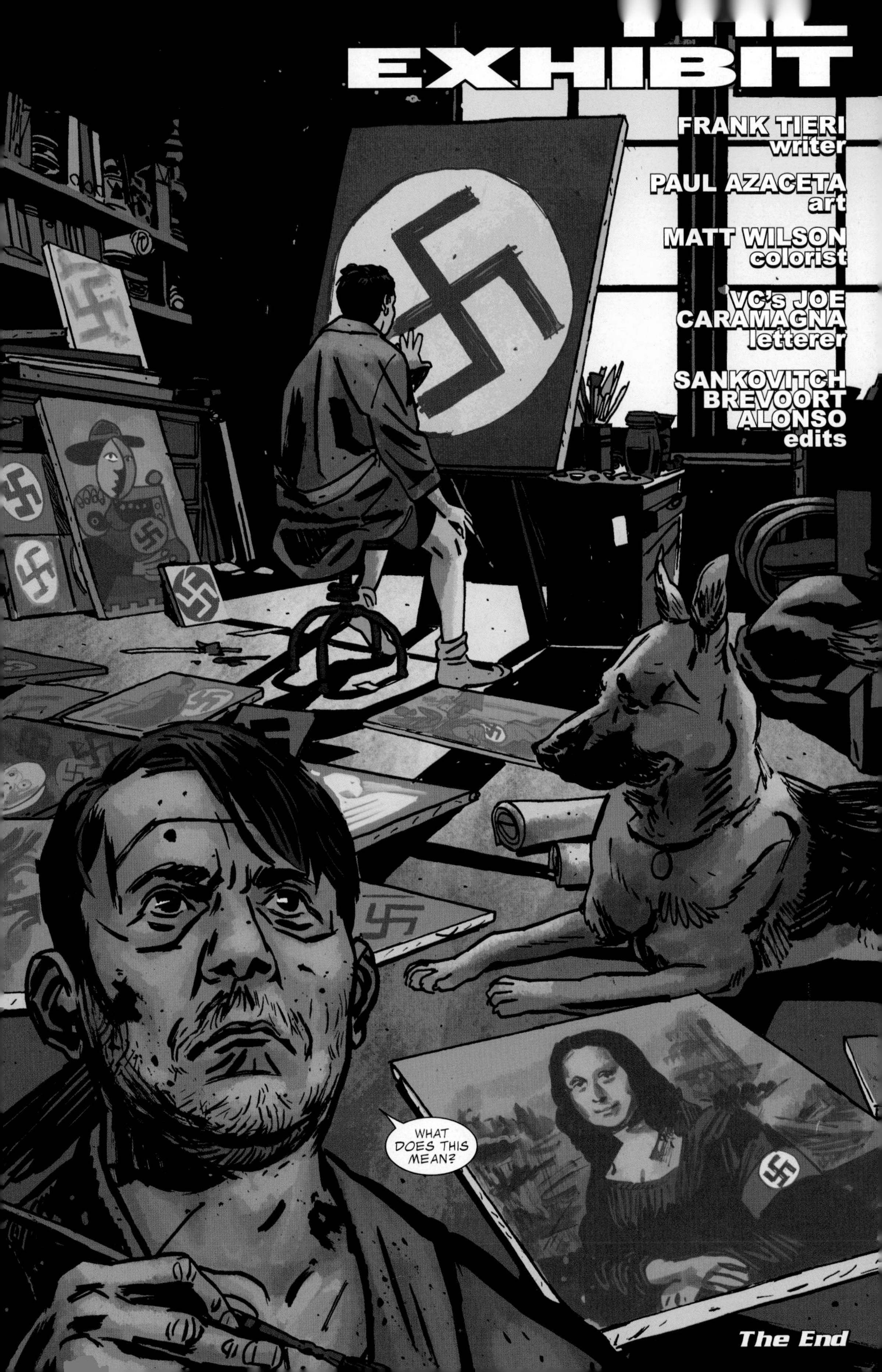
EXHIBIT
FRANK TIERI
writer
PAUL AZACETA
art
MATT WILSON
colorist
VC's JOE CARAMAGNA
letterer
SANKOVITCH
BREVOORT
ALONSO
edits
WHAT DOES THIS MEAN?
The End

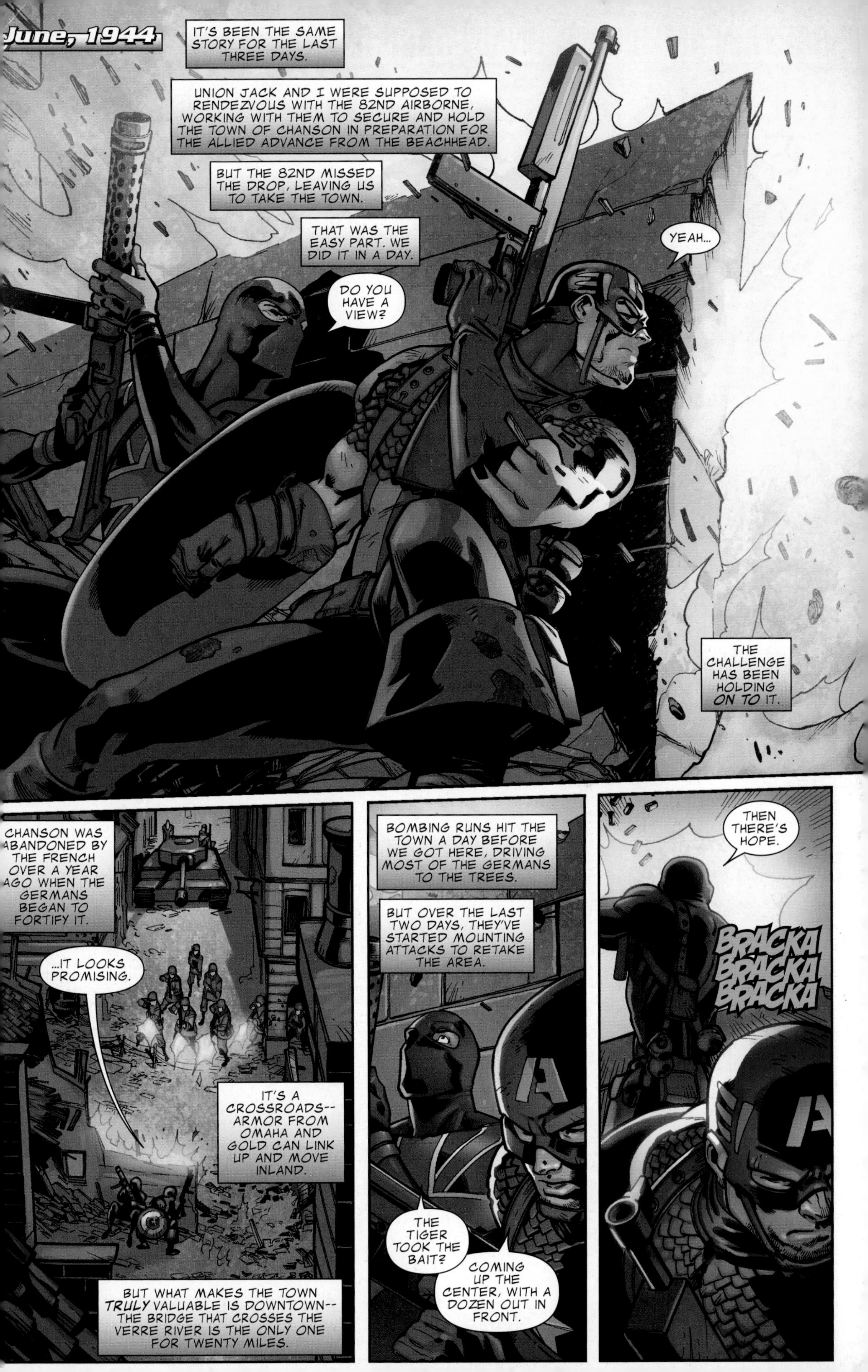

June, 1944
IT'S BEEN THE SAME STORY FOR THE LAST THREE DAYS.
UNION JACK AND I WERE SUPPOSED TO RENDEZVOUS WITH THE 82ND AIRBORNE, WORKING WITH THEM TO SECURE AND HOLD THE TOWN OF CHANSON IN PREPARATION FOR THE ALLIED ADVANCE FROM THE BEACHHEAD.
BUT THE 82ND MISSED THE DROP, LEAVING US TO TAKE THE TOWN.
THAT WAS THE EASY PART. WE DID IT IN A DAY.
DO YOU HAVE A VIEW?
YEAH...
THE CHALLENGE HAS BEEN HOLDING *ON TO* IT.
CHANSON WAS ABANDONED BY THE FRENCH OVER A YEAR AGO WHEN THE GERMANS BEGAN TO FORTIFY IT.
...IT LOOKS PROMISING.
IT'S A CROSSROADS-- ARMOR FROM OMAHA AND GOLD CAN LINK UP AND MOVE INLAND.
BUT WHAT MAKES THE TOWN *TRULY* VALUABLE IS DOWNTOWN-- THE BRIDGE THAT CROSSES THE VERRE RIVER IS THE ONLY ONE FOR TWENTY MILES.
BOMBING RUNS HIT THE TOWN A DAY BEFORE WE GOT HERE, DRIVING MOST OF THE GERMANS TO THE TREES.
BUT OVER THE LAST TWO DAYS, THEY'VE STARTED MOUNTING ATTACKS TO RETAKE THE AREA.
THE TIGER TOOK THE BAIT?
COMING UP THE CENTER, WITH A DOZEN OUT IN FRONT.
THEN THERE'S HOPE.
BRACKA BRACKA BRACKA

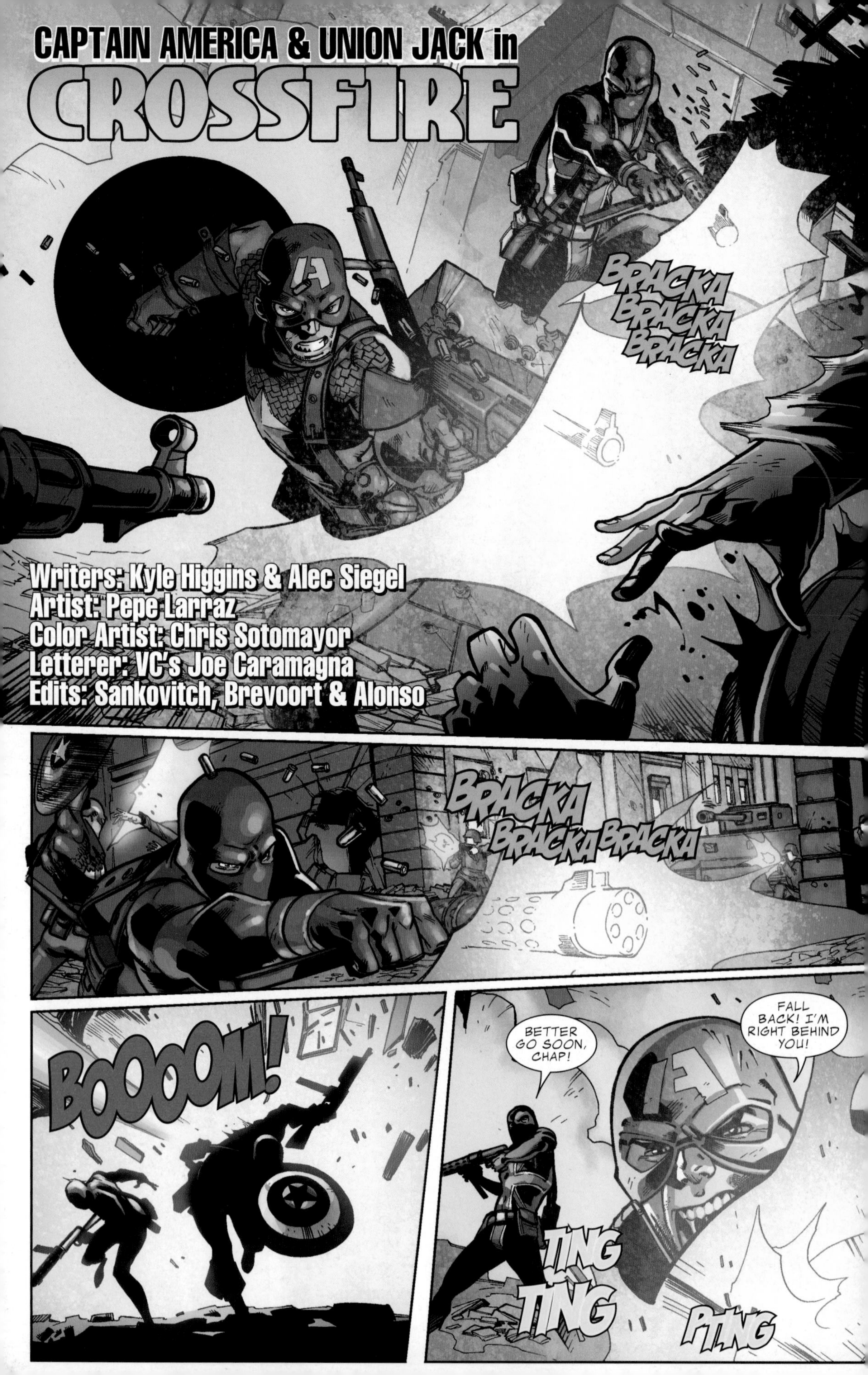
CAPTAIN AMERICA & UNION JACK in
CROSSFIRE
BRACKA BRACKA BRACKA
Writers: Kyle Higgins & Alec Siegel
Artist: Pepe Larraz
Color Artist: Chris Sotomayor
Letterer: VC's Joe Caramagna
Edits: Sankovitch, Brevoort & Alonso
BRACKA BRACKA BRACKA
BOOOOM!
BETTER GO SOON, CHAP!
FALL BACK! I'M RIGHT BEHIND YOU!
TING
TING
PTING

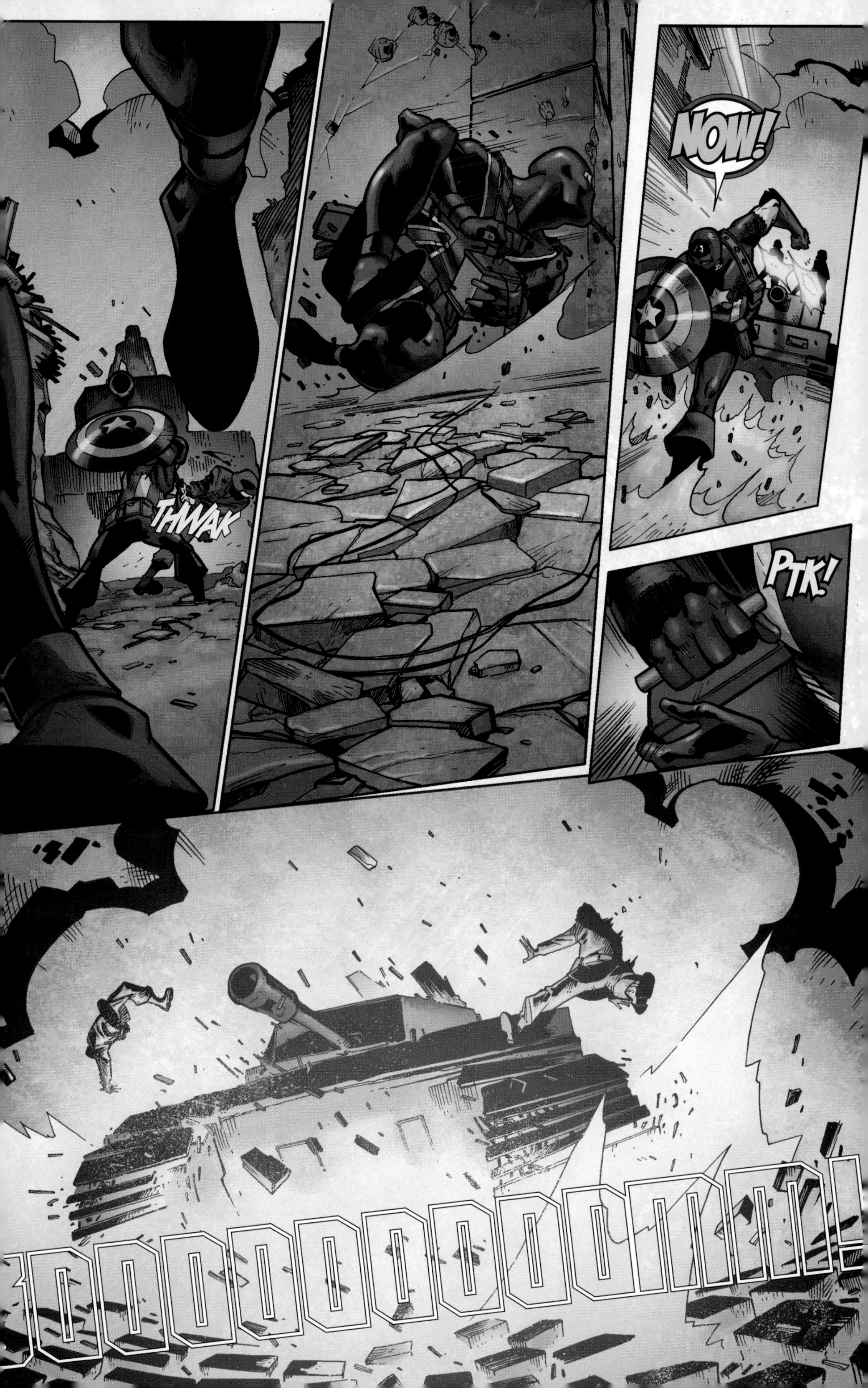
THWAK
NOW!
PTK!
BOOOOOOOOOMM!

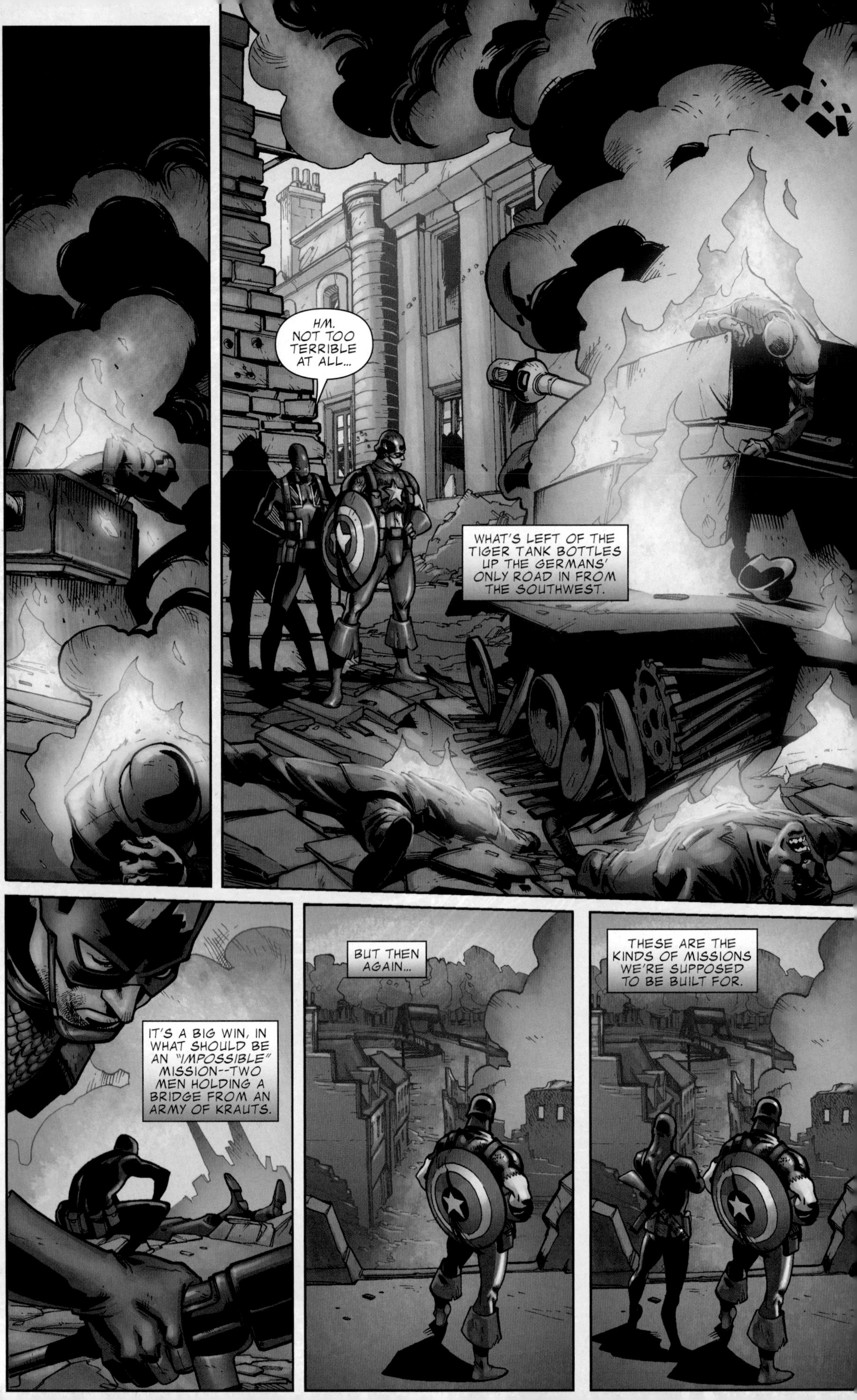
HM. NOT TOO TERRIBLE AT ALL...
WHAT'S LEFT OF THE TIGER TANK BOTTLES UP THE GERMANS' ONLY ROAD IN FROM THE SOUTHWEST.
IT'S A BIG WIN, IN WHAT SHOULD BE AN "IMPOSSIBLE" MISSION--TWO MEN HOLDING A BRIDGE FROM AN ARMY OF KRAUTS.
BUT THEN AGAIN...
THESE ARE THE KINDS OF MISSIONS WE'RE SUPPOSED TO BE BUILT FOR.

THE NEXT TWO DAYS ARE QUIET. NO SIGN OF TROOP MOVEMENT AT ALL.

WE WONDER OUT LOUD IF THEY MIGHT BE FALLING BACK AS THE ALLIES MARCH CLOSER, MAYBE EVEN RETREATING BECAUSE "THE FLAGS" ARE HERE.

BUT WE'RE NOT THAT LUCKY.

TREE LINE. TWO HUNDRED YARDS.

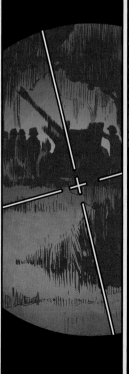

SO IT'S BLOODY ARTILLERY THEN. GONNA TRY AN' DRIVE US OUT...

AND THAT'S WHEN THINGS GET INTERESTING.

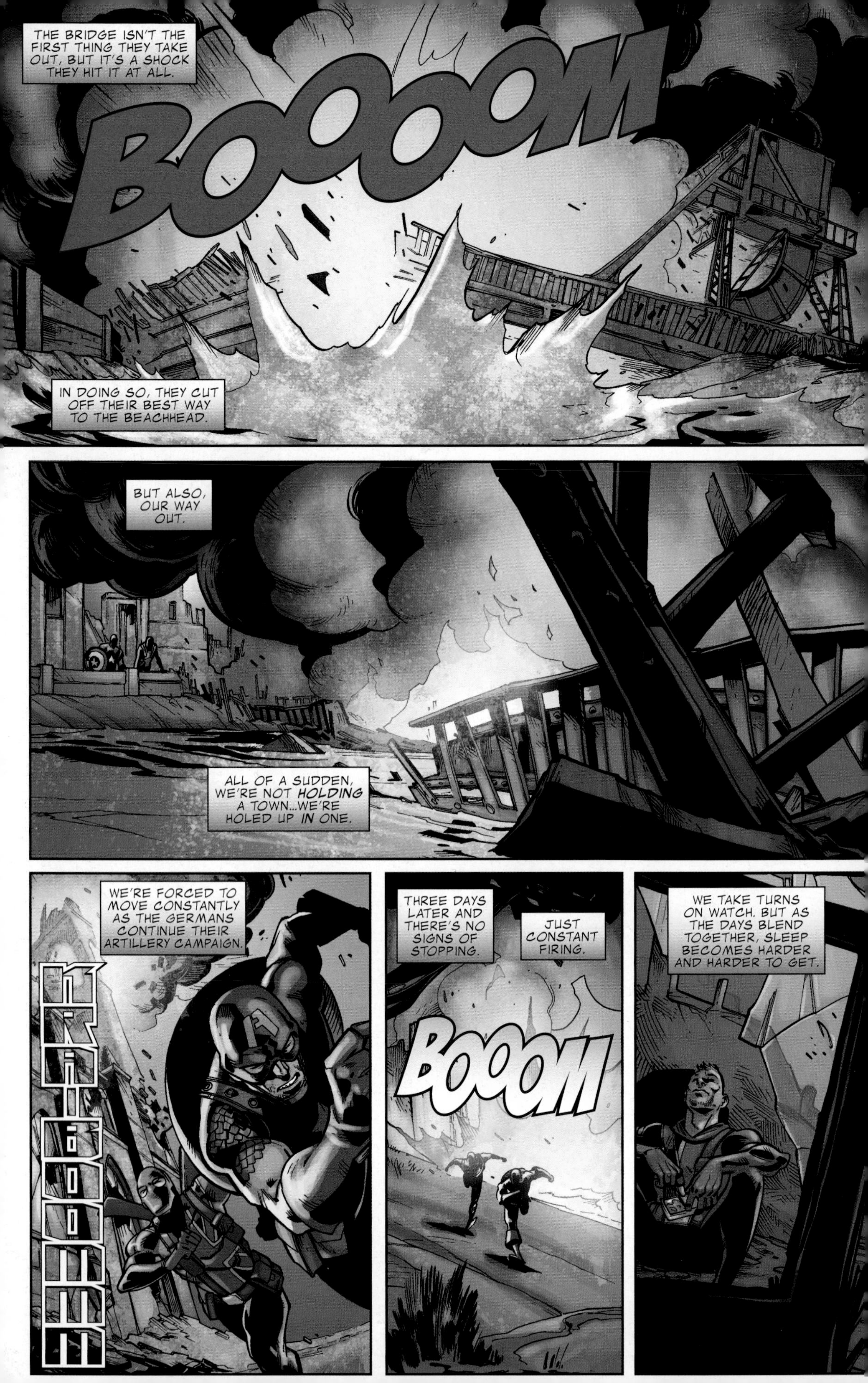
THE BRIDGE ISN'T THE FIRST THING THEY TAKE OUT, BUT IT'S A SHOCK THEY HIT IT AT ALL.
BOOOOM
IN DOING SO, THEY CUT OFF THEIR BEST WAY TO THE BEACHHEAD.
BUT ALSO, OUR WAY OUT.
ALL OF A SUDDEN, WE'RE NOT HOLDING A TOWN...WE'RE HOLED UP IN ONE.
WE'RE FORCED TO MOVE CONSTANTLY AS THE GERMANS CONTINUE THEIR ARTILLERY CAMPAIGN.
THREE DAYS LATER AND THERE'S NO SIGNS OF STOPPING.
JUST CONSTANT FIRING.
BOOOM
WE TAKE TURNS ON WATCH. BUT AS THE DAYS BLEND TOGETHER, SLEEP BECOMES HARDER AND HARDER TO GET.

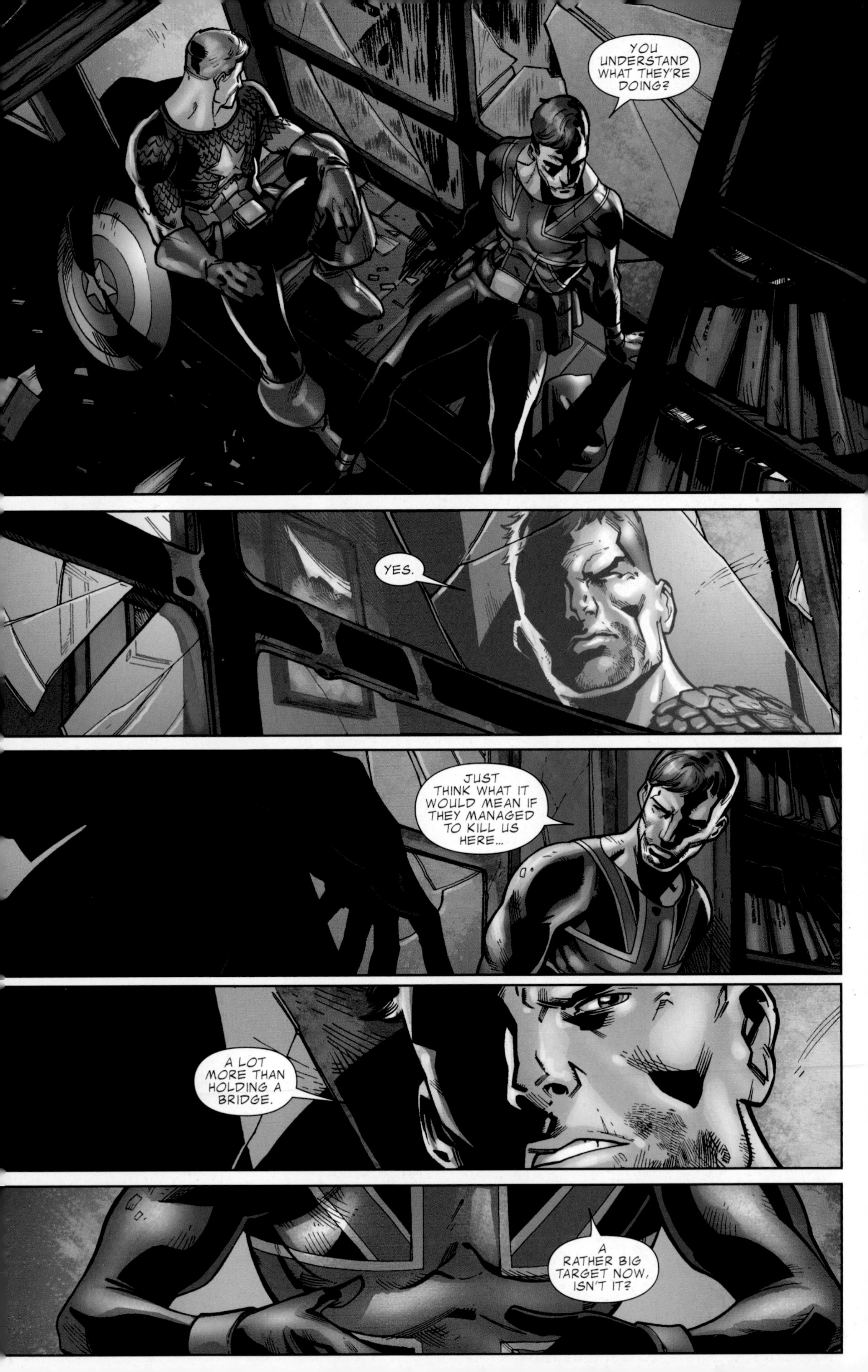
YOU UNDERSTAND WHAT THEY'RE DOING?
YES.
JUST THINK WHAT IT WOULD MEAN IF THEY MANAGED TO KILL US HERE...
A LOT MORE THAN HOLDING A BRIDGE.
A RATHER BIG TARGET NOW, ISN'T IT?

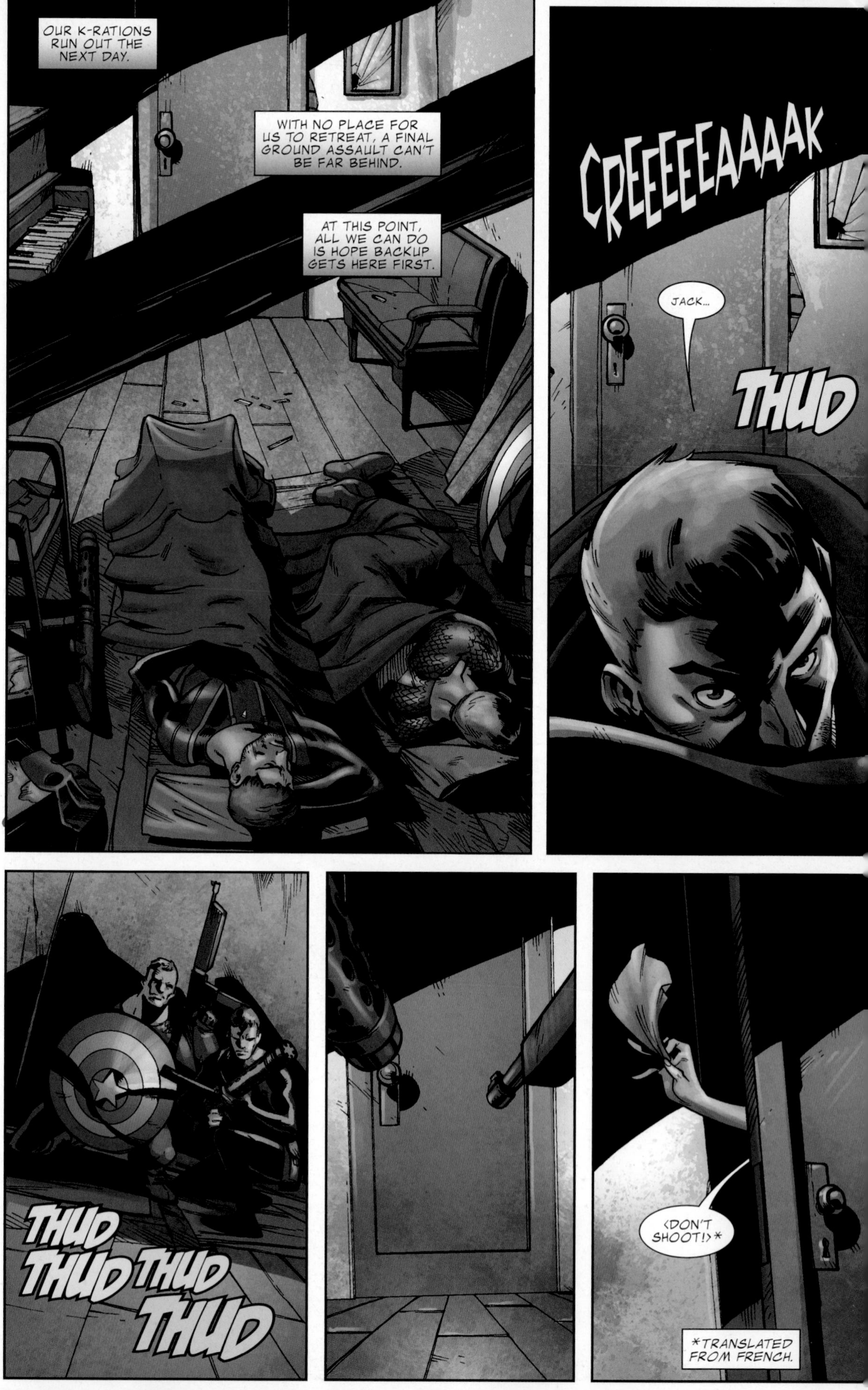
OUR K-RATIONS RUN OUT THE NEXT DAY.
WITH NO PLACE FOR US TO RETREAT, A FINAL GROUND ASSAULT CAN'T BE FAR BEHIND.
AT THIS POINT, ALL WE CAN DO IS HOPE BACKUP GETS HERE FIRST.
CREEEEEAAAAK
JACK...
THUD
THUD THUD THUD THUD
‹DON'T SHOOT!›*
*TRANSLATED FROM FRENCH.

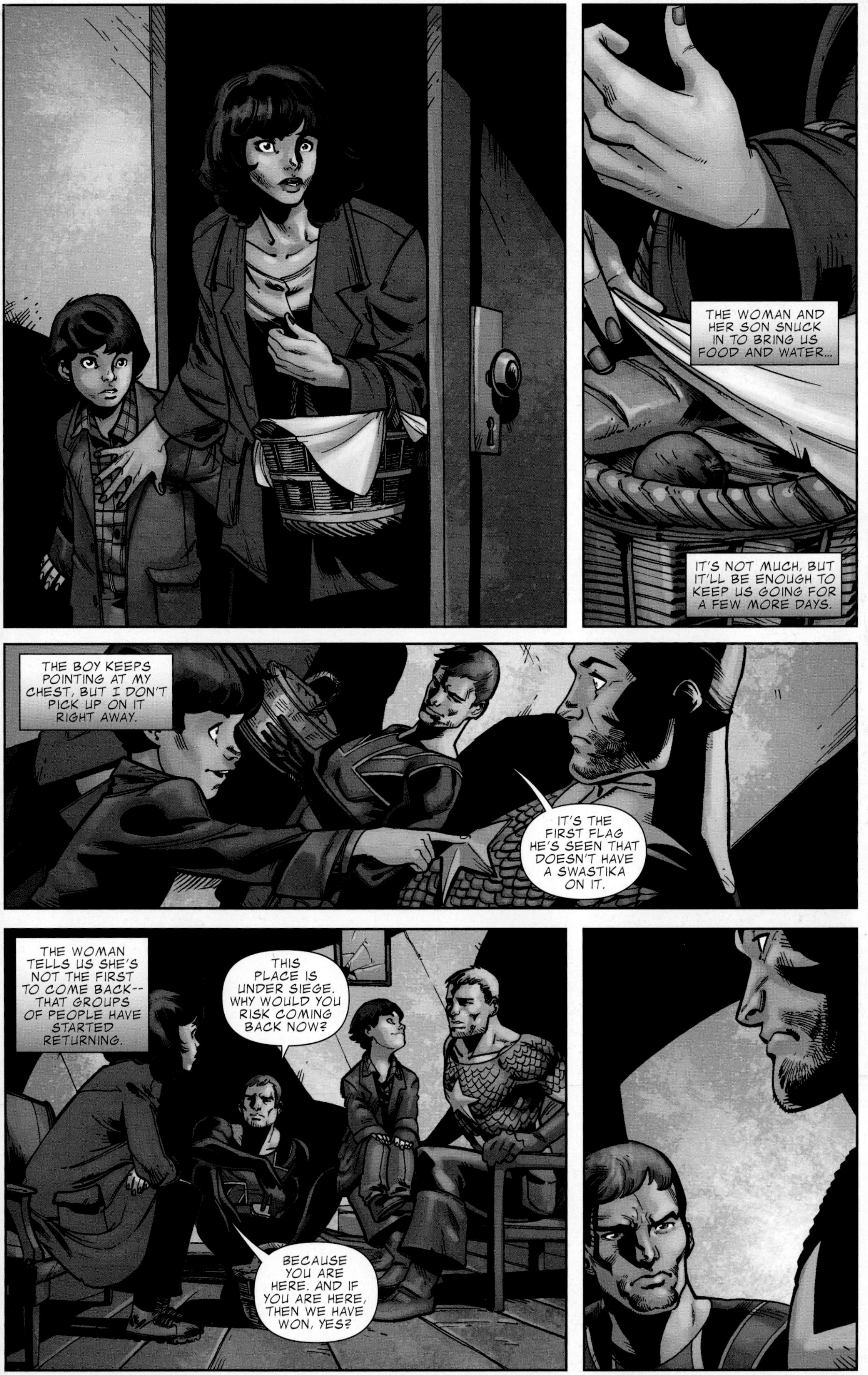
THE WOMAN AND HER SON SNUCK IN TO BRING US FOOD AND WATER...
IT'S NOT MUCH, BUT IT'LL BE ENOUGH TO KEEP US GOING FOR A FEW MORE DAYS.
THE BOY KEEPS POINTING AT MY CHEST, BUT I DON'T PICK UP ON IT RIGHT AWAY.
IT'S THE FIRST FLAG HE'S SEEN THAT DOESN'T HAVE A SWASTIKA ON IT.
THE WOMAN TELLS US SHE'S NOT THE FIRST TO COME BACK--THAT GROUPS OF PEOPLE HAVE STARTED RETURNING.
THIS PLACE IS UNDER SIEGE. WHY WOULD YOU RISK COMING BACK NOW?
BECAUSE YOU ARE HERE. AND IF YOU ARE HERE, THEN WE HAVE WON, YES?

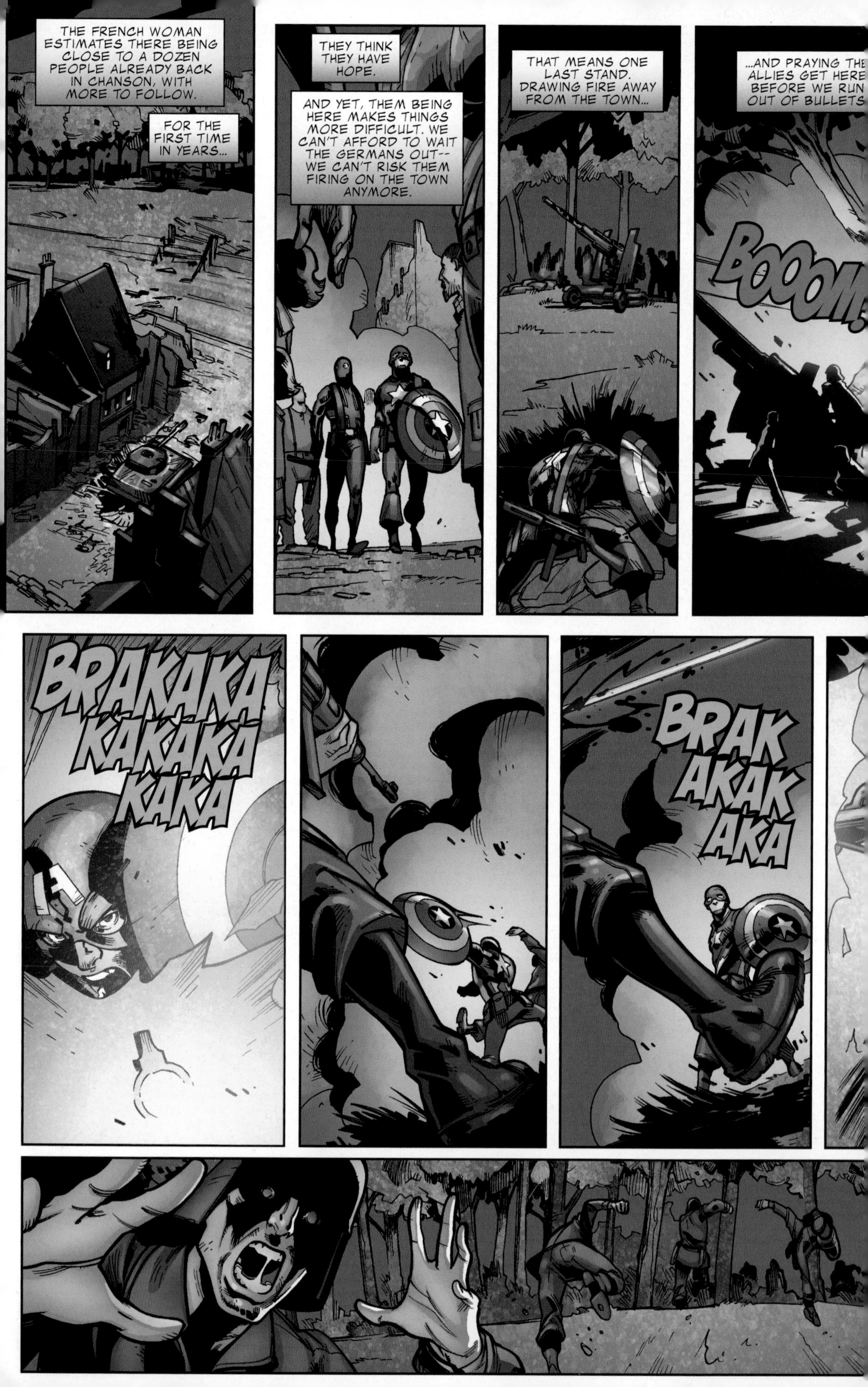
THE FRENCH WOMAN ESTIMATES THERE BEING CLOSE TO A DOZEN PEOPLE ALREADY BACK IN CHANSON, WITH MORE TO FOLLOW.
FOR THE FIRST TIME IN YEARS...
THEY THINK THEY HAVE HOPE.
AND YET, THEM BEING HERE MAKES THINGS MORE DIFFICULT. WE CAN'T AFFORD TO WAIT THE GERMANS OUT-- WE CAN'T RISK THEM FIRING ON THE TOWN ANYMORE.
THAT MEANS ONE LAST STAND. DRAWING FIRE AWAY FROM THE TOWN...
...AND PRAYING THE ALLIES GET HERE BEFORE WE RUN OUT OF BULLETS.
BOOOOM!
BRAKAKA KAKAKA KAKA
BRAK AKAK AKA

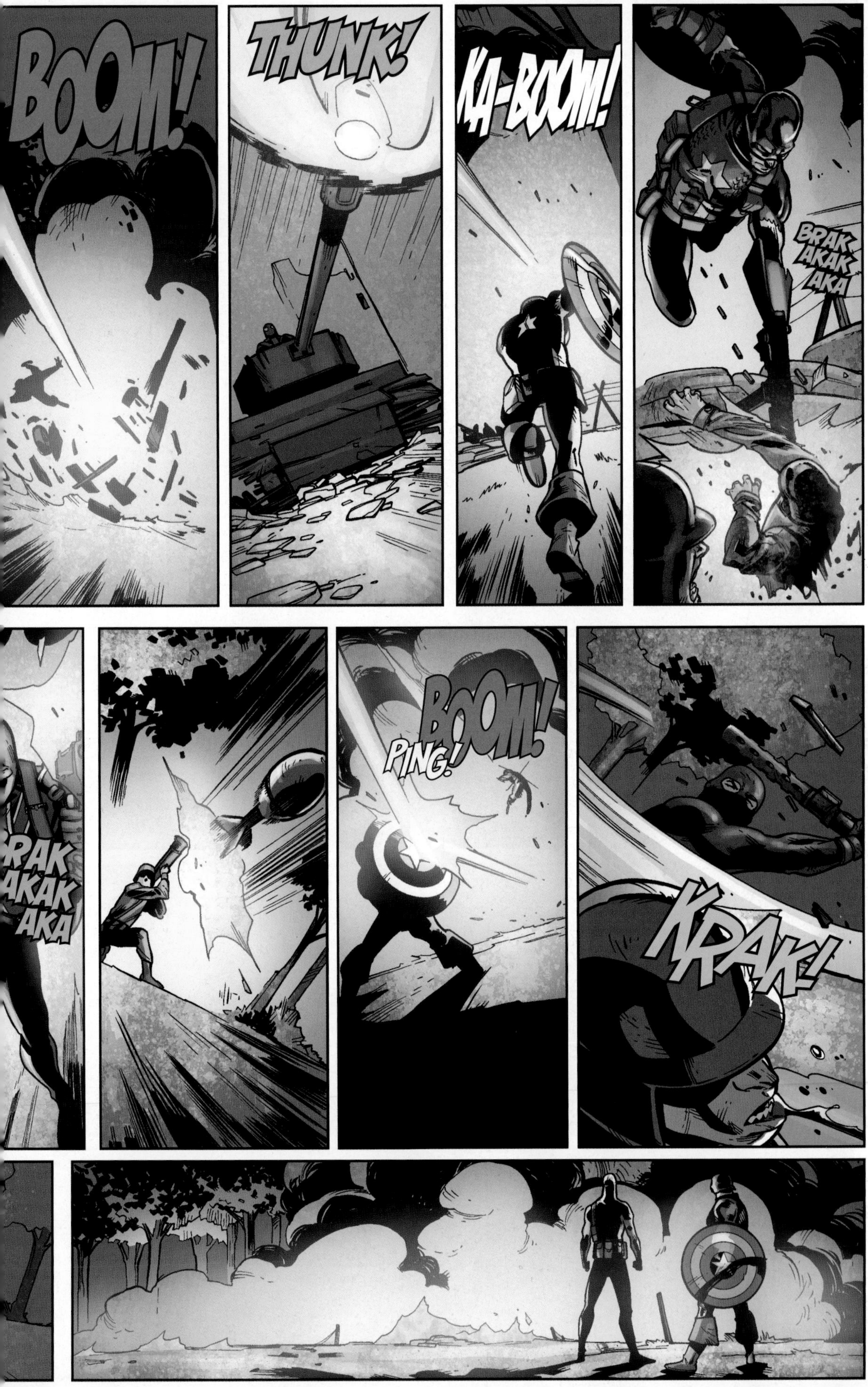
BOOM!
THUNK!
KA-BOOM!
BRAK AKAK AKA
RAK AKAK AKA
BOOM!
PING!
KRAK!

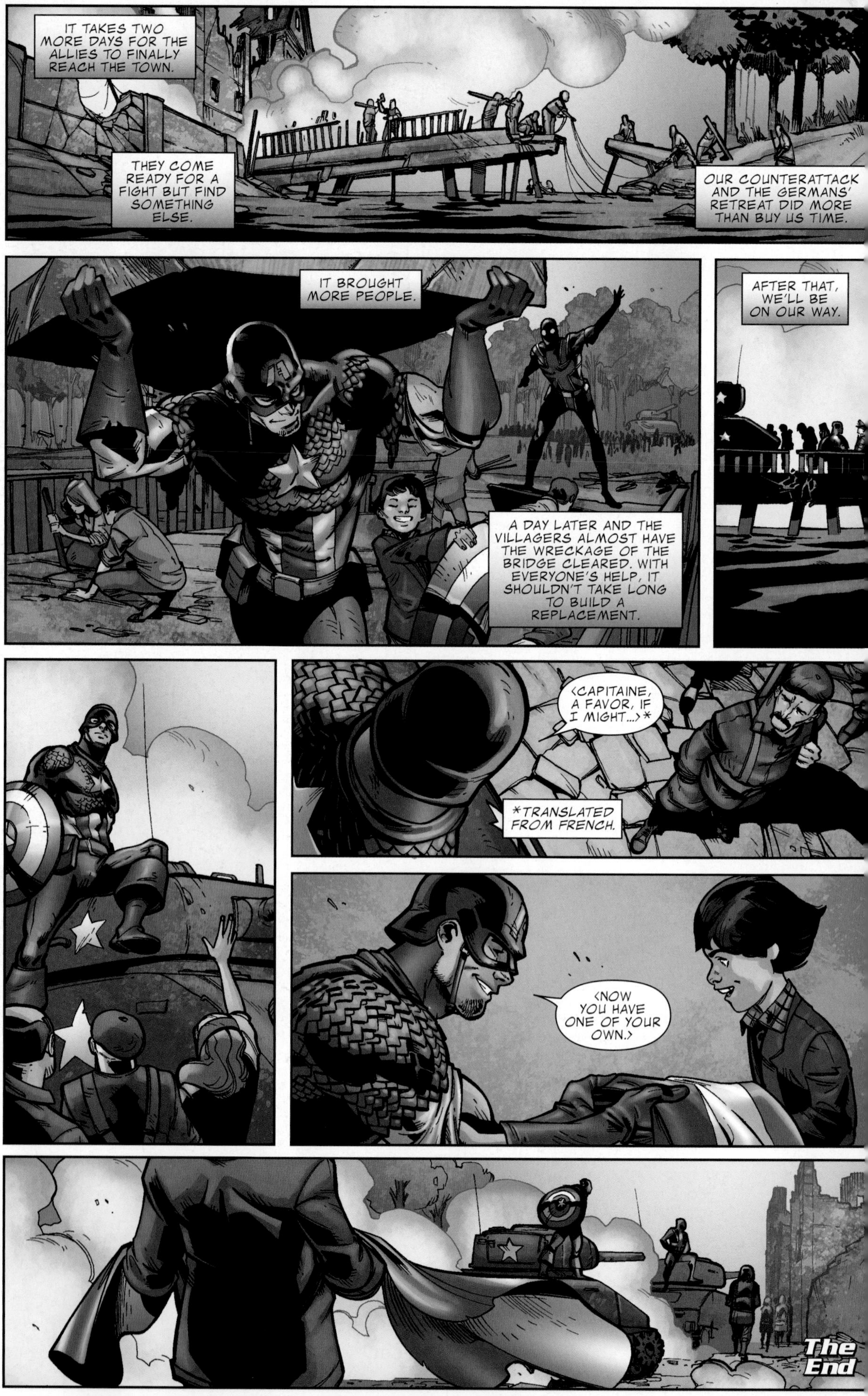
IT TAKES TWO MORE DAYS FOR THE ALLIES TO FINALLY REACH THE TOWN.
THEY COME READY FOR A FIGHT BUT FIND SOMETHING ELSE.
OUR COUNTERATTACK AND THE GERMANS' RETREAT DID MORE THAN BUY US TIME.
IT BROUGHT MORE PEOPLE.
A DAY LATER AND THE VILLAGERS ALMOST HAVE THE WRECKAGE OF THE BRIDGE CLEARED. WITH EVERYONE'S HELP, IT SHOULDN'T TAKE LONG TO BUILD A REPLACEMENT.
AFTER THAT, WE'LL BE ON OUR WAY.
<CAPITAINE, A FAVOR, IF I MIGHT...>*
*TRANSLATED FROM FRENCH.
<NOW YOU HAVE ONE OF YOUR OWN.>
The End

★★★ **BRUBAKER** AND **"BUTCH"** ★★★
ARE **CAPTAIN AMERICA'S** CREATIVE BROTHERS-IN-ARMS

BEHIND THE LINES

★ BY CHRIS ARRANT ★

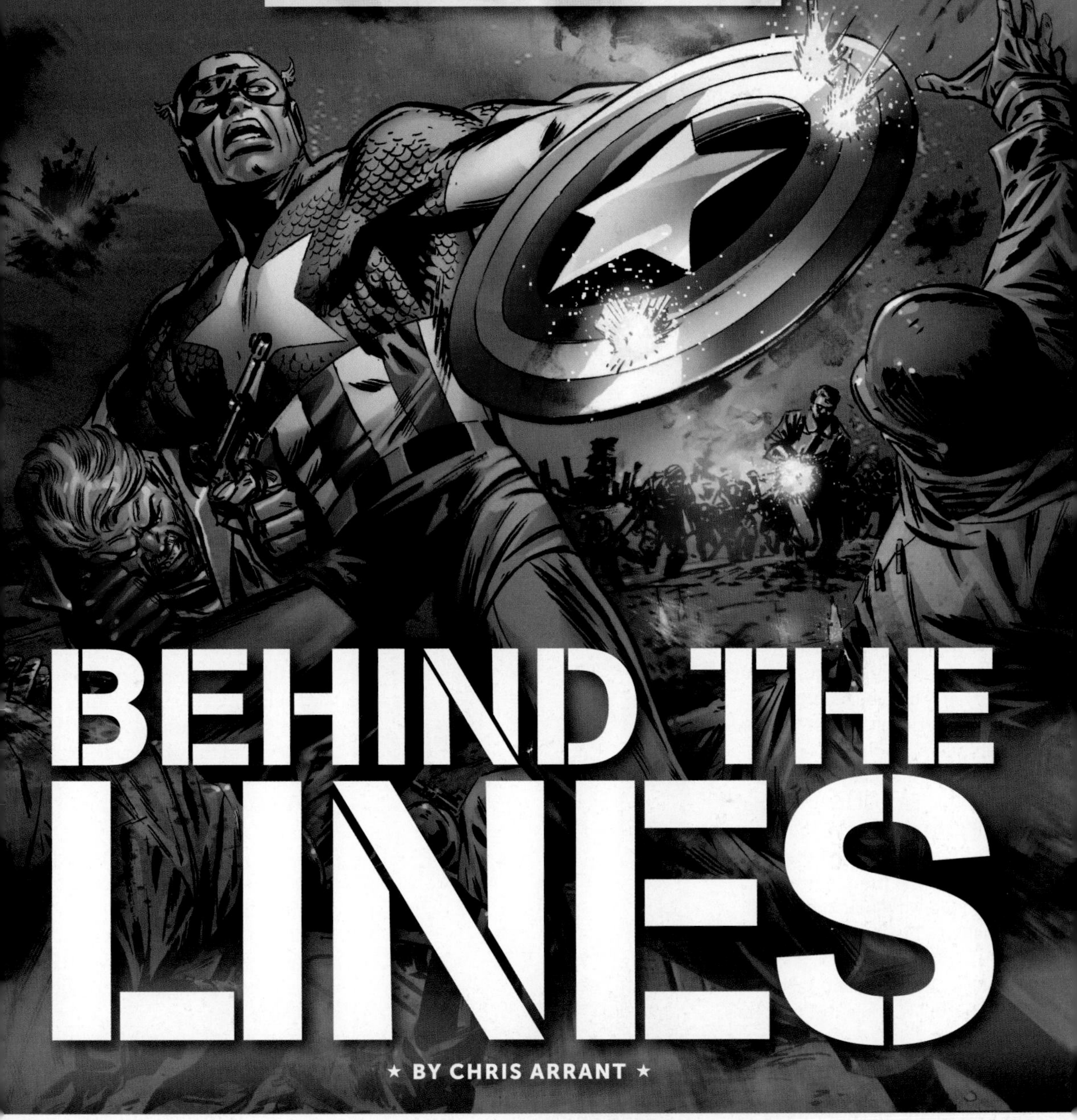

ART FROM *CAPTAIN AMERICA #600* BY BUTCH GUICE.

Ask anyone who's seen action what they'd most like to take into battle, and they'll rank a trustworthy partner at the top of the list. Any gun will run out of ammo, but a combat-ready brother-in-arms will never let you down. And in *Captain America*, longtime series scribe Ed Brubaker has had just that — times two — first with artist Steve Epting, invaluable to the writer in setting the tone for his run out of the gate, and now with Jackson "Butch" Guice, who's seen James "Bucky" Barnes through from his awkward first days as the new Captain America into his comfort zone as America's Sentinel of Liberty.

It's hard to believe that as the character rounds his 70th year, the title is as fresh as the day Joe Simon and Jack Kirby launched it during the months before World War II. Brubaker has been writing *Captain America* for nearly six years now, making it the noted crime writer's definitive work; Guice's experienced and steady hand has made it evident this is the book for which he's spent his whole career preparing. With the major motion picture *Captain America: The First Avenger* set for release later this year Brubaker and Guice have charted a course from the return of Steve Rogers and the ascension of Bucky Barnes as Cap to the last days of the Winter Soldier and a bitter homecoming in the cold wastelands of Russia.

SPOTLIGHT: It's good to talk to you two! You recently wrapped up the "Trial of Captain America" arc, which ended with Bucky giving in and taking the blame for the things he did under mind-control as the Winter Soldier. That seems like a big step for him. How will it affect things going forward with the series?

ED: It takes Bucky out of the country in the near future, just when he's trying to do what he obviously thought was the right thing. In our last story arc, he realized that as Captain America, when is it not the fault of the guy in the costume for what happened? Bucky took that a little bit too far, but his thinking is that it's the honorable thing to do — to stand up for acts that were committed, even though he doesn't feel completely responsible for it personally. While the trial was going on, you also saw Bucky began to embrace his new life and sacrifice his life for his friends. But now he's being shunted back to his worst nightmare — Russia, where he was turned into the Winter Soldier — and must finally face up with that portion of his life. Now he's in a Russian gulag, a Thunderdome type of place.

SPOTLIGHT: Bucky's been through a lot as an ex-boy soldier, an ex-spy and now an ex-con. But the actions we saw in *Captain America #615* — during the trial, as well as with Bucky risking it all to save his friends the Falcon and Black Widow — show that he's in a far different place than when he first came back onto the scene.

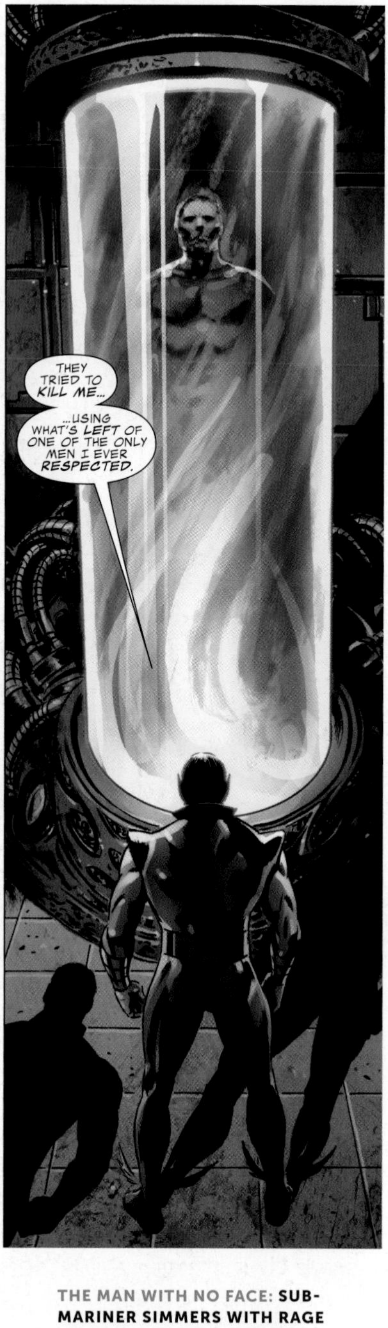
THEY TRIED TO KILL ME...
...USING WHAT'S LEFT OF ONE OF THE ONLY MEN I EVER RESPECTED.

THE MAN WITH NO FACE: SUB-MARINER SIMMERS WITH RAGE AS A VILLAIN FROM BUCKY'S PAST USES AND ABUSES THE ORIGINAL HUMAN TORCH. (ART FROM *CA #48* BY GUICE.)

ED: I think it's been a kind of redemption arc in some ways. He was a badass during World War II, and I think he — like most any soldier — had some awful stuff happen during the war that's taken forever to recover from. And the fate he ended up suffering after the war — enduring brainwashing as the Winter Soldier — became his own personal nightmare, and there's always a remnant of that with him. There are memories still inside him from the Winter Soldier days, and he blames himself for that. In a way, there are two warring sides of himself: one side that blames him for acts he committed as the Winter Soldier, and the other side telling him it wasn't his fault. That's how I've sort of pictured it in my head.

Once he got his memories back, thanks to Steve, he got on the road to redemption. With the "Trial of Captain America" arc, he came face-to-face with that. And now back in Russia, he's going to where the roots of it all were.

SPOTLIGHT: I've always thought Bucky was unique in that he didn't have a "normal" childhood. Steve Rogers grew up on the Lower East Side and was going to art school when the war broke out. Bucky never had anything like that.

ED: That's right. Bucky was a military brat and got orphaned on a military base, so he was raised as a military kid. As far as him being a "boy soldier," there were a lot of 16-year-olds in World War II — so he wasn't rare in that instance.

SPOTLIGHT: Butch, what's it like trying to draw this new person

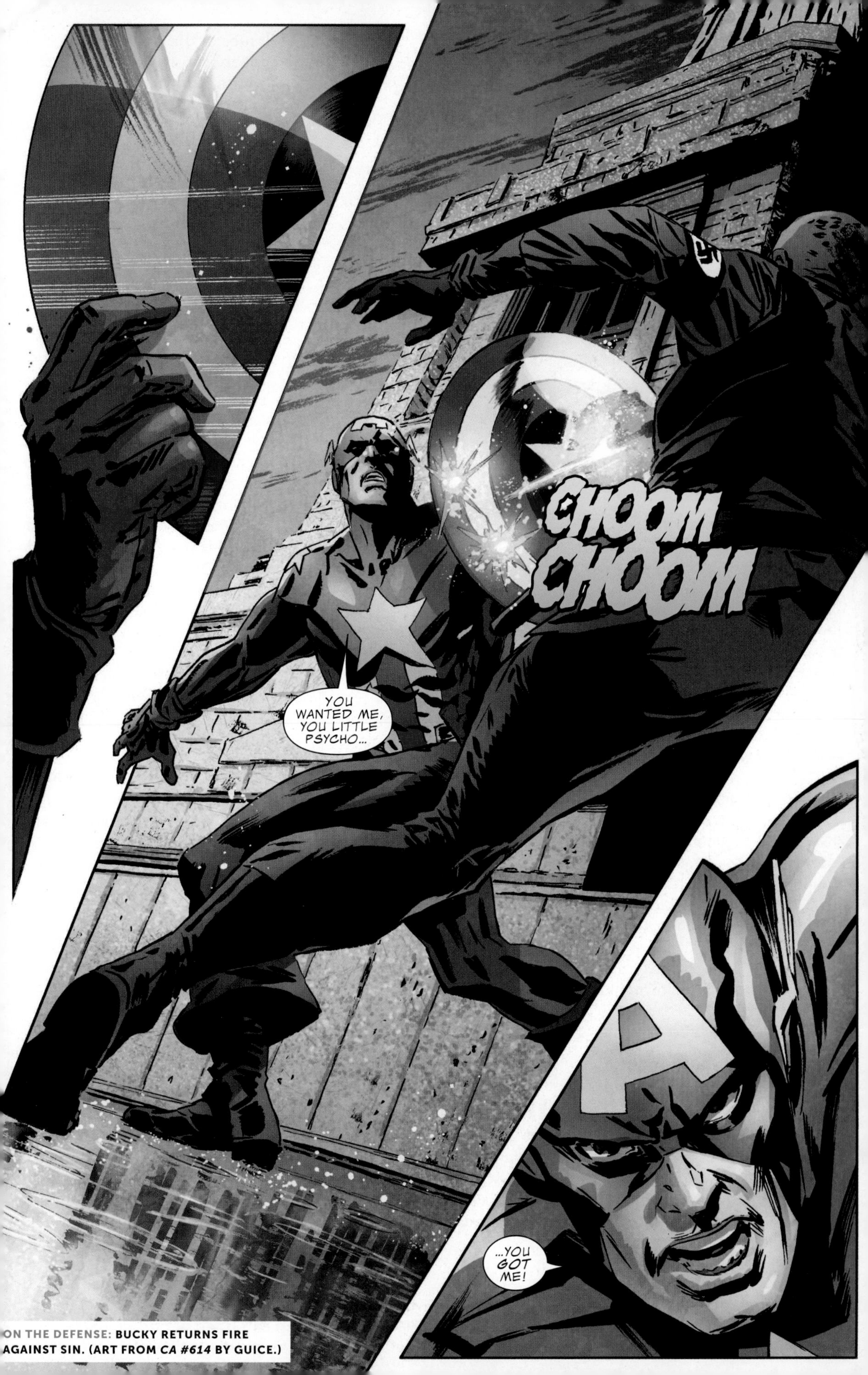
CHOOM CHOOM
YOU WANTED ME, YOU LITTLE PSYCHO...
...YOU GOT ME!

ON THE DEFENSE: **BUCKY RETURNS FIRE AGAINST SIN. (ART FROM *CA* #614 BY GUICE.)**

CAP ACTION! GUICE AND INKER RICK MAGYAR RECALL FORMER CAP ART GREATS JACK KIRBY AND GENE COLAN IN *CA #609*.

issues of the ongoing series, collaborated with Bryan Hitch on the *Reborn* miniseries, followed that up with a one-shot, and then rejoined the main series as the full-time artist. What's it like to be able to settle into a character and really put some miles on him and not jump around from one book to another?

BUTCH: Great! I admire and respect the ability certain artists possess to drop into a title at any point and effortlessly — or at least appear so — put their own confident, individual stamp on the visual look of a character and title. Unfortunately, I've never had that particularly elusive skill set. I have found there is always this slow-simmering creative building process which needs to take place for me — a mental taking stock of what is working and what needs fixing, a lot of back and forth in the creative bag of tricks — before I start to feel genuinely comfortable with what I'm producing.

So yes, this extended opportunity working on the *Captain America* book has been a very enjoyable experience.

SPOTLIGHT: Ed, what's it like teaming up with a veteran like Butch, who's so knowledgeable about the medium?

ED: It's pretty amazing, especially when he's able to pencil and ink himself. He's the complete package. He has his own style and is able to bring in the style of artists he grew up with like Jack Kirby, John Buscema and Jim Steranko. He's bringing artistically the same kind of influences I bring as a writer. When I write, I think back to Kirby and Steranko's work on *Captain America*. In fact, there's a montage in an upcoming issue where I asked Butch to do it like Steranko — and Butch out-Steranko'd Steranko. It really is kind of amazing to get someone so mentally attuned to do a modern take on that kind of artist.

under the Captain America mask — with a new mask all together?

BUTCH: Even after nearly thirty years of doing this for a living, it takes a certain amount of time and effort to find the character running around in my imagination. Then one day, unexpectedly, there they are staring back at you on the page. Those are always great days at the board. James Barnes has been an evasive one to solidify in my mind. When he's in his Winter Soldier persona, I have no difficulty seeing the character in my head — but put him in the Cap costume, and he instantly collides with my already deeply ingrained mental imagery of Steve Rogers as Captain America. In a way, that's the story Ed has been telling all along since I've been on the book. I do find it amusingly ironic that this battle of perception between Caps has also caused me no end of banging my head on the art table in artistic frustration.

SPOTLIGHT: You've been working on the Captain America character in some way, shape or form since 2008 when you inked previous artist Steve Epting's pencils. Since then, you've drawn several

> # "But now he's being shunted back to his worst nightmare — Russia... — and must finally face up with that portion of his life."
> **– WRITER ED BRUBAKER ON BUCKY**

out-Steranko'd Steranko. It really is kind of amazing to get someone so mentally attuned to do a modern take on that kind of artist.

SPOTLIGHT: You've worked with a variety of artists, from fresh talents with hot styles to steady hands like Butch and Steve Epting. You've been with Butch for an extended period now. Has that helped further the collaborative process?

"…I guess the most unique challenge for me has been to avoid a complete breakdown."

– ARTIST BUTCH GUICE ON DRAWING *CAPTAIN AMERICA*

ED: Definitely. Butch and I have been working together for over a year now, and we've developed a high level of trust in each other's abilities. I've seen Butch's work for over twenty years, and I have this sort of feeling that I've seen the best he can do, so I know where he might go when I propose something in the script. I know he's not the type to skimp on backgrounds or avoid setting a scene. There's a lot of communication between us, and we let each other know when we want to try something different with a particular scene. I give him a heads up about something coming in a script — or if he sees something in the script he wants to experiment on, then he'll ask. Because of the time we've worked together, and the time we've been professionals in the industry, we've built up a lot of trust.

SPOTLIGHT: Butch, you've literally drawn all the greats in comics — Superman, Flash, Iron Man, the X-Men, Dr. Strange — even some Terminators and Aliens! Before you started this book, what was your appraisal of the character?

BUTCH: Captain America was a favorite of mine when I was a kid, reading comics and daydreaming about possibly drawing them myself some day for Marvel. Of course, in those daydreams, I was a much better artist and looked and sounded like Steve McQueen. As a result, when Tom Brevoort emailed asking if I would be interested in taking on the book as a full time assignment, there was this genuine head-rattling moment — extreme excitement mixed with panicked certainty some

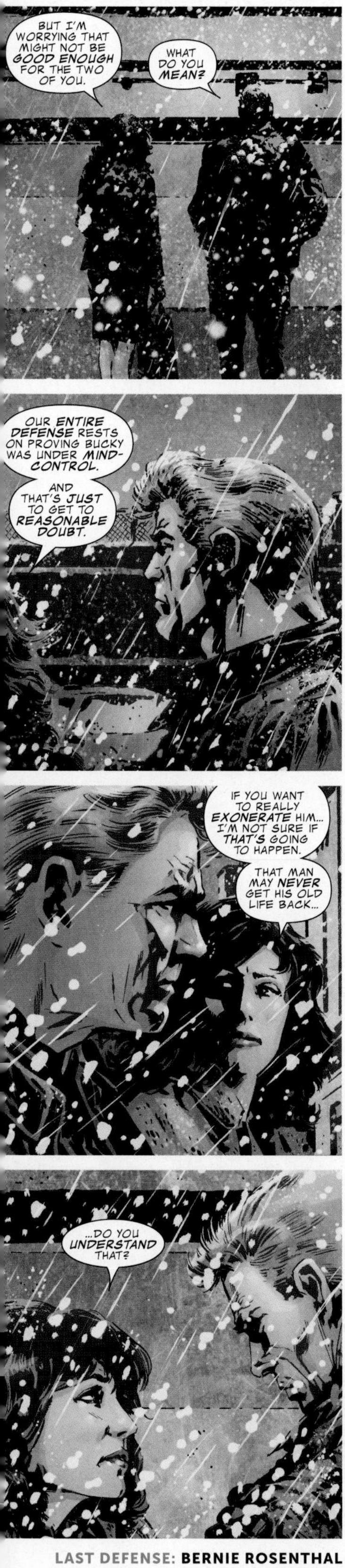
BUT I'M WORRYING THAT MIGHT NOT BE GOOD ENOUGH FOR THE TWO OF YOU.
WHAT DO YOU MEAN?
OUR ENTIRE DEFENSE RESTS ON PROVING BUCKY WAS UNDER MIND-CONTROL.
AND THAT'S JUST TO GET TO REASONABLE DOUBT.
IF YOU WANT TO REALLY EXONERATE HIM... I'M NOT SURE IF THAT'S GOING TO HAPPEN.
THAT MAN MAY NEVER GET HIS OLD LIFE BACK...
...DO YOU UNDERSTAND THAT?

LAST DEFENSE: BERNIE ROSENTHAL RETURNS IN "THE TRIAL OF CAPTAIN AMERICA" IN YET ANOTHER GREAT CHARACTER MOMENT WRITTEN BY ED BRUBAKER. (ART FROM *CA #612* BY GUICE.

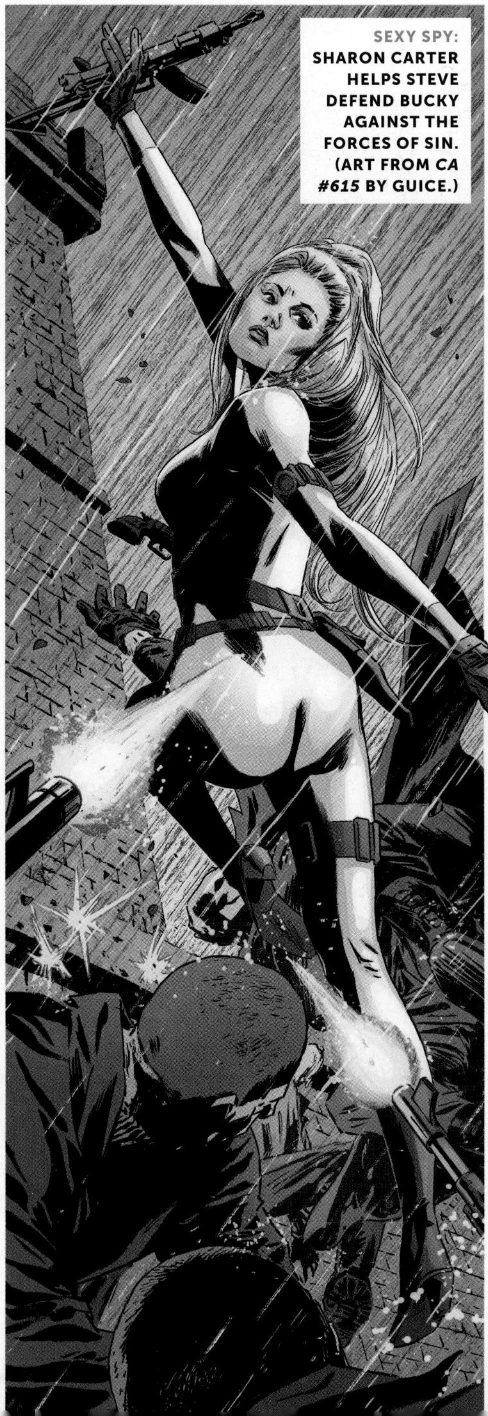

SEXY SPY: SHARON CARTER HELPS STEVE DEFEND BUCKY AGAINST THE FORCES OF SIN. (ART FROM *CA #615* BY GUICE.)

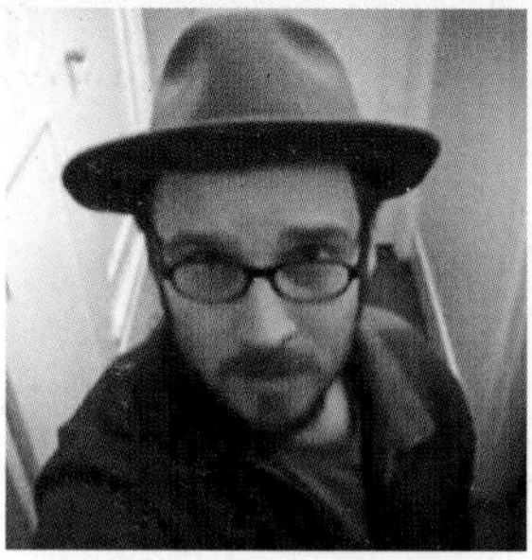

WRITER ED BRUBAKER

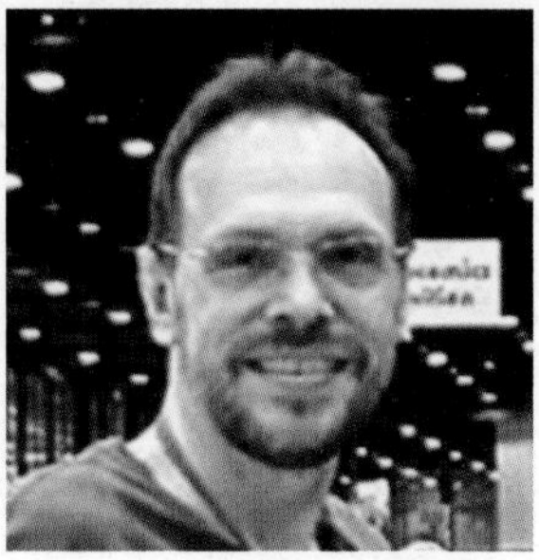

ARTIST BUTCH GUICE

mistake had occurred. I quickly replied yes before he could realize he had sent the email to the wrong guy.

Since then, all the rest has been a full-blown, blind panic knowing I'm following in the artistic legacies of Kirby, Steranko, Colan, Romita, Buscema, Epting and all the other greats who have contributed to Captain America over the years. So I guess the most unique challenge for me has been to avoid a complete breakdown.

SPOTLIGHT: Ed, you've become one of the longest-running writers on *Captain America* in its more than sixty year history. Can you compare how you handled writing those first issues with how you're treating it now? And did you think you'd make it this far?

ED: I never thought I'd stay on *Captain America* as long as I have. At the beginning, I figured I would do two or three years. Before this, my longest run on a title was DC's *Catwoman*, which was three-plus years of my life.

I try not to compare my early issues with what I'm doing now. I still put just as much thought into it as when I started. I am more comfortable with all the characters — but I've always had a certain comfort with Steve Rogers, Sharon Carter and Nick Fury. These are the characters I grew up reading. I never really felt like I struggled to find my voice for the title, as I just continued the voice I saw naturally occurring from the character's history.

I was really lucky to be able to write the book that was my favorite as a young reader. And even though it had its up and downs over the years, there were some amazing high points — from the Steranko run to Englehart's, Kirby's crazy stuff and the work John Byrne did with Roger Stern. When I started *Captain America*, I came in and brought my voice to see what I'd like to see them do next. And I got the cherriest gig of doing the thing that virtually every writer on the title before had pitched to do, but never been able to: bring Bucky Barnes back.

If you haven't been keeping up with Ed's Captain America *for the last six years, especially the last year's worth of issues with the estimable Butch Guice at the art boards, you have severe psychological problems. May we suggest a trip to Dr. Faustus? Or you could just save yourself the co-pays and pick up the next issue of* Cap!

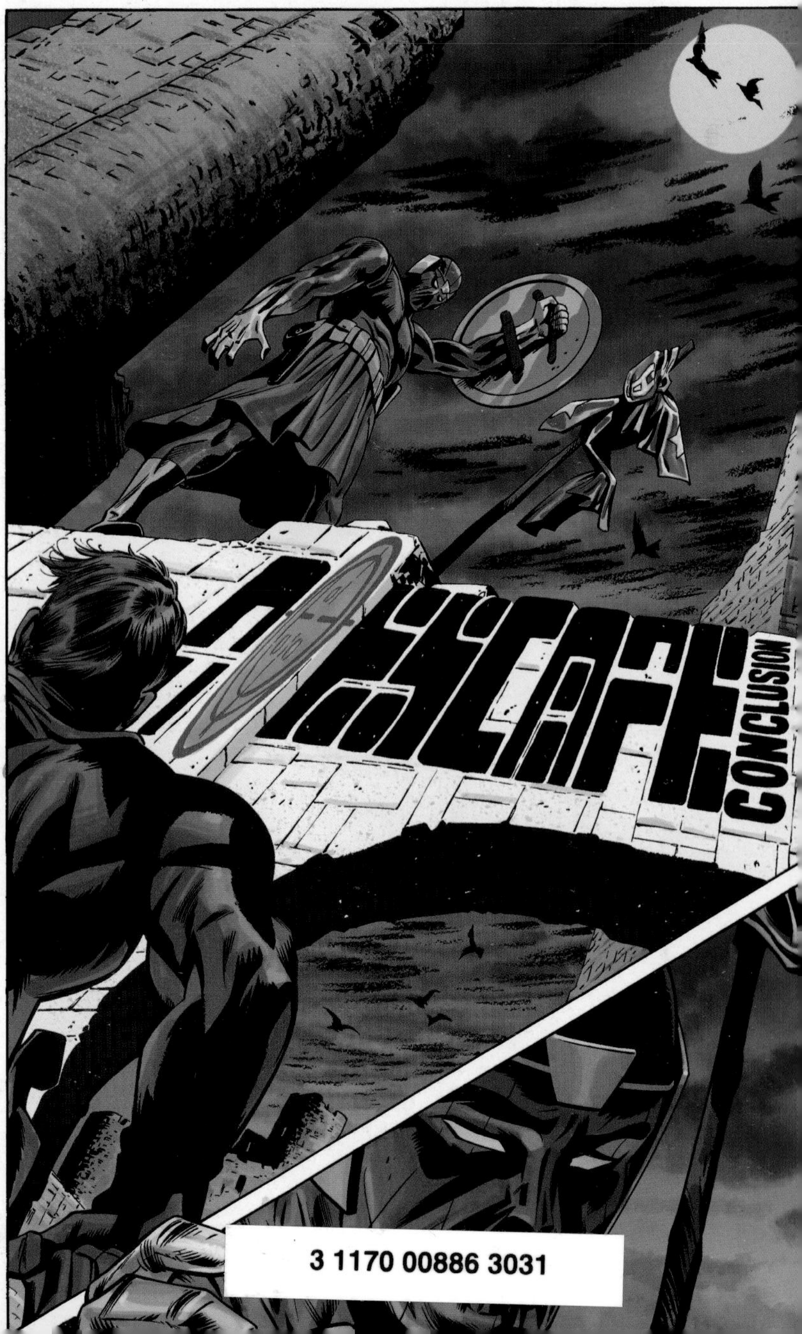
CONCLUSION

STERANKO HOMAGE: BUTCH GIVES A NOD TO ONE OF HIS ART HEROES IN THIS PAGE FROM *CAP #610*.